Foreign Policy Analysis

Foreign Policy Analysis

Continuity and Change in Its Second Generation

Laura Neack   Jeanne A. K. Hey

Patrick J. Haney

Miami University

PRENTICE HALL, Englewood Cliffs, New Jersey 07632

Library of Congress Cataloging-in-Publication Data

Foreign policy analysis: continuity and change in its second
   generation/edited by Laura Neack, Jeanne A. K. Hey, Patrick J.
   Haney.
       p. cm.
     Includes bibliographical references and index.
     ISBN 0-13-060575-1
       1. International relations—Research.   2. International relations—
   Study and teaching.   I. Neack, Laura.   II. Hey, Jeanne A. K.
   III. Haney, Patrick, Jude.
   JX1291.F663 1995
   327.1'01—dc20   94-38260
                                                                 CIP

Chapter 2 was adapted and expanded from Comparative Politics, Policy, and International Relations *edited by William Crotty. Copyright © 1991 by Northwestern University Press. Reprinted with permission.*

Chapter 3 was adapted and expanded from Defining Power: Influence and Force in the Contemporary International System *by John M. Rothgeb, Jr. Copyright © 1993. Reprinted with permission of St. Martin's Press, Incorporated.*

Editorial/production supervision: Lauren Byrne
Editorial director: Charlyce Jones Owen
Cover design: Maureen Eide
Buyer: Bob Anderson

©1995 by Prentice-Hall, Inc.
A Simon & Schuster Company
Englewood Cliffs, New Jersey 07632

Printed in the United States of America
10 9 8 7 6 5 4 3 2 1

ISBN 0-13-060575-1

PRENTICE-HALL INTERNATIONAL (UK) LIMITED, *London*
PRENTICE-HALL OF AUSTRALIA PTY. LIMITED, *Sydney*
PRENTICE-HALL CANADA INC., *Toronto*
PRENTICE-HALL HISPANOAMERICANA, S.A., *Mexico*
PRENTICE-HALL OF INDIA PRIVATE LIMITED, *New Delhi*
PRENTICE-HALL OF JAPAN, INC., *Tokyo*
SIMON & SCHUSTER ASIA PTE. LTD., *Singapore*
EDITORA PRENTICE-HALL DO BRASIL, LTDA., *Rio de Janeiro*

*To our teachers
and for our students*

► CONTENTS

▶ PREFACE

This book is designed to be an integrated, cohesive volume on foreign policy theory and analysis. Foreign policy analysis, as a distinct field having its nascence in the 1960s, is well into its second generation of ideas and scholarship. Despite the considerable achievements in the field in its short history, those of us who teach foreign policy analysis encounter multiple obstacles when we attempt to find a general foreign policy theory and analysis book for our students. First, there is no single, comprehensive text or anthology of articles that discusses the development of the study of foreign policy with reference to the linkages between the generations of scholarship. Second, there is no single, up-to-date collection of essays that can be used to introduce students to the theoretical perspectives and analytic approaches shaping the ever-evolving study of foreign policy. This book, we think, will serve teachers and students well as a foundation text for advanced undergraduate and graduate foreign policy courses. Further, as a "state-of-the-discipline" book, this volume serves those of us (most of us!) in our dual function as well—as foreign policy scholars.

    The idea of a "second generation" of scholarship is unique to this foreign policy book. We discuss our use of the generational concept and what we imagine as the distinctions between the first and second generations in chapter 1, and so we will save most of that discussion for later. However, allow us a few preliminary thoughts on "generational change" in the study of foreign policy. First, the concept is controversial and can put some people immediately on guard. "Generation gaps" are, of course, notorious in most cultures; generations are commonly seen as being at odds with one another, as not understanding one another, with each rejecting what the other values. In a limited sense, we see some of the scholarship in this volume as distinct from and critical of the "first-generation" scholarship as presented in chapter 1 and as Deborah Gerner discusses it in chapter 2. Some of the work here is critical of the limitations and biases of the first generation, and some "returns" to theoretical traditions that were often enough not embraced by the first generation. And so there is some tension here between generations and some of the guardedness over the generational concept is warranted. But, as we indicate in chapter 1 and at many points throughout this book, generations are not just in opposition to one another. Indeed, and quite importantly, second generations come from first generations; others brought us here, and their work and help must be acknowledged and honored. In the same way that we assert the distinctiveness of the second generation from the first, we also stress the continuities between the scholarships and point to the foundations laid for us by first-generation foreign policy scholars. And so, as these things go, there is also in this book less tension between the generations than dynamism generated out of a shared pursuit of a cherished interest.

■ Acknowledgments

This is a collaborative effort that has benefited from the assistance and insights of many, and so we have many people to thank. We particularly want to acknowledge the help of Mickey East, Deborah Gerner, Joe Hagan, Chuck Hermann, Karen Mingst, Brian Ripley, Jerel Rosati, John Rothgeb, Phil Schrodt, and the following reviewers of the original prospectus and the completed manuscript: Joseph Lepgold, *Georgetown University*; David T. Yamada, *Monterey Peninsula College*; Gary Prevost, *St. John's University*; and Larry Elowitz, *Georgia College*. We also express thanks to Dotti Pierson and Dlynn Armstrong in the political science department of Miami University, and Nicole Signoretti and Charlyce Jones Owen at Prentice Hall. The order of our names on the book and on our joint introductory chapter reflects that it was Laura Neack who had the idea to put together this book. Recognizing her initiation of the project, we list her name first, with the others following in reverse alphabetical order.

In addition, Laura Neack thanks Karen Mingst for being a teacher *extraordinaire*; Karen, Spike Peterson, and John Rothgeb for being so easy to work with; Phil Russo for the use of his speaker phone; and her family, especially Rog and Harry (who remains disappointed because this book contains no pictures).

Jeanne Hey would like to thank Sheila Croucher, Steven DeLue, Joe Hagan, Elizabeth Hey, E. B. Hey Jr., Jeanne C. Hey, Margaret Hermann, Charles Hermann, Lynn Kuzma, William Mandel, Michael Pagano, Katherine Roberson, Douglas Shumavon, Michael Snarr, and especially Thomas Klak.

Patrick Haney would like to thank Alexander George, Misty Gerner, Harold Guetzkow, Harry and Sue Haney, Chuck Hermann, John Lovell, Bill Mandel, Anthony Matejczyk, Mike McGinnis, Lin Ostrom, Jim Perry, Brian Ripley, Phil Schrodt, Keith Shimko, Doug Shumavon, Dina Spechler, Harvey Starr, John Williams, and his students who ask tough questions.

L.N.
J.A.K.H.
P.J.H.

▶ ABOUT THE AUTHORS

Deborah J. Gerner received her Ph.D. from Northwestern University and is associate professor of political science at the University of Kansas.

Joe D. Hagan received his Ph.D. from the University of Kentucky and is associate professor of political science at West Virginia University and faculty associate at the Mershon Center of The Ohio State University.

Patrick J. Haney received his Ph.D. from Indiana University and is assistant professor of political science at Miami University.

Charles F. Hermann received his Ph.D. from Northwestern University and is director of the Mershon Center and professor of political science at The Ohio State University.

Jeanne A. K. Hey received her Ph.D. from The Ohio State University and is assistant professor of political science and international studies at Miami University.

Karen A. Mingst received her Ph.D. from the University of Wisconsin and is professor and chair of political science at the University of Kentucky.

Bruce E. Moon received his Ph.D. from The Ohio State University and is associate professor and chair of the department of international relations at Lehigh University.

Laura Neack received her Ph.D. from the University of Kentucky and is assistant professor of political science at Miami University.

V. Spike Peterson received her Ph.D. from The American University and is assistant professor of political science at the University of Arizona.

Brian Ripley received his Ph.D. from The Ohio State University and is assistant professor of political science at the University of Pittsburgh.

Jerel A. Rosati received his Ph.D from The American University and is associate professor and graduate director of international studies in the Department of Government and International Studies at the University of South Carolina.

John M. Rothgeb Jr. received his Ph.D. from the University of Kentucky and is professor of political science at Miami University.

Philip A. Schrodt received his Ph.D. from Indiana University and is professor of political science at the University of Kansas.

Keith Shimko received his Ph.D. from Indiana University and is associate professor of political science at Purdue University.

Foreign Policy Analysis

ONE

Generational Change
in Foreign Policy Analysis

Laura Neack, Jeanne A. K. Hey,
Patrick J. Haney, MIAMI UNIVERSITY

Our purpose in bringing this volume together is to highlight the progression in the study of foreign policy that has been taking place over the last half century by presenting to colleagues and students examples of the variety of ways that the study of foreign policy is being pursued. As will be evident, the study of foreign policy is a diverse set of activities, dedicated to understanding and explaining the foreign policy processes and behaviors of actors in world politics. The evolution of this field, as one would expect, has included both continuity and change, and this volume assembles a broad sampling of the field that shows this record of continuity and change. In our thinking about this process of evolution, we have found it helpful to focus on the provocative concept of "generational change."

The ideas of a "second generation" and a "first generation" carry many implications. *A second generation follows on the existence of and builds upon the efforts of its predecessor.* A second generation is nurtured by and relies upon the strengths of its predecessor. A second generation carries on the work of a first generation and passes along the heritage to a potential third generation. *At the same time, a second generation is distinct from a first generation,* thus it leaves its own mark upon the world. A second generation oftentimes, directly or indirectly, speaks to those things that have been overlooked or not completed by the first generation. So there are elements about a second generation that can appear oppositional, accusatory, or even rebellious to the first.

This volume on foreign policy analysis in its "second generation" demonstrates second-generation scholarship in the variety of ways it embraces as well as moves beyond the first generation. Our use of the idea of a second generation has met and probably will meet with some opposition and concern. When we suggest that foreign policy analysis as a field of study has moved into a second generation, we imply some departure from the past and its ways of knowing. This departure should not be seen as simply oppositional, for the second generation (as these things go) would not exist if not for the efforts of the first.

We brought this book together in an act that implicitly indicates that the first generation's work has been important but remains incomplete. As can be seen throughout, the first generation of foreign policy scholarship was critical to establishing many of the foundations for the second generation. Deborah Gerner's essay that immediately follows this chapter presents a broad overview of the first generation as it consciously developed as a "field" of study. The reader is encouraged to consider what lines of inquiry were included in the "field," as presented by Gerner, that carry through into some of the second-generation chapters in this volume. The reader should further consider what theoretical traditions are omitted from Gerner's review of the first generation, traditions that play key roles in many of the other chapters in this volume. Recognizing the inclusion and exclusion of certain theoretical traditions from the first-generation "field" is crucial to understanding why we declare foreign policy analysis to be in a broader-reaching second generation.

As a final introductory note, we need to state the obvious here: the study of foreign policy is not a new phenomenon. As long as there have been political units engaging in relations with other political units, people have thought about and studied the problems of relations with the other or foreign group. What is new is the attempt to structure the activities of scholars engaged in the study of foreign policy into a coherent, identifiable field of study. This, then, is our first fundamental assertion (and not one that is just our own): the study of foreign policy is different from the study of international relations and comparative politics, and the effort to distinguish and delineate this field is a relatively new phenomenon. The pioneering scholars in this endeavor are referred to here as the first generation. These were certainly not the first people to study foreign policy, but they were the first group to try to delineate a field of foreign policy analysis. How they tried to do this, what they emphasized as well as disregarded in their demarcations of the field, and what environmental motivations conditioned their efforts are all important to consider in order to appreciate the efforts and distinctiveness of the second-generation scholars.

■ The First Generation: "Comparative Foreign Policy"

The study of foreign policy has entered a "second generation" in two ways. In a limited sense, there is now a second generation of *scholars* working in the field, trained by those who pioneered and consolidated the field. This second generation has benefited from the insights and experience of two decades of systematic foreign policy research performed by the first generation of foreign policy scholars. Thus, some second-generation scholars have the luxury of coming into an established field of research, rather than the task of trying to begin one. To paraphrase a recent review of the field, new scholars in the field interested in building theory about foreign policy have "a significant theory building heritage" that their predecessors lacked (Hermann and Peacock 1987, 30).

In a broader sense, the study of foreign policy has entered a second generation of *scholarship,* which at its most fundamental level means a different way of thinking about the study of foreign policy. In this sense, many "first-generation" scholars as well as scholars who were actively engaged in foreign policy analysis but were not part of the first-generation "field" fit into the designation of second-generation scholars. This second-generation perspective is actually a broad set of approaches bound together by a common focus on studying foreign policy and an.acceptance of eclecticism in theory building. This shift can be seen even in how we refer to the field. The first generation of scholarship typically was labeled "comparative foreign policy," whereas the second generation is referred to as "foreign policy analysis." It is important to recognize here that the generations we refer to frequently overlap temporally. Some scholars continued to pursue first-generation questions into the period in which second-generation scholarship began. While we see a general evolution from a first to a second generation, the shift is neither complete nor specific to a particular year.

The first-generation analysis of foreign policy, or comparative foreign policy (CFP), had as one of its primary goals a desire to move away from noncumulative descriptive case studies and to construct a parsimonious explanation of what drives the foreign policy behavior of states. It sought to do so using modern social science techniques and comparative analyses of the behavior of states. Along the way, it was hoped that a relatively uniform pursuit of theory about foreign policy would contribute to the establishment of a normal science in the Kuhnian sense (see Kuhn 1962; on comparative foreign policy as a normal science, see East, Salmore, and Hermann 1978; Hermann and Peacock 1987; McGowan and Shapiro 1973; Rosenau 1966, 1987a). In order to do this, many first-generation scholars adopted quantitative, positivist (scientific) models of theory building and methodologies. This disposition toward positivist theory building required that scholars assemble "data" of the foreign policy behavior of states, often in the form of event counts, and explore sources of foreign policy behaviors through discrete, separate levels of analysis (e.g., Azar and Ben-Dak 1975; Kegley et al. 1975; McGowan and Shapiro 1973; Rummel 1972). The explanations produced in this pursuit were intended to be general (even generic) in nature, stressing ideal nation-types, societal characteristics, and behavioral modes, including those linked to systematic decision-making models (e.g., East and Hermann 1974; McGowan 1974; Moore 1974; cf. Rosenau 1967a, 1967b, 1967c, 1968a, 1968b).

There were also, and at the same time, a large number of foreign policy scholars who remained largely outside the CFP paradigm, opting for different views of theory building both from CFP and often from each other. Important research, for example, by Graham Allison (1971), Michael Brecher (1972, 1980), I. M. Destler (1972), Alexander George (1969, 1972), Alexander George and Richard Smoke (1974), Morton Halperin (1974), Roger Hilsman (1971), Ole Holsti (1962, 1970), Samuel Huntington (1961), Irving Janis (1982), Nathan Leites (1951, 1953), and Kenneth Waltz (1967), did not fall under the CFP paradigm. Nor did there emerge from this set of foreign policy scholars (or others) a call for a unified approach to the study of foreign policy similar to that put forward by those working within the CFP paradigm. As CFP was the first attempt to unify the approach to the study of foreign policy, we have found it useful to think of it as a first generation of foreign policy scholarship.

First-generation scholars, then, were a relatively small core of analysts concerned with the construction of a rigorous body of research that would together form a unified "field." Within this context Rosenau proposed a "pre-theoretical" framework as a way to orient foreign policy research toward being systematic, scientific, and quantitative (1966). His pre-theory framework, which sought to focus attention on the different and discrete levels of causation of foreign policy behavior (e.g., individual, role, government structure, society type, international relations, and global system), was to be a step that in some ways was modeled on Robert Merton's concept of "middle range theory" (1957). Middle-range theories offer explanations of particular, limited phenomena rather than explanations that encompass the entire universe being studied (in this case, foreign policy). Rosenau's "pre-theory" was to serve as a research guide that might lead, in time, to some accumulated understanding of how, for instance, role perception might lead to certain foreign policy choices, and to some understanding of how the level of a country's development might limit the foreign policy choices available to it. Enough middle-range theories, over time, could be fitted together into a general or grand theory that would explain the multiple sources of, variations in, and implications of foreign policy.

Despite the fact that Rosenau proposed a "pre-theory," some first-generation scholars—including Rosenau—quickly identified the field as a "normal science," that is, a scientific field with a central general or grand theory around which research proceeded using a common strategy of inquiry or methodology. Ongoing research within such an established "normal science" involved "mopping-up" activities that sought to answer details left over after solving the larger puzzle of the field's universe. Several of the most prominent scholars in CFP published glowing but questionable pronouncements about the progress in the field. Consider the following two examples:

A field of scientific (comparative) foreign policy analysis has not only emerged but is also proceeding in the "mopping up" activities of "normal science." (Kegley and Skinner 1976, 303, as quoted in Korany 1986b, 42)

All the evidence points to the conclusion that the comparative study of foreign policy has emerged as a *normal* science. For nearly a decade many investigators have been busily building and improving data banks, testing and revising propositions, using and departing from each other's work. It has been an astonishingly rapid evolution…because of the steady and growing flow of research products … and of the convergence around particular variables and methodologies. Our differences now are about small points. (Rosenau 1976, 370, as quoted in Korany 1986b, 42)

This progress report about the study of foreign policy was exaggerated. There was some convergence of practice around quantitative methodology and scientifically based ways of knowing—specifically, a shared commitment to positivism—among scholars who called their field "comparative foreign policy." However, a shared set of theoretical commitments and the central paradigmatic core of the field never came into focus. By the 1980s many had noted that the field as defined by CFP had not attained all of its goals (e.g., Caporaso et al. 1987; Hermann and Peacock 1987; Kegley 1980; Moon 1987).

As stated earlier, the theoretical traditions and findings established in this first-generation scholarship are discussed in detail in Deborah Gerner's essay in this book (chapter 2). As indicated by Gerner, the scope and range of first-generation scholarship have been considerable, but so are the subjects and issues that have been excluded from the "field." The exclusion of certain theoretical traditions seems to have occurred because of the first generation's desire to construct a rigorous field that was largely positivist in orientation and predisposed to quantitative analysis. Understanding the positivist orientation of the first generation and the rejection of positivism as the sole logic of inquiry in the second generation can be enhanced by an awareness of the political context in which each generation of scholarship has been conducted.

■ The First Generation and Positivism

To understand the positivist orientation of CFP it is helpful first to understand the politics of the "real world." Scholarship is never immune to real-world politics; indeed, scholarship reflects the political trends of the day. The study of CFP (the first generation), like the study of international relations and comparative politics, clearly reflected the "ways of knowing" that dominated social science research in the 1950s and 1960s. As the hegemony of positivism in international relations and comparative politics waned in the 1970s and 1980s, so too did positivism loosen its grip on the study of foreign policy, allowing for an opening in the field that, in turn, allowed the second generation to coalesce. Beyond understanding that CFP reflected the politics of the day, it is equally important to understand a related phenomenon: the study of foreign policy has been influenced by theoretical and conceptual developments in the fields of international relations and comparative politics.

Ray Maghroori (1982) and Howard Wiarda (1985) have discussed how the theoretical and methodological developments in the fields of international relations and comparative politics, respectively, can be mapped onto a time line against real-world events in the twentieth century. An understanding of the development of these fields helps us to understand the origins of the first generation of foreign policy analysis.

The appropriate starting point for this discussion is the end of World War II. The lessons from the two world wars as well as from the interwar period helped reestablish the dominance of the realist paradigm and "power politics" in international politics. Even attempts to foster (idealistic) cooperation among states within the new United Nations were backed with a realist belief in military might—as seen in the Security Council's permanent memberships and veto power given to the victors of World War II. As the cold war between the superpowers developed, the realist preoccupation with the study of military security and strategic balances was reinforced.

During the same period, the study of comparative politics was dominated by scholars who had learned to fear mass politics from both ends of the political spectrum. Fascist Italy, imperialist Japan, and Nazi Germany had taught them the dangers of mobilized masses from the extreme right end of the spectrum, while the politics of the Soviet Union exemplified the dangers of mobilized masses from the left. The study of comparative politics after World War II became infused with a normative imperative to study and model the "good" moderate participatory politics found in the United States and Western Europe (Wiarda 1985, 12). The dominant theoretical perspective in the field became modernization theory—sometimes called developmental economics—with its emphasis on state building along the Western model. As the cold war emerged and deepened, the modernization-developmental model became the formula by which Western states, especially the United States, examined, judged, and intervened in developing states to protect them from the dangers of the mass politics of the left being exported by the Soviet Union.

During the 1950s, American academia was greatly influenced by the cold war and its arms and space races. A principal strategy of the United States in the cold war involved scientific advancements and the recruitment of academics to the cause. Federal funding for "scientific" research created a strong impetus among social scientists to become more "scientific" (and perhaps less "social" or "historical"). This contributed to the beginnings of the positivist era in the social sciences, with its focus on hypothesis testing and quantification.

International and comparative politics were thus dominated by positivism during the 1950s and into the 1960s. Two important lines of inquiry that emerged in international politics during this period were formal decision-making models for understanding policymaking and mathematical, game-theoretic models of arms racing, alliance building, and war. In comparative politics, modernization theory was formalized in an institutionally focused state-building model against which states could be judged as developing or failing to develop. Research in both fields became highly quantified as well, especially in international relations.

Comparative foreign policy emerged within this positivist era of international and comparative politics. This research environment was consistent with James Rosenau's (1966) call for the study of foreign policy to become a normal science with a dominant paradigmatic core and central methodological framework (e.g., Raymond 1975). The first-generation foreign policy analyses that focused on models of foreign policy behavior, quantitative methods, and the use of event data to link ideal nation-types and foreign policy behaviors were informed by this positivist origin (e.g., East and Hermann 1974; Moore 1974b; see also chapter 2, in which Gerner discusses this at greater length). U.S. federal funding opportunities for academics, as well as the abundance of data on the world's countries being generated by the United Nations and the Western states' intelligence apparatuses helped solidify and legitimate this approach to foreign policy analysis.

The real-world events of the 1960s, however, were to cause scholars in international and comparative politics as well as foreign policy scholars to rethink their fundamental assumptions in the 1970s. The huge increase in the number of independent states in the 1960s caused by decolonization infused international and comparative politics with new voices, orientations, and issues. The power of numbers to be exercised by "Third World" states within the UN General Assembly, and later the economic power harnessed by the Organization of Petroleum Exporting Countries (OPEC) in the 1970s, encouraged international relations scholars to come to terms with nonmilitary bases and definitions of power and less-than-great power states. Further, the problems of Third World countries were not primarily military and strategic, but also involved issues of economic development and dependency, as well as issues of state and nation building, creating a need for more diverse theoretical and conceptual tools in the study of international politics (Azar and Moon 1988).

As the number of countries and issues confronting international politics expanded dramatically into the 1970s, so too did the voices from both Western and non-Western scholars who operated under a nonrealist, non-Western paradigm. Many of these scholars from developing countries proposed a historical, structural accounting of the international system informed by Marxism and generalized as (although not limited to) dependency theory (see Cardoso and Faletto 1979; Frank

1981; see also Wallerstein 1979). Some scholars in the West also defected from the realist flock and began to discuss alternative explanations of international politics. These alternative accountings are generally described as part of an omnibus pluralist/transnationalist/complex interdependency approach (e.g., Barnet and Muller 1974; Keohane and Nye 1974). As these alternative or contending paradigms emerged in the study of international politics, strict positivist methodology was challenged as being inappropriate to the study of the emerging, contextualized theoretical accountings of international politics. By the end of the 1970s, more complex qualitative and quantitative research efforts were being conducted even among those scholars who still adhered to realism (or neorealism).

Within the study of comparative politics, modernization theory also came under scrutiny during the 1960s and 1970s. Wiarda states that the theory faced two challenges: one intellectual and one societal-political (1985, 18). Intellectually, Wiarda writes, the theory, "was accused by critics of ignoring the phenomenon of class and class conflict, the play of international and market and economic forces, and dependency. The cold war origins and overtones of the developmental (modernization) approach came under strong attack, and developmentalism was further criticized as perpetuating myths and stereotypes about developing nations that were down-right destructive of cherished traditional institutions within these societies" (1985, 18). The societal-political challenge reflected the "widespread questioning of all institutions and forms of authority" in the United States and in the world. Wiarda continues: "This was especially the case as it was revealed that some of those responsible for articulating the developmentalist perspective were also among the government policy advisers who were helping to design and carry out what were widely perceived as ill-advised U.S. foreign policies with regard to the Third World and especially Vietnam" (1985, 19).

Scholars from developing countries and Western "area specialists" who had rejected modernization theory were able to exploit the cracks in the crumbling modernization theory paradigm and assert the importance of studying complex domestic processes in comparative politics (Wiarda 1985; see, e.g., Ferris and Lincoln 1981; Muñoz and Tulchin 1984; Valenzuela and Valenzuela 1978). The study of domestic processes took a variety of forms in the 1970s, including the study of domestic class-based divisions caused by colonialism and perpetuated in postindependence dependent relations, political economy, state corporatism, and state-society relations (e.g., Chilcote 1985; Verba 1985). The unifying feature of comparative politics from the 1970s onward was not a central paradigmatic core but a central methodological agreement on the comparative method.

The impact of other voices and other worldviews on international and comparative politics was felt similarly by those who studied foreign policy. As the realist and developmentalist hegemonies were ended in international and comparative politics, respectively, the divisions between the two fields were often difficult to determine. This was especially true in the case of political economy approaches to international and comparative politics (e.g., Caporaso 1988; Moon 1983; Rosenau 1988; Therborn 1986). This blurring of the divisions between the two fields occurred at the junction of the fields that foreign policy was supposed to bridge in its early days (Rosenau 1987a). In its first generation, however, foreign policy analysis did not bridge international and comparative politics, as it was largely informed and structured by the theoretical orientation and conceptualizations of international politics and claimed to be borrowing only the comparative method from comparative politics (e.g., McGowan 1975).

By the start of the 1980s, however, a variety of theoretical and methodological accountings from *both* international and comparative politics were adopted by foreign policy scholars. The impact of these accountings is evident in the contextualized, multisourced, sometimes multileveled foreign policy analyses undertaken in the 1980s and into the 1990s.

■ Areas for Growth in the Second Generation

The first generation of the study of foreign policy accomplished a great deal (see, e.g., Caporaso et al. 1987; Hermann and Peacock 1987). In the broadest sense, CFP moved scholarship beyond work that was, to date, largely atheoretical and descriptive. It generated a body of concepts and data about foreign policy behavior, and it attempted to do so in systematic ways. But there were many theoretical traditions within the study of international relations that were acknowledged as important to foreign policy scholars in a general sense, and then typically not included in the realm of CFP. Similarly, much knowledge being generated by the study of comparative political systems was not well integrated into first-generation foreign policy scholarship.

In a broad sense, everything in international relations speaks to foreign policy issues. The first generation (CFP), however, tended to neglect many of the grand and middle-range theories in international relations that addressed foreign policy issues. These were rarely considered *systematically* in comparative foreign policy. Thus, a student could take a course in CFP and not be exposed to a number of important grand theories in international relations that had much to say about foreign policy.

For example, CFP scholarship tended to ignore the foreign policy contributions of the grand theories of political realism, globalism (and the related world-system theory), and complex interdependency/transnationalism, as well as the middle-range theories developed from these. Realist theories, for instance, have premised discussions of alliance behavior (Walt 1987), security dilemmas (Jervis 1978), deterrence (Brodie 1978; Morgan 1977; Snyder 1961), and bargaining behavior (Schelling 1966) in ways that speak directly to particular foreign policy behaviors of states. Similarly, neorealist theories have discussed the foreign policy behaviors of states called hegemons, challengers, and supporters (Gilpin 1987; Kindleberger 1981; Krasner 1976). Globalist theories that have spoken about foreign policy behaviors and motivations include discussions of imperialism and imperialist states (Frank 1981; Hobson 1965) and discussions of the roles played by the countries of the core, semiperiphery, and periphery in the capitalist world system (Wallerstein 1979). Complex interdependency theorists have built upon older discussions of functionalism and sector integration (Haas 1958; Haas and Schmitter 1964; Schmitter 1970), communications patterns (Deutsch 1966), and "ecological" discussions of the interactions between leaders, their states, and the external environment (Papadakis and Starr 1987; Sprout and Sprout 1971). More recent transnationalist scholarship has focused on foreign policies developed out of multiple state-nonstate linkages (Moon 1988; Keohane and Nye 1977), interstate conflict management through international organizations (Haas 1983; Zacher 1979), and the use of multilateralism as a form or tool of statecraft (Holbraad 1984; Karns and Mingst 1992).

The first generation also tended to discount the contributions that comparative politics scholarship could make to the understanding of foreign policy. In some respects the first generation was imitating international relations: both fields focused heavily on the individual and system levels of analysis (sometimes conflating the two levels, as in discussions of decision-making models and unitary, rational national actors), relegating domestic political factors to a position of secondary importance. This is not to suggest that first-generation scholarship and international relations scholarship never focused on domestic politics. Indeed, as Deborah Gerner, Brian Ripley, Patrick Haney, and Joe Hagan indicate in this volume, the first generation paid considerable attention to institutionally situated decision-making models and public opinion (among other state-level sources of foreign policymaking). Often, however, these state-level sources of foreign policymaking were studied using the single case of the United States, making the *comparability* of these studies questionable. Some first-generation scholarship, such as that by Maurice East (1973, 1975), Michael Brecher (1972), and Brecher, Steinberg, and Stein (1969), as well as research projects such as CREON[1], did seek to break out of the American-centric, great power–centric mode to consider the foreign policy behavior of less powerful states. However, the knowledge generated by comparativists studying the domestic systems of states other than the United States that bore directly on a general understanding of foreign policy was often neglected even by these first-generation attempts to be more comparative.

For example, comparativists have had much to say on the role of the state in social transformation and the implications of this interaction for the state's foreign relations (Crahan and Smith 1992; Finkle and Gable 1971; Mander 1969; O'Donnell, Schmitter, and Whitehead 1986; Skocpol 1979). Political economic explanations of the interaction between domestic developmental and foreign economic policies have been generated primarily from comparative political studies (Balassa 1982; Evans 1979; Johnson 1982; Moon 1983, 1985). Similarly, while regional specialists studying developing areas have had much to say on the types of foreign policy opportunities available to dependent states (Cardoso 1973; Hey and Kuzma 1993; Ferris and Lincoln 1981; Mehta 1985), only rarely were these topics included in reviews of or edited volumes on the study of CFP (Korany 1986b).[2]

All of these theoretical traditions from both fields are embraced by the second generation of foreign policy analysis as relevant and informative. The eschewing of the need to have a field organized around a central paradigmatic and methodological core has freed foreign policy analysts to draw upon multiple literatures that speak to the central preoccupation: foreign policy theory and behavior.

One recent collection of research essays—*New Directions in the Study of Foreign Policy,* edited by Charles F. Hermann, Charles W. Kegley Jr., and James N. Rosenau (1987)—has attempted to reclaim some of the theoretical traditions of international relations and accommodate some understandings of the sources of foreign policy generated from comparative politics. *New Directions* is a forward-looking volume; indeed, in one of the introductory chapters the authors state: "it has become clear that fuller explanations of foreign policy phenomena require multi-level and multi-variable explanatory frameworks" (Hermann and Peacock 1987, 30). The volume goes beyond first-generation presentations of foreign policy analysis in that most of the chapters do *not* dwell explicitly on the continuing desire for a central paradigm and central methodology in the field. Still, this quest is not entirely abandoned in *New Directions*. James Rosenau's introduction to the book clearly suggests that the search for the central paradigm and methodology is not over but has moved on to a higher level of sophistication:

> It is perhaps a measure of movement into a new, more mature era of inquiry that philosophical and methodological argumentation is conspicuously absent from these essays. Where earlier works were pervaded with efforts to clarify the epistemological foundations and methodological premises on which the analysis rested, here such matters are largely taken for granted. Gone are the triumphant paragraphs extolling science, the holier-than-thou espousal of quantification. . . . No longer do researchers need to parade their commitments to scientific methods. Now, instead, they just practice them. (Rosenau 1987a, 5–6)

The introductory chapter in *New Directions* by Charles Hermann and Gregory Peacock assesses the study of foreign policy as a field to date, most of it revolving around first-generation themes and approaches such as decision-making theories, event data projects, and Rosenau's several pre-theory discussions. Hermann and Peacock conclude with a call for further "multi-level, multi-dimensional" research, some of which emerges in the edited volume's chapters.

For example, Bruce Moon's chapter in *New Directions* on political economy and Margaret Karns and Karen Mingst's coauthored chapter on international organizations appear to be grounded in different theoretical frames than the traditional one described by Hermann and Peacock. Other chapters in *New Directions*, however, report recent advances in research areas explored by foreign policy analysts for some time. The three chapters by Neil Richardson, Charles Kegley, and Stephen Walker are illustrative of these more first-generation themes. In this sense, *New Directions* is a bridge to the present volume in that it incorporates new and old foreign policy analysis themes.

■ Foreign Policy Analysis in Its Second Generation

This presentation of scholarship from the second generation of foreign policy analysis does not focus on what must be done to make the field a "field." Moreover, the idea of a "field" is different in this volume: the "field" we propose is a wide circle of scholarship dedicated to helping shape a broader understanding of foreign policy. This volume contains scholarship derived from varied theoretical traditions in international relations and comparative politics, as well as from the important traditions established by the first generation of foreign policy scholarship. Some of the works included here continue themes from the first generation, some pick up on theoretical themes previously disregarded in CFP and carry them forward, and some do both. Some of the scholarship is multileveled in approach, and some explores a single level in rich detail. Because this is just one book attempting to present a far-reaching circle of scholarship, we do not bring, nor do we claim to bring, all the voices that speak to foreign policy together here.[3]

Scholars in foreign policy analysis more and more see any theory of foreign policy as having to be built in a contingent way, focusing on context, informed by empirical analysis. Such theory is likely to be conditional and bounded, recognizing that single-cause explanations are not sufficient to explain foreign policy behaviors and processes. Rather, explanations crafted for certain circumstances or certain actors, that recognize that actors can "substitute" one foreign policy choice for another when pursuing goals, and explanations that may be time-, region-, or issue-bound, are more likely to be pursued by foreign policy analysts in the second generation (cf. Most and Starr 1989; Papadakis and Starr 1987). Research that seeks to build such theory may still focus on only one level (e.g., individuals or societies), but that level is generally seen as part of a larger context of action (e.g., Katzenstein 1976; Moon 1988; Montville 1991).

Furthermore, a diverse collection of methods are recognized as useful and appropriate for building these explanations of foreign policy. While many foreign policy analysts use quantitative methods and large data sets to study foreign policy (often in new and exciting ways, as Philip Schrodt explains in chapter 9), many use qualitative methods such as comparative case studies and the in-depth explanations of area specialists to understand foreign policy behaviors and processes. There has been renewed attention to using these types of methods in rigorous, systematic ways with the goal of theory building in mind.

Finally, the "model" for science in the social sciences may be shifting away from that of the physical and chemical sciences toward that of the biological sciences, informed more by "evolutionary epistemology" (see, e.g., Gould 1989; Krasner 1988, 1984; Mayr 1982). But, to some extent, this perspective also reflects disappointment with the results of first-generation research (cf. Hermann and Peacock 1987; Rosenau 1987a).

Thus, second-generation foreign policy analysis can be summed up in the following points:[4]

- Second-generation scholarship is conducted using a wide variety of methodologies embracing a diversity of quantitative and qualitative research techniques.

- Second-generation scholarship draws from as many critical theoretical perspectives as it draws from methodologies; indeed, the need for a paradigmatic core and central methodology is rejected as unnecessary and diversionary in this generation of foreign policy study.

- Second-generation scholarship rejects simple connections and considers contingent, complex interactions between foreign policy factors.

- Second-generation accountings of the domestic sources and processes of foreign policy draw heavily upon insights generated by comparativists and area specialists and more systematic and consistent attention is given to non-American cases.

- Second-generation scholars are conscious of the contextual parameters of their work and explicitly seek to link their research to the major substantive concerns in foreign policy.

In bringing together the diverse scholarship in this volume we have tried to reject the limitations of "comparative foreign policy" and to embrace multiple theoretical traditions that inform us about foreign policy. There is a metaphor that describes our effort here, one used by a contributor to this volume to describe some of her own scholarly efforts. In the introduction to her edited volume, *Gendered States: Feminist (Re)Visions of International Relations Theory*, V. Spike Peterson describes her book's mission as that of "opening feminist-IR conversational spaces." Peterson explains, "The metaphor of 'conversations' and reference to 'openings' are very much to the point: I want to emphasize the processual, interactive dynamics and fluid boundaries of conversations, as well as the exploratory nature of shifting perspectives and gaining new vistas" (Peterson 1992b, 16). And so, to borrow the metaphor, we try here to "open" a "conversational space" that includes scholarship built upon the first generation along with scholarship built upon traditions not included in the first generation. Within this opened space we hope to share with the reader a number of perspectives and "new vistas" on foreign policy. In some respects, the opening of this conversational space is the essence of the second generation of foreign policy analysis.

■ Continuing Themes and Areas of Innovation Developed in This Book

The essays in this volume attempt to illustrate and capture the essence of second-generation scholarship in foreign policy analysis. Each includes and/or builds on first-generation scholarship. Each chapter occupies a different point on a continuum spanning the first and second generations, that is, between continuity and change in foreign policy analysis. The book itself is divided into two parts. The first part, including this chapter, sets the context for the second-generation scholarship represented in the second part. Following this chapter, Deborah Gerner's essay, "The Evolution of the Study of Foreign Policy" (chapter 2), provides a broad overview of the development of *comparative foreign policy* as a field of first-generation study. The reader will see how some second-generation work builds upon the themes discussed by Gerner. Gerner's chapter is a necessary complement to the previous discussion on the generational differences in foreign policy analysis.

In the third contextual chapter, "The Changing International Context for Foreign Policy," John Rothgeb outlines and reviews the major modifications the international system has undergone since the end of World War II and since the end of the cold war. Within this framework Rothgeb identifies and discusses two "parallel universes"—the first composed of the advanced industrialized countries and the second composed of less developed countries—and the different foreign policy goals, tools, and behaviors associated with each. Finally, Rothgeb offers some ideas about how the changing international context for foreign policy influences the way in which we study foreign policy.

The second part of this volume presents a broad sampling of second-generation research. In chapter 4, "A Cognitive Approach to the Study of Foreign Policy," Jerel

Rosati provides an overview of advances in research relating cognitive processes to foreign policy analysis. This body of work is an extension of the foreign policy *decision-making* research, begun in the first generation by Snyder, Bruck, and Sapin (1962). Rosati demonstrates that second-generation psychological approaches to foreign policy analysis have yielded a sophisticated body of theory and evidence demonstrating that at least part of a state's foreign policy behavior can be explained by an understanding of what happens in the minds of foreign policymakers.

Keith Shimko's "Foreign Policy Metaphors" (chapter 5) provides an example of the research Rosati introduces. Shimko reviews research that relates decision makers' use of analogies and metaphors to their foreign policy behavior, and discusses the use of metaphors in foreign policy analysis. Then, Shimko demonstrates how the "drug war" and "falling dominoes" metaphors have shaped policymakers' thinking and behavior about U.S. policy toward international drug trafficking and security policy, respectively. Shimko's chapter is an example of a second-generation application to a field (political psychology) that has been part of foreign policy studies since the 1960s.

In "Cognition, Culture, and Bureaucratic Politics" (chapter 6), Brian Ripley blends cognitive and group studies to shed light on such issues as the relationships between organizations' leaders, the persistence of particular organizational values and beliefs, and institutional resistance to foreign policy change. Ripley draws upon rich research traditions here and attempts to blend in complementary ways what has often been treated separately. Ripley uses U.S. decision making during the 1968 Tet Offensive to illustrate this approach to the study of foreign policy.

Patrick Haney's essay (chapter 7) borrows heavily from a series of approaches used by first-generation scholars: public management, U.S. presidential studies, organization theory, psychology, and group decision-making studies. In "Structure and Process in the Analysis of Foreign Policy Crises," Haney reviews progress toward linking a decision-making group's structure to process during crisis decision making. Haney argues that together the disparate literatures provide a limited understanding; he suggests that an "institutional perspective" may contribute to a more theoretically fruitful linkage between structure and process in group behavior.

Joe Hagan discusses and expands on first-generation research on the domestic political sources of foreign policy behavior. His "Domestic Political Explanations in the Analysis of Foreign Policy" (chapter 8) reviews the variety of literatures contributing to our understanding of the many domestic influences on foreign policy behavior (particularly the role of domestic opposition groups). Hagan builds on scholarship in domestic and leadership politics and introduces the need for contingent explanations. Hagan's analysis is deeply embedded in area studies' case study literature, a departure from most CFP analyses. Like Haney, Hagan goes on to recommend specific strategies for moving current research into more productive areas.

Philip Schrodt speaks specifically to the difficulties experienced by nearly all foreign policy scholars in finding data for foreign policy analysis. His "Event Data in Foreign Policy Analysis" (chapter 9) considers the use of event data in past and current research. Schrodt argues that with careful attention to the multilevel requirements of second-generation foreign policy data, event data can be a fertile source of theory building in foreign policy analysis.

In "The Politics of Identity and Gendered Nationalism" (chapter 10), V. Spike Peterson introduces the "newest" variable or research framework examined in this book: gender. Peterson incorporates two understudied concepts, gender and nationalism, in the analysis of foreign policy. As Peterson explains, "this chapter explores the politics of identity and the problematics of nationalism through a gender-sensitive lens. It argues that gender is a structural feature of the terrain we call world politics, shaping what we study and how we study it." Peterson's chapter forms part of a growing body of research relating gender to the study of foreign policy and international relations.

Bruce Moon, in "The State in Foreign and Domestic Policy" (chapter 11), contends that there are analytic problems surrounding realism's focus on the "state" as the primary unit of analysis, particularly when examining the foreign policy of peripheral states. Moon argues that peripheral states have different foreign policy goals and tools than core states (the focus of most realist studies) and are therefore poorly accounted for by traditional foreign policy models. Moon calls for greater consideration of the political dynamics and material interests influencing peripheral countries' foreign policy decisions. Moon's chapter resonates with much current research in Third World national security studies (e.g., Azar and Moon 1988; Job 1992; Thomas 1987).

In a related essay entitled "Foreign Policy in Dependent States" (chapter 12), Jeanne Hey reviews the literature on the foreign policy behavior of countries that are economically dependent on core states. Hey holds that most of this literature relies on quantitative methods and realist-based theoretical foundations that cannot explain dependent foreign policy behavior. She develops four distinct dependent foreign policy theoretical models, incorporating variables from the individual, domestic, and international levels of analysis, and argues that each has explanatory value under certain conditions. While the models borrow from first-generation concepts and from dependency theory, the theoretical expectation that dependent states will demonstrate a multitude of foreign policy behaviors is quite new. Like Moon, Hey incorporates political economy into the study of foreign policy.

In "Linking State Type with Foreign Policy Behavior" (chapter 13), Laura Neack reviews the mostly reductionist and atheoretical first-generation attempts at statistically associating ideal-state types and foreign policy behavior. The "pacific democracies" literature formed a more sophisticated body of research examining whether democracies engage in war less often than nondemocracies. Neack argues that even this literature fails to incorporate the complexity needed to understand the foreign policy behavior of democracies. She concludes that "middle power theory" is an example of second-generation contextualized research linking state type and foreign policy behavior that contributes to theory building in foreign policy analysis.

In an essay that aims specifically at linking first-generation ideas to second-generation contributions (chapter 14), Karen Mingst answers James Rosenau's call for linking domestic and international factors in foreign policy analysis. In "Uncovering the Missing Links: Linkage Actors and Their Strategies in Foreign Policy Analysis," noting that too few scholars have heeded Rosenau's plea, Mingst develops a typology of linkage actors and the strategies that they employ in attempting to influence foreign policy decisions. She incorporates actors at all levels into the typology, from local grass-roots movements to international governmental and nongovernmental organizations.

Charles F. Hermann concludes the volume with an epilogue in which he discusses the issues raised by the individual chapters and the challenges for building theory about foreign policy posed by the changing global environment. Hermann uses the end of the cold war as a prism through which to view the state of theory about foreign policy and the challenges that await foreign policy analysis now and in the future.

These essays provide a second-generation approach to foreign policy at all levels of analysis. They build on and diverge from the theoretical emphases of those identified as "comparative foreign policy" scholars. As we discuss here and as will be evident in the chapters that follow, the field of foreign policy analysis has moved from a first to a second generation of scholarship. While there is much overlap across these generations, scholarship in the field now is building on the work of the previous decades to advance our understanding of foreign policy processes and behaviors in new ways. The chapters that follow—individually and collectively—represent the broad range of research areas that contribute to the theoretically rich field of foreign policy analysis.

■ Acknowledgments

We would like to thank Mickey East, Colin Elman, Deborah Gerner, Joe Hagan, Chuck Hermann, Karen Mingst, Brian Ripley, Jerel Rosati, Phil Schrodt, Keith Shimko and those who attended the 1993 APSA panel at which an earlier version of this chapter was presented, as well as anonymous reviewers of the manuscript for their insightful comments.

■ Notes

1. CREON, or the Comparative Research on the Events of Nations project, is explained in detail in the essay by Philip Schrodt in this book (see chapter 9).

2. In this volume, see the essays by Moon (chapter 10) and Hey (chapter 11) on these topics.

3. Indeed, there are interesting advancements in areas of study that speak to issues of foreign policy that are not part of this volume. These areas would include but are not limited to the study of foreign economic policy, foreign policy change, culture and foreign policy, rational models, artificial intelligence, war, war termination, and crisis bargaining.

4. Our profound thanks to Joe Hagan for helping us focus and summarize our thoughts here.

TWO

The Evolution of the
Study of Foreign Policy

Deborah J. Gerner, UNIVERSITY OF KANSAS

■ Editors' Introduction

In "The Evolution of the Study of Foreign Policy" Deborah Gerner reviews in brief form the concepts and research foci that shaped the contours of the first generation of the study of foreign policy, especially that identified as "comparative foreign policy." Gerner discusses the important lines of research that helped define the field of study, such as the early decision-making research by Snyder, Bruck, and Sapin, Rosenau's "pre-theory," and Allison's "bureaucratic politics" paradigm. Her review proceeds by a levels-of-analysis framework and sets the context from which some of the research presented in this volume has emerged.

The reader will note certain themes throughout Gerner's essay that will reappear in some later chapters as well. Other themes and concepts that will be discussed in the rest of the book are quite new to the study of foreign policy. The reader should consider the following questions when reading this chapter: What were the main foci of the field in its first generation? What types of questions were being asked in foreign policy research? On what sources of foreign policy did research concentrate in its first generation? What types of methods were used to study foreign policy? What types of interesting questions or empirical puzzles about foreign policy can you think of that were not addressed during this period? ■

Although no subfield in political science is completely self-contained, the study of foreign policy is somewhat unusual in that it deals with both domestic and international arenas, jumping from individual to state to systemic levels of analysis, and attempts to integrate all of these aspects into a coherent whole. Since at least the 1950s, though, researchers of foreign policy have tried to define an independent field of study that examines foreign policy. Reflecting the broad scope of analysis of such a discipline, the field of foreign policy analysis has always been diverse and dynamic, with scholars pursuing an assortment of substantive topics through a variety of methodological approaches. Today the study of foreign policy is quite diverse, as more and new voices enter the field and add their efforts to the continuing goal of understanding and explaining foreign policy. The central focus of foreign policy analysis is on the intentions, statements, and actions of an actor—often, but not always, a state—directed toward the external world and the response of other actors to these intentions, statements, and actions. Beyond this, however, there is no clear consensus on how the field should be defined. For good reason, Rosenau has called foreign policy a "bridging discipline," one with "limitless boundaries" that must deal with "the continuing erosion of the distinction between domestic and foreign issues, between the sociopolitical and economic processes that unfold at home and those that transpire abroad" (1987a, 1, 3).

Foreign policy analyses can be descriptive, evaluative, or analytical. *Descriptive* studies establish the facts regarding foreign policy decisions, policies declared publicly, actions taken, and the official and de facto relationships among state and nonstate international actors. Foreign policy *evaluation* considers the consequences of foreign policy actions and assesses whether the goals were desirable and if they were achieved. This chapter examines the evolution of research concerned with the *analytical* study of foreign policy: the societal, governmental, and individual inputs that affect foreign policy choices—the main emphases of the first generation of foreign policy scholarship. It begins with a summary of multilevel frameworks and data collection activities, then discusses briefly some substate sources of foreign policy: public opinion and political structures; bureaucratic structures and processes; cognition, perception, personality, and belief systems; artificial intelligence approaches; and decision making under conditions of crisis. In each section I try to highlight the development of the first generation of the study of foreign policy by discussing briefly what I see to be key examples of research and theory development and representative examples of scholarship in each area.

This chapter illustrates the evolution of the study of foreign policy through its first generation. Some of the chapters that follow discuss the issues first mentioned here in greater detail and discuss how research in these areas continues and changes in the second generation of foreign policy scholarship. In its effort to review first-generation scholarship broadly, this chapter does not cover a variety of approaches to the study of foreign policy that are included in this volume, such as those found in the chapters by Jeanne Hey, Bruce Moon, Laura Neack, Karen Mingst, V. Spike Peterson, and John Rothgeb. Indeed, the very inclusion in this volume of these approaches indicates some of the ways in which foreign policy analysis as a field is changing and broadening.

■ Frameworks, Classification Schemes, and Data Development Activities

Initial efforts to make foreign policy research more systematic than the traditional studies that predated World War II and to create a general explanation of foreign policy were expressed in the form of multilevel typologies and frameworks. These frameworks were essentially laundry lists of the potentially relevant factors that needed to be considered in order to understand the foreign policymaking process. The goal was to identify the relevant sources of foreign policy. These sources or variables exist at a variety of levels of analysis (e.g., individuals, bureaucracies, societies).

Underlying these frameworks was a growing recognition that traditional analyses of foreign policy—based upon realpolitik and its assumption of a unitary state actor and its focus on national interest, power, and fully rational and efficient decision making—was insufficient to fully explain foreign policy decisions. This research was also influenced by the challenges of the behavioral revolution, with its neopositivist orientation and its long-term goal of developing empirically verifiable cross-national theories of foreign policy.[1] This section reviews some of the most important attempts to achieve this goal.

One of the first attempts to develop a systematic framework was Snyder, Bruck, and Sapin's *action-reaction-interaction* model. For Snyder and his colleagues, "the key to the explanation of why the state behaves the way it does lies in the way its decision makers as actors define their situation" (1954, 65). That "definition of situation" results from the relationships and interactions of the members of the decision-making unit, existing in a particular international and domestic environment, as well as from each individual's personal attributes, values, and perceptions. This approach, which incorporated insights from psychology and sociology, was a clear departure from the idea of the state as a monolithic actor pursuing its unified "national interests." The general framework developed by Snyder et al. was later applied by Snyder and Paige (1958) and by Paige (1968) to analyze the U.S. decision to intervene in Korea in 1950.

In retrospect, it is easy to criticize the work of Snyder, Bruck, and Sapin for its complexity and its failure to specify how variables were related to one another and were ranked in importance. At the time, however, the framework was a significant step forward for foreign policy research because of its explicit definitions, its indications of underlying assumptions, its emphasis on a decision as a unit of analysis, its effort to untangle the meaning of the actions or decisions of a "state," and, particularly, its goal of creating a structure within which the foreign policy of any country—not just the United States—could be analyzed.

James Rosenau's 1966 "pre-theory" article was a second and highly influential attempt to create a general explanation of foreign policy. Rosenau moved several steps beyond Snyder, Bruck, and Sapin by calling for testable "if-then" propositions, grouping the multitude of potentially relevant sources of foreign policy decisions into five categories, and proposing ways to rank the importance of these variable clusters depending on the specific issue and attributes of the state (e.g., size, political accountability/level of democracy, level of development). The five clusters of foreign policy sources that Rosenau developed—idiosyncratic (later called "individual"), role, governmental, societal, and systemic variables—have served as the basis for analysis in numerous articles, foreign policy textbooks, and collections of readings over the past three decades. Still, Rosenau's "pre-theory" was just that, as Rosenau himself (1984) was quick to acknowledge. It was a typology for organizing research on foreign policy, rather than a fully specified model. As such there was some ambiguity in the concepts used. For example, the dependent variable—foreign policy behavior—was never clearly specified, and the idiosyncratic category contained a mishmash of variables, some of which pertain to general belief systems, others to the unique attributes of a specific leader.

Michael Brecher's case studies of Israel (1972, 1975; cf. Brecher with Geist 1980) were a further effort to develop a framework for understanding foreign policy decisions. Building on the work of Harold Sprout and Margaret Sprout (1956, 1957, 1965), Brecher developed an *input-process-output* model that identifies and classifies the factors that are important in the decision-making process. Of particular interest is the attention this perspective gives to the relationship between the operational or external environment (military and economic capacity, political structure, interest groups, external factors) and the decision makers' interpretations or perceptions of that environment, which Brecher labeled the *psychological environment*. Brecher also introduced a descriptive set of policy issue areas (military-security, political-diplomatic, economic-developmental, cultural-status) that he suggested influence the foreign policy decision. He stopped short, however, of providing specific hypotheses relating the individual variables in the system.

A more recent multilevel approach considers the impact of decision structures on foreign policy (Hermann, Hermann, and Hagan 1987; Hermann and Hermann 1989). This work tries to make sense of the diverse theories about the decision-making process by suggesting that the type of *ultimate decision unit* and the nature of the decision-making process within the decision unit affect both the actual choice and its impact domestically and internationally. Three categories of decision units are identified: *a predominant leader* (who has the power to make the choice for the government); *a single group* (all the individuals necessary for allocation decisions participate in the group, and the group makes decisions through an interactive process among its members); and *multiple autonomous actors* (the decision does not involve any single group or individual that can independently resolve differences existing among the groups or that can reverse any decision the groups reach collectively).

A key part of this argument is that different factors will be relevant for each type of decision unit. When there is a predominant leader, for example, the personality attributes of that individual, his or her degree of sensitivity to the international and domestic environment, and his or her belief system will be of central importance. Although these factors will also be significant for each member of multiple autonomous groups, other variables, such as the nature of the relationships among the groups, enter into the calculus. This approach has been used to study foreign policymaking across national settings (e.g., Hermann and Hermann 1989) and is being applied to specific countries with a wide variety of attributes as the project continues to develop.

One issue that has constrained multilevel foreign policy research—as well as single-level analyses—is the static conceptualization of many of the frameworks and models developed:

> The macro question "when and why do certain policy activities occur?" leads to an enumeration of potential explanatory sources—the nature of the international system, the immediate policy actions of other actors in the environment, the structure of the actor's society or economy, the nature of the domestic political system, the personal characteristics of leaders. . . . But time, evolutionary processes, system transformations, or primary feedback mechanisms are seldom considered. The impact of foreign policy on the subsequent condition of explanatory variables or the possibility that explanatory variables might respond dynamically to one another is rarely explored (Caporaso et al. 1987, 37).

The problem with a nondynamic conception of foreign policy is obvious: it does not reflect reality! Foreign policy is a highly interactive activity that involves continuous communication and feedback. Any approach that is unable to incorporate time and change in foreign policy will have difficulty accurately explaining why foreign policy occurs in the particular ways it does. Coping with the difficulty of constructing dynamic explanations has been a central problem of many foreign policy studies.

The development of multilevel frameworks for the analysis of foreign policy inspired the creation of cross-national event data collections to evaluate these frameworks and to attempt to capture the interactive nature of foreign policy. Event data are nominal or ordinal codes recording the interactions between international actors as reported in the open press. Event data break down complex political activities into a sequence of basic building blocks that can then be aggregated into summary measures of foreign policy exchanges. Event data are valuable because they allow scholars to examine interaction patterns of discrete actions and communication involving international actors—the basic "stuff" of foreign policy—in a systematic way. This is, however, an approach ill suited to studying a number of crucial foreign policy questions, such as the decision *not* to undertake a particular action, since nonevents are excluded from the data sets. In addition, cross-national event data collection often has an unintentional bias toward the Western industrialized world, due to the unavailability of data for Third World states or because the variables chosen come out of Western conceptions of political processes, structures, and ideologies.[2]

Although few scholars would deny the importance of multiple levels of analysis for understanding foreign policy choices, the majority focus their own research on one dimension such as public opinion, group dynamics, or cognition. This choice of focus often reflects individual researchers' judgment of which level of analysis is likely to be most fruitful and, it is hoped, can contribute to a more general understanding of foreign policy when combined with other scholarship at other levels of analysis. The remainder of this chapter examines some of these specific types of foreign policy inputs.

■ Societal Sources of Foreign Policy

All foreign policy decisions occur in a particular domestic context. This environment includes the values, national character, political culture, and historical traditions of a society, its structural attributes (size, level of industrialization, form of government, etc.), and the particular political issues that are important at any given time. In the late 1960s and the 1970s, a number of empirical studies examined the relationship between foreign policy and state attributes.[3] While this research identified some useful generalizations—for instance, the importance of state size in predicting variations in foreign policy behavior (see Sullivan 1976, 135; Jensen 1981, 222–24)—the approach was less productive than scholars had originally anticipated. More recently, attention has also been focused on the multiplicity of nongovernmental actors—multinational corporations, ethnic and special-interest groups, the media, the general public—that attempt to influence the foreign policy choices made by the elites, either through conventional political participation (e.g., voting, letter-writing campaigns) or through nonconventional means of political expression (e.g., protests, demonstrations, strikes, riots, and coups d'état).[4]

The evidence on the relationship between foreign policy and mass opinion is not entirely clear and often appears contradictory. Scholars variously argue that public opinion *determines* foreign policy, that public opinion is *irrelevant* to the foreign policy process, or that public opinion *follows* the chief executive on foreign policy matters rather than influencing decision making.[5] Furthermore, current analyses suggest that public opinion may be influential for certain types of issues or under certain conditions and irrelevant in others. Looking at the United States, Hinckley (1988, 1992) finds that mass opinion toward foreign affairs, like elite opinion, is fractured along several dimensions and thus cannot be easily predicted without reference to specific foreign policy issues.[6] The challenge for foreign policy researchers is to identify the circumstances in which public opinion plays a critical role and those in which its impact is more marginal.

The significance of public opinion as a determinant of foreign policy may well be greater in other countries than it is in the United States. In the case of the latter, public opinion has become more important as an explanatory factor in recent years only because it is increasing from such a small base. For much of the world, however, the connections between foreign and domestic concerns are more visible and explicit. Thus we might expect a higher level of public interest in and awareness of foreign policy issues. Bruce Moon (in chapter 11 of this volume) argues, for instance, that in many states positive public perceptions of foreign policy can serve as a major source of legitimation for the government, particularly when such legitimacy is difficult to achieve through domestic policies or when the state was created by outside powers. Thus, the role of public opinion in defining foreign policy choices needs to be understood in the context of the particular global position of each state and the relationship between the state and the population.[7]

Research on the importance of public opinion often presupposes that democratic regimes are more politically constrained than are their counterparts in authoritarian regimes. This assumption stems partly from a failure to recognize the diversity of ways in which opposition can be expressed. Hagan (1987, 1994) investigates the impact of domestic opposition on foreign policy behaviors in a cross-national analysis of thirty-eight countries during the 1960s and concludes that domestic opposition is a significant influence in the overall substance and style of foreign policy for a wide variety of countries, not only those with democratic systems. Another aspect of regime opposition is considered in a study of anti-Americanism among U.S. allies by Hudson and Sims (1992) that incorporates elements from human needs theory and exchange theory to explain why a regime (e.g., France under Mitterrand in 1982 and 1983, Spain under González-Marquez in the mid-1980s, the Philippines under Aquino in 1990) might seemingly turn against the United States to improve its position relative to an anti-American domestic opposition movement.[8] As this suggests, implicit in research on public opinion and foreign policy is an understanding of the role of the state. In recent years scholars have begun to formulate more carefully exactly what is meant by "the state" and to articulate the implications of various theoretical approaches.[9]

■ Bureaucratic Structures and Processes

A second general approach to the study of foreign policy focuses on the impact of bureaucratic structures, subcultures, and decision-making processes on the eventual choices made.[10] Hilsman (1952, 1959) and Schilling, Hammond, and Snyder (1962) were among the earliest scholars of bureaucratic policies and foreign policy. In the 1970s, research by Allison (1971), Allison and Halperin (1972), and Gelb and Betts (1979) was particularly significant in the development of the field.

Allison's well-known volume on the Cuban missile crisis, *Essence of Decision,* proposes three complementary approaches to explain the decision-making process that occurred in October 1962. The rational actor, organizational processes, and bureaucratic/governmental politics models are each used to illustrate the insights provided by the varying conceptual lenses.[11] *Model I* (rational actor) argues that foreign policy choices are the purposive actions of unified, rational governments, based on plausible calculations of utility and probability, to achieve definable "state goals." *Model II* (organizational processes) reflects the theory that foreign policy can best be understood as the choices and outputs of a group of semifeudal, loosely allied organizations within the government that are looking out for their own interests and following standard operating procedures. *Model III* (bureaucratic/governmental politics) maintains that foreign policy is the result of intensive competition among decision makers and bargaining along regularized channels among players positioned hierarchically within the government bureaucracy, each with his or her own perspective on the issues at hand. It is the "pulling and hauling" of the individual actors that results in the final outcome (cf. Allison and Halperin 1972). While Allison's models have frequently been criticized (see, e.g., Bendor and Hammond 1992), they remain an important starting point for a great deal of current foreign policy research.

One of the best-known efforts to apply bureaucratic decision-making theories to a concrete case is the analysis by Leslie H. Gelb with Richard K. Betts (1979) of the U.S. decision-making processes on Vietnam from World War II until 1968. Gelb and Betts respond to the conventional wisdom that since the U.S. involvement in Vietnam was not "rational" it must have come about through mistakes in the bureaucratic process. They contend instead that U.S. failures reflected the policy preferences of the actors and agencies influencing the decision-making process. "The paradox is that the foreign policy failed, but the domestic decision making system worked. . . . Vietnam was not an aberration of the decision making system but a logical outcome of the principles that leaders brought with them into it" (1979, 2).

Building on the general theorizing of Allison and others, a number of more recent studies explicitly address the impact of organizational structures and the interaction of governmental players—the chief executive and his or her staff, the legislative body, the foreign affairs bureaucracy, the Defense Department—on foreign policy. One of the key issues is the extent to which bureaucracies either enhance or jeopardize prospects for rational decision making. Another question is what happens when a part of the foreign policy bureaucracy comes to see itself as an autonomous (nonaccountable) actor and begins to operate in ways counter to an agreed-upon policy or against the wishes of the president.[12]

The bureaucratic approach to foreign policy analysis has most often been used to describe the decision-making process in the United States and Western Europe. There are at least two reasons for this. First, bureaucratic analyses require detailed, accurate data about what goes on inside the government: what the standard operating procedures are, how individuals bargain with each other, what agencies have actual (as opposed to official) responsibility for which issues or activities. This information is not easily obtained even in the relatively open United States. In many countries it is extremely difficult to acquire. Furthermore, most of the scholars who are trained in this approach in the United States and Western Europe tend to focus their research on these areas as well. Second, bureaucratic factors are most often significant in countries with massive and complex governmental structures. This group is limited at present to relatively few states. Nonetheless, some scholars have attempted to test the bureaucratic approach on countries outside of the industrialized world.[13]

■ Cognitive Processes and Psychological Attributes

Individual-level theories focus on decision makers in order to understand how an individual's belief system, the way an individual perceives, interprets, and processes information about an international situation, and idiosyncratic personal attributes explain foreign policy choices. Research on these dimensions was once viewed with skepticism. Such factors were thought to be either outside the realm of political science (and perhaps unknowable) or a mere residual after systemic, societal, and governmental factors had been taken into account. Therefore, psychological elements of decision making were simply left inside a "black box."

In recent years, however, personality attributes, cognitive processes, attitudes, and belief systems have played a more prominent role in foreign policy research. Much of the current research on the psychological aspects of foreign policy has evolved from the work of Holsti (1962, 1970, 1982), George (1969, 1979b), and Walker (1977, 1983) on the "operational code"; the cognitive mapping approach developed by Axelrod (1976a) and Bonham and Shapiro (1976); and the small-group dynamics explored by Janis (1982, 1989).[14]

An example of how personality is studied is Margaret Hermann's research on the personal characteristics of world leaders to determine the circumstances under which these will represent a significant influence on foreign policy decision making. In a series of articles (e.g., 1978, 1980, 1984), Hermann examines leaders' operational codes or views of the world, political styles, interest and training in foreign affairs, conceptual complexity (sensitivity to the environment), and political socialization, as well as their constituencies and the functions they perform in relation to those constituencies. All of these, Hermann argues, need to be taken into account in order to assess leaders' impact on foreign policy.[15]

The issue of perception is crucial to any consideration of individual-level sources of foreign policy (see Vertzberger 1990; Voss and Dorsey 1992). Simon (1957a, 1985) and Braybrooke and Lindblom (1963) were among the first scholars to examine why rational decision making—whether in foreign or domestic policy—so often fails to occur. Among scholars of decision making, Simon is probably best known for his development of the concepts of "bounded rationality" and "satisficing," which challenge the rational actor framework while working within it. Bounded rationality emphasizes the psychological and intellectual limits of human beings: the normal desire to simplify the world, the tendency to take shortcuts in thinking that violate formal logic, the inability of most people to hold a complex set of variables in mind simultaneously. Given these human limits, Simon argues, fully rational decision making is impossible. Instead, people satisfice: they examine sequentially the choices facing them until they come upon one that meets their minimum standards of acceptability, one that will "suffice" and "satisfy."

Braybrooke and Lindblom also reject the "synoptic conception" of decision making that assumes that the values, consequences, and probabilities of all options are known and carefully considered by the decision maker. Like Simon, they recognize that time and resource constraints may not allow such a comprehensive analysis, even assuming that all the necessary pieces of information can, in theory, be known. Given this situation, the definition of a problem is crucial in determining the solution chosen. Other factors, such as the abilities of the decision maker and the values held by that person, will also limit the alternatives considered and ultimately chosen.

More recently Jervis (1968, 1976) has also investigated the ways in which rational decision making can get sidetracked. Jervis begins with the question: How and why does one actor misperceive the actions and intentions of another? The pressures toward premature cognitive closure, the failure to recognize the influence of preexisting beliefs (including the tendency to see other states as more hostile—and other actions as more disciplined and coordinated—than is usually the case), perceptual satisficing, and wishful thinking are all identified as factors that can lead to misperception. Jervis's research has significantly extended our understanding of the relationship between individual and group decision making in the foreign policy realm. It has been criticized, however, for failing to distinguish between static and dynamic aspects of perception and for ignoring group dynamics and societal-cultural variables (see Vertzberger 1990, 17–18).

Another aspect of cognitive studies is a focus on individual and communal belief systems. For more than a decade, Holsti and Rosenau have investigated the changes in foreign policy beliefs and perceptions of U.S. opinion leaders. They find that the elite foreign policy consensus (that saw communism as the single most important threat to U.S. interests) that existed during the cold war era was shattered during the Vietnam War. The result was the creation of "sharply divergent views on the nature of the international system and the appropriate international role for the United States" that are so different they can be considered competing belief systems (1984, 30, 31; see also 1979, 1986b). Holsti and Rosenau identify three belief systems present immediately after the Vietnam War—cold war internationalism, post–cold war internationalism, and semi-isolationism—and suggest that these divisions continued into the 1980s before beginning to recede with the end of the cold war. These belief systems appear to have given way to a renewed consensus in favor of active internationalism that nonetheless differs on the specifics of U.S. involvement in world affairs (1990b).

Several articles challenge the specific categories used by Holsti and Rosenau to classify elite attitudes, but they do not dispute the basic notion of fundamental splits among foreign policy elites (as well as the mass public). Combining these dimensions results in at least eight different types of elites. Wittkopf (1986, 1987, 1990) suggests there are two critical dimensions—militant internationalism and cooperative internationalism—that, when combined, create four types of foreign policy attitudes among elites and the general public: hard-liners, internationalists, isolationists, and accommodationists. In a reassessment of Wittkopf's research, Holsti and Rosenau (1990a) confirm that there is strong support for his classification approach as applied to foreign policy elites. In contrast, Chittick and Billingsley (1989) argue that elite as well as mass beliefs are structured along at least three different dimensions: universalism-isolationism, multilateralism-unilateralism, and militarism-nonmilitarism.

These categories have practical applications. McCormick (1985), for example, finds that belief system (which he labels ideology) is a good predictor of congressional votes on several nuclear freeze proposals in the early 1980s. Examining only the Senate, Carter (1989) concludes that ideology is one factor (along with party identification and, to a lesser extent, economic benefit) that explains senators' roll call votes in the 1980s on defense issues such as spending for weapons procurement. It should be noted that research in this area places heavy emphasis on the case of the United States.

Psychological research on foreign policy is likely to undergo some changes in the next few years as the effects of the "cognitive revolution" in psychology diffuse. Newer methods emphasize human information processing at a relatively micro level, rather than focusing on more macro concepts such as "personality." Some of these approaches are found in the artificial intelligence literature discussed in the following section, but there are insights about human interpretation and recall of events, attitudes, and assessments of risk (e.g., Kahneman, Slovic, and Tversky 1982) as well as the impact of language, cognitive development, and culture (Sampson and Walker 1987) that are relevant to foreign policy analysis even in the absence of computer models of those processes.

■ Artificial Intelligence

A number of models of foreign policy have been developed in recent years using artificial intelligence (AI) methods (the phrase *computational modeling* has also been applied to this research). Artificial intelligence models employ case-specific information in order to model the foreign policy process. This approach is capable of modeling complex decision-making processes that involve past actions, bureaucratic bargaining, and information flow rather than being restricted to the simplistic model of maximization by rational unitary actors that characterized many earlier formal models. As with the studies of cognition and perception, artificial intelligence research is also valuable because it focuses attention on the notion of choice in foreign policymaking.[16]

The most common AI technique applied to foreign policy is "rule-based modeling." In the late 1970s computer scientists discovered that many problems requiring human expertise could be solved by the simple application of a large number (five hundred to five thousand) of idiosyncratic rules. Unlike statistical methods, these "expert systems" also seem to capture some of the characteristics of how humans actually solve problems. Humans are not particularly adept at either statistical reasoning or logical reasoning from first principles; instead, most human problem solving appears to involve the nonstatistical application of idiosyncratic rules.

Rule-based systems are especially attractive when one is modeling the behavior of organizations, since a great deal of organizational behavior is explicitly rule-guided. For example, rule-based models appear able to capture many of the standard operating procedures implemented by low-level bureaucrats in the U.S. Departments of State and Defense (Job and Johnson 1991; Taber 1992). These standard operating procedures can be exceedingly complex and particularized for different situations and countries—the ruled response to the kidnapping of a U.S. citizen in Ethiopia, for instance, may be very different than the response to a similar kidnapping in Italy—and hence the behavior of the organization is more likely to be captured by a rule-based model than by an explanatory model that is more parsimonious and general. Rule-based models have been less successful, however, in dealing with the less regularized problem solving that is found in crisis situations or with decisions that involve political controversy or change.

Rule-based models in foreign policy research have generally taken two forms. The most common uses fairly simple versions of the if-then structure of expert systems. Behaviors that have been modeled include Chinese foreign policy (Tanaka 1984), general characteristics of foreign policy behavior (Hudson 1987), rules for Vietnam War involvement (Majeski 1987), Soviet crisis response (Kaw 1989), and Sino-Soviet negotiations (Mills 1990). These systems were coded by the authors' deriving the rules either through interviewing experts or through study, intuition, and experimentation.

Rule-based systems can be extended substantially beyond the if-then rules of expert systems, particularly when complicated data structures are introduced that approximate the wealth of information available to a decision maker. Several AI models have tried to replicate some of the actual rules used by actors in an international system, thereby attempting to gain process validity as well as outcome validity.[17]

Artificial intelligence modelers have also attempted to model the cognitive process itself. The primary approach is the use of analogy or precedent, originally developed in a series of papers by Alker and others (1972, 1976, 1980). This approach is based on the idea that decision makers seek the "lessons of the past" in dealing with crises and continually modify those lessons depending on the success or failure of the policy. For example, the CIA overthrow of Iranian leader Mussadegh in 1953 was used as a precedent for the overthrow of Arbenz in Guatemala in 1954. Those two "successful" interventions were then used as the model for the ill-fated Bay of Pigs invasion against Castro in 1961. The failure at the Bay of Pigs was attributed in part to the low level of U.S. military support; this was corrected by the massive use of U.S. troops in invading the Dominican Republic in 1965, Grenada in 1983, and Iraq in 1990–91. Although the use of historical analogies and metaphors is not without risk, humans use them all the time.[18]

A precedent-based computer model involves at least three elements. First, the model must accessibly store information concerning a set of historical precedents in the computer. Humans acquire precedents through some combination of induction and explicit teaching; this is less straightforward for a computer. Second, there must be an explicit means of comparing a current situation with the information (knowledge) stored in the database to determine which situation or situations will be employed as the precedent. Finally, the system must have some means of correcting mistaken analogies through feedback and a means of acquiring new information. The importance of precedent is almost universally accepted by AI researchers in foreign policy, but constructing actual models based on that principle still appears to be a major challenge and has not been as successful as initially anticipated. If the technical problems can be overcome, precedent-based AI models may provide a realistic approximation of how decision makers use history and a systematic means of studying that aspect of the foreign policymaking process.

■ The Emphasis on Decision Making during Crises

An explicit emphasis on "crisis" has been important to foreign policy scholars at least since the late 1950s, in spite of the seemingly endless debate on what defines a crisis and whether "crisis" should be an independent, dependent, or intervening variable in the analysis (see, e.g., Brecher 1977; Hermann 1969b, 1972).[19] A set of research identified collectively as the Stanford 1914 Crisis Study was one of the earliest efforts to take seriously the goal of an interdisciplinary, scientific approach to foreign policy decision making under crisis. The goal was to use a single specific crisis—the outbreak of war in 1914—to develop a general model of interstate foreign policy behavior. Initially, the group planned to create a complete minute-by-minute chronology of the period just prior to the beginning of the war. Although this chronology proved unmanageable and was not completed, the progress that was made allowed researchers to focus on the various perceptions and misperceptions that appeared to trigger acts that intensified the crisis (see Zinnes 1976, chapter 7).

Holsti, North, and Brody (1968) based their research on this initial research effort. Their approach used content analysis within the framework of a stimulus-response model taken from psychology to examine the interaction between decisional units. They began with the assumption that there was congruence between the stimulus (or input) in a crisis and the response (or output), but they quickly realized that for this to hold true—particularly in a crisis situation—one must incorporate perceptual variables rather than look only at so-called objective reality. Their research therefore sought to explore the importance of perceptual variables in crises. Although the researchers did not present a true decision-making model because they did not deal with the internal dynamics leading to particular responses, their work does illustrate a keen sensitivity to the psychological issues that underlie contemporary perceptual studies, as well as illuminating how early scientific research looked at crisis.

Snyder and Diesing (1977) and Lebow (1981) also focused on decision making in crisis situations. These analyses were both based on a series of detailed case studies of international crisis situations in the late nineteenth century and the twentieth century, with the goal of building a theory of international crisis behavior. Snyder and Diesing began with theories about aggregate bargaining behaviors, but they also examined "the effects of international system structures and the decision making activities of the actors on the bargaining process" (1977, xi). Thus, they shifted from systemic factors to an examination of perception, group processes, and other individual- and domestic-level variables. The majority of their investigation dealt with sixteen intensive and five less detailed case studies of crises in the period 1898–1970; these were undertaken to provide consistent information on a clear set of common hypotheses and questions.

The most interesting part of the research by Snyder and Diesing (1977) is the chapter on decision making, which draws on the research by Jervis (1976) and others. Snyder and Diesing identified fifty cases of strategic decisions and used them to test three theories of decision making: (1) utility maximization, or classical rational theory; (2) bounded rationality, taken from Simon's satisficing model; and (3) bureaucratic politics, as defined by Allison and Halperin. The first two are "problem-solving" theories; the third looks at political processes occurring inside the decision-making unit. Snyder and Diesing argued that utility maximization and bounded rationality may be complementary rather than competing theories, and that the bureaucratic politics approach, with its focus on the "internal political imperatives of maintaining and increasing influence and power" (1977, 355), should be viewed as supplemental to, rather than in competition with, the other two. Snyder and Diesing also pointed out that bureaucratic politics, as it is usually discussed, has both rational and nonrational components that are often confused, with the nonrational dimension accounting for attitudes, values, beliefs, and cognitive sensitivities (cf. Robinson and Snyder 1965).

Snyder and Diesing concluded that although the basic assumptions of utility maximization theory do not hold in crisis situations, "the fit of bounded rationality to crisis bargaining decisions is excellent, especially in the area of strategy revision" (1977, 405–7). Bounded rationality and bureaucratic politics theories apply in different circumstances. The former fits best when a limited number of individuals are involved in the decision-making process. The latter is most useful in explaining the coalition-building activities that occur when a large number of actors have input in the decision.

Lebow began his analysis with twenty-six historical crises divided into three categories (justification of hostility, spin-off crises, brinkmanship) based on their origins, patterns of development, and probability of resolution of each crisis. A *justification of hostility* situation is one in which there is a deliberate effort to create a crisis in order to provide the excuse to go to war. *Spin-off crises* involve secondary confrontations in which neither party really wants the conflict and will try to resolve the situation in a peaceful fashion if this can be accomplished while protecting the "national interest." *Brinkmanship* (the most common form of crisis) occurs "when a state knowingly challenges an important commitment of another state in the hope of compelling its adversary to back away from [its] commitment" (Lebow 1981, 57).

These three types of crises are intended to illustrate patterns rather than to directly predict or explain whether a specific crisis will lead to war. While Snyder and Diesing approached their material from a bargaining perspective, Lebow was more interested in the political-military environment of the crisis and the thought processes of the decision makers, in particular, cognitive consistency and misperception. The focus on crisis has continued to be a central part of the study of foreign policy, focusing on decision making (including that by individuals, small groups, and large groups), bargaining, crisis management, and the onset of war.[20]

■ Conclusion

Significant advances have been made in the study of foreign policy since scholars began to define the field in the 1950s. The state of our substantive knowledge has increased, as have our theoretical and conceptual skills for trying to understand and explain foreign policy. Yet the field of foreign policy analysis as it enters its second generation of scholarship is replete with still-unsolved intellectual puzzles.

If there is a single conclusion that can be drawn from surveying the evolution of the study of foreign policy in its first generation it is that there has been a shift away from trying to build grand theory—trying to explain all aspects of foreign policy for all countries at all points in time—in favor of trying to build midrange theories that are empirically grounded, culturally sensitive, and often issue- or domain-specific. In their discussion of efforts to understand and explain foreign policy behavior, Most and Starr observe:

> There may well be a variety of social laws, each of which is true but which should be expected to hold only under certain—perhaps very special—conditions. While it is possible that universals—always true laws—exist . . . it is difficult to think of very many empirical universals that have been identified even by physical scientists. Thus, it may be useful to recognize that there could very well be laws that are in some sense "good," "domain-specific," or "nice" even though the relationships that they imply are not necessarily very empirically general. Rather than assuming that there need be a single, "always true," law which accounts for a given phenomenon whenever and wherever it has occurred or will occur, it may be more productive to think of laws each of which is always true under certain conditions (or within certain domains) but which is only "sometimes true" empirically because those conditions do not always hold in the empirical world (1989, 117).

By taking a more modest approach, researchers in the second generation of foreign policy analysis, while building on the foundation of the first generation, enhance their prospects for advancing our understanding of pieces of the diverse and fascinating field of foreign policy analysis. The chapters that follow in this volume serve to illustrate in far greater detail the breadth of the field of foreign policy analysis, the many voices that try to explain foreign policy. Here I have tried to briefly sketch the development of research that has focused on foreign policy in its first generation— the field as it saw itself from the 1950s through the 1980s. In the following chapters a broader and more eclectic field of foreign policy analysis is presented in a way that illustrates the continuing evolution of the field as it tries to understand and explain foreign policy.

■ Acknowledgment

This chapter was adapted and updated with permission from Deborah J. Gerner, "Foreign Policy Analysis: Renaissance, Routine, or Rubbish?" in *Political Science: Looking to the Future,* vol. 2, ed. William Crotty (Evanston, Ill.: Northwestern University Press, 1991); and from Debor ┑ J. Gerner, "Foreign Policy Analysis: Exhilarating Eclecticism, Intriguing Enigmas," *International Studies Notes* 16, no. 3/17, no. 1 (Fall 1991/Winter 1992): 4–19.

■ Notes

1. Cohen and Harris (1975) summarize much of this early research, and Vertzberger (1990, chapter 1) provides a useful discussion of the importance of using multiple levels of analysis.

2. Philip Schrodt discusses event data and the many data collection activities that have taken place within the study of foreign policy in his essay in this volume (see chapter 9).

3. For example, see East 1978; East and Hermann 1975; Moore 1974a and b; Rummel 1972a; Salmore and Salmore 1978; Sawyer 1967; Wilkenfeld 1968; and Wilkenfeld et al. 1980. See also the essay by Laura Neack (chapter 13) in this volume.

4. See the essays by Joe Hagan (chapter 8) and Karen Mingst (chapter 14) in this volume for discussions of these issues.

5. See Holsti (1992) for a summary of this debate.

6. Recent examples of issue-specific research include public opinion and U.S. policy toward South Africa (Metz 1986; Rogers 1992); economic pressure groups and U.S. trade policy (Destler and Odell 1987); activism on nuclear arms control and disarmament issues (DeHaven 1991; Oudsten 1989; Solo 1988); public opinion on U.S. involvement in Central America (Sobel 1989); public input on U.S. defense policy (Hartley and Russett 1992; Russett 1990; Russett and Graham 1989); the influence of presidential popularity and other domestic factors on the decision to use force (James and Oneal 1991); the impact of peace activism on Israeli foreign policy formation (T. Hermann 1992); the SALT II debate in the United States (Skidmore 1992); public responses to changing U.S.-Soviet relations (Peffley and Hurwitz 1992); and the public opinion politics of the international drug trade (Friman 1992).

7. See also the essay by Joe Hagan (chapter 8) in this volume.

8. See also Jeanne Hey's essay (chapter 12) in this volume.

9. For two very different treatments of the state, see Evans, Rueschemeyer, and Skocpol (1985) and Ikenberry, Lake, and Mastanduno (1988).

10. For a more complete discussion of the bureaucratic politics approach, see the essays by Ripley (chapter 6) and Haney (chapter 7) in this volume.

11. Brian Ripley discusses this research approach in greater detail in his essay (chapter 6) in this volume.

12. Bock (1987), Crabb and Holt (1989), Crabb and Mulcahy (1986), Destler (1972, 1983), Hilsman (1990), Inderfurth and Johnson (1988), Johnson (1989), and Lenczowski (1990) are representative of this often descriptive and occasionally normative and prescriptive research tradition.

13. Dawisha's (1980) study of the Soviet Union is one notable example, as is Korany's (1986a) application to the Third World. See also, for example, the research by Kasza (1987) and Weil (1975).

14. These and other psychological dimensions of foreign policy are examined in Cottam (1986), Hermann (1986), Rosati (1987), Shimko (1991), and Singer and Hudson (1992). In this volume the essays by Jerel Rosati (chapter 4) and Keith Shimko (chapter 5) discuss cognition, while the essay by Brian Ripley (chapter 6) addresses the links between individuals and groups.

15. The role of personality in foreign policy formulation is also investigated in Shepard's (1988) replication of Etheredge's (1978a, 1978b) research on interpersonal generalization theory. Kellerman and Rubin (1988) present a set of case studies on the personalities of specific Middle East leaders; Snare (1992) provides a comparison of methods of assessing the relationship between personality and foreign policy behavior; and Winter (1992) contains a general assessment of this research approach.

16. Cimbala (1987), Hudson (1991), and Sylvan and Chan (1984) provide a number of examples; see also Benfer, Brent, and Furbee (1991), Garson (1990), Purkitt (1992), and Schrodt (1994a) for useful reviews of this literature.

17. Situations that have been modeled using this approach include Saudi Arabian foreign policy (Anderson and Thorson 1982); the Cuban missile crisis (Thorson and Sylvan 1982); Middle East international politics (Phillips 1987); Japanese energy and foreign policy decision making (Sylvan, Goel, and Chandresekaran 1990); U.S. policy toward Asia (Taber 1992); and U.S. policy toward Central America (Job and Johnson 1991).

18. The arguments for precedent are reviewed in Anderson (1981), Khong (1992), Pazzani (1989), and Schrodt (1985), as well as in articles employing precedent-based modeling such as Mefford (1987) and Schrodt (1989, 1991). See also Vertzberger (1990, chap. 6) and the essay by Keith Shimko (chapter 5) in this volume.

19. See also the essay by Patrick Haney (chapter 7) in this volume for a further discussion of research on crisis decision making.

20. A large portion of crisis research has focused on the United States and other advanced industrial countries.

THREE

The Changing International
Context for Foreign Policy

John M. Rothgeb Jr., MIAMI UNIVERSITY

■ Editors' Introduction

In the next context-setting chapter, John Rothgeb discusses the broader political context in which foreign policy analysts and practitioners operate. This chapter, like several of the concluding chapters in this volume, derives from an international relations orientation that clearly speaks to foreign policy issues. Here Rothgeb contends that the foreign policies of states in the emerging, post–cold war international system will continue to be differentiated by key organizing features of the post–World War II era, particularly those that maintain the distinctions between the advanced industrialized countries and the non-Western developing countries. Rothgeb describes these two groups of states as two "parallel universes" between which states' foreign policy objectives and tools of statecraft vary markedly. The reader should think about how this dualistic international system resembles the core-periphery system that premises later essays by Bruce Moon (chapter 11) and Jeanne Hey (chapter 12). Further, Rothgeb reminds us that we must confront the broader political environment when studying foreign policy, a theme that will be reasserted later by V. Spike Peterson (chapter 10) and Laura Neack (chapter 13).

When reading this chapter, the reader should consider the following questions: Rothgeb contends that war between the Western advanced industrialized countries has become an impossibility. How likely is this to hold true given the movement in the world toward trade blocs? Could the use of "Super 301" sanctions by the U.S. against Japan signal the beginning of a series of "trade wars" within the Western world? What conditions would be necessary for the non-Western world to similarly "give up" the use of military force as a legitimate tool of statecraft? Finally, given the remarkable differences between these two "parallel universes," is it possible for foreign policy scholars to develop general statements about foreign policy behavior that apply to all states universally? ■

This chapter provides the reader with a description of the international system in which foreign policy is conducted. The *international system* is defined as the patterns of interaction that exist among the actors around the world who pursue policies designed to further their foreign goals and interests.[1] As the editors have noted, second-generation analysts regard foreign policy as a complex phenomenon that only can be understood properly when one investigates carefully the social, political, psychological, economic, and other forces that work both within and between international actors to define the context in which foreign policy is formulated.[2] The international system is an important element in the creation of foreign policy because the behavior of any one actor tends to elicit counterresponses from other actors. These counterresponses redefine circumstances and confront actors with the need for new policy selections. Thus, the international system affects foreign policy by way of the constant interactions that occur between actors, with each interaction forcing the affected actors to reevaluate their needs and adjust their policies.

The central argument in this chapter is that while the international system remains anarchic and is dominated by interactions among independent states, the degrees and types of conflicts among states, the types of issues that structure the foreign policy behavior of states, the goals that states pursue, and the resources used to conduct foreign policy all have changed or are in the process of changing.[3] In other words, the structure of the international system remains much the same, but the nature of the competition and the patterns of conflict within the system have shifted.

Until recently, these changes have been obscured in part by the military and political rivalry between the superpowers that formed the basis of the cold war. The end of that conflict, however, is permitting analysts to devote full attention to new international circumstances and to their implications for the conduct of foreign policy as the world moves toward the twenty-first century. International politics remains competitive, and international actors continue to pursue divergent objectives and seek to protect themselves and their interests by trying to manipulate the behavior of others. However, many countries now define their goals and vital interests in new ways and have new conceptions of what resources are most appropriately used to conduct foreign policy and exercise power. In addition, a careful look at recent patterns of international interactions points to the evolution of what might be referred to as *parallel international universes*. While these universes do interact with one another, they appear to operate according to different rules and to involve very different casts of characters. As a result, in order to obtain an accurate understanding of policy behavior it is increasingly important for foreign policy analysts to specify carefully the international context in which the policy is formulated.

The following pages illustrate and elaborate upon these points. The next section describes the characteristics of the international system as scholars traditionally have depicted them. The basic issues that currently structure foreign policy are then discussed. Finally, the chapter closes by examining the emergence of the parallel international systems just mentioned.

■ The Traditional International System

Traditional descriptions of the international system usually begin with the observation that the state is the dominant actor in an international game that is played under anarchic conditions. The state is a sovereign entity, which means that it has the right to control a given expanse of territory, and the people living on it, and to make and enforce such rules, or laws, as it deems necessary. *Anarchy* refers to the absence of any international or world government that can regulate international activities. In a world of independent actors and no government, foreign policy is conducted in a competitive atmosphere in which each actor must safeguard its own interests and usually is wary of arrangements that infringe on its independence.[4]

Given the competitive nature of international politics, a country's ability to bend others to its will, that is, to exercise power, is essential to its self-preservation and to the attainment of its foreign policy objectives. Conflict among nations results as an outgrowth of these circumstances because countries frequently pursue clashing interests. Indeed, many see conflict as the essence of international politics, and the relative power relationships among international actors usually are treated as a key to the study of foreign policy. The late Hans Morgenthau, one of the most respected scholars in the field of international relations, argued that "international politics is of necessity power politics" (Morgenthau 1948, 33). More recently, another author has written that "there is really only one approach which enables students to appreciate the essence of the field [of international politics]. The approach, for want of better terminology, is power politics" (Gray 1977, 2).

Within this framework, the relative military capabilities of differing nations traditionally have been an important area for study. The reason is related to the role war has played in the international arena. E. H. Carr recognized that "potential war being thus a dominant factor in international politics, military strength becomes a . . . standard of political values" (1939, 109). Harold Sprout and Margaret Sprout agree that "power . . . has been seen historically in military terms" (1971, 165). Joseph Nye concurs, stating that for most analysts "war has been the ultimate indicator of national military strength" (1990, 78).

In this sort of international climate, when countries have incompatible foreign policy goals that their governments and people feel strongly about, military resources often determine the winner and loser. While actual fighting generally is avoided, the threat to fight and a state's military strength can be counted on to figure prominently in negotiations. In the international system, "the power to hurt—the sheer . . . unproductive power to destroy things that somebody treasures, to inflict pain and grief—is a kind of bargaining power" (Schelling 1966, v). A country's military capabilities, combined with the perception that it is willing to use them, is a vital backstop to the various diplomatic, political, economic, and other techniques that it might employ. As Klaus Knorr noted, "Historically, military power has tended to be superior . . . to other forms of power. Ever since the world became politically organized in terms of independent states, each claiming military sovereignty, force has been regarded as the ultimate arbiter in the settlement of conflicts" (1975, 19). In fact, the role of the military has been treated as so dominant that many scholars have discussed other national characteristics, such as a country's population, its political organization, its geographic position and topography, its endowment of natural resources, and its economic capacity almost solely in terms of how they contribute to the ability of a state to make war.[5]

World leaders also have spoken of the importance of the military for foreign policy. When Winston Churchill proclaimed "Thank God for the French Army" before the House of Commons after Hitler came to power in Germany, he pointed to what he felt would guarantee British safety from the German menace (Churchill 1948, 68). Former Secretary of State Cordell Hull expressed his appreciation for the military by noting, "When I came to the State Department I thought for a time, when talking to Axis diplomats, that they were looking me in the eye; but I soon discovered that they were looking over my shoulder at our armed forces and appraising our strength. Here, I came to feel, was the controlling factor in their acts and utterances toward us" (1948, 457). From antiquity until the middle of the twentieth century one could with accuracy describe the international system as dominated by the great military powers.[6] Such nations set the rules for conducting foreign policy, they defined international political structures, they settled disputes with and among smaller states, and they determined the distribution of international resources. Relative military capabilities also defined the pecking order among the largest countries, for "recognition as a great power [was] normally the reward of fighting [and winning] a large-scale war" (Carr 1939, 109).

■ The Changing International System

In the years since World War II, serious analysts increasingly have been forced to wonder about the nature of the international system and the predominance assigned to the military as an instrument of foreign policy. The rise to international prominence of such nonmilitary powers as Japan and Germany, the collapse of the Soviet Union, the liberation of Eastern Europe, the unification movement in the European Community, and the strength of the newly industrializing states in the Pacific all lead to questions about traditional views. Many other developments also could be cited as evidence of rapid change. Indeed, some recent authors have speculated that an international revolution is under way and that the rules of international politics are shifting dramatically.[7]

Among the most fundamental of the contentions of those who argue the case for international revolution is the idea that wars are so dysfunctional that they have become obsolete and that military strength no longer has much applicability in the international arena.[8] Analysts adopting this point of view usually cite the absence of warfare since 1945 and the increased economic interdependence among the advanced industrialized countries as important supporting evidence for their views.[9]

These beliefs are not universally accepted and are challenged on several grounds. For one thing, as Kenneth Waltz has noted, "the structure of international politics has not been transformed; it remains anarchic in form" (1988, 626). That is, no international political community has emerged to provide a form of world government. Foreign policy still is conducted within the same basic decentralized international framework that has existed for centuries (Gilpin 1981, 7). Michael Sullivan (1990, 52–53) points to another reason for doubting that substantial changes have occurred, that being that international wars have been fought no less frequently since 1945 than during other eras. Finally, many argue that the importance of a state's armed forces has not declined and that the military remains an essential instrument of foreign policy because it both provides the security shield behind which international commerce is conducted and serves as a nation's guarantee of safety.[10]

In considering this debate about international change, two issues stand out. One has to do with how countries define their international goals and interests and what resources they regard as most appropriate for conducting foreign policy. Another relates to the different patterns of behavior found within and between differing clusters of actors. These points will serve as the basis for evaluating the validity of the arguments pertaining to whether the international system has been transformed.

Goals and Issues

Many scholars have noted that nations traditionally have focused their foreign policies on the pursuit of military and territorial security.[11] The foregoing discussion has illustrated this. A variety of new goals and issues have emerged, however, that lead to new definitions of security. It no longer is at all proper to depict nonmilitary issues in the following terms: "When states cooperate with one another to maintain postal or transport services, or to prevent the spread of epidemics or suppress the traffic in drugs, these activities are described as 'non-political' or 'technical'" (Carr 1939, 102). While such a description may have been accurate when it was written in the middle years of this century, it is now inappropriate. Forty years ago, epidemics and drug trafficking, no matter how tragic, may have been seen as nonpolitical, and consequently as not involving the vital interests of nations. Today matters are different. In recent years, opinion polls consistently have indicated that the American public (for one) regards such concerns as the AIDs epidemic and drug trafficking as major issues, both domestically and internationally. Even such a "technical" issue as agricultural subsidies has provoked such an outcry among French farmers during the Uruguay Round of the General Agreement on Tariffs and Trade (GATT) negotiations that the French government was forced to make it a major foreign policy issue and to break ranks on several occasions with its partners in the European Community.

Perhaps the most salient of the nonmilitary concerns now facing states relates to economics. Governments began paying closer attention to managing both their domestic economies and international commercial networks in the years between the world wars. Two forces pushed them in this direction. One was the devastation of World War I. Another was the extreme dislocation that occurred during the Great Depression, which created such a threat to political stability, both domestic and international, that governments were compelled to assume a role as a provider of welfare services (see Kindleberger 1973).

Once governments acknowledged their responsibilities in the economic arena, new standards were set for determining their legitimacy. States found that they had new goals. As Wolfram Hanrieder has remarked: "Modern governments have become increasingly sensitive to demands for a wide variety of welfare services and have taken on the responsibility for mass social and economic welfare. The improvement through state intervention of the material…well-being of its citizens has become one of the central functions of state activity. The satisfaction of rising claims by citizens has become a major source of the state's legitimation and of a government's continuance in office" (1978, 1278).

The unprecedented destruction of World War II reinforced the need for state action. Also pushing in this direction were the needs of both the East and the West to pull together resources for the cold war confrontation and the belief that carefully managed economic growth would prevent a resurgent Axis threat (see Rothgeb 1993, 64–80). In addition, the emergence in recent decades of a host of new states further magnified the state's economic responsibilities, for one of the most compelling concerns of these countries is promoting economic growth and development in order to overcome the poverty that afflicts them (see Duvall and Freeman 1983; Holsti 1975).

A greater economic role for the state carries with it important international implications, for the complexity of modern industrial societies demands greater access to foreign markets and resources to meet one's economic goals. The Bretton Woods economic system was created after World War II to meet these needs. Along with the evolution of mammoth international corporations, the development of the European Community, and the leadership of the United States, the Bretton Woods institutions paved the way for the vast increases in economic interdependence found among many international actors since 1945.

This growth in interdependence and its importance for the maintenance of a sound domestic economy have placed the economic relationships between nations in the forefront of the issues that are now at the core of foreign policy. The fanfare surrounding the yearly economic summits of the Group of Seven (the United States, Canada, Japan, the United Kingdom, Germany, France, and Italy), the debates over the North American Free Trade Agreement (NAFTA), and the controversies over Japan's balance-of-payments surpluses are examples of the new importance of commercial issues. Another is the fact that by the late 1980s Americans were more concerned with economic than with military threats to the prestige of the United States (Nye 1990, 141).

This focus on economics has had implications regarding foreign policy resources. When the definition of national interests centers on protecting and controlling territory, people, and natural resources, the military is absolutely important and serves as the instrument of final resort. As attention shifts to other concerns, then so must the focus on resources. If one wishes to induce others to change their economic policy in order to secure greater access to markets or to obtain more investment, economic instruments are more appropriate than military force. The same is true for fighting pollution, epidemics, and drugs. In each case, military solutions are not practical. Thus, one finds the military consigned to an ever smaller role in the contemporary world.

This does not mean, however, that there is *no* role for the military, or that war is a thing of the past. The Persian Gulf War illustrated this by demonstrating that even the interests of the strongest and most advanced countries can be threatened by heavily armed states guided by leaders who believe that the use of military force can yield benefits. This war also showed that the international arms market makes an array of dangerous weapons available to anyone with the ability to pay. Consequently, the military remains an important tool of foreign policy because wars continue to occur in some parts of the world and military establishments are the key to national security both for those states that are directly involved in a war and for those that rely upon the belligerents. Nevertheless, as is described subsequently, a time may be coming, if it has not already arrived, when military resources will play almost no part in the relations between selected members of the international system.

■ Parallel International Universes

When speaking of international change, one must do more than talk about shifting issues and conflicts. By nature, change is almost always uneven, affecting some actors one way, others in another way, and still others almost not at all. Thus, it is important to specify who is affected by change and how. This brings one to the question of the evolution of parallel international universes in which differing countries have very different patterns and qualities of interactions with one another. Nye refers to this change when he says that "the games of world politics are being played by different actors with different piles of chips at different card tables" (1990, 182).

Describing the world as composed of groupings of different types of countries is not new. Many authors discussed the post–World War II international system as consisting of three or more "worlds," with a state's level of economic development, ideological predispositions, and alliances serving as the keys for differentiating one world from another.[12] This scheme was popularized by the cold war, which created two "natural" political-military clusters of countries and a third nonaligned group. The concurrent differences between developed and developing states reinforced these distinctions by drawing attention to variations in levels of wealth, types of cultural and religious practices, and histories of international imperialism. The present concept of parallel international universes extends these earlier discussions. As just noted, the previous treatments of differing "worlds" focused on a state's development, ideology, and political-military alignments. The current discussion, however, is concerned with the basic conduct found within and between groups of states.

The Western World

The decreased importance of the military as a determinant of the relations between some countries is a good place to start examining these differences. In the current international system, a group has emerged that includes states that have become exceptionally reliant upon one another in many ways and that at the same time have reached the point in their relations where they no longer pose any military threat to each other. The particularly interesting aspect of this situation is that it exists among countries that generally are regarded, both individually and collectively, as the world's most powerful, both in an economic and in a military sense. In the past, militarily powerful states had such mutual suspicion that it led them to regard one another as threats, which produced considerable tension and even occasional wars. At present, however, the advanced industrialized countries in Europe, North America, and East Asia, which may be referred to as the Western world, have reached the point where it is inconceivable that they would ever turn to military force, or that they would even hint at the use of such force, as a means for settling disputes among

Table 3.1 Average Income for Selected Regions

	1960	1970	1980	1987
Africa	365	458	875	533
Asia	253	255	368	310
Latin America	955	1,146	2,364	1,424
North America	7,725	10,194	11,727	13,163
European Community	3,258	4,808	9,812	9,658

Note: All figures are in 1980 United States dollars.
Source: United Nations, *Yearbook of National Accounts Statistics,* various years.

themselves. The very countries that fought to the finish in a total war just fifty years ago now have set the military aside, probably forever, as an instrument for conducting statecraft among themselves. As one analyst has put it, "today the [Western] European core of the international system is a vast zone of peace" (Holsti 1986, 369).[13]

The absence of military conflicts with one another is not the only thing that sets these countries apart. They also possess the world's most advanced economies and have the world's highest standards of living. The figures in Table 3.1 illustrate this by comparing the per capita income among Western countries with the incomes in other parts of the world.

Table 3.2 Imports for Selected Countries and Regions

	1948	1958	1968	1978	1988
United States	24,615*	37,014	78,170	231,375	319,142
	168**	212	389	1,061	1,296
United Kingdom	27,921	28,928	44,766	99,442	131,773
	557	558	810	1,782	2,309
France	11,827	16,072	33,061	103,551	123,629
	290	360	662	1,943	2,213
Germany	4,764	21,092	47,641	152,744	173,919
	102	404	821	2,491	2,842
Canada	9,062	14,914	27,024	54,980	74,817
	702	877	1,299	2,340	2,883
Italy	5,289	9,215	24,317	71,449	96,295
	116	189	461	1,260	1,676
Japan	2,351	8,691	30,702	99,661	130,103
	29	95	304	867	1,061
Latin America	25,601	30,057	35,556	93,416	67,415
	157	153	134	272	157
Sub–Saharan Africa	6,186	10,172	13,688	39,176	19,385
	37	49	51	122	41
Asia	20,687	23,496	36,714	115,630	NA
	26	30	32	94	NA

Note: All figures are in 1980 United States dollars.
 * Represents total trade in millions.
 ** Represents per capita trade.
 NA means that the relevant data were not available.
Source: United Nations, *UN Statistical Yearbook,* various years.

In addition, members of the Western world have a high degree of commitment to international commerce, and to this end have created and currently manage the primary international economic and commercial organizations described earlier. Beyond this, their societies and their economies are extensively tied to one another through a variety of transnational linkages, and their governments engage in substantial collaborative efforts to coordinate policy.

The extent of the commercial linkages found in the Western world and the degree to which they have grown over time are depicted in Tables 3.2 and 3.3, which contain figures for the total and per capita trade of the countries comprising the Group of Seven (the leading members of the Western world) and for several developing regions. As can be seen readily, the Group of Seven (G7) countries have become ever more involved in international trade since 1948. Indeed, by 1988 the volume of trade for each of the G7 countries had become so high that it exceeded the totals for entire regions of the developing world. In addition, the per capita trading figures for Western countries in 1988 were at least ten times the comparable levels in developing regions.

The lack of violence among these countries and their commitment to international commerce should not be taken as meaning that they do not have conflicts with one another, for they do. However, while these countries do continue to compete and to engage in conflict, their relations with each other are of a different order

Table 3.3 Exports for Selected Countries and Regions

	1948	1958	1968	1978	1988
United States	43,108*	50,808	80,849	178,676	223,481
	294**	291	402	819	907
United Kingdom	21,836	25,481	36,324	90,709	101,020
	437	491	657	1,626	1,770
France	6,911	14,662	30,035	96,973	116,522
	169	329	602	1,820	2,085
Germany	2,058	25,235	58,728	179,861	224,498
	44	484	1,012	2,934	3,668
Canada	10,687	14,456	29,792	58,310	78,377
	830	848	1,434	2,481	3,020
Italy	3,700	7,384	24,080	70,951	88,274
	81	152	456	1,251	1,537
Japan	888	8,244	30,667	123,422	183,969
	11	90	303	1,074	1,500
Latin America	25,636	27,536	33,310	79,946	75,446
	157	140	125	233	175
Sub–Saharan Africa	5,979	9,054	13,901	31,790	18,892
	36	44	52	99	40
Asia	17,869	18,367	26,430	109,039	NA
	22	23	23	89	NA

Note: All figures are in 1980 United States dollars.
  * Represents total trade in millions.
  ** Represents per capita trade.
  NA means that the relevant data were not available.
Source: United Nations, *UN Statistical Yearbook,* various years.

of magnitude from those that they have with other countries or that other countries have among themselves. In the West, conflict now takes place along economic fault lines, with questions relating to market access, foreign investment, and the coordination of fiscal and monetary policies serving as the primary areas of contention. Under these circumstances the tools for conducting foreign policy center on political persuasion, for the complex interrelationships among these actors dictate that they refrain from threatening one another, with either their military or their economic resources, lest they upset the international commercial networks that they all rely upon. In effect, a form of implicit deterrence exists among the members of the Western world that bars any one state from unduly pressuring or upsetting the others. As a result, studying the foreign policies of these states dictates that the analyst be intricately familiar with economic and commercial theory, interdependence, and the subtleties of deterrence.[14]

The Non-Western World

Alongside this group of what may be regarded as immensely privileged states is another category of countries. This collection of societies is far more amorphous and diverse than the first group. Its members include the very poorest countries of the world, newly industrializing middle-income countries, nations made wealthy because they are blessed by natural resources that are in great demand internationally, and Communist and ex-Communist states.

One characteristic of this second group of countries is the degree to which they still exhibit militarily based violence. This is seen both internally and externally. Domestically, the use of force is found in the employment of military coups d'état to change governments and in insurgency movements designed to promote revolutions.

Table 3.4 Incidence of Civil Wars and Interventions, 1945–89

	1945–49	1950–59	1960–69	1970–79	1980–89	Total
Western Europe	0	0	0	0	0	0
North America	0	0	0	0	0	0
Latin America	4	4	2	2	3	15
North Africa/Middle East	1	2	3	4	2	12
Sub–Saharan Africa	0	0	5	3	6	14
Asia (excluding Japan)	2	4	4	6	2	18
Other (all non-Western)	1	0	0	0	0	1
Total	8	10	14	15	13	60
Type of Intervention						
Western Developed in Developing	1	1	4	1	1	8
Developing in Developing	0	0	1	6	1	8
Other	0	0	0	1	0	1
Total	1	1	5	8	2	17

Note: Civil wars were counted only for the time period in which they began. Interventions were counted more than once if countries from more than one category were involved.
Source: Singer (1991, 60–65).

As Table 3.4 shows, from 1945 to 1989 no advanced industrialized state has experienced such a disturbance. In the same period, all civil wars have occurred within countries from developing regions.[15] The data further reveal that domestic problems of this sort are distributed widely among all regions of the developing world. One point worth mentioning is that advanced countries have intervened in the troubles in developing regions on eight occasions, indicating the degree to which at least some members of the Western world are prepared to intervene forcefully in the affairs of less-developed countries when they perceive that important issues are at stake.

Internationally, one finds that the wars fought in the last four decades always have involved developing countries. Table 3.5 demonstrates this clearly, showing that in the years from 1945 to 1989 there have been no wars in which Western countries have fought one another.[16] On five occasions, however, Western countries have fought underdeveloped countries, with these conflicts centering for the most part on questions relating either to the collapse of imperialism or to the cold war (see Holsti 1986, 369). Interestingly, developing countries, which largely have been left out of the Western system described previously, have engaged in a considerable degree of conflict, fighting twenty wars among themselves, constituting over three-fourths of all wars fought in the period.

A second feature of non-Western countries is the degree to which so many were dominated by stronger states in the past and, in some cases, continue to experience such domination.[17] In the past, control was a result of the predominantly military supremacy of the European imperialist powers in Latin America, Africa, and Asia, and of the Soviet Union in Eastern Europe. At present, domination comes more from the use of economic resources that allow outsiders to control, at least in part, the access that non-Western states have to key international economic resources and to control as well some of the most important economic management functions within these states.[18]

In addition, non-Western countries increasingly find themselves subjected to economic coercion, as advanced states seek to use their reliance on the West for essential goods and services to manipulate their behavior through the use of economic sanctions.[19] As can be seen in Table 3.6, from 1950 to 1989 the overwhelming majority (65 of 109) of economic sanctions have involved attempts by Western countries to force developing governments to alter their behavior. By comparison, Western

Table 3.5 Incidence of International War, 1945–88
Classified According to Type of Actor and Target

	1945–49	1950–59	1960–69	1970–79	1980–88	Total
Western vs. Western	0	0	0	0	0	0
Western vs. Developing	0	2	1	1	1	5
Developing vs. Developing	1	2	6	8	3	20
Other	0	1	0	0	0	1
Total	1	5	7	9	4	26

Note: A war is counted more than once if it fits more than one actor/target category. Wars are counted only for the time periods in which they began.

Source: Singer (1991, 60–65).

Table 3.6 The Incidence of Economic Sanctions, 1950–89
Classified According to Type of Actor and Target

	1950–59	1960–69	1970–79	1980–89	Total
Western against Western	2	0	1	1	4
Western against Developing	4	12	28	21	65
Developing against Western	5	0	3	0	8
Developing against Developing	1	3	3	3	10
Other	4	7	3	8	22
Total	16	22	38	33	109

Note: Sanctions are recorded only for the time period during which they were initiated. When multiple actors and targets are involved, each one is counted separately.

Source: Hufbauer, Schott, and Elliott (1990, 16–27).

countries rarely are a target of sanctions. Developing countries have aimed eight such acts against the West, with only three in the last thirty years and none from 1980 to 1989. And Western states almost never use sanctions against one another (four total, and only one from 1980 to 1989), which reinforces a point made earlier: the intricate interrelationships among the members of the Western world restrain them from threatening or attempting to coerce one another in any way. Yet again, one finds evidence of very different patterns of conduct within the West and between the West and the developing world.

Another characteristic of non-Western countries has to do with their patterns of international interactions. For the most part these nations tend to have far fewer diplomatic, political, and economic contacts with one another than they have with the advanced industrialized states. As one might expect, this has had a profound effect upon their ability to coordinate policy in order to solve some of their most pressing problems.[20] The barriers that these countries experienced when trying to organize to push for a New International Economic Order and to set up effective natural resource cartels are two examples of how much their isolation from one another hampers collective action.[21]

Thus, the world appears to be divided into at least two parallel international universes that, while they exist together in the same international time-space, operate by very different sets of foreign policy rules. In the West, one has highly stable societies where foreign policy increasingly is devoted to fine-tuning and managing relations among highly interdependent countries that cannot afford to coerce one another. For non-Western countries, the threat of domination, both military and economic, and the absence of the benefits of interdependence and of the domestic stability found in the West place the prospect of coercion more squarely on the foreign policy agenda.

■ Conclusion

This chapter has examined the nature of the international setting in which foreign policy is conducted. Traditionally, the international system has been described as anarchic and foreign policy making authority as decentralized. In this situation, security concerns motivate all members of the international system and the basic function of foreign policy revolves around protecting oneself from the threats posed by others, with a nation's military capabilities serving as the most important of its foreign policy resources. Evidence has been presented to show that the international system has undergone significant changes since 1945. New issues are now the focus of foreign policy, and very distinct patterns of relationships are found within and between different groups of international actors. These changes suggest that second-generation scholars must adopt at least two basic analytical strategies if they are to obtain a proper appreciation for the manner in which international systemic forces will shape foreign policy in the coming years. The first of these strategies juxtaposes the operation of past international configurations with those of the present, while the second examines how the Western world differs from the non-Western world.

In making the first comparison a vital question for exploration concerns the forces affecting the evolution of the international system, the degree to which these forces continue to influence the current international arena, and the probability that they will have future effects. Within the context of the present essay it has only been possible to outline briefly some of the forces that might be responsible for the changes that have occurred; more in-depth investigations are in order. It is particularly important that attention be paid to the way in which interdependence, the development of nuclear weapons of mass destruction, and the evolution of new international actors and institutions have interacted to change the international system and to alter the conduct of foreign policy.

In addition, scholars must assess carefully the applicability to the present and the future of theories that were designed to explain past systems. One must consider the utility of principles derived from the study of such issues as the balance of power, polarity, deterrence, and military alliances for explaining contemporary foreign policy behavior. After all, these theories are based on the notion that military competition is dominant. For example, as it has evolved since 1945, deterrence theory has focused almost entirely on military confrontations, and especially on the use of nuclear weapons. Little attention has been paid to how economic resources may be used for deterrent purposes or to the operation of deterrence among actors that are intertwined commercially. And yet, as was noted in the discussion of the Western world, the relationships found among these actors appear to have created a new role for an implicit form of deterrence. The result is a conceptual gap that must be filled if scholars are to understand how advanced states influence one another's foreign policy behavior.[22]

Closer attention also must be devoted to trying to understand the changing nature of interdependence through time and to comparing the meanings of foreign policy in worlds where conflict is economic rather than military. The figures in Tables 3.2 and 3.3 illustrate the rapid expansion since 1948 of interdependence based on trade. These tables, however, tell only part of the story, for international commercial linkages, particularly international investments of all sorts, have virtually exploded in recent decades. The result is an interdependence that goes far beyond anything that scholars have envisioned in the past, with effects on foreign policy that analysts have barely started to conceptualize.[23]

When comparing the Western and non-Western worlds at least four questions come to mind. The first centers on the relative effects of dependence and interdependence in these very different international universes and how this affects foreign policy. As noted previously, interdependence has expanded greatly among Western states. This has not been the case in non-Western areas, where increased international linkages have had different meanings and the impact on foreign policy has varied. It is important to continue the exploration of questions relating to whether and how a reliance on the West leads to restricted foreign policy choices for developing countries and whether some types of interdependence can contribute to economic development without deleterious political effects. In addition, the effects of interdependence among non-Western countries must be examined to determine how these actors may structure their foreign policies to achieve a greater pooling of resources to solve mutual problems. As noted earlier, cooperation along these lines has been difficult in the past.

The second question considers how advanced and less-developed countries conceptualize foreign policy, including the international goals they regard as appropriate to pursue, the techniques they use in pursuing these goals, the international rules they feel they must follow, and how they develop their foreign policies. One of the basic distinctions between Western and non-Western worlds centers on their differing conceptions of foreign policy. The result has been confusion and conflict. This mandates careful comparisons of the use of foreign policy.

The third question is closely related to the second, for it also is necessary to examine carefully the communications problems that one confronts when transmitting signals from one international universe to the other. The very different configurations of actors found in the present international arena has created, and is bound to continue creating, fundamental difficulties in sending foreign policy messages; these difficulties must be studied carefully if they are to be surmounted.

Finally, the conditions under which actors use force must be studied with care. While Western states appear to have forsaken force as a foreign policy instrument against one another, one still finds considerable violence among non-Western states and between Western and non-Western countries. Second-generation scholars need a clear understanding of how and why force is used. International violence remains too great a source of tragedy; perhaps careful analysis can eliminate some of this misery.

■ Acknowledgment

Copyright (c) 1993. From *Defining Power: Influence and Force in the Contemporary International System* by John M. Rothgeb Jr. Reprinted with permission of St. Martin's Press, Incorporated. Portions of the text have been changed or omitted.

■ Notes

1. A more complete discussion of this definition of the international system may be found in Young (1978) and Gilpin (1981). This definition and the discussion of the traditional views of the international system that follows are based on what scholars commonly refer to as the realist point of view of international politics. An exceptional description of realism may be found in Waltz (1979). Although it is beyond the scope of this essay to discuss them, the reader should note that dependency and world systems theorists

provide alternative views of the nature of the international arena. The seminal works of these analysts are found in the writings of Frank (1969), Galtung (1971), and Wallerstein (1976).

2. See Karen Mingst's essay (chapter 14) in the current volume for an excellent discussion of the actors in international politics.

3. This thesis agrees with Blainey's contention that it is "unwise to regard international relations since 1945 as an old game obeying completely new rules. It is a slightly different game obeying the same rules" (1988, 121). It should be noted that the discussion in this chapter focuses on the state and does not consider the development of the many new actors found in international politics. One reason for this is that foreign policy generally is seen as the province of the state.

4. For more complete discussions of anarchy and its effects on foreign policy, see Bull (1977), Young (1978), Gilpin (1981), and Waltz (1988). Competing conceptions of the degree to which the international system is anarchic are presented by dependency and world systems theorists. For these views, one may consult Frank (1969), Galtung (1971), and Wallerstein (1976).

5. One of the earliest of these types of discussions is found in Schuman (1941, 291–95). Others include Morgenthau (1948, chapter 9), Van Dyke (1966, chapter 11), Organski (1968, chapters 7, 8), and Spanier (1987, chapter 7).

6. Even those who have studied the foreign policy of smaller states have recognized the degree to which great powers have controlled the international scene. One example is East (1973, 556–76); another is Rothstein (1968).

7. Several authors who discuss such rapid change are Kaysen (1990), Mueller (1989), Ray (1989), and Rosecrance (1986).

8. See Mueller (1989) for a particularly compelling discussion of this subject.

9. See Mueller (1989). An excellent source describing the incidence of international war since 1945 is Singer (1991).

10. For a discussion of these points, see Gilpin (1975) and Nye (1990).

11. For example, see Hanrieder (1978) and Rosecrance (1986).

12. One of the earliest discussions of the notion that the international system was divided into three "worlds" is found in Horowitz (1966); another is presented in Martin (1962).

13. The same point is made in Buzan (1984, 605), and in Russett and Starr (1992, 408).

14. These themes are discussed in more detail in Rothgeb (1993).

15. A *civil war* is defined as a situation in which organized armed violence occurs between a recognized government and some portion of its domestic opposition. For a discussion of the civil wars since 1945, see Singer (1991).

16. A *war* is defined as an instance of international violence in which two or more recognized states engage in armed hostilities toward one another and where there are at least one thousand battle deaths. For a discussion of wars since 1945, see Singer (1991).

17. For a discussion of this sort of domination, see Cohen (1973) and Rothstein (1977).

18. Discussions of how the International Monetary Fund and the World Bank restrict the policies of developing countries are presented in Payer (1974) and Broad (1988). The role of multinational corporations is described in Rothgeb (1989).

19. Economic sanctions are defined as a "deliberate government-inspired withdrawal, or threat of withdrawal, of customary trade or financial relations" in support of foreign policy goals. See Hufbauer, Schott, and Elliott (1983, 2).

20. The diplomatic, political, and economic interactions of the states in this category are described in Addo (1974) and in Galtung (1971).

21. For a discussion of the New International Economic Order, see Cooper (1977) and Laszlo et al. (1978). The problems confronted in setting up resource cartels are described by Jabber (1978) and Mingst (1976).

22. Rothgeb (1993, 165–81) has taken a first step in this direction with the analysis of economic deterrence.

23. Frieden (1991) and Rogowski (1989) are among the scholars who have begun to touch on the implications for foreign policy of these vast increases in interdependence.

A Cognitive Approach to the Study of Foreign Policy

Jerel A. Rosati, UNIVERSITY OF SOUTH CAROLINA

■ Editors' Introduction

In this chapter Jerel Rosati introduces the role of cognitive studies in foreign policy analysis. As Rosati illustrates, cognitive analyses consider the role of policymakers' beliefs and images and are present in both the first and second generations of foreign policy analysts. Indeed, much of what this chapter discusses can be found in literature focusing on the "individual" level of foreign policy analysis. Rosati makes explicit the changes occurring in cognitive studies throughout the evolution of foreign policy analysis and emphasizes the contributions of recent, second-generation, cognitive studies. This chapter complements the following chapter by Keith Shimko, which looks specifically at the metaphors (a cognitive concept) leaders use in developing foreign policy.

In considering the role of cognitive sources of foreign policy, can you think of any modern examples of foreign policy makers whose beliefs and images influenced foreign policy? For example, would President Clinton's belief system have led him to a different policy in the Gulf War than the one pursued by President Bush? What type of belief system might have been behind Iraqi leader Saddam Hussein's decision to invade Kuwait? Consider your own belief system. How would it influence your foreign policy actions if you were a policymaker? How important are cognitive factors as compared to other sources of foreign policy (e.g., bureaucratic, domestic political, systemic)? ■

How do policymakers view the world? What affects the beliefs and images of policymakers over time? What impact do the beliefs of policymakers have on foreign policy making and the practice of foreign policy? These are the kinds of questions about the role of cognition that interest many students of foreign policy and are addressed in their scholarship, hence contributing to knowledge and understanding about the formulation and conduct of foreign policy. Although the value of a cognitive approach should be obvious, it has not always received the attention it deserves in the study of foreign policy.[1]

Traditionally, foreign policy has been explained from a *rational actor* perspective common to the realist and power politics tradition. The assumption has been that governments, and their political leaders, think and act in a rational manner in their quest for power and order. Such rationality assumes that individuals perceive the world accurately and arrive at decisions through an open intellectual process: goals are ordered, a search is made for relevant information, a wide range of alternatives is considered, and the option that maximizes the benefits while minimizing the costs is selected. Since policymakers act rationally in pursuit of power and order, there is no need to delve into their psychological predispositions or closely examine the governmental policymaking process. Instead, one should focus on how the international system constrains foreign policy action, treat the government as a rational actor, and speak in terms of an overriding shared national interest in the making of foreign policy.

A cognitive approach challenges much of Western thought and practice premised on the assumption of individual rationality (see Allison 1971, 10–38; Simon 1957b; Snyder, Bruck, and Sapin 1962; Steinbruner 1974, 25–46). Where the rational actor perspective assumes individual open-mindedness and adaptability to changes in the environment, a cognitive approach posits that individuals tend to be much more closed-minded due to their beliefs and the way they process information—thus, they tend to resist adapting to changes in the environment. A cognitive perspective emphasizes the importance of examining the individuals involved in the policymaking process, for they are likely to view their environment differently. This approach has grown in visibility, prominence, and sophistication since the 1950s as social scientists have attempted to be more systematic in identifying and explaining major patterns of foreign policy.

This chapter is organized along three lines so the reader can arrive at a better understanding of the development of a cognitive approach and its relevance for contributing to an understanding of the theory and practice of foreign policy. First, a brief history of the evolution of political psychology and its impact on a cognitive approach to the study of foreign policy is provided. Second, a number of significant research programs and individual studies are highlighted to illustrate different cognitive approaches to the study of foreign policy. Finally, an assessment is made of what has been learned by a cognitive approach to foreign policy over the past few decades and what issues require future attention. Together, this should provide the basis for clarifying how a cognitive approach can contribute to a better understanding of the dynamics of foreign policy.

■ The Political Psychological Study of Beliefs and Foreign Policy

Scholars and individuals have been interested in examining the beliefs of individuals and the workings of the human mind throughout the ages. Yet it was not until the 1930s, with the development of psychology as a discipline of study, that systematic efforts to apply psychological approaches to the study of politics and international relations really began. The evolution of *political psychology* and its relevance to international relations and foreign policy is marked by three distinct periods. With each new period the political psychological study of beliefs has grown tremendously in sophistication and has contributed to a powerful understanding of the theory and practice of foreign policy.[2]

Early Efforts

Early efforts were made beginning in the 1930s and continuing through the early 1950s to apply explicitly psychological concepts to the study of politics, especially the nature of war and peace. Most of this research focused on national stereotypes, attitudes toward war, and public opinion on foreign policy issues (Kelman 1965b; Klineberg 1950; Pear 1950). Unfortunately, while most of these early efforts were made by scholars and individuals who were well versed in psychology, they usually lacked a strong foundation in the study of international relations and world politics. This was best exemplified by the studies on individual irregularities and pathologies that were directly projected onto the nation-state, the "war begins in the minds of men" approach, and national character studies of the war proneness of different societies.

This well-intentioned effort by many psychologists to apply different psychological concepts and knowledge about the individual "directly" to the complex arena of the state and world politics was not well received by students of international relations (see Holsti 1976, 16–20; Jervis 1976, 3–10). Most international relations scholars found these studies unrealistic and believed they were not relevant to the study of foreign policy and world politics (see, e.g., Waltz 1959). The problem was clearly stated by Herbert Kelman in *International Behavior: A Social-Psychological Analysis:* "Only if we know where and how these individuals fit into the larger process, and under what circumstances they operate, are we able to offer a relevant psychological analysis" (1965b, 6). Clearly, until political psychology was well grounded in politics and international relations such studies would likely remain naive and simplistic.

Although the initial effort to incorporate psychological approaches into the analysis of international behavior failed to influence the field, some scholars began to question the lack of psychological input into the study of international relations and foreign policy. Quincy Wright, in his magnum opus, *The Study of International Relations,* proposed that psychology belongs at the "core" of the discipline: "International relations cannot, therefore, be confined to intergovernmental relations and conclusions based on the assumption that they [i.e., psychological studies] fail to provide an adequate foundation for prediction and control. The minds of individuals who constitute the world's population, the influences that affect them, and the influences they exert, both domestic and foreign, must be taken into account by examining their minds" (1955, 433).

The First Generation of Scholarship

Beginning in the mid-1950s, the contribution of psychological approaches to the study of international relations grew in importance due to the interaction of the "peace research" movement and the "behavioral" revolution in the social sciences (see Kelman 1965b; Kelman and Bloom 1973). A number of psychologists, sociologists, economists, anthropologists, and other scientists became interested in applying the knowledge and techniques of their disciplines to the problems of war and peace. At the same time, many international relations scholars became interested in making their field more empirical and scientific. Nowhere was this interaction greater than among those who advocated a decision-making approach to the study of foreign policy (see Snyder, Bruck, and Sapin 1962).

In comparison to the early efforts by psychologists, the late 1950s and 1960s represented the beginning of a qualitative leap forward for psychological approaches and their application to the study of international relations. Psychological approaches increasingly were applied from an international relations and political perspective. Two groups of specialists "emerged and interacted closely with one another: students of international relations, with a political science background, who are thoroughly grounded in social-psychological concepts and methods; and social psychologists (as well as students of other disciplines outside of political science) who have systematically educated themselves in the field of international relations" (Kelman and Bloom 1973, 263).

These developments meant that the systematic study of the *beliefs* and *images* of foreign policy makers grew in popularity and significance during the 1960s and 1970s. The working assumption was that the ideas and thoughts about the environment held by policymakers affect the foreign policy–making process. Policymaker images "may be partial or general. They may be subconscious or may be consciously stated. They may be based on carefully thought-out assumptions about the world or they may flow from instinctive perceptions and judgements. In any event all decision-makers may be said to possess a set of images and to be conditioned by them in their behavior on foreign policy" (Brecher, Steinberg, and Stein 1969, 86–87).

Much of the psychologically oriented research on foreign policy was influenced by the study of *attitudes* and attitudinal change in psychology that began as early as the 1930s (see Calder and Ross 1973; Oskamp 1977). Most of the work on attitudes and attitudinal change in psychology during this time was based upon theories of *cognitive consistency,* including cognitive dissonance, congruity, and balance theory (see Abelson et al. 1968; Festinger 1957; McGuire 1969; Oskamp 1977). The assumption behind cognitive consistency is that individuals make sense of the world by relying on key beliefs and strive to maintain consistency between their beliefs. Under cognitive consistency, individuals maintain coherent belief systems and attempt to avoid acquiring information that is inconsistent or incompatible with their beliefs, especially their most central beliefs. In other words, "individuals do not merely subscribe to random collections of beliefs but rather they maintain coherent systems of beliefs which are internally consistent" (Bem 1970, 13).

The study of the impact of propaganda and communications on individuals reinforced research on cognitive consistency (McGuire 1969; Oskamp 1977; Sears and Whitney 1973). The literature on *persuasive communications* at the time indicated that most individuals are indifferent to persuasive appeals, especially political propaganda, and when they are attuned they tend to be surrounded by people and communications with which they sympathize. In other words, incoming information typically gets interpreted in accordance with an individual's existing central beliefs and predispositions.

The prevalence of cognitive consistency, and the tendency of most communications to reinforce an individual's belief system, found in the first generation of political psychological research provided the foundation for many studies of foreign policy decision making since the 1960s. This psychological literature and its relevance for the study of foreign policy were brought together by Robert Jervis (1976) in *Perception and Misperception in International Politics.*[3] Jervis provided a significant service to the advancement of a cognitive approach to foreign policy through his rich survey of the processes of perception for foreign policymakers, including a discussion of how cognitive consistency affects decision makers, how decision makers learn from history, how attitudes change, and an analysis of common patterns of misperception among policymakers. Not only did he illustrate the relevance of a cognitive approach for foreign policy and international relations, he also used such a perspective to critique what he saw as simplistic assumptions of both deterrence theory and the spiral model of state interaction in world politics. As Jervis concluded, "It is often impossible to explain crucial decisions and policies without reference to the decision-makers' beliefs about the world and their images of others" (1976, 28).

Second-Generation Scholarship

Beginning in the 1970s, psychology underwent what has been referred to as a "cognitive revolution" in the study of attitudes and how individuals process information. The revolution involved a different conception of the individual and his or her interaction with the environment: away from a "passive agent who merely responds to environmental stimuli" to a concept of the individual as more likely to selectively respond to and actively shape his or her environment; away from an individual who "strives for consistency" toward an individual who is more likely to act as a "problem solver" in order to make sense of a complex environment involving great uncertainty (George 1980b, 56; see also Fiske and Taylor 1991, 9–14; Lau and Sears 1986c). Responding to developments in cognitive theory, psychological research increasingly moved beyond the study of cognitive consistency to a more sophisticated study of attitudes and information processing often referred to as social cognition theory and schema theory.[4]

Social cognition theory and *schema theory* assume that individuals are "cognitive misers" who tend to rely on existing beliefs and schema—that is, mental constructs that represent different clumps of knowledge about various facets of the environment—for interpreting information. Although schema necessarily simplify and structure the external environment, they are the basis from which individuals are able to organize new information, use their memory, and intelligibly make sense of the world around them. The more complex and uncertain the environment, the more likely individuals will rely on simple schema and cognitive heuristics—shortcuts in information processing—to make sense of the world and the situation at hand (Fiske and Taylor 1991; Lau and Sears 1986b; Milburn 1991).[5]

The social cognition theory and schema theory approach to attitudes and beliefs builds upon and extends the previous work on cognitive consistency but is based on a more complex and sophisticated understanding of the nature of attitudes and how information is processed by the mind. Social cognition theory and schema theory emphasize the dominant role of preexisting beliefs in interpreting new information, much like cognitive consistency theory. Yet, where the theory of cognitive consistency assumes the existence of a belief system with a high degree of coherence and interdependence between beliefs that are extremely resistant to change, a social cognition perspective depicts individual belief systems as much more fragmented internally, with different beliefs or schema being invoked under different situations for making sense of the environment. This suggests a greater likelihood that some beliefs may change over time. From this perspective, although the beliefs held by an individual may appear incompatible and contradictory to an outside observer, the overall *belief system* is likely to make sense to the individual of concern, suggesting a rather complex cognitive process. Although more sophisticated than cognitive consistency theory about the workings of the human mind, cognitive psychology and social cognition nevertheless continue to represent an alternative to the rational actor perspective.

Two major works published near the beginning of the so-called cognitive revolution anticipated many of these developments in the area of social cognition theory and schema theory, integrating them into the study of foreign policy. One, already discussed, was *Perception and Misperception in International Politics* by Robert Jervis (1976). The other was another landmark in cognitive approaches to the study of foreign policy, entitled *The Cybernetic Theory of Decision* by John Steinbruner (1974). Actually, Steinbruner's title was somewhat of a misnomer; his book really developed a "cognitive theory of decision" that made three significant contributions. First, Steinbruner demonstrated that the rational actor model (what he called the analytic paradigm) has great difficulty in explaining governmental decision making and performance, especially under real-world conditions of complexity and uncertainty. Second, he synthesized a large body of knowledge from the fields of cybernetics and cognitive theory in developing a cognitive process model as an alternative to the rational actor model. He argued that relatively simple decisions could be explained by a simple cybernetic process of "satisficing" and "incrementalism" commonly found in bureaucracy. However, to explain more complex decisions one had to turn to a cognitive process model (or cognitive paradigm) in order to understand the regularities of how the mind deals with uncertainty. According to this model, the mind "constantly struggles to impose clear, coherent meaning on events" (Steinbruner 1974, 112), relying on "cognitive structures" involving memory, centrality, consistency, simplicity, and stability. Finally, Steinbruner not only demonstrated how individuals arrive at decisions under the cognitive process model but discussed how the model applies within a larger collective decision-making context as occurs within the government: "In essence, it is cognitive operations of the human mind working in interaction with the organizational structure of the government which set workable limits on highly diffuse decision problems" (Steinbruner 1974, 14). Ultimately, what Steinbruner did was present a coherent and powerful theoretical foundation for the cognitive study of foreign policy.

■ Major Foreign Policy Studies

The evolution of the psychological study of attitudes provided the foundation for a number of research programs and studies employing a cognitive approach to the study of foreign policy, especially since the first generation of scholarship. The most significant approaches and studies over time will be highlighted here; these both reflect the evolution of the cognitive study of foreign policy and have contributed to its development.[6] These works vary in terms of conceptual orientation, substantive focus, and research strategy, as discussed subsequently.

Images of the Enemy and Mirror Images

The earliest and most popular studies employing a cognitive approach in a systematic fashion have focused on general images held by political elites, especially images of the "other" and self-images. Such a cognitive approach to foreign policy has been a particularly powerful source for better understanding international conflict and war.

One of the most powerful studies from the first generation of scholarship has been Ole Holsti's (1962, 1967; Finlay, Holsti, and Fagen 1967, 25–96) work on the *image of the enemy*.[7] Holsti believed that the concept of the enemy helped to explain and sustain international conflict over time. In order to better understand U.S.-Soviet hostility and the evolution of the cold war, he employed a case study to examine the image of the Soviet Union held by former Secretary of State John Foster Dulles. Holsti (1967, 17) assumed that hostile images of the enemy, represented by Dulles's image of the Soviet Union, tended to be self-perpetuating, which could be explained by the psychological literature on cognitive dynamics.

Dulles's image of the Soviet Union was derived from a content analysis of his public statements "supplemented by contemporary newspapers, secondary sources, questionnaires sent to a number of Dulles's closest associates, and memoirs written by those who worked closely with him" (Holsti 1967, 18). Holsti found that Dulles's extremely hostile image of the Soviet Union was very rigid and resistant to change regardless of changes in Soviet behavior. This was consistent with the psychological literature on cognitive dynamics based on the nature of attitudes, cognitive consistency, and persuasive communications.[8] Dulles resisted new information inconsistent with his image of the Soviet Union by engaging in a variety of psychological processes: discrediting the information, searching for other consistent information, reinterpreting the information, differentiating between different aspects of the information, engaging in wishful thinking, and refusing to think about it. According to Holsti, the self-perpetuation and resistance to change found in Dulles's image of the Soviet Union was based on an "inherent bad faith" model of the enemy: "As long as the Soviet Union remained a closed society ruled by Communists, it represented the antithesis of values at the core of Dulles' belief system. Furthermore, information that might challenge the inherent-bad-faith model of the Soviet Union generally came from the Soviets themselves—a low-credibility source—and was often ambiguous enough to accommodate more than one interpretation" (1967, 24).

The study of *mirror images* is consistent with the study of the image of the enemy but involves the images held by both parties in a hostile relationship. The concept of mirror images refers to the fact that each party holds an image that is diametrically "opposite" the other: each party has a positive and benevolent self-image while holding a negative and malevolent image of the enemy. Ralph White (1966, 1968) popularized the notion of mirror images in *Nobody Wanted War: Misperception in Vietnam and Other Wars*.[9] Analyzing the two World Wars and focusing on the

Vietnam War, White discussed how each party in a conflict situation holds a "diabolical enemy-image" and a "virile and moral self-image" that become the source of selective inattention, absence of empathy (for the other), and military overconfidence. Although the result of diverse social and psychological sources, such "black-and-white" thinking leads to escalation and war. As White concluded, "The ethnocentric black-and-white picture is a transcultural, almost universal phenomenon, the details of which vary greatly from nation to nation, but the essence of which remains much the same. … In view of this it is not surprising that there is a 'mirror image' quality in the reality-worlds of combatants" (1968, 275).

The Operational Code

One of the most popular approaches for describing a political leader's belief system has been the development of what has been called the *operational code,* based upon Nathan Leites's (1951, 1953) study of communism in the Soviet Union. However, it was not until Alexander George (1969) refined the concept that the operational code became popular as a research program in the area of foreign policy involving numerous scholars. The operational code is based on the concept of cognitive consistency, for it assumes an overall coherent and interconnected set of beliefs about the nature of political life.[10]

The operational code approach consists of two fundamental types of beliefs—philosophical and instrumental beliefs organized around ten questions. *Philosophical beliefs* refer to assumptions and premises regarding the fundamental nature of politics, political conflict and one's opponents, the future, and historical development. *Instrumental beliefs* refer to beliefs about strategy and tactics concerning political action, risk taking, timing, and means for advancing one's interests. The operational code serves as a guide to political decision making: the individual's philosophical beliefs help diagnose the definition of the situation, while the instrumental beliefs affect the likely choice of action (see George 1979b).

One of the more interesting uses of the operational code has been Stephen Walker's (1977) study of former National Security Adviser and Secretary of State Henry Kissinger.[11] Walker examined the interface between Henry Kissinger's operational code and his bargaining behavior during the Vietnam conflict. The study was particularly informative in depicting how Kissinger saw the world, including the role of great powers, and his understanding of the use of force and negotiations in interacting with an adversary. Walker also found a close relationship between Kissinger's operational code (through his academic writings) and his conduct of the Vietnam negotiations (through governmental and secondary sources). While the operational code has been a powerful cognitive approach for determining the "content" of political leaders' foreign policy beliefs, Walker's study represents an early landmark in actually examining the relationship between foreign policy beliefs and behavior.

Cognitive Mapping

In the early 1970s an attempt was made to examine the beliefs of policymakers in a more specific and rigorous way through the use of a *cognitive map.* A cognitive map refers to a specific set of beliefs, and their interconnectedness, as they exist in the mind of a decision maker concerning some aspect of the environment. It is a "specific way of representing a person's assertions about some limited domain, such as a policy problem" (Axelrod 1976, 55). The foundation of *cognitive mapping* is based upon the early formulations of Robert Axelrod (1972, 1973) and Michael Shapiro and G. Matthew Bonham (1973), derived from the literature on cognitive consistency and schema theory.

From the work of Shapiro and Bonham (see, e.g., Bonham 1976), a decision maker goes through five basic cognitive steps when he or she perceives a new international situation that may require a policy response: initial amplification (of relevant beliefs), search for antecedents (explaining the events), search for consequences (of likely future behavior of actors involved), search for policy alternatives, and policy choice. Given the focus on specific mental constructs and causal beliefs over different information-processing stages, the cognitive mapping approach allows for a mathematical modeling and computer simulation of the mind. Such an approach has been particularly useful for examining specific decisions and analyzing the cognitive complexity of decision makers in a variety of contexts, as demonstrated by the collection of studies in *Structure of Decision: The Cognitive Maps of Political Elites*, edited by Robert Axelrod (1976b).[12]

Attribution Theory and International Conflict

Since the 1950s psychologists have been interested in understanding how people perceive the causes of human behavior, resulting in the generation of a body of knowledge known as *attribution theory*. It was not until the late 1960s and 1970s, however, that attribution theory grew in prominence and began to influence the study of political psychology. Attribution theorists have attempted to identify the various types of attribution errors and biases that people commonly make. For example, the "fundamental attribution error" is the tendency to attribute (explain) our own behavior in terms of external or situational causes. This would be akin to someone saying, "The situation forced me to do what I did." However, this error also entails attributing the behavior of others to internal causes. In this case the same person might say, "The other person acted as he or she did because he or she is mean-spirited." This is further affected by the "self-serving bias," which is the tendency to take credit for good or positive behaviors but to deny responsibility for bad or negative behaviors, and the "halo effect," which is the tendency to see friends in a positive light and enemies in a negative light (Baron and Byrne 1981; Freedman, Carlsmith, and Sears 1970; Jones 1972; Nisbett and Ross 1980).

Attribution theory has not received as much attention from scholars who take a cognitive approach to the study of foreign policy as have other psychological concepts discussed previously. Nevertheless, an important study employing this perspective, along with consistency theory, was conducted by Daniel Heradstveit (1979) in *The Arab-Israeli Conflict: Psychological Obstacles to Peace*.[13] Based on interviews of political activists conducted in Egypt, Israel, Jordan, Lebanon, and Syria, Heradstveit found strong support for the existence of the fundamental attribution error in explaining the behaviors of participants in the Arab-Israeli conflict. In fact, he found that the inference of internal causes of the opponent's behavior is enhanced when the observer dislikes the actor who performs the blameworthy act, which is consistent with the self-serving bias and the halo effect. As stated by Heradstveit, "If I have a devil-image of the opponent and the opponent behaves in an indisputably friendly way, I can still maintain my beliefs about the opponent by explaining his friendly behavior as caused by environmental influences and constraints. His disposition to act in an unfriendly way remains the same, but certain characteristics of the situation have forced him to be *temporarily* friendly. In other words, the opponent is not given responsibility (credit) for what he is doing" (1979, 74). Such research based on attribution theory contributes to a further understanding of the rise and rigidity of the image of the enemy and mirror images during times of conflict.

More Recent Studies

Beginning in the 1980s a number of individuals built upon earlier work in an effort to further extend knowledge and understanding of the role of cognitive approaches to the study of foreign policy. Much of this work emphasized the need to synthesize available knowledge and to be more eclectic in the study of foreign policy, reflecting the growing diversity and interdisciplinary nature of the study of international relations. Four studies that reflect such concerns and have contributed to them are highlighted here.[14]

One important study has been *Origins of Containment: A Psychological Explanation,* by Deborah Larson (1985), which employs cognitive social psychology to explain the origins of the cold war. Larson specifically attempted to explain the changes that transpired in the beliefs of key U.S. policymakers—W. Averell Harriman, Harry S. Truman, James F. Byrnes, and Dean Acheson—toward the Soviet Union from 1944 to 1947 in terms of five rival theories of attitude change: the Hovland attitude change approach (involving persuasive communications), cognitive dissonance theory (the classic cognitive consistency approach), attribution theory, self-perception theory (which makes the unique argument that individual beliefs are derived from observing one's own behavior), and schema theory. Through an analysis of the archival evidence, Larson concluded that Harriman, Truman, and Byrnes, unlike Acheson, did not have coherent, structured belief systems; instead, their inconsistent and contradictory beliefs resulted in each eventually developing an enemy image of the Soviet Union in his own way. In fact, since "U.S. policymakers used different types of cognitive processes to interpret information about Soviet behavior…No one theory of attitude change explains the origins of American leaders' Cold War belief system" (Larson 1985, 342). Instead, self-perception, schema, and attribution theories were all useful in explaining the individual policymakers' beliefs about the Soviet Union over time. Accordingly, the Larson study is particularly powerful in demonstrating the complexity and messiness of individual belief systems and cognition, especially during times of considerable uncertainty.

Another important cognitive study is *Perceptions and Behavior in Soviet Foreign Policy,* by Richard Herrmann (1985; see also 1984, 1988). Building on the work of Richard Cottam (1977), this study addressed "the problem of inferring the perceptions and motives of a nation's leaders" in order to better understand Soviet foreign policy (Herrmann 1985, xix). Drawing on attribution and cognitive consistency theory, Herrmann developed a framework that presents three common types of perceptions policymakers have of rival countries and their likely implications for foreign policy behavior: the "enemy" stereotype that produces a defensive foreign policy pattern; the "degenerate" stereotype that produces an expansionist foreign policy pattern; the "child" stereotype that produces an imperialist foreign policy pattern. Based on an examination of the stereotypical justifications invoked in Soviet speeches, public statements, and foreign policy behavior, Herrmann found that the Soviet image of the United States resembled the classic enemy stereotype in 1967, evolved into a more complex and less stereotypical enemy image in 1972, and then reverted to a more stereotypical enemy image in 1979, although more differentiated and less intense than in 1967. Herrmann's cognitive approach and empirical findings contribute to an understanding of the motives underlying foreign policy behavior in general and Soviet foreign policy in particular, especially in its implications for U.S. foreign policy.

Another significant cognitive study of foreign policy produced during the eighties is *The Carter Administration's Quest for Global Community: Beliefs and Their Impact on Behavior,* by Jerel Rosati (1987; see also 1984, 1990). Given the reports of policy disputes between high-level officials, especially Secretary of State Cyrus Vance and National Security Adviser Zbigniew Brzezinski, and conflicting interpretations of President Jimmy Carter's foreign policy views during the late seventies, Rosati saw the Carter administration as an excellent case study for applying some of the insights of social and cognitive psychology to advance an understanding of U.S. foreign policy. Employing a content analysis of public statements made by Carter, Vance, and Brzezinski throughout their four years in office, Rosati found that in 1977 the Carter administration initially had an optimistic worldview that was shared by the principal policymakers, that individual differences emerged in 1978 when Brzezinski's image of the Soviet Union hardened, that the administration's image fragmented in 1979 as Carter began to waver between Vance's optimism and Brzezinski's increasing pessimism, and that by the beginning of 1980 a new consensus emerged based on a pessimistic image of an increasingly unstable world in which Soviet power had to be contained. The stability of Vance's image and the change in Brzezinski's and Carter's images were explained through use of the literature on cognitive consistency, persuasive communications, individual personality, the impact of external events, and the role of domestic politics. Ultimately, Rosati found that the greater the consensus in beliefs among individual policymakers, the greater the likelihood that the Carter administration's foreign policy behavior was congruent with those beliefs. Not only does the study shed light on the nature and significance of U.S. foreign policy during the Carter years, but it also demonstrates the power of a broad cognitive approach for contributing to an understanding of continuity and change in policymakers' beliefs over time and their impact on foreign policy behavior.

Finally, there is the important study by Yuen Foong Khong (1992), *Analogies at War: Korea, Munich, Dien Bien Phu, and the Vietnam Decisions of 1965,* which focuses on "how and why policymakers use historical analogies in their foreign policy decision-making" (Khong 1992, 8). It specifically addresses the question of whether the use of "lessons of history" invoked by policymakers actually shapes policy or primarily serves as its justification. Relying on the public record, interviews, and archival documents, Khong demonstrates that the lessons policymakers drew from Munich, Dien Bien Phu, and, most importantly, the Korean War had a powerful influence on the decision-making process relative to Vietnam because they predisposed them toward military intervention. In other words, policymakers use analogies not merely to justify policies but also to perform specific cognitive tasks essential to political decision making: to help define the nature of the situation facing the policymaker, to help assess the stakes, and to provide policy prescriptions. The Khong study contributes to an improved understanding of why humans analogize and why policymakers often use analogies poorly due to a common cognitive process.

■ What Do We Know? Where Should We Go?

In surveying the development of political psychology and cognitive approaches to foreign policy, it should be relatively clear that much knowledge has accumulated concerning the role of policymakers' beliefs and images on foreign policy. In this section I briefly review what has been learned about the cognitive study of foreign policy and discuss some questions that remain unanswered or need to be addressed in the future.

Content of Beliefs

One feature all cognitive approaches share is that they provide an excellent perspective for determining the actual *contents of the beliefs and images* held by individual policymakers. A myriad of cognitive approaches can be drawn upon. For instance, the operational code emphasizes a policymaker's broad beliefs about politics; the image of the "other" focuses on the policymaker's perceptions and beliefs concerning a particular actor in world politics; cognitive mapping tends to examine a policymaker's foreign policy beliefs toward very specific issues. Whether a broad or narrow perspective is taken, a cognitive approach allows one to examine any aspect of a policymaker's foreign policy beliefs to contribute to a better understanding of foreign policy. This is particularly important because historians and observers of contemporary politics often make judgments and disagree about the contents of policymakers' beliefs. In this respect, a cognitive perspective allows for a more sophisticated foundation to examine the contents of the beliefs of policymakers. In the study of U.S. foreign policy, for example, cognitive approaches have contributed to a better understanding of the origins of the cold war (Larson 1985), American perceptions of Soviet communism during the "high" cold war era (Holsti 1967), the American decision to intervene in Vietnam (Khong 1992), the years of détente as represented by the beliefs of Henry Kissinger (Walker 1977), and the rise and decline of a world order approach during the Carter administration (Rosati 1987).

In order to describe foreign policy beliefs and images, it is important to determine the relevant policymakers involved in the formulation of policy. Most scholars who have systematically studied the foreign policy perceptions and beliefs of political leaders from a cognitive perspective have tended to focus on one key leader, such as Holsti's (1967) study of John Foster Dulles or Walker's (1977) study of Henry Kissinger. Also, a government and sometimes even a society has been treated as a single actor—that is, the equivalent of a single individual—such as in White's (1968) general discussion of mirror images or Heradstveit's (1979) analysis of the

Arab-Israeli conflict. Although analyzing an individual leader minimizes the empirical problems of identifying the content of beliefs, it considerably simplifies the "collective" nature of most decision making and the differences in beliefs that one might find across individuals (Steinbruner 1974). Some of the more recent work in this area has attempted to be more sophisticated in the cognitive analysis of foreign policy, as demonstrated by Larson's (1985) study of Harriman, Truman, Byrnes, and Acheson within the Truman administration; Rosati's (1987) study of Carter, Brzezinski, and Vance (and Muskie) within the Carter administration; and Khong's (1992) study of Lyndon Johnson and his advisers during the Vietnam policymaking process. More studies need to identify the critical individuals within the policymaking process and examine the contents of their beliefs and the decision-making dynamics between them so as to better understand the formulation and conduct of foreign policy.

Also, most of the work on the contents of beliefs has centered on the policymakers of the great powers, especially the United States, and has focused on the "high policy" issues of national security and international conflict, a possible legacy of the initial interest by political psychologists in addressing the paramount questions of war and peace.[15] Clearly, cognitive studies of images of the enemy and mirror images; crises (see, e.g., Holsti 1990; Lebow 1981); deterrence theory (see, e.g., Jervis, Lebow, and Stein 1985; Snyder 1978); and intelligence warning and surprise attack (see, e.g., Betts 1978; Wohlstetter 1962) have contributed to a better understanding of the dynamics of international conflict and war. At the same time, much more needs to be done in systematically examining the contents of beliefs about "low policy" issues such as international economics and the environment and in studying images of other actors from other parts of the world using a cognitive perspective.[16]

The Structure of Beliefs

The development of political psychology and the cognitive study of foreign policy has contributed to a better understanding of the *structure of beliefs* in the minds of individuals in a political setting. Both cognitive consistency theory and schema theory agree that central beliefs are consequential, although they differ about the level of coherence and interconnectedness between beliefs. On the one hand, the literature on cognitive consistency theory emphasizes that individuals acquire beliefs and images that are interconnected and form coherent belief systems. This was the basis, for example, of some of the earlier research approaches, such as the study of the image of the enemy as represented by Holsti's (1967) examination of John Foster Dulles or the study of an individual's general orientation toward political life found in the operational code approach. On the other hand, the literature on social cognition theory and schema theory describes cognitive structures within the minds of individuals as quite complex and messy. From this perspective, people's beliefs tend to be much less coherent, less interconnected, and more contradictory than originally conceived by cognitive consistency theory.

As the more recent studies demonstrate, both cognitive patterns are likely. Larson's (1985) study of the origins of the cold war found that only Acheson had a coherent belief system about world politics. Harriman, Byrnes, and especially

Truman had much less coherent beliefs and were more prone to make sense of world developments and Soviet behavior in ways that were consistent with schema, attribution, and self-perception theory. It was only in 1947 that a more coherent belief system crystallized for these policymakers around an enemy image of the Soviet Union and a policy of containment. Likewise, Rosati (1987) found both sets of cognitive patterns operating in his study of the Carter administration. Whereas Vance and Brzezinski maintained relatively coherent belief systems throughout, Carter's beliefs became increasingly inconsistent during 1978 to the point that, by 1979, he was constantly wavering between Vance's more optimistic image and Brzezinski's increasingly pessimistic one, until eventually siding with Brzezinski's interpretation of world politics in 1980.

What can possibly account for these contrasting cognitive structures suggested by cognitive consistency and schema theory? It appears that much depends on the individual, on his or her background, personal development, and role. According to studies on the *differences between "experts and novices,"* coherent images of phenomena are more likely to be formed if individuals have developed considerable expertise and experience relative to those phenomena. Fragmented, inconsistent, and contradictory beliefs are more likely to exist for phenomena about which individuals have given little thought or have acquired little knowledge and experience (see, e.g., Lau and Erber 1985; Lau and Sears 1986c; Milburn 1991). From this perspective it is not surprising that Acheson, Brzezinski, and Vance—each an expert in foreign policy with considerable experience—developed relatively coherent belief systems, while Harriman (to a lesser extent), Byrnes, Truman, and Carter as politicians and nonexperts were more prone to uncommitted thinking (see Larson 1985, 346).

Such an interpretation is consistent with the emphasis placed by cognitive theorists over the years on the *importance of the situation* for perception and cognition (Fiske and Taylor 1991; Milburn 1991; Rokeach 1968). Different situations are likely to trigger different schemas and sets of beliefs.[17] This is one of the major conclusions drawn by Herrmann (1985) in his work on the role of the enemy, degenerate, and child stereotypes in Soviet foreign policy. And such differences in images are likely to vary among individuals. Although individuals are likely to have little difficulty making sense of situations that are relatively stable and familiar in terms of their beliefs, situations of great complexity and uncertainty may result in significant cognitive inconsistency and confusion, especially if individuals do not have considerable knowledge and well-developed belief systems for imposing some degree of understanding on the environment. This may help account for why Truman administration policymakers were vulnerable to such inconsistency in their beliefs and dependent on the mechanisms of schema, attribution, and self-perception theory (Larson 1985)—clearly, the immediate post–World War II years were a time of great uncertainty and flux in global developments, similar to the current collapse of communism and the rise of the so-called post–cold war era. This may also explain why policymakers are prone to rely on historical analogies, as Khong (1992) found in his study of Vietnam decision making. Such cognitive responses by policymakers in differing times and settings needs to be explored further.[18]

Continuity and Change in Beliefs

A cognitive approach to foreign policy also contributes to an understanding about the extent to which policymakers' beliefs are likely to change over time. Cognitive theory, as informed by the literature on both cognitive consistency and schemas, is based on the premise that *central beliefs* are the most consequential in understanding the process of perception and cognition. As described by Milton Rokeach, "First, not all beliefs are equally important to the individual; beliefs vary along a central-peripheral dimension. Second, the more central a belief, the more it will resist change. Third, the more central the belief changed, the more widespread the repercussions in the rest of the belief system" (1968, 3; see also Bem 1970).

Beyond this common core, cognitive consistency and schema theory differ as to the likelihood and nature of attitudinal change. Cognitive consistency theory tends to emphasize the overall rigidity of belief systems due to their interconnectedness and, should change occur, the abrupt and all-encompassing nature of belief system change. As explained by Jervis (1976, 170), "If a person's attitude structure is to be consistent, then incremental changes among interconnected elements cannot be made. Change will be inhibited, but once it occurs, it will come in large batches. Several elements will change almost simultaneously." A number of studies from different cognitive research programs support such an explanation. Holsti (1967) found that Dulles's enemy image of the Soviet Union was fundamentally constant over time. Heradstveit (1979) found stability in Arab and Israeli images throughout the 1970s, while Bonham, Shapiro, and Trumble (1979), employing cognitive mapping, found no difference in the belief systems of American policymakers before and after the 1973 Yom Kippur War. Harvey Starr (1984) reviewed the literature on Henry Kissinger's foreign policy beliefs and found considerable stability in his pre-office, official, and post-office beliefs. Finally, Ben-Zvi (1978) found that the images of Japan held by American leaders were dramatically altered following the attack on Pearl Harbor and the fighting of the war in the Pacific, as predicted by cognitive consistency theory.

Schema theory, on the other hand, stipulates that beliefs are much more isolated and inconsistent with each other, and hence are less resistant and more open to piecemeal, incremental changes over time. This is what Larson (1985) found in her study of the origins of the cold war: the years 1944 to 1947 represented constant fluctuation in the beliefs of Harriman, Byrnes, and Truman, who moved sporadically but inevitably toward an enemy image of the Soviet Union. Likewise Rosati (1987) found that not only did Carter experience changes in his beliefs and increasingly waver between Vance's and Brzezinski's opposing views over a period of two years, Brzezinski also experienced considerable change in his worldview over time: relatively optimistic during 1977, skeptical of Soviet behavior and its implications for world order after the Ethiopian-Somali war in early 1978, and increasingly pessimistic about Soviet expansionism by 1979.

What the various studies suggest is that *patterns involving both belief stability and change* may in fact occur. According to cognitive consistency theory, the more coherent and interconnected the belief system, the more resistant to change and, should change occur, the more likely that it will be abrupt and profound. At the same time, from the perspective of schema theory, the fragmented and inconsistent nature of most people's beliefs indicates that incremental changes may also occur with some frequency. Both patterns were observed by Larson (1985) and Rosati (1987) in their studies of Truman and Carter administration policymakers over time. In this respect it is important to remember that while consistency theory and schema theory have different implications for belief system change, both emphasize the level of centrality of beliefs: the more central the belief, the more stable and resistant it is to change.

These two patterns of stability and change are consistent with the earlier discussion of the structure of beliefs, and probably for the very same reasons: much depends on individual background and personal development, the role occupied, and the situation at hand. According to Rosati (1987, 30), "While individuals strive to maintain consistency and the communication of information acts to reinforce one's belief system, images may still undergo change under certain conditions." He specifically highlighted the role of individual personality, external events, and domestic forces to explain the continuity of Vance's image and the changes in Brzezinski's and Carter's images. As summarized by Rosati (1987, 102–3):

> While Carter's personality was open to new information, Brzezinski's insecurity and rigid personality prompted his return to a previously held image. Major events played a critical role in shaping their alternative views: Soviet and Cuban interventionism in Africa was particularly crucial for Brzezinski; the Iranian hostage crisis and the Soviet invasion of Afghanistan for Carter. And finally, the development of a more pessimistic image for Brzezinski and particularly for Carter was reinforced by the changing mood of the country in a more nationalistic and conservative direction.

Larson (1985) also offered a rich explanation, although less systematic in conceptualization, in examining continuity and change in the beliefs of Truman policymakers. Clearly, further study of the patterns of continuity and change in the beliefs of policymakers is warranted.

Beliefs and Their Impact on Behavior

A considerable amount of research has been conducted in analyzing the significance of individual attitudes and beliefs: describing their content, structure, and relative degree of stability over time. All of this work has been based on one fundamental assumption: that beliefs are major sources of behavior and, therefore, explain and predict human action. Unfortunately, this assumption is so embedded in the attitudinal research that the *relationship between beliefs and behavior* has rarely been tested and demonstrated. The following comment by Fishbein and Ajzen (1975, 355) pertains to the present day: "Despite the commitment of the social sciences to the study of human behavior, relatively little research in the attitude area has investigated overt behavior as such." The results of the few studies conducted in social and political psychology have been inconsistent and indicate that the link between individual beliefs and behavior is quite complex and varied (see Barner-Barry and Rosenwein 1985; Calder and Ross 1973; Deutscher 1973; Oskamp 1977; Wicker 1969).

A similar problem exists with a cognitive approach to foreign policy. Holsti (1976, 52), in his review of the literature, found that the linkage between foreign policy beliefs and behavior has rarely been tested. "It is not uncommon to find in the conclusion a statement to the effect that, 'the preceding analysis of X's belief system established its utility for understanding X's political behavior.' Less often do we find an explicit and compelling demonstration of why this is the case." George (1979b) has outlined two basic techniques for determining the impact of policymakers' beliefs on behavior: the process-tracing procedure and the congruence procedure. Each has been applied, although only in very select cases, to better understand this relationship between beliefs and behavior.

The *process tracing procedure* "seeks to establish the ways in which the actor's beliefs influenced his receptivity to and assessment of incoming information about the situation, his definition of the situation, his identification and evaluation of options, as well as, finally, his choice of a course of action" (George 1979b, 113). By closely examining the process of decision making, process tracing is able to establish causality. However, it tends to be oriented around a specific case study and requires large amounts of detailed information about the decision-making process not readily available. The major study operating within a process-tracing perspective is Larson's (1985) study of the Truman administration.[19] Relying on archival data, Larson found that although individual beliefs did influence individual behavior, what was more surprising was that policymakers' beliefs about the Soviet Union often flowed from their decisions, as suggested by self-perception theory. These contradictory patterns indicate the complexity of the belief-behavior relationship, which, as suggested earlier, may have been accentuated by the fluidity and uncertainty of the immediate post–World War II era.

The *congruence procedure* examines the level of consistency between the content of the beliefs and the content of the decision outcome. Since the congruence procedure focuses on the level of association between beliefs and behavior, it cannot determine causality although it requires much less specific information about the decision-making process and allows for broad generalizations over time. The few studies conducted also point to the existence of contradictory patterns. Starr (1984) found that Kissinger's images of the Soviet Union and China were not consistent with American behavior toward the Soviet Union and China. However, when Walker (1975, 1977) examined the relationship between Kissinger's beliefs and his bargaining behavior toward the Soviet Union, the Arab-Israeli conflict, and the Vietnam War, he found consistency. Loch Johnson (1977, 85) studied the operational code of Senator Frank Church and found a strong correlation between Church's "beliefs and subsequent voting behavior which reinforces my impression (as participant observer) of his belief-behavior consistency." In Rosati's (1987) comparison of the beliefs of Carter, Brzezinski, and Vance with the administration's major foreign policy behavior over four years, he found both sets of belief-behavior patterns. He found that the Carter administration's foreign policy behavior was extremely consistent with its beliefs during 1977 and 1980, in contrast to 1978 and 1979, when the consistency between behavior and beliefs declined considerably. The major factor accounting for these differing patterns was the level of consensus in beliefs among Carter's policymakers—a high level of shared beliefs promoted congruent foreign policy behavior, but little congruency existed when consensus in beliefs broke down.

One of the impressive aspects of the study of Vietnam policymaking by Khong (1992) is that he relies on both procedures—process tracing and congruence—to demonstrate how historical analogies affect decisions. Despite such efforts to explain decision-making and foreign policy behavior as a function of the beliefs held by policymakers, this is a topic that needs considerably more exploration and study. Ultimately, as described by George, beliefs "serve as a prism or filter that influences the actor's perception and diagnosis of political situations and that provides norms and standards to guide and channel his choices of action in specific situations. ... Neither his diagnosis of situations nor his choice of action for dealing with them is rigidly prescribed and determined by these beliefs" (1980b, 45). Although beliefs often impact behavior, many other causal factors also play a role in influencing foreign policy behavior.

The Context and Study of Beliefs

If a cognitive approach is to provide a useful understanding of foreign policy, the scholar must remain sensitive to the role other psychological characteristics have along with governmental, domestic, and global dynamics in forming both policymaker beliefs and foreign policy. The early work on cognitive approaches to foreign policy was sensitive to such complexity.[20] For example, Holsti (1967) discussed the effect of personality on Dulles's image of the enemy, while White (1968) highlighted the psychological, social, and cultural sources of mirror images. However, as social scientists became increasingly specialized and systematic in their studies of political psychology during the late sixties and seventies, contextual factors such as the role of personality and the larger environment were increasingly ignored. As Ben-Zvi (1976–77, 90) has observed, the cognitive literature in foreign policy has tended to "de-emphasize the multitude of interwoven factors."

Over the past decade a number of political psychologists have pointed out the need for a broader conceptualization that integrates psychological characteristics associated with emotion, motivation, and *personality* within a more cognitive approach to better understand human behavior and interaction. Lebow (1981), for instance, has demonstrated how the management of brinkmanship crises is heavily affected by both cognitive and motivational characteristics of policymakers. Likewise, Tetlock and Levi (1982) concluded in their review of the literature that the future will likely see the integration of cognitive and motivational explanations. In his study of the Carter administration, Rosati (1987) explained policymaker image stability and change from a cognitive perspective that also incorporated the role of individual personality. Walker (1990) reviewed how the operational code originally had a broad conceptualization that included the integral role of personality, which he argues needs to be reintegrated in future research. This is consistent with the observation by Fiske and Taylor concerning the growing trend in the study of social cognition: "Having developed considerable sophistication about people's cognitive processes, researchers are beginning to appreciate anew the interesting and important influences of motivation [personality] on cognition" (1991, 13).

Such sensitivity to the need to integrate other relevant factors to better explain foreign policy within a cognitive perspective has grown over the years. Jervis (1976), for instance, relied upon a "two-step" model in which perceptions and beliefs served as the "proximate" cause of foreign policy decision making that also was affected by the role of bureaucracy, domestic determinants, and the international environment.

Likewise, Larson (1985, 326) provided a "multilevel explanation" in which "theories at different levels of analysis—systemic, domestic political, and individual cognitive processes—were applied to historical case material" to provide a rich explanation of the origins of American cold war policies. Similarly, Rosati's (1987, 168) study "was based on a framework that integrates theoretical work developed at four different levels: the individual, group, societal, and the international environment," including an examination of the role of personality, external events, and domestic forces to explain continuity and change in the beliefs of Carter administration officials. Such a *multilevel foundation* is needed to ensure that cognitive studies of foreign policy do not fall victim to the charge of reductionism and irrelevance that they experienced early on.

In fact, one of the promises of a cognitive approach is that beliefs usually act as a *causal nexus*—that is, as a filter through which other factors pass (George 1979b; Rosati 1987, 168–70). Beliefs are naturally positioned between the environment and behavior. Gordon Allport, one of the founders of attitudinal research in psychology, long ago recognized the potential of beliefs to serve as a causal nexus: "Background factors never directly cause behavior, they cause attitudes (and other mental sets) and the latter in turn determine behavior" (1931, 173). In order to better understand foreign policy, such a perspective must be embedded within a decision-making context that identifies the relevant policymakers and is sensitive to the nature of the policy-making process (see, e.g., de Rivera 1968; Rosati 1981, 1987, 17–19; Snyder, Bruck, and Sapin 1962; Steinbruner 1974). The major advantage of treating beliefs as a causal nexus is the synthesis of both environmental and psychological factors for understanding foreign policy. At the same time, since the focus of a cognitive approach is on the "psychological environment" of the policymaker, the scholar must remain sensitive to integrating the direct influence of the "objective environment" as well so as to ensure a comprehensive understanding of foreign policy (see Sprout and Sprout 1965).

The discussion of the context of beliefs and the need for multilevel explanations parallels the evolution of *research strategies* employed to study beliefs and their impact on foreign policy. Most studies have taken a case study approach, usually relying on some form of content analysis of information (such as public statements, private memoranda, oral interviews), often supplemented by other sources, to infer the beliefs of policymakers (see, e.g., Tetlock 1983b). Earlier studies tended to be more historical, qualitative, and often eclectic in examining beliefs, as represented by the initial work on images of the enemy, mirror images, and the operational code. With the rise of behavioralism, studies became much more systematic and quantitative, particularly those using the cognitive mapping approach. More recent studies have attempted to integrate the strengths of these two orientations by being both theoretically and methodologically systematic. These have also been open to diverse and increasingly eclectic research strategies—some more qualitative (see Herrmann 1985; Larson 1985, 1988), others more quantitative (see Herrmann 1986), and some employing both techniques (see Khong 1992; Rosati 1987). Such recent advances in methodological diversity and sophistication are consistent with the general rise of "postpositivism" in the study of international relations (see Lapid 1989), offering much promise to the future application of cognitive approaches to the study of foreign policy.

■ Conclusion: The Power of a Cognitive Approach

As we have seen, a cognitive approach provides considerable explanatory and predictive power in the study of foreign policy. Although much remains to be done to resolve the contradictory findings and to address the gaps of knowledge that continue to exist, the second generation of scholarship has become increasingly sensitive to studying the role of beliefs and perception in all of its complexity. Past studies have demonstrated that the beliefs and cognitive processes of policymakers affect how they see the world and what actions they take within the policymaking process. Not only does such a cognitive perspective provide invaluable insights into the formulation and conduct of foreign policy, it helps us better understand the dynamics of world politics (Rosati 1987, 170–79).

As stated by Richard Ned Lebow in *Between Peace and War*, "The proximate causes of conflict [such as the role of beliefs and perceptions] may even be as important as the underlying ones if a crisis can determine whether long-standing tensions are ultimately eased or lead to war" (1981, 4). This explains the disproportionate amount of attention that international crises have received in the study of foreign policy—a time when individuals and their psychological characteristics can dramatically affect the outcome. How crises are resolved "can determine whether war breaks out or peace is maintained. They can also intensify or ameliorate the underlying sources of conflict in cases where war is averted" (Lebow 1981, 334). Consequently, a cognitive perspective also has considerable policy relevance for the policymaker and the citizen, for it can contribute to the diagnosis of the situation surrounding policy by minimizing common perceptual errors while enriching an understanding of the psychological aspects of human and international interaction (see, e.g., Tetlock 1986; White 1986). Ultimately, a cognitive perspective serves as a useful corrective to the rational actor perspective that many scholars, policy analysts, and practitioners, as well as individual citizens, often rely on to make sense of the dynamics of foreign policy and world politics.

■ Acknowledgments

I would like to thank Jean Garrison, Michael Link, Roger Moore, Robert Shaw, and Steve Twing for their helpful comments and suggestions.

■ Notes

1. A point of clarification: political scientists usually make a distinction between the concept of *cognition* (involving beliefs, perception, and the processing of information) and the concept of *personality* (involving emotion and ego-defensive and motivational characteristics). Psychologists, on the other hand, usually treat "personality" as a broad, generic concept that incorporates beliefs, perception, emotion, motivation, and all other individual psychological characteristics (see Greenstein 1975, chapter 1). This chapter reflects the perspective of the political scientist, preferring to distinguish between cognition and personality so as to add clarity to the discussion.

2. Informative overviews of the general study of political psychology and its application to international relations over the years can be found in Kelman (1965a), Knutson (1973), Hermann (1977), Falkowski (1979), Hopple (1982), Hermann (1986), White (1986), and Singer and Hudson (1992). For a wide-ranging essay on the integral nature of "the image" for knowledge and life in a variety of contexts, see Boulding (1956).

3. An excellent earlier overview can be found in de Rivera (1968).

4. According to Richard Lau and David Sears (1986a) in their introduction to political cognition, "Social cognition began to dominate the study of attitudes in social psychology only by the late 1970s, the central journal had incorporated the term by 1980, and the first major textbook in the area had appeared by 1984" (Fiske and Taylor 1984, 7).

5. For early statements anticipating this perspective while cognitive consistency theory still reigned supreme, see Bem (1970) and Rokeach (1968).

6. This is a more fruitful approach than attempting a comprehensive review of the vast body of cognitive-oriented scholarship in foreign policy that has accumulated over the years. There are also other relevant bodies of knowledge that impact on cognition, including the role of personality, group and organizational decision making, and the societal-cultural context. For an excellent but incomplete review of the literature, see Vertzberger (1990; see also Tetlock and McGuire 1985). It also should be pointed out that there has been a strong tradition of biographies, histories, and policy studies that often invoke analysis, although informally and implicitly, from a psychological (and cognitive) perspective. Although these works are often quite informative and insightful (see, e.g., Tuchman 1984), the focus of this review is on foreign policy studies that are informed explicitly by psychological theory and research in the area of cognition.

7. For other studies of images of the enemy, see Ben-Zvi (1975), Lampton (1973), Stuart and Starr (1981–82), and Welch (1970), as well as the collection of essays in Farrell and Smith (1967) and Finlay, Holsti, and Fagen (1967); the two-step mediated stimulus-response model applied to state interaction during the World War I and Cuban missile crises (Holsti, Brody, and North 1965; Holsti, North, and Brody 1968; North 1967); as well as the analysis by historian Daniel Yergin (1977) of the origins of the cold war due to the displacement of the "Yalta" axioms during the Roosevelt administration by the "Riga" axioms under the Truman administration. A more conceptual discussion of national images can be found in Boulding (1959).

8. Holsti (1967) also discusses the role of personality on attitude change.

9. For other mirror image studies, see Bronfenbrenner (1961), Gamson and Modigliani (1971), and Stoessinger (1967, 1971). See also Charles Osgood's (1966) "graduated and reciprocated initiatives in tension-reduction" (GRIT) for reducing international conflict applied in the context of cold war mirror images.

10. For an excellent overview of the evolution of the operational code approach and its relationship to the literature on cognitive consistency, see Walker (1990).

11. For other studies using the operational code approach, see Holsti (1970), Johnson (1977), Starr (1984, Stuart and Starr 1981–82), and Tweraser (1974).

12. Other examples of cognitive mapping can be found in Bonham and Shapiro (1977), Bonham et al. (1978), and Hart (1977).

13. Other foreign policy studies emphasizing the perspective of attribution theory include Heradstveit and Bonham (1986) and Heuer (1980).

14. Although it is relatively common today to find psychobiographies and international relations scholarship that integrate a psychological perspective within their work, only a few have focused on a cognitive approach and applied it to the study of foreign policy.

In addition to the four scholars highlighted in this section, see the studies by Cottam (1986), McCalla (1992), and Shimko (1992), as well as the edited volume by Sylvan and Chan (1984). For sources that offer broader reviews of political psychology in general and its application to international relations, see note 2.

15. The major exception to the rule has been the more varied literature on cognitive mapping.

16. One clearly must be sensitive to the implications of applying a Western, especially American-oriented, cognitive approach to different societies with different cultures. See Price-Williams (1985), Putnam (1973), Pye (1986), and Shweder and Sullivan (1993).

17. As Lau and Sears have stated, "Certain information will be highly relevant to some people's schemata (and therefore easily processed, stored, and later recalled) and at the same time totally irrelevant to other people's schemata (and therefore not processed or remembered)" (1986c, 355).

18. These differences have led scholars to examine the level of "cognitive complexity." Drawn from cognitive consistency and schema theory, the assumption is that policymakers who demonstrate greater cognitive complexity have a more sophisticated understanding of the world, are more open to new information, and are less likely to choose strident alternatives when making decisions. See, for example, some of the cognitive mapping studies (Axelrod 1976) and the work of Philip Tetlock (1983a, 1985).

19. See also Ben-Zvi (1975). There have been numerous in-depth foreign policy historical and case studies developed over the years that may be informative about policymaker beliefs and their impact on foreign policy, but most do not emphasize a cognitive approach to foreign policy. Jervis (1976) provides an excellent review of this literature for illustrating patterns of perception and misperception in foreign policy.

20. See, for example, de Rivera (1968); Farrell and Smith (1967); Finlay, Holsti, and Fagen (1967); Snyder, Bruck, and Sapin (1962).

FIVE

Foreign Policy Metaphors: Falling "Dominoes" and Drug "Wars"

Keith L. Shimko, PURDUE UNIVERSITY

■ Editors' Introduction

In this chapter Keith Shimko examines the possible utility of the concept of "metaphors" for foreign policy analysis. Shimko's chapter emerges from a long line of research at the individual level of analysis and the emphasis on the importance of political psychology and cognition in foreign policy decision making. The following chapter extends the discussion by Jerel Rosati in the previous chapter but focuses attention in more depth on a concept that has not received much attention from political psychologists and foreign policy scholars—foreign policy metaphors. Recently "analogies" and "analogical reasoning" have received substantial attention by foreign policy scholars. But as Shimko points out, the related but analytically different concept of "metaphors" has yet to be systematically explored by foreign policy analysts. Through an examination of the common "domino" and "war" metaphors, Shimko discusses the possible roles of metaphors in foreign policy decision making. In so doing, he shows one future path for research in the area of cognition and foreign policy.

With what foreign policy metaphors besides "domino" and "war" are you familiar? How might these metaphors frame a debate about what to do in a foreign policy problem? How would an analyst of foreign policy try to study the presence and effect of metaphors in foreign policy? ■

The analysis of foreign policy is the study of choices made within constraints. It is concerned with why decision makers pursue the policies they do and is interested in those forces—international, societal, governmental, and idiosyncratic—that set the range of choices available to decision makers and influence the eventual choice made among possible actions. It is a truism of decision-making research that while policies are implemented in the "objective" world, they are formulated and crafted in the "subjective" world—that is, the world as it exists in the minds of decision makers, the situation they think they confront. This is the same distinction drawn by Harold Sprout and Margaret Sprout more than three decades ago in their discussion of "cognitive behaviorism," a label they used to "designate the simple and familiar principle that a person reacts to his milieu as he perceives it…in light of past experience" (1957, 314). A number of psychological approaches to the study of foreign policy, such as operational code analysis (George 1969; Holsti 1970; Starr 1984; Walker 1990), national images (Holsti 1962; Shimko 1991), analogical reasoning (Hybel 1990; Khong 1992; May 1973; Neustadt and May 1986; Schuman and Rieger 1992), and cognitive mapping (Axelrod 1976b; Hart 1976), have shared the assumptions of what Sprout and Sprout called cognitive behaviorism. Each assumes that an adequate understanding of policy formulation and choice requires an understanding of how decision makers think, what they think, and why they think what they think.

While the basic assumptions that have guided research on the cognitive dimensions of foreign policy have remained unchanged, the research itself has evolved. More recent work on the psychological components of decision making differs from earlier efforts in several respects. First, the "second generation" of research has been more explicit in its application of cognitive theories and concepts. Second, contemporary research has tried to move beyond the preliminary, illustrative, and sometimes anecdotal approach of earlier research (compare, e.g., the work of Schuman and Rieger [1992] as well as Khong [1992] on historical analogies to the pioneering work of May [1973]).[1] This is particularly true when second-generation researchers expand on topics that were introduced by earlier scholars. Third, the second generation has itself introduced new areas of research within the general cognitive approach, which is what this essay attempts.

The components of a decision maker's psychological milieu, as the variety of research on beliefs systems indicates, are numerous. They range from very specific beliefs about particular countries (e.g., that Soviet nuclear capabilities are superior to those of the United States) to very abstract and general beliefs (e.g., why nations go to war). This is one reason why research on the cognitive dimensions of foreign policy is so diverse. It is the combination of all of these beliefs that ultimately influences decisions. While the study of certain psychological variables is well developed, others have been neglected. The study of the role of metaphors is one such area. Deborah Larson is certainly correct in observing that "the role played by metaphors in foreign policy making is still unexplored" (1985, 55). This initial examination of the role of metaphors shares the same assumption that united all cognitive approaches to decision making but focuses on an aspect of the decision maker's thought and decision process that has been ignored by most previous work on the psychological foundations of foreign policy decision making.

■ Analogies, Metaphors, and Cognitive Psychology

The world around us is uncertain. There are many things we would like to know before we make decisions that we do not, and often cannot, know. Our environment is complex in that we are constantly bombarded with information and stimuli, sometimes important and sometimes not. The uncertainties, ambiguities, and complexities of life are unavoidable. This is true not only in our immediate, personal lives but also (perhaps even more so) in the more distant realm of politics and international relations. The recognition of these uncertainties and complexities is the starting point for much of cognitive psychology, which is devoted to understanding how people deal with the uncertainties and complexities of life that confront them. How, for example, do people decide to behave in situations in which they have never before found themselves? Why do people react to certain people in similar or different ways? How do people anticipate the consequences of their actions when the outcome is dependent upon how others, whose behavior they cannot control, will respond? In other words, how do people make sufficient sense of an uncertain and complex world in order to act coherently? The question is the same no matter what sort of human behavior we are attempting to understand, from the most mundane actions of regular people to the dramatic decisions of political leaders.

Cognitive psychologists have shown that people routinely use several mechanisms to bring order to complexity, resolve ambiguities, and comprehend new situations. Many of these mechanisms rely on comparisons. When people are confronted with problems, situations, or people, they have not confronted before, they try to make comparisons to problems, people, and situations they have dealt with in the past. In this way people use their knowledge of other events or people to compensate for their lack of knowledge of new events and people. They fill in the blanks of current events with knowledge accumulated from past experiences. Analogical thinking is one such type of comparative thinking that has received substantial attention from students of foreign policy. The "Munich analogy," for example, refers to attempts to draw comparisons between more recent events, whether the Soviet Union in Eastern Europe in the late 1940s or Saddam Hussein in Kuwait in the 1990s, and the experiences and "lessons" of the 1930s (the lesson being that one should not attempt to "appease an aggressor"). Metaphorical thinking is another cognitive process based on comparisons in that it involves viewing one phenomenon as being like another. Though similar, there are significant differences between analogical and metaphorical reasoning. These differences are important because they lead to different consequences for studying and understanding their roles in decision making.

What exactly is a metaphor, and how is it different from an analogy? According to Susan Sontag, who borrows her definition from Aristotle, a metaphor involves "saying a thing is or is like something–it–is–not" (1989, 93). Linguists Lakoff and Johnson describe the essence of a "metaphor a[s] understanding and experiencing one kind of thing in terms of another" (1980, 5). It is not difficult to think of metaphors that are commonplace. We frequently refer to time as "money" which we can "spend," "waste," "squander," and even "save." We discuss ideas as if they are "food" (for thought). We put forward ideas for people to "savor," "chew on," and "digest." And how frequently do we hear expressions such as "love is like…," with the blank being filled in with a colorful metaphor? These are all metaphors because they describe something as being like something it is not—time is not money and ideas are not food. These are attempts to describe, explain, and understand one concept in terms of another.

The key difference between analogies and metaphors is the nature of the comparison being made. Analogies are generally comparisons drawn from the same realm of experience, whereas metaphors tend to be comparisons between things from very different realms. Analogies are what we might classify as "within-domain" comparisons, while metaphors are "across-domain" comparisons (Vosniadou and

Ortony 1989, 7). If we say that John is like his father, we are making an analogical comparison because we are trying to convey something about one person by comparing him to another person. But if we said that John is like a lion in his cunning and like a rock in his steadiness, we are using a metaphor because we are comparing a person to something quite different. Similarly, if we compare Soviet-American relations in 1949 to the West's dealings with Nazi Germany in the 1930s or the Vietnam War to the Korean War, we are drawing analogies. But if we describe Soviet-American relations as a "game" involving high "stakes," "gambles," and even "bluffs," we are being metaphorical in comparing an international crisis to something from a very different realm of experience—a game of chance. Whether a comparison is being made within or between domains may not always be obvious. Larson (1985), for example, reports that Truman often drew parallels between his early experiences in local Jackson County (Missouri) politics and international diplomacy. While still in the realm of politics, the comparison was not within the realm of international politics. Some metaphors involve comparisons between things much further removed from one another.

The fact that both analogies and metaphors involve cognitive comparisons suggests that much of the empirical and theoretical work on historical analogies is relevant for understanding the role of metaphors because many of the underlying cognitive processes are the same. The cognitive dynamics involved in analogical and metaphorical thinking are relatively easy to understand when placed in the context of what has become known as script or schema theory[2] (see Conover and Feldman 1991; Khong 1992, 25–37; Kuklinski, Luskin, and Bolland 1991; Larson 1994; Lodge and McGraw 1991). The basic logic of script or schema theory is quite simple: when people confront objects, people, or situations they have not encountered before, they search their memories for previous objects, people, or situations that resemble the new ones in ways that are readily apparent to them. People then use their stored knowledge of the previous events, people, and objects as tools for comprehending the new ones.[3]

Analogical and metaphorical reasoning involves two analytically distinct, though empirically entwined, processes. The first might be called retrieval—that is, people search through their memories for something that resembles the thing or situation they are trying to understand. Once something similar has been found, the individual can say that the present situation or object is like whatever he or she has determined resembles it. The metaphors and analogies are invoked because of their accessibility (i.e., it is something in the individual's experience) and perceived similarities or, to use Sontag's nice phrasing, their "felt aptness" (1989, 24). Cognitive psychologists generally refer to this initial invocation of the comparison as "mapping" (Sternberg 1977, 136).

The second aspect of analogical and metaphorical reasoning is most important for our purposes and involves the process by which knowledge is "created." Having located something in their experience that is similar to the object or situation confronting them in certain key respects, people assume that the objects or situations are alike in other respects as well. In this way knowledge about one person, object, or situation is created by the transfer of knowledge from another. Thus analogies and metaphors, in Khong's words, allow people "to go beyond the information given"

(1992, 28). This information, or created knowledge, is part of the basis on which decisions are made.

■ Analogies, Metaphors, and Decision Making

Although the cognitive dynamics of analogical and metaphorical reasoning are the same, the implications for decision making are not. The cognitive dynamics are the same because both types of reasoning are attempts at understanding based on comparisons and the transfer of knowledge. The decision-making ramifications are different because metaphors and analogies involve different types of comparisons. The key distinction, which has already been pointed out, is the domain of comparison. Analogies are comparisons within domains, whereas metaphors are comparisons across domains. In terms of decision making this is important because the more removed something is from that to which it is being compared, the less helpful it is likely to be for devising specific policies.

To understand the importance of this distinction between within-domain and across-domain comparisons for decision making, it is useful to begin by examining the role of historical analogies and then determine which of the decision functions performed by analogies can and cannot be fulfilled by metaphors. According to Khong, whose treatment of historical analogies remains the most satisfying, analogies perform a set of "diagnostic tasks":

> First and foremost, analogies help define the nature of the problem or situation…by comparing the new situation to previous situations with which the policymaker is more familiar…. The second and third diagnostic tasks follow: analogies give the policymaker a sense of the political stakes involved and they also imply or suggest possible solutions to the problem as defined…. The fourth, fifth and sixth diagnostic tasks all pertain to evaluating the implicit polic[ies] prescribed…by "predicting" their likelihood of success, "assessing" their moral rightness, and "warning" of the dangers associated with them (1992, 20–21).

Khong goes on to demonstrate persuasively how decisions made about the conduct of the Vietnam War in 1965 were influenced by analogies to the Korean conflict: the situation and stakes were defined as being similar, the response of adversaries to possible U.S. actions was anticipated to be the same, and policies that were successful in Korea were evaluated favorably in the context of Vietnam, while those that failed in Korea were discounted. What is particularly interesting is Khong's ability to show how specific diplomatic and war-fighting strategies in Vietnam were evaluated in the context of the Korean analogy.

We cannot, however, expect metaphors to play the same role as historical analogies in decision making. In particular, metaphors cannot exert the same influence on policy details as do historical analogies. Analogies of the sort Khong examined are largely attempts to draw parallels between one international crisis and another or a previous war and a current one (i.e., they are within-domain comparisons). This being the case, the degree of "help" or "guidance" offered to the policymaker is greater than if the crisis or war were being compared to something very different. That is, the more removed something is from that to which it is being compared, the less helpful it is for offering specific policy advice to the decision maker. In terms of the six diagnostic tasks mentioned by Khong, metaphors will be more helpful for the first three (more general) functions than for the last three (more specific) functions.

The difference between the decision-making functions of metaphors and historical analogies can be capsulized in the distinction between "problem framing" and "problem solving." The first three diagnostic tasks identified by Khong involve problem framing—that is, defining the situation, analyzing the issues and stakes involved, and perhaps suggesting a general approach. The second set of tasks deals with problem solving—that is, identifying specific courses of action and evaluating their prospects for success or failure. Vosniadou and Ortony hint at this basic distinction when they observe that "within-domain models [analogies] tend to focus on *problem solving tasks*" (1989, 11). The implication is that across-domain comparisons focus on a different set of tasks, namely, problem framing. There has been considerable attention in the cognitive literature, particularly in what has become known as "decision heuristics," to the importance of problem framing. Kahneman and Tversky (1984) present results of experiments demonstrating that different frames lead to different choices even though problem situations (i.e., the payoff matrix) remains the same.[4] Problem framing answers the question: What sort of situation am I confronting? Problem solving answers the question: What exactly should I do now? Thus, while historical analogies can, as Khong demonstrates, perform both problem-framing and problem-solving tasks, metaphors are more important for the former. In particular, metaphors can be expected to play a critical role in the first task Khong mentions—what has become known as "problem representation." Metaphors provide an underlying intellectual framework for understanding or making sense of a situation, not a detailed guide to policy.

■ Metaphors and Foreign Policy: Falling "Dominoes" and Drug "Wars"

It is not very difficult to compile a long list of metaphorical allusions and constructs that are routinely employed by foreign policy decision makers. Some of these are vivid and immediately recognized as metaphors. We are told, for example, that Latin America is in the United States' "backyard" in which no outside interference will be tolerated. During the cold war, communism was considered and portrayed as a "disease" that was contagious and could "spread" in the absence of sufficient effort to contain it. Military escalation involves a series of "steps" or "rungs" along a "ladder." Bombing raids are described as "surgical." Initial military involvement poses the risk of "going down" a "slippery slope." Further bombing might be justified in a war as the thing that will "break the enemy's back." In the early 1980s some thought there was a "window" of vulnerability in the strategic nuclear force of the United States through which the Soviets might be able to launch a successful first strike and thus destroy the United States with impunity (Shimko 1992). Geographic areas are categorized as "vacuums" into which nations are drawn: in the wake of the 1956 Suez crisis Eisenhower claimed that "the existing vacuum in the Middle East must be filled by the United States before it is filled by Russia" (in Walt 1987, 67). According to Lakoff, "The discourse over whether the U.S. should go to war in the Gulf was a panorama of metaphor. Secretary of State Baker saw Saddam as 'sitting on our economic lifeline.' President Bush saw him as having a 'stranglehold' on the U.S. economy. General Schwarzkopf characterized the occupation of Kuwait as a 'rape'" (1991, 25).

The metaphorical nature of such constructs is obvious. There are other concepts, however, that are so widely accepted and integrated into the discourse of foreign policy that the metaphorical origins often pass unnoticed. For example, two or more hostile countries building armaments are usually considered to be involved in an arms "race." This metaphor is so widely used that it is almost impossible to discuss the acquisition of arms without using it and its associated terminology of being "ahead," "behind," or "catching up." Feminist scholars have pointed out that the language of international relations and strategy is replete with sexual imagery and metaphors that, they argue, have consequences for who may enter into a policymaking dialogue and what types of tactics and strategies are permissible within such a dialogue (e.g., Cohn 1987).

Not every metaphor is important for understanding policy. Some are almost certainly nothing more than clever or colorful rhetoric designed to convey a point in a dramatic fashion, such as some of the metaphors Lakoff mentions from the Gulf war. The expression "mother of all battles" is undoubtedly a metaphor but probably an irrelevant one in terms of how either side actually conducted the war. If we are interested in metaphors that are conceptual (i.e., are playing a role in people's under-standing of an issue) as opposed to merely rhetorical, we want to look for those metaphors that *appear with regularity* and are accompanied by a whole *series of expressions* and ideas that are related to the central metaphor, particularly when the metaphor itself is not being specifically invoked.[5] Thus, the "mother of all battles" is not a good candidate for a conceptual metaphor; the arms "race" is.

The discourse of the cold war was filled with metaphors. In fact, the expression "cold war," coined by Walter Lippmann in the 1940s to characterize the emerging U.S.-Soviet rivalry, was actually a double metaphor itself, with both "cold" and "war" being used metaphorically. The metaphor most linked with the cold war has been the so-called domino principle. Along with the metaphor of communism as a "disease" with the potential to spread like the plague, the imagery of nations as dominoes "falling" to communism was probably the most common metaphor for Soviet/communist expansion. President Eisenhower put forward the domino metaphor in its most vivid expression when he spoke of communist expansion in Southeast Asia: "You have the broader considerations that might follow what you would call the 'falling domino' principle. You have a row of dominoes set up, you knock over the first one, and what will happen to the last one is the certainty that it will go over very quickly" (in MacDonald 1991, 112).

The domino metaphor is a plausible candidate for a metaphor that influenced U.S. cold war policy because it was frequently invoked by U.S. policymakers. More importantly, U.S. strategic analysis was frequently characterized by a manner of thinking and speaking that was an extension of the domino metaphor. Even when the specific metaphor was not being invoked consciously, it was not uncommon to hear policymakers employ the language of the metaphor—for example, nations and governments facing communist challenges were in danger of "falling" and "toppling," the "fall" of one nation could set off a "chain reaction," and friendly governments could be "propped up" with U.S. "support."

The domino metaphor was not the only, or even the most important, factor shaping the analysis of the world situation confronted by U.S. policymakers, and in many ways the domino metaphor reinforced an analysis that drew on other constructs, such as the Munich analogy. Nonetheless, the domino metaphor helped frame the strategic environment in particular ways that implied predictions about the consequences of actions (and inactions) and the eventual stakes involved in certain conflicts. Perhaps the most important and obvious aspect of the international situation characterized by the domino metaphor is the interdependent nature of world events. The central element of the metaphor, as is evident in Eisenhower's explanation, is the idea that developments in one country have ramifications beyond its borders. The problem, however, is that the interdependence of actual dominoes that are lined up together is extreme, even absolute; the fall of the first domino inevitably leads to the fall of the second, and so on in a mechanistic fashion. Although events in one area of the world often have ramifications in others, the level of strategic interdependence is seldom (if ever) as severe as the imagery of falling dominoes suggests.

Other facets of the domino metaphor might not be as readily apparent. In addition to highlighting the notion of strategic interdependence, the domino metaphor also obscures differences between the dominoes (i.e., nations). When dominoes are lined up in a row, they are interchangeable, differing only in their cosmetic characteristics (i.e., the number of dots), which have nothing to do with their propensity to fall once struck by the adjacent domino. This blurring of national differences combined with the exaggeration of strategic interdependence is what most have identified as the major shortcoming of the domino metaphor as applied to international relations. LaFeber argues "The domino theory was (and remains) one of the most dangerous ideas to attract Americans. As experts on Asia tried to tell Johnson in 1965: 'a first reality to bear in mind: despite elements of similarity, no Southeast Asian nation is a replica of the other'" (1989, 231). Karnow similarly argues "the American crusade, propelled as it was by the 'domino theory'…disregarded the complex nationalistic diversity of Southeast Asia" (1983, 43).

There were further ramifications of this imagery. By framing the strategic environment as being composed of states lined up as a row of identical dominoes just waiting to be pushed over, "the domino theory fails to discern the local roots of discontent and the various local conditions that can weaken a government" (Glad and Taber 1990, 70). That is, the source of each domino's "fall" is external—that is, the pressure exerted by the fall of the previous domino. In the context of U.S. strategic analysis, this explanation reinforced a tendency to see local revolutions with leftist orientations as being instigated and manipulated by external involvement—that is, the Soviet Union and/or China. Furthermore, the falling of the dominoes can be stopped only with external intervention—left to their own devices their fall is inevitable. Thus, the domino metaphor framed the problem of communist expansion in a way that emphasized strategic interdependence, external forces, and national similarities. The metaphor did not give any specific policy advice concerning how to stop the dominoes from falling (beyond the general advice that policymakers should stop the forces that begin the falling of the dominoes), but it did help frame the strategic environment in a way that prompted decision makers to do something. Returning to the diagnostic tasks laid out by Khong, we can see how the domino metaphor helped define the strategic situation and gave some sense of the stakes involved (i.e., failure to intervene to stop the fall of one domino would lead to the fall of others).

A concept more commonly used in a metaphorical sense is that of war. People frequently try to frame a problem as a war when they want to eliminate or end something they view as undesirable, harmful, or threatening. In recent years we have witnessed "wars" on poverty, hunger, AIDS, cancer, and even government waste. The wide variety of issues to which the war metaphor has been applied attests to its elasticity. The reasons for the common use of war as a metaphor are simple. First, war is a widely and readily accessible concept; everyone knows what a war is. Second, war is a complex and multifaceted phenomenon. Since there are so many aspects of war, there are many dimensions along which something can be like a war.

The policy implications of framing an issue as a war are difficult to determine because the concept of war carries so many possible connotations. Sontag emphasizes one possible implication of the war metaphor: "War-making is one of the few activities that people are not supposed to view 'realistically'; that is, with an eye to expense and practical outcome. In all-out war, expenditure is all-out" (1989, 99). Thus one of the consequences of framing an issue as a war might be support for all-out expenditure to "combat" that which people are trying to eliminate. But there are other possible, and perhaps less desirable, consequences of representing something as a war. Times of war are not normal times. In addition to being periods of focused effort and all-out expenditure, "wartime" might also be viewed as a period when some of the normal luxuries of life (e.g., material comforts or political liberties) are "sacrificed" to the war effort. As a result, framing an issue as a war could lead to calls for restrictions on behavior and rights that are typically protected but come to be viewed as unaffordable luxuries during wartime. Perhaps more than anything else people associate war with insecurity, violence, and the use of military force to achieve certain objectives. In war, problems are usually viewed as having military dimensions and military solutions. This being the case, we might hypothesize that when a situation that is not a war is framed as a war, there is the possibility that it may come to be viewed as having a military component. Thus, framing an issue as a war, I would suggest, may increase the likelihood that people will look for a forceful or military approach.

The concept of war is used both literally and metaphorically in foreign policy. In terms of the metaphorical uses of "war" that frame foreign policy issues, there are probably few better examples than the current "war on drugs" in the United States. The first major "war on drugs" was announced by President Nixon in 1971. Declaring drugs "public *enemy* number one," Nixon called for an "all-out *offensive*" (Wisotsky 1986, 3, emphasis added). Since President Reagan announced the next major "war on drugs" in the 1980s the language of war has surrounded this issue. Reagan spoke of his "new federal *strategy* which is designed to *mobilize* all our *forces* to stop the flow of illegal drugs" (WCPD 1982, 1532, emphasis added). "For the first time, the federal government is *waging* a planned, concerted *campaign*…we've taken down the *surrender flag* and run up the *battle flag*. And we are going to *win* the *war* on drugs" (WCPD 1982, 1253, emphasis added). Though denying there was any militarization of the war on drugs, Melvyn Levitsky, assistant secretary of state for international narcotics in the Bush administration, argued that the United States was "*mobilized* and engaging in a real *war effort*" against drugs. Even though the "*main front* in this *war* is at home," there were international dimensions as well. The United States, in his view, "need[ed] to *attack* all aspects of the drug chain…[because] our *fight* against illegal drug use…cannot be *won* on any single *front* alone. It must be *waged* everywhere." He urged the United States to "stick with [its] *strategy*" because "*fighting* drugs is tough." He was confident that the United States would ultimately "*defeat* the scourge of drugs in this country and internationally" (1991, 360–67, emphasis added). In congressional testimony, Lee Brown, then commissioner of the New York Police Department and later "drug czar" in the Clinton administration, making reference to the recent war in the Persian Gulf, argued that "we need to *wage a war* of equal intensity closer to home [where] people are being killed.…I submit to you that if we are going to do *battle* against drugs, we must do no less here at home than is being done in the Middle East" (U.S. Congress 1990, 8–9, emphasis added). These words and expressions—"enemy," "offensives," "war," "mobilization," "fronts," "strategy," "attacks," "fight," "wage," and "defeat"—are all part of the language of war, and they are indicative of how the drug problem has been framed in the minds of decision makers and the broader American public.

Viewing the drug problem as a war can have ramifications both domestically and internationally. While the war on drugs has yet to run its course, some of the consequences of framing the problem as a war are already evident. Domestically, a number of commentators have expressed concerns about the implications of the war metaphor (although usually without explicitly recognizing the underlying metaphorical thinking). Tom Wicker, for example, argues that "a war on drugs, emphasizing combat, arrests and jailings could produce a wartime mentality—the spirit that anything goes, including the sacrifice of constitutional freedoms in the battle against drugs" (in Johnson 1992, 89). A student of cognitive psychology might argue that while Wicker is perceptive, he has the situation reversed—it is not combat, arrests, and jailing that created the wartime mentality, but the mentality that leads to the combat, arrests, and jailings.

What might some of the other consequences be, particularly when we look at the foreign policy dimensions of the drug problem? In order to speculate on this issue one needs to consider what sort of images are evoked by the concept of war— that is, what do people think of and associate with the phenomenon of war? Certainly among the constellation of images that are part of war is violence and the use of military force. One needs to be careful, however, about the implications of the war metaphor in this regard. Merely because a problem is framed as a war does not mean people will assume there is a military solution. For some problems the use of military force is obviously not part of the solution, no matter how commonly used the war metaphor is. There are limits to what can be transferred in the process of metaphorical thinking; a metaphor cannot transform objective reality completely.[6] There was, for example, no military component to the "war" on poverty. For the "war" on poverty other elements of the concept of war were more important (e.g., all-out effort and expenditure). But if there is a conceivable military option for dealing with a problem, framing it as a war may increase the chances that such an option will be pursued. The drug problem is one in which the military could conceivably play a role.

Since the most recent war on drugs was declared in the early 1980s, one of the recurring policy problems that has faced policymakers has concerned the role of the military in fighting the war at home and overseas. Chairman of the Senate Judiciary Committee Joseph Biden (D-MD) claims that "drug trafficking is—without question—the no. 1 security threat in this hemisphere…the full diplomatic, economic and military power must be marshalled in response" (in Bernards 1990, 161). At issue have been the military's potential contribution to domestic law enforcement, drug interdiction, and military aid and advice to foreign governments (particularly in Central and South America) to assist in their efforts to find and destroy drug crops. The U.S. military has been generally resistant to demands that it become more involved in the drug war, perhaps realizing that its purpose and mission is to fight "real" wars, not metaphorical wars. Nonetheless, the military has slowly given in to civilian pressures and increased its contribution to the drug war gradually throughout the 1980s and early 1990s.

According to Wisotsky, "Reagan…succeeded in literally militarizing what had previously been a rhetorical war by deploying the military forces of the United States in drug enforcement operations" (1986, 5). A few examples highlight this ongoing militarization. In 1984 the U.S. Navy was involved in efforts off the coast of Colombia to stop the transport of illegal drugs (Magnuson 1990), and in 1986 U.S. special forces participated in the training and support of Bolivian police in raids against cocaine laboratories in what was code-named Operation Blast Furnace (Abbott 1988). The FY 1989 National Defense Authorization Act, among other provisions, established the Department of Defense as the "lead agency" in the interdiction of illegal narcotics being smuggled into the United States. Overall, according to Perl, the 1989 act is part of "an ongoing trend to enhance direct military involvement in the nation's anti-drug campaign" (1989, 100). As if to confirm this new role, in 1989 the United States announced that fifty to one hundred U.S. military personnel would be sent to Colombia to assist in the fight against drug production (Halloran 1989), and that U.S. military trainers would be sent to Peru for similar purposes (Brooke 1990). There was also, of course, the December 1989 invasion of Panama; though the invasion was justified on the grounds of promoting democracy and securing the canal, U.S. troops arrested General Manuel Noriega and brought him to the United States for trial on drug smuggling and money laundering charges.

During the Bush administration, Secretary of Defense Richard Cheney was particularly supportive of an increased military role in the war on drugs, arguing that "the detection and countering of the production, trafficking and use of illegal drugs is a high priority national security mission of the Department of Defense." He pointed to three phases of the drug problem—production abroad, transport to the United States, and distribution in the United States. "The United States armed forces," he claimed, "can assist in the attack on the supply of drugs in each of these phases" (1990, 222–23). While Cheney and other administration officials were hesitant to specify exactly what role U.S. armed forces could or would take abroad to deal with drug production and smuggling, Cheney indicated that he saw a definite role for U.S. forces in fighting the drug war abroad. A July 1989 National Security Council report urged an expansion of the role of the U.S. military in the Andean countries and did not rule out the use of combat forces in the future (Berke 1989).

These two cases—falling dominoes and the drug war—illustrate how metaphors can influence behavior by framing issues. Metaphors, like analogies, do this by highlighting some features of reality while downplaying others. According to Lakoff and Johnson, "The very systematicity that allows us to comprehend one aspect of a concept in terms of another will necessarily hide other aspects of a concept. In allowing us to focus on one aspect of a concept…a metaphorical concept can keep us from focusing on other aspects of the concept that are inconsistent with that metaphor" (1980, 10). Viewing geopolitical dynamics as falling dominoes and the drug problem as a war highlights certain facets of these problems while obscuring others. In this way metaphors "have the power to [help] define reality" (Lakoff and Johnson 1980, 157).

■ Conclusion

As was stated at the outset, the study of foreign policy decision making is the study of choices made within constraints. Foreign policy problems do not present their own solutions or policy choices; indeed, they do not even present themselves as "problems." Decision makers frame issues as problems and go on to define what type of problems they are. How a problem is defined or represented in the minds of decision makers can be expected to influence how they choose to respond to the problem. This was one of the central insights of the first generation of research on the psychological and cognitive bases of foreign policy decision making. All of this is another way of saying what Sprout and Sprout observed (1969) nearly four decades ago—people react to their environment according to their perceptions and understandings of it. It is within this tradition that I developed the present argument on the potential importance of metaphors for framing foreign policy issues.

Garrett Hardin notes that "it is probably impossible to approach an unsolved problem save through the door of metaphor." Furthermore, "since metaphorical thinking is inescapable it is pointless to weep about our human limitations. We must learn to live with them, to understand them, and to control them" (1977, 261). Drawing on cognitive theory, I have argued that metaphorical thinking, like analogical thinking, is probably "inescapable" because people have no choice but to rely on what they already know to understand what they do not know and on past experiences to understand and solve new problems. This essay is not, though, an attempt to dwell on the psychological bases of foreign policy failures or foibles. There is no *a priori* reason to assume that metaphorical thinking has led to more failures than successes (or vice versa), even with the two examples discussed in this chapter. There are undoubtedly cases where metaphors have been helpful as well as harmful. There are certainly cases where metaphors have provided creative new ways of looking at problems that have led to worthwhile solutions. People can debate which particular instances of metaphorical thinking fall into which category. But these issues are secondary to those of whether and how metaphors influence behavior and policy. If the metaphors used by policymakers exert no influence on the course of action they eventually follow, then the metaphors are neither helpful nor harmful, simply irrelevant. Given what we know about cognitive processes and the importance of analogical thinking, though, there is no reason to believe that metaphors are irrelevant. In fact, there are good reasons to suspect otherwise. One of the tasks for the future of foreign policy analysis is to examine the theoretical and empirical importance of metaphors of foreign policy.

■ Notes

1. This is not intended to be a criticism of earlier research. Initial attempts to draw attention to new areas of research are often illustrative, speculative, and anecdotal. As people become persuaded that these new areas of research are potentially worthwhile, we can expect scholars to become more rigorous in their approach. Indeed, the present essay, focusing on an issue that has thus far received little attention, is itself somewhat illustrative, speculative, and anecdotal.

2. I group script and schema theory together here even though there are some differences between the two. In doing so I am following the lead of Khong, who argues that "schemas, scripts, and analogies may thus be considered knowledge structures whose functional similarities are much more impressive and pertinent than their differences" (1992, 25). I would add metaphors to Khong's grouping of schemas, scripts, and analogies.

3. Two examples will suffice to illustrate the logic of script or schema theory. Whenever we walk into a restaurant, we tend to behave in certain ways. We wait to be seated because we assume we will be (unless there is a sign telling us to seat ourselves). We wait for our menus because we expect them to be delivered. We make our selections. We tell the server what we want. Then we assume our food will arrive shortly. But how do we know whenever we walk into a restaurant that these things will happen? In fact, we do not know; we think, suspect, anticipate, and predict. We "know" this because past experience of what happens in restaurants leads us to expect this and we act accordingly. We really do not know our food will be delivered until it is in front of us, but we act on the assumption that it will because that is what has always happened—that is the "script" we associate with the situation. As another example, imagine a young boy who has grown up around dogs. He will have developed a mental image of what dogs look like (four legs, snout, a tail, etc.) and how they behave (friendly, like to be petted, etc.). Upon encountering a wolf for the first time, the boy will search his memory for something that looks like the wolf. The closest thing might be his image of a dog. The boy is then likely to respond to the wolf as if it were a dog, with potentially less than desirable results. The point is that a script or scheme is a mental picture of something familiar that is invoked in order to make sense of something unfamiliar. Scripts and schema are forms of "mental economics" by which "knowledge can be *created* from recorded knowledge" (Michalski 1989, 122, emphasis added). Analogies and metaphors are essentially scripts and schemas that serve as cognitive mechanisms for "creating" knowledge upon which decisions can be made.

4. Sylvan and Thorson (1992) have recently drawn on this literature to examine problem representation during the Cuban missile crisis. Prospect theory also focuses on how differences in the way a problem is framed can lead to different decisions being made. For a discussion of prospect theory and related issues, see Hogarth and Reder (1987) and the special issue on prospect theory in the journal *Political Psychology* (June 1992).

5. For a fuller discussion of how we might draw the difficult distinction between a rhetorical metaphor and a conceptual metaphor, see Shimko (1994).

6. The same is true of analogies. For example, merely because one war is invoked in comparison to another does mean that all the lessons of the previous war are transferred. If bombing industrial targets proved to be successful before, this does not mean this strategy will be applied again, particularly if the new adversary has no industrial centers to bomb.

SIX

Cognition, Culture, and Bureaucratic Politics

Brian Ripley, UNIVERSITY OF PITTSBURGH

■ Editors' Introduction

In this chapter Brian Ripley discusses theory and research in bureaucratic politics, a research tradition brought most clearly into the study of foreign policy in Graham Allison's study of the Cuban missile crisis in Essence of Decision. *Ripley brings together two lines of research that have often been treated separately—individual-level concerns with cognition and the group-level phenomena of organizational culture and bureaucratic politics. To the extent that these issues are treated together in foreign policy analysis, they have often been labeled "role-level" phenomena. Here Ripley's concern is with reinvigorating the type of research exemplified by Allison's work, but which has of late fallen out of use as researchers have focused primarily on only one issue at a time, such as political psychology, organizational dynamics, or rational models of decision making. Ripley argues that the choice of research approach need not be an "either-or" decision, but that instead a research approach that reaches across levels of analysis and blends individual- and group-level concerns may lead not only to a reinvigoration of the bureaucratic politics approach but to significant new insights into the nature of political decision making performed by individuals within groups.*

Questions to keep in mind when reading this chapter include: What is at the heart of the bureaucratic politics perspective? Most of the work on bureaucratic politics has been on the American case. To what type of information would we need access in order to determine the impact of the bureaucratic politics model in the foreign policy making of other countries? Why would this approach be more suited to the study of highly institutionalized states? Reflecting not just on this chapter but also on the preceding ones, what is at the heart of the cognitive approach to foreign policy? What examples can you think of in which these two issues have come together in foreign policy making? How profitable is the approach discussed by Ripley for understanding the roots of foreign policy? ■

Can the study of "bureaucratic politics and foreign policy" survive the next generation of foreign policy analysis? A concerted effort to diagnose problems in Graham Allison's (1969, 1971) classic work on bureaucratic politics is long overdue and must be undertaken in order to revive the study of organizational decision making in foreign policy. Most executive-branch decisions in U.S. foreign policy are the result of problem solving by high-level advisory groups and officials working in bureaucratic agencies. Therefore it is important to understand what bureaucrats do (and how and why they do it) if we are to appreciate the true nature of the foreign policy process.

In this chapter the study of bureaucratic politics is reconsidered in light of theories and concepts from social cognition and organizational culture. Social cognition is the study of human reasoning, especially the way in which individuals make judgments about people and situations. Organizational culture refers to the routines and rituals that influence decision making in corporate boardrooms or government agencies. Together, social cognition and organizational culture help reveal new insights about the nature of bureaucratic politics in foreign policy. The Johnson administration's response to the 1968 Tet Offensive provides some examples to illustrate this updated approach.

■ Allison's Models

Allison's three models of the Cuban missile crisis have been a familiar feature in foreign policy analysis for more than two decades. The 1962 nuclear standoff between the United States and the Soviet Union over Soviet missiles in Cuba is open to many interpretations. Allison's purpose was to apply alternative perspectives to analyzing the same crisis. His clever use of "conceptual models" was itself a contribution to foreign policy analysis since it demonstrated the consequences of choosing among different assumptions when attempting to explain a foreign policy event.

A model helps an analyst interpret a complex real-world phenomenon (such as foreign policy decision making), identify the most important features, and understand how those features are interrelated. A model need not be a precise description of reality, although a thoroughly unrealistic model may fail to convey crucial ideas. Consider how a tourist depends upon a reliable map to get around in an unfamiliar city. A cartographer designs a map to *represent* important features of reality, such as vivid landmarks or major intersections, rather than attempting to recreate all the minute details of a city. Aided by such a map, the tourist knows what to look for and where to find it amid the confusing welter of busy streets and unfamiliar neighborhoods. What's more, one can create several different maps of the same city (e.g., one map that emphasizes historic landmarks, another that highlights parks and bike trails) depending upon the cartographer's preferences and the intended audience.

Allison provided three "maps" or, in his words, three sets of "conceptual lenses" for analyzing the same foreign policy crisis. Model I ("rational actor") summarizes classical realist thinking about foreign policy decision making.[1] In the mid-1960s, classical realism was the dominant intellectual tradition among foreign policy intellectuals and practitioners alike. Hans Morgenthau, one of the most important contributors to classical realism, suggested that whenever we engage in foreign policy analysis "we put ourselves in the position of a statesman who must meet a certain problem of foreign policy under certain circumstances, and we ask ourselves what the rational alternatives are from which a statesman may choose who must meet this problem under these circumstances (presuming always that he acts in a rational manner), and which of these rational alternatives this particular statesman, acting under these circumstances, is likely to choose" (1985, 5).

The rational actor model is quite consistent with Morgenthau's call to treat decision making as a choice among rational alternatives. According to Allison, "rationality refers to consistent, value-maximizing choice within specified constraints" (1971, 30). In the Model I representation of reality, one assumes the existence of a single, rational decision-making unit rather than a collection of individuals with different motives or contending perspectives.

Decision making by a rational actor is depoliticized: an apolitical "statesman" is free to select the most desirable foreign policy option without concern for the personal foibles of top advisers or the constraints posed by domestic policy processes. In short, the rational actor decides on the basis of national interest—easily defined and efficiently achieved. Variations on the rational actor model can be identified in the work of many contemporary scholars interested in explaining nuclear bargaining strategies, deterrence, and the outbreak of conflict (e.g., Bueno de Mesquita 1981; Morrow 1989; Powell 1990).

Allison's second model ("organizational process") depicts foreign policy as the output of large "semi-feudal, loosely allied" organizations. Rather than "looking over the shoulder" of a rational statesman, the Model II analyst accepts the fact that foreign policy problems are the province of multiple, quasi-independent actors. Each organization (and suborganization) is ruled by a collection of rigid decision-making routines, known as "standard operating procedures," or "SOPs" (Allison 1971, 89).

Standard operating procedures are a logical response to an organization's need to solve similar kinds of problems on a regular basis. Whereas Model I presumes the existence of an optimal solution to a specific problem, Model II adopts an assembly-line logic of matching routine problems with routine solutions. Organizations make impersonal, incremental decisions; a solution that worked adequately in the past is applied to a new problem. Organizations must adopt these procedures in order to function efficiently. Unfortunately, efficiency comes at a price. Unusual, novel problems throw a wrench in the organizational machinery as the existing repertoire of SOPs is searched and found wanting. Eventually the novel problem either gets attached to the least objectionable solution or else the process breaks down.

The incremental nature of Model II is compounded by the organizational equivalent of Murphy's Law: anything that can go wrong will go wrong. In decentralized organizations a single agency is responsible for one highly specialized piece of a foreign policy problem. Driven by the impersonal logic of SOPs, the specialized agency may fail to recognize contradictions in the larger, overarching policy. Unintended consequences abound, resulting in fits of frustration for top-level decision makers who sense they are losing control of a crisis situation. As John F. Kennedy once remarked, "There is always some son-of-a-bitch who doesn't get the word."

Scholars who adopt Model II depict foreign policy decision making as a rule-governed process of pattern recognition and adaptation. Steinbruner's (1974) concept of "cybernetics," for example, suggests a Darwinistic process where a foreign policy organization monitors change in the external environment, receives information "feedback," and modifies its behavior in an attempt to survive. The U.S. defense planning and budgeting process has been modeled in this way (Marra 1985). Recent advances in artificial intelligence (or computational) models of political decision making have produced sophisticated applications of the organizational processes approach. Recent research on U.S. foreign policy responses to events in Asia (Taber 1992) and on Japan's sensitivity to disruptions in global energy supplies (Sylvan, Goel, and Chandrasekaran 1990) draws many insights from Allison's Model II.

Finally, Model III ("governmental politics") builds on the metaphor of a "game" played by high-ranking officials, such as a president's top foreign policy advisers. Better known as "bureaucratic politics," this model depicts foreign policy as the result of competitive maneuvering and compromise by decision makers who interact frequently, know each other well, and hold different beliefs about policy.

In Model III the state's "national interest" is not a given, nor can it be inferred by analyzing the views of a single all-powerful decision maker. Instead, bureaucrats *bargain* with each other to define the "national interest." Sometimes the bargaining is based on strongly held foreign policy views, but often parochial concerns such as career advancement, prestige, or desire for personal power define the bargaining positions. In the end, according to Model III, foreign policy decisions are a "resultant" of arduous negotiations among highly skilled advocates. As Allison puts it: "To explain why a particular formal governmental decision was made, or why one pattern of governmental behavior emerged, it is necessary to identify the games and players, to display the coalitions, bargains, and compromises, and to convey some feel for the confusion" (1971, 146).

From the outset, Model III attracted a great deal of critical attention from foreign policy analysts (e.g., Art 1973; Ball 1974; Caldwell 1977; Freedman 1976; Krasner 1971; Perlmutter 1974; Rosati 1981; Smith 1984/85). The critics identified several basic problems with the bureaucratic politics model. For example, some thought the model underestimated the influence of the chief executive in foreign policy, since it treated the president as only slightly more powerful than the other bureaucratic players. Others argued that the Cuban missile case study was based on questionable evidence. Most common was the criticism that bureaucratic politics was not a very effective model, because it requires an analyst to wade through too much detailed information about a particular foreign decision in order to draw conclusions. After all, a model is supposed to simplify the task of analysis—not make it more complicated!

Recent appraisals (Bendor and Hammond 1992; Welch 1992) highlight many of the same concerns. The new critics have produced persuasive reinterpretations of the bureaucratic politics model, noting problems with the logic, concepts, and historical accuracy of Allison's work. The critics make a strong case for the weakness of bureaucratic politics compared with other models of the policy process. Despite its past popularity, the bureaucratic politics model may be facing intellectual extinction at the hands of a new generation of foreign policy analysts. If that happens, the field would lose a remarkably insightful way of thinking about the "politics" of foreign policy making.

Cognition and Culture

I argue that foreign policy analysis ought to continue to explore in its second generation the conception of political decision making that Allison brought into the field in *Essence of Decision.* One way to revive bureaucratic politics is to maintain the most compelling, plausible aspects of the model while modifying it to take account of promising new approaches in the study of foreign policy decision making. Given the powerful insights cognitive psychology has contributed to the study of foreign policy,[2] it makes sense to build on this solid foundation in the revitalization of bureaucratic politics.

The notion of a foreign policymaker as a "naive scientist" (i.e., a person who attributes causality to events, and develops and tests informal "hypotheses" about his or her environment) has considerable resonance in the decision-making literature (George 1979b; Larson 1985, 34–42; Vertzberger 1990, 48). Much of the existing work concerns the manner in which individuals reason about substantive problems, such as Harry Truman's attempts to draw inferences about Soviet behavior after World War II (Larson 1985). But individuals *also* reason about social interactions and processes, such as their organizational interests and affiliations in the foreign policy bureaucracy (Voss and Dorsey 1992, 17–19).

Emerging work in the field of social cognition, especially "social intelligence" and "self-regulation," is quite consistent with Allison's claims about bureaucrats. According to Allison, bureaucrats have an abundant desire to influence the president or other high-ranking officials on matters of foreign policy. Successful bureaucrats understand the need to present themselves in a way that makes a positive impression on their peers and, of course, their leader. The concept of "social intelligence" helps us understand the way people use knowledge, goals, and strategies for presenting themselves when interacting in social situations (Fiske and Taylor 1991, 512; cf. Fiske 1993; Showers and Cantor 1985). Susan T. Fiske posits that top-ranking officials "spend an inordinate amount of cognitive energy analyzing the president's personality in order to predict future behavior as it relates to their own concerns" (1993, 250). Clearly, there are concepts from social cognition that merit further attention by advocates of the bureaucratic politics approach to foreign policy analysis.

In addition to social cognition, the organizational culture approach provides some clues about the behavior of bureaucrats in large organizations (Feldman 1993, 278–79; Frost et al. 1991; Martin 1992; Ott 1989; Peters 1990; Schein 1992). In an extensive literature review, Ott (1989) defines the core elements of an organizational culture as its artifacts, values and beliefs, and basic underlying assumptions. Deeply embedded, shared expectations allow organizations to function and help participants "make sense" of the decision-making process. Culture can be defined more simply, to borrow an oft-cited phrase, as "the way things are done around here."

How are "things done" in bureaucratic politics? According to Allison, foreign policy officials assume the role of players in an ongoing game of influence and prestige. Bureaucrats invited to participate in a foreign policy advisory meeting steel themselves for a high-stakes competition rather than calm, objective deliberations. Participants who cannot persuade or will not compete soon find themselves on the outside looking in.

Culture and cognition reinforce one another in the analysis of decision-making situations. Consider an example from the legal system. Judges and jurors render verdicts, a task with both cognitive and cultural dimensions. Legal arguments rely on precedent-based problem solving and can be explained by cognitive theories involving categorization, scripts, memory cues, and styles of information processing (e.g., Bennett and Feldman 1981; Carroll and Weiner 1982; Hastie and Pennington 1991). On the other hand, a juror is not merely a cognitive problem solver reasoning in the solitude of a laboratory. The U.S. trial process is cloaked in ritual. Robes and formal attire, a swearing-in ceremony, highly stylized forms of questioning, and secret jury deliberations help define participant roles and provide a set of metacognitive constraints on legal problem solving. Decision makers operate in both a cognitive *and* a cultural environment.

One of the enduring findings of Allison's Model III is that decision makers cannot escape ingrained bureaucratic habits even under the most extraordinary conditions. Options remain shrouded in ambiguity. Policy debates are not free from ritual or gamesmanship. In the case of the Cuban missile crisis, the overwhelming cognitive need to solve a problem did not completely eliminate the participants' strongly felt cultural need to make sense of the experience.

A revitalized bureaucratic politics approach to foreign policy should answer an overarching question: How do members of interdependent, competitive, hierarchical decision groups reason about the policy process, and what impact does such reasoning have on foreign policy outputs?[3] Bureaucratic politics might best be understood as the examination of three closely related concepts: "bureaucratic roles" (how participants see themselves and others contributing to the decision process), "procedural scripts" (the structures, strategies, and premises that make pragmatic sense in a decision process), and "cultural rationales" (the attempt by participants to define appropriate behavior and invoke symbols to help give meaning to their decisions). The political maneuvering of Lyndon Johnson's advisers in the aftermath of the 1968 Tet Offensive helps illustrate each concept.

■ Bureaucratic Politics and the Tet Offensive

The Tet Offensive in January 1968 resulted in a highly visible failure for the Johnson administration's Vietnam policy and provided the impetus for a major reappraisal of U.S. policy in Vietnam (Berman 1989; Schandler 1977; Wirtz 1991). Robert S. McNamara, a major figure in Vietnam planning during the Kennedy and Johnson administrations, was replaced as secretary of defense by Clark Clifford in early 1968. Clifford, a well-established Washington "insider," was recruited on the basis of his personal friendship with Johnson as well as his presumed "hawkish" views on Vietnam. Ironically, Clifford became the catalyst for a reassessment of U.S. policy objectives.

During March 1968, Clifford engaged in a campaign of persuasion to alter Johnson's position on the war. The new secretary of defense helped build a coalition of bureaucratic support for a shift in Vietnam policy, acting as a mediator between harsh critics of the war and his old friend Lyndon Johnson. Clifford's strategy, along with advice from other sources, confirmed what Johnson already suspected: the

United States was failing to meet its objectives in Vietnam. Moreover, the objectives themselves were in doubt. The situation was unlikely to be altered substantially by sending additional U.S. troops, although such action would surely wreak havoc for President Johnson in domestic politics.

By the end of March 1968, Johnson decided to change course in Vietnam. In a dramatic televised speech on March 31, 1968, Johnson announced a partial bombing halt in Vietnam and offered a public invitation to begin negotiations with Hanoi. He also announced his withdrawal from the presidential race given the domestic ramifications of U.S. policy in Vietnam. How can one explain the Johnson administration's decision making during this period? The combination of *bureaucratic roles, procedural scripts,* and *cultural rationales* provides part of the answer.

Bureaucratic Role

Bureaucratic politics involves an interplay between individuals and their roles. A specific position, such as secretary of state, carries with it a number of formal obligations and informal expectations. In short, "positions define what players both may and must do" to fulfill their responsibilities in a decision-making group (Allison 1971, 164–65). Likewise, a powerful individual brings his or her own well-developed personal style to the position, perhaps redefining the job for future occupants. Finally, bureaucrats may be called upon to play different kinds of roles in different settings. The secretary of defense may act as a staunch policy advocate in a presidential advisory group but then assume the role of a neutral arbiter when chairing an interagency task force.

The traditional interpretation of the maxim "where you stand depends upon where you sit" illustrates some of the problems with an overly restrictive definition of bureaucratic role. In some respects Allison's work lends support to a mechanistic view of role where the "face of an issue" is derived exclusively from organizational interests. According to this logic bureaucrats restrict their policy proposals to those with the most obvious direct implications for agency involvement. For example, the Marine Corps commandant should bark "send in the marines" in response to every conceivable problem encountered by the decision group. Research in this vein has been inconclusive; at best one can argue that bureaucratic participants adopt positions consistent with their roles without these positions necessarily being caused by the role (Smith 1984/85).

Examination of actual foreign policy cases reveals a more complex, less rigid relationship between role and issue position.[4] While bureaucrats often propose solutions that conveniently involve a direct role for their agency, few would expect the ploy to work every time. Experienced bureaucratic game players know how to look out for their career and agency interests without being brutally obvious about it. They pick fights carefully, and exhibit reflexive behavior. Ever aware of context and peers, the skilled advocate can sense when a proposal is no longer relevant, when a question is "dumb," and when a line of argument will be considered invalid by the group.

The concept of "bureaucratic role" could be expanded to capture what Allison refers to as the bureaucrat's "style of play" and a "code of conformity" based, among other things, on career tenure and long-term expectations (1971, 179–80). Social roles can be defined as shared expectations about how a particular person in a group ought to behave, and in some respects are the result of an ongoing negotiation between the individual and the group (Levine and Moreland 1990, 601; Moreland and Levine 1982). Bureaucrats belong to one or more interdependent groups (i.e., groups where there is regular interaction and the members are reliant on others in some significant way). Roles allow individual members of a group to work together according to ascribed roles and negotiated boundaries.

Consider an example of "social roles" outside the foreign policy context. Suppose your roommate, an accounting major handy with figures, generally takes care of paying major bills such as rent and utilities in your shared apartment. She has played that role since you started rooming together. Each month you contribute your share of the expenses without giving it a second thought. Nothing needs to be said, because you know the bills will be paid. In fact, your roommate may be offended if you start "nagging" about the bills, since it suggests a lack of confidence on your part. You would be challenging your roommate's role and quite possibly overstepping the boundaries of your own.

Some foreign policy advisers fulfill a bureaucratic role based on a strong personal convictions, highly valued skills, or close association with others in the group. In other cases, ambiguity over bureaucratic role creates barriers to effective advocacy and information processing. In the case of Vietnam, some of Johnson's advisers felt constrained in both the substance and the style of the advice they could offer because of well-understood roles.

Participant roles (whether self-defined or group-defined) place limits on avenues of advocacy. Clark Clifford reports that he and Bill Moyers had doubts about U.S. escalation as far back as the summer of 1965. Yet when Clifford attended a foreign policy advisory meeting in his role as "a personal friend" of Johnson, he chose silence over active participation in the deliberations (Clifford 1991, 414). Moyers had growing doubts about the war, but "felt he could not play a role in policymaking because his job as Press Secretary constrained him from active policy formulation" (Clifford 1991, 416). In a corollary to Allison, "where you sit" determines the rules of engagement on the bureaucratic battlefield.

Although constrained in some respects, outsiders can often play by a different set of rules than those who must conform to an official insider role (Allison 1971, 180). As Clifford's informal involvement on Vietnam became more routine, his status changed from "the President's friend" to an informed outsider, free to speak his mind on controversial issues: "An outside adviser can serve the role of a Doubting Thomas when the bureaucracies line up behind a single position, or help the President reach a judgment when there is a dispute within the government. They can give the President a different perspective on his own situation; they can be frank with him when White House aides are not" (Clifford 1991, 424).

During his "transition period" from informal adviser to secretary of defense, Clifford took on yet another role. With McNamara still the secretary, Clifford recalls, "I was not burdened by any of the formal responsibilities of the Secretary of Defense, and thus, half-private citizen and half-Cabinet member, I was free to concentrate almost exclusively on Vietnam" (1991, 475–76).[5] Clifford's role-transition phase provided a perfect opportunity for key Defense Department bureaucrats (such as Paul

Warnke and Morton Halperin) to revive long-held doubts about fundamental strategy in Vietnam. As Halperin put it: "We had worked for McNamara, and we believed in what McNamara was doing, and we had to decide if we could really work with Clifford. We had to really—not educate him—but turn him around. And this was quite deliberate. Clifford, in effect threw us a ball by saying, 'Prepare a draft report'" (cited in Schandler 1977, 150).

The process of negotiating Clifford's relationship with his new staff—a mutual exercise of testing boundaries and establishing limits—helped change the dynamics of policy advocacy on Vietnam. Clifford played a different bureaucratic role than did his predecessor, opening the door to new lines of argument on the future of U.S. involvement in Vietnam.

Procedural Scripts

Successful bureaucrats rely on an arsenal of institutional strategies and tactics for problem solving.[6] Just as bureaucratic roles are important for determining appropriate relationships, a bureaucrat's understanding of the "rules of the game" within a particular decision group can facilitate efforts at bargaining, persuasion, and coalition building (Allison 1971, 170–71).[7] In a world of ambiguous policy problems, knowledge about the policy *process* helps decision makers "decide how to decide" and "learn how to learn."[8]

The U.S. failure during the Tet Offensive gave rise to a classic example of bureaucratic "gamesmanship" by General Earle Wheeler, chairman of the Joint Chiefs of Staff. Wheeler's behavior is consistent with Allison's notion that "deadlines and events raise issues and force busy players to take a stand" (1971, 168). As Schandler observes, General Wheeler and the Joint Chiefs of Staff saw Tet as an opportunity to force the president's hand and to achieve their long-sought goal of a mobilization of reserve forces (1977, 101).

The request reflects the familiar tendency of bureaucrats to act as vociferous advocates on behalf of their policy preferences, at times basing arguments on overly optimistic forecasts or "worst-case scenarios." The troop request included a politically volatile recommendation to call up U.S. military reserve units that might have been rejected immediately in a different context. But after Tet, the troop request took on the form of an ultimatum for Johnson and his top advisers: either approve the request for two hundred thousand troops, thereby placing the U.S. on an all-out war footing, or deny the request, raising questions about U.S. commitments in Vietnam and elsewhere (Schandler 1977, 120).

Widely shared, well-understood procedural scripts help a decision maker anticipate the moves of a fellow bureaucrat. Sometimes anticipation contributes to policy failure when one bureaucrat's expectations about the actions of a colleague are incorrect (Ripley and Gardner 1992). In other cases a pragmatic understanding of decision rules may help a bureaucrat modify his or her behavior to capitalize on the patterned behavior of another group member. In effect, General Wheeler was operating according to a "procedural script" that helped him anticipate the responses of his bureaucratic counterparts. Under most circumstances, Wheeler's move might have succeeded. In this case it backfired because Clifford altered "the rules of the game."

The "Clifford Task Force," composed of high-ranking military officials and midlevel Department of Defense bureaucrats, met between February 28 and March 4 to discuss the troop request. Many task force members expected the bargaining over numbers of troops to follow a well-established pattern. Assistant Secretary of Defense Paul Warnke said: "I thought of [the troop request] as the same sort of exercise that McNamara always went through with Westmoreland. Westy would come in with a request and then that request would be sort of massaged, and Bob and Westy would agree on a figure, always something less than Westy had asked for, but always the request was granted" (cited in Schandler 1977, 138).

To the surprise of military and civilian members of the task force, Clifford altered the "procedural script." As presiding member of the task force, Clifford was made aware of the serious disputes arising within the bureaucracy over policy in Vietnam. Due in part to his evolving bureaucratic role (discussed earlier) civilian members of the task force began feeding Clifford detailed, pessimistic assessments of American prospects in Vietnam (Schandler 1977, 143). Clifford adopted a probing, skeptical style when questioning military experts (Clifford 1991, 493). He pressed them on underlying assumptions rather than allowing them to confuse the issue with platitudes or questionable statistics. What started as a calculated tactical move by Wheeler (based on a familiar procedural script) ended up in a soul-searching dialogue about U.S. strategy in Vietnam.

Cultural Rationales

Rituals are pervasive in bureaucratic decision making because they endow deliberations with special meaning and establish boundaries of appropriateness, decorum, and fair play. The first two concepts, bureaucratic role and procedural script, reinforce a decision maker's identity and provide pragmatic clues for anticipating the moves and countermoves of bureaucratic competition. The third concept, "cultural rationale," speaks to the decision maker's desire to justify long-standing traditions or idiosyncratic features that define every decision-making group.

Students of U.S. foreign policy often compare the well-established "cultures" perpetuated by foreign service officers in the Department of State, or the proud traditions of various branches of the armed forces (Kegley and Wittkopf 1991, 365–71; Rosati 1993, 147–50). Comparable "cultures" or traditions develop within a decision-making group as it evolves over time, or as it conforms to the style of a powerful, charismatic leader.

Lyndon Johnson's political experience taught him the importance of consultation. In some cases consultation was motivated by very pragmatic goals. Johnson cultivated a network of political contacts, often by telephone, to provide the latest bits of information or offer reactions on the political feasibility of a decision (Best 1988b). During the 1964 presidential campaign Johnson relied on three groups of advisers: one for day-to-day operations, another for strategy and tactics, and "a third group second-guessing the first two groups" (Clifford 1991, 398).

Consultation also served important symbolic purposes for Johnson. For example, getting a large number of advisers "on board" a proposal could provide valuable insurance in the event of a policy failure. Consultation also allowed Johnson to convey respect for the opinions of a politically important ally or demonstrate the extent of his patience and tolerance. Why bother to consult even after a decision has been reached? Consultation represents the way things "ought to be done" given the far-reaching implications of a presidential decision.

Clifford's familiarity with at least one "cultural rationale" in the Johnson White House resulted in a master stroke of bureaucratic advocacy. The secretary of defense arranged for a meeting between Johnson and the so-called "Wise Men," a group of distinguished former statesmen. Although unfamiliar with day-to-day operations in Vietnam, the "Wise Men" held strong views about U.S. strategy. In addition, the group (which included Dean Acheson, George Ball, General Omar Bradley, McGeorge Bundy, and General Matthew Ridgway) had the stature to question U.S. policy since many had been (to use Acheson's phrase) "present at the creation" of containment strategy.

The hastily arranged meeting conformed well to the tradition of White House consultation. In an earlier meeting these staunch defenders of U.S. containment policy reassured Johnson about Vietnam and urged him to keep the faith. By the time of their March 1968 meeting, however, the senior statesmen of U.S. foreign policy had undergone a serious transformation in their thinking about Vietnam. Rather than bolstering Johnson's policy, many members of the group urged the president to find an honorable (but hasty) way to withdraw the U.S. commitment to Vietnam. Once the members had delivered their pronouncement, it became exceedingly difficult for Johnson to reject the results of consultation.

In 1965 a Johnson administration foreign policy adviser named George Ball tried and failed to force a reappraisal of fundamental objectives on Vietnam (Berman 1982). Although in hindsight much can be said for Ball's "tactical withdrawal" arguments, Johnson and top advisers remained unconvinced. In the aftermath of Tet, Clark Clifford succeeded where George Ball failed, not because Clifford had better ideas or because he had spent more time studying the issues. Clifford didn't bring any new ideas or additional information about Vietnam into the White House in 1968. He did, however, bring a lifetime of experience in the practice of presidential advising, and tremendous insight into the mind and moods of Lyndon Johnson. Clifford orchestrated, schemed, and plotted a campaign of dissent virtually from the day he entered the White House. The combination of bureaucratic role, procedural scripts, and cultural rationales helped convince Johnson that U.S. policy toward Vietnam had to change.

■ Conclusion

Examining the way bureaucrats reason about the policy process provides an appropriate avenue for revitalizing the Model III approach to foreign policy analysis. The Johnson administration's reaction to the Tet Offensive helps illustrate the concepts of *bureaucratic roles* (how participants see themselves and others contributing to the decision process), *procedural scripts* (the routines, strategies, and premises that structure a decision process), and *cultural rationales* (symbols and traditions that define appropriate behavior and give meaning to bureaucratic interactions). Although successful foreign policy bureaucrats may differ substantially in personality, power, or issue positions, they share one common characteristic: a highly nuanced understanding of the policy-making process. Perhaps this understanding is the true "essence of decision" in foreign policy analysis.

The attempt to understand the politics of policy-making processes has been a continuing theme in foreign policy analysis. Allison was not the first to introduce such a focus into the field, and he has certainly not been the last to urge such a focus in our research. I have argued that in its second generation, foreign policy analysis must continue to examine the issues and concepts that Allison presented as the bureaucratic politics perspective. Analysts should do so by drawing on research from the study of political psychology and social cognition in order to reinvigorate our studies of political decision making in bureaucratic settings. In this way we can continue to pursue the "essence" of foreign policy making.

■ Acknowledgments

The author gratefully acknowledges editorial suggestions by the editors of this volume and research support from the Mershon Center Research Training Group on the Role of Cognition in Collective Political Decision-Making, National Science Foundation (DIR-9113599), Ohio State University.

■ Notes

1. The classical realist tradition of Hans Morgenthau, E. H. Carr, and other earlier writers is distinguished here from the structural realism of Kenneth Waltz (1979). See Keohane (1987) for an elaboration of this distinction.

2. See the essays by Rosati (chapter 4) and Shimko (chapter 5) in this volume on this literature.

3. Foreign policy *outputs* refer to the results of the decision process, while foreign policy *outcomes* imply a much broader scope. A foreign policy *output* such as a U.S. decision to retaliate against Iraq cannot, by itself, provide a complete explanation of the ultimate *outcome* of such action.

4. Indeed, Allison lists a number of factors that compete with career and organization interests (such as misperception, miscommunication, and reticence) in defining the "face of an issue" (Allison 1971, 178–79).

5. Clifford claims he tried to make the most of his status as the "new boy in town" (Clifford 1991, 493).

6. The concept of "standard operating procedures" (SOPs) might be a perfectly acceptable (even preferable) alternative to "script" were it not for the fact that the vast literature of "cybernetics" has transformed SOPs into a set of rigid, cyborglike responses (see Marra 1985; Steinbruner 1974). I have something much more flexible and responsive in mind here.

7. Refer to Bettenhausen and Murningham (1985) and Martin (1982) for a slightly different interpretation of the "script" concept as applied to organizations.

8. Indeed, the deceptively simple question "Can governments learn?" requires a complex answer (Etheredge 1985). A recent review by Huber (1991) suggests the richness of research on "organizational learning" by presenting numerous questions on which the field focuses, ranging from "searching," "organizational experiments," "cognitive maps and framing," "unintentional learning," and even "unlearning."

SEVEN

Structure and Process in the Analysis of Foreign Policy Crises

Patrick J. Haney, MIAMI UNIVERSITY

■ Editors' Introduction

In this chapter Patrick Haney reviews research on decision making in foreign policy groups during international crises, on the management of these groups by leaders, and explores the links that exist between "structure" and "process" in crisis decision making. Professor Haney argues that much of the research on crisis decision making focuses on individual and small group behavior, since these are seen as the most important actors during crises; while much of the research on decision making management focuses on policy-making in large organizations and institutions and their effects on the process of decision making, since these institutions are seen as central in routine policymaking situations. Haney argues that these two perspectives can profitably be merged by bringing an "institutional" perspective to bear upon decision making during crises to see how the structures established by leaders to manage a foreign policy crisis can have patterned effects on the process of decision making that these groups employ. This chapter builds upon the research discussed in earlier chapters, and in particular complements Ripley's chapter, which also makes an argument for reaching across levels-of-analysis to examine decision making. This chapter also directs us to subsequent chapters by pointing to the importance of large institutions in foreign policy and how they can shape foreign policy behavior.

Questions that the reader should consider when reading this chapter include: What are the similarities and differences between making decisions about policy during routine situations and crisis situations? What are the factors that affect decision making during crises? Which of these factors can leaders try to control or manage? What examples of crisis decision making can you think of that might be better understood by applying the "institutional perspective" that Haney discusses? ■

Imagine that a newly elected American president, or British prime minister, or Russian president, were to ask international relations and foreign policy scholars how a set of advisory groups should be organized and managed in order to cope with policymaking, especially during crises. That does not seem like such an extraordinary request. After all, management studies of businesses and other productive enterprises have long focused on the relationship between the organization of work and the outputs of work (e.g., Hayes, Wheelwright, and Clark 1988; Melan 1989). Research in the field of public management has also focused on the importance of organizational structures on the flow and output of work. Indeed, there is even a two-volume handbook addressing these issues in public management research (Starbuck and Nystrom 1981).

Furthermore, there has been increasing attention in recent studies to the relative merits of different organizational "configurations" and their impact on the process and quality of work generally performed by governments (e.g., Boardman and Vining 1989; Chubb and Moe 1990; Dilulio 1989; Donahue 1989; March and Olsen 1989; Oakerson 1987; Mintzberg, Raisinghani, and Theoret 1976; Savas 1987; Wilson 1989; Wise 1990; Vaughan 1990). Unfortunately, the head of state who asks for help in ascertaining the relationship between structure and process in foreign policymaking may be disappointed, especially if that leader is looking for ideas about how to structure advisory arrangements for crisis situations. Foreign policy analysts would be hard-pressed to identify bodies of cumulative theory and systematic empirical analysis of the relationship between structure and process in crisis decision making.

Some preliminary answers, however, may be derived from a variety of literatures that study foreign policy decision making, crises, and the American presidency. Indeed, in a recent review of the literature on advisory networks and the American presidency, Hult notes that the bulk of attention to these issues comes in the area of foreign policy (1993, 121). In the field of foreign policy analysis, interestingly enough, we do know quite a bit about advisory "structures," on the one hand; and we know a fair amount about foreign policy decision making "processes," on the other. What foreign policy analysts have largely not done, however, is to examine the link *between* structure and process: how does structure affect process in decision making? And how does this relationship work during crises?

In this chapter I discuss research on foreign policy structures and processes and their interrelationship in crisis decision making with a selective review of the literature that begins as a mirror of much of the field of foreign policy analysis and the study of crises: with a largely separated discussion of the state of theory and knowledge about policymaking *structures,* and then about *processes* of decision making in foreign policy crises. The reader will note that much of this literature is rooted in the context of the United States, as much (though not all) of the research in the area has focused on the study of U.S. foreign policy. At the end of each of these sections I discuss research that has tried to bridge the gap between these two issue areas. In the final part of the chapter I consider a perspective on politics and the study thereof—an institutional perspective—that places the issues of structure and process in a position of prominence and suggests ways that we might better do our work of analyzing foreign policy and decision making during international crises.

■ Foreign Policy Structures

In this context, the term *structure* refers to the organizational configurations within which foreign policymaking takes place. This can include a broad set of formal institutions and how they are organized (e.g., the U.S. Department of State, the National Security Council), and/or may also include a focus on how much smaller decision-making groups are structured or configured in a crisis. The suggestion that policymaking structures need to be part of the focus of foreign policy analysis can be found in the early emphasis on the study of foreign policy decision making. Snyder, Bruck, and Sapin, while urging that research attention be focused on the explanation of discrete decisions, remind us of the importance of the context of decision: "The definition of the situation which we consider to be central to the explanation of state behavior results from decision-making processes in an organizational context....To ignore this context omits a range of factors which significantly influence the behavior of decision-makers (and therefore state behavior), including not only the critical problem of how choices are made but also the conditions under which choices are made" (1962a, 87).

Following on this discussion, Robinson and Snyder argue that there are three major clusters of factors that explain decision outcomes: the occasion for decision, the individual, and the organizational context in which the individual operates (1965, 439–40). With respect to organizational factors, they assert that decision makers do not act only in an individual capacity when they make foreign policy decisions, they also act within an organizational environment. An integral part of the study of policymaking, then, must be the "organization" cluster of variables (cf. de Rivera 1968, 207–44; Frankel 1963).

There has been much scholarly attention to the structures of routine foreign policymaking, much of which has sought to document the organizational configuration of specific departments or foreign policy organizations, or to track the structure of the relationships between various foreign policy organizations in policymaking. A long line of research has been performed within the U.S. government focusing on the organization of the government and on the organization of the foreign policy apparatus of the United States. Concluding its review of the organization of the executive branch of the U.S. government in 1937, the "Brownlow Commission" argued that the president "needs help" for policymaking—more staff, better structures, and better management of those staffs and organizations (see Hess 1988). These recommendations have led over time to the development and expansion of the "Executive Office of the President," a large staff that works for the president and vice-president to coordinate and plan policymaking. The Eberstadt report, issued in 1945, focused specifically on the problem of foreign policy coordination and recommended the establishment of a "national security council" to facilitate such coordination (see Jackson 1965). Former President Hoover directed two commissions (1949 and 1955) that examined the organization of the executive branch of the U.S. government and the policymaking needs and functions of that branch (see Jackson 1965). And in 1961 the "Jackson Subcommittee" in the U.S. Senate examined the organization of the executive branch and, like the earlier Eberstadt report, focused attention on the way the National Security Council is organized for policymaking (Jackson 1965; cf.

Hunter 1988; Prados 1991). Finally, the *Report of the Commission on the Organization of Government for the Conduct of Foreign Policy* (1975) explored the organization and administration of foreign policy. As I stated earlier, these studies have largely sought to describe and examine the structures of foreign policymaking and to recommend how to reorganize these units.

Foreign policy research has also examined American presidents' management of foreign policy bureaucracies, such as Hilsman's discussion of foreign policymaking within the Kennedy administration (1967) and the studies by Destler (1972), Destler, Gelb, and Lake (1984), and Allison and Szanton (1976) of the U.S. foreign policy bureaucracy (cf. Barnet 1971; McCamy 1964). Research in this tradition has been largely descriptive (and sometimes critical) of the organization and management of the foreign policy bureaucracy by particular presidents, and has focused on the difficulties that leaders face in trying to manage foreign policy bureaucracies.

Advisory Structures and Studying Crises

Case studies of crises and biographies and autobiographies provide a wealth of descriptive information about decision-making groups. The recent memoirs of McGeorge Bundy (1988), Clark Clifford (1991), and Paul Nitze (1989), for example, reflect on the activities of presidents' advisers across a variety of foreign policy issues. Case studies such as Quandt's (1977, 1993) studies of U.S. policymaking in the Middle East provide grist for our theoretical mills. Unfortunately, case studies are rarely written with the expressed purpose of trying to extract lessons about the relationship between decision structures and decision-making processes during crises. Nor have many foreign policy analysts tried to return to case studies and extract from them general lessons about the relationship between structure and process.

A substantial amount of attention in the social science literature also has been given to the structure and organization of advisory groups in policymaking, such as Cronin and Greenberg's (1969) review of the U.S. advisory system (cf. Herken 1992; Schilling 1962; Sickels 1974). Kernell and Popkin (1986) focus on the changing nature of presidents' chiefs of staff, noting the increasingly important role of the chief of staff to the president as a manager of (one who structures) policymaking (cf. Benveniste 1977; Burke 1984; George 1980b; Meltsner 1990; Plowden 1987). In his study of advisory structures to U.S. presidents, Barrett (1988) draws on data from appointment logs and other sources to discuss the important role of President Johnson's advisers in the execution of the Vietnam War. From this evidence he contests the argument that Lyndon Johnson was a victim of groupthink or that he acted nearly alone in running the Vietnam War, showing, rather, the broad spectrum of advisers and advice that Lyndon Johnson received about U.S. policy in Vietnam (cf. Best 1988a, 1988b; Best and DesRoches 1991). Moens (1991) investigates the role of Carter's advisers leading up to and following the fall of Iran's Shah. And in a recent review of the literature on "advising," Hult (1993) argues that future research in this area should focus on the "networks" of advisers that are at work during different types of policymaking (e.g., domestic policy, foreign policy, crises) so that stronger propositions about the role of advisers may be derived.

Research has also sought to understand how U.S. presidents have organized the White House for policymaking and have begun to explore the possible effects of those structures on policymaking. In *Organizing the Presidency* (1988), Hess tracks the ways that modern U.S. presidents have structured White House operations. Besides describing the organizational styles of each administration, Hess discusses how presidents "learn" from the perceived organizational mistakes of each former president in an effort to fine-tune the structure of policymaking. For example, John F. Kennedy perceived problems in policymaking due to President Eisenhower's formalistic and hierarchical policymaking structures, so President Kennedy designed a less-structured, collegial organization for policymaking, which created its own difficulties (1988, 74–87).

Burke and Greenstein (1989) examine the importance of advisory groups as well as presidential personality and the political environment during two cases of American decision making about Vietnam—Eisenhower in 1954 and Johnson in 1964–65. They seek to explain why two presidents who were faced with very similar problems responded in such very different ways. Their analysis indicates that the way presidents organize advisory groups may have an important impact on the process of decision making, but that the individual president's style and the political climate also affect the process of decision making.

Johnson explores how a president "manage[s] a team of men to provide him with information, staff out his alternatives, and otherwise extend his reach" (1974, xxii) so that the president can be successful at leadership and policymaking. Johnson focuses on how the White House is organized for general policymaking,[1] identifying three generic models of organization that presidents have used—a formalistic, a competitive, and a collegial model of decision making. The formalistic model is characterized by an orderly policymaking structure that seeks to benefit from diverse perspectives but also discourages open conflict. The competitive model encourages conflicting points of view but can become disorderly and fail to provide clear, concise advice to the president. The collegial model attempts to provide structure and discourage conflict, though it may lead to an overloaded foreign policy agenda and its maintenance may exact a price as well (cf. George 1980b; Hermann and Preston 1994; Orbovich and Molnar 1992; Pika 1988).

The reader should note that many of the studies mentioned here *suggest* that a link exists between structure, process, and policy performance; that is, they assume a relationship to exist between sound organizational structures and sound policymaking and policy. What they have largely failed to do, however, is to explicate the links between foreign policy structures, policymaking processes, and policy outputs in ways that would allow us to draw even contingent generalizations about the relationships between these variables. For example, what lessons might we draw about the role and impact of advising more generally from the research that examines President Johnson's advisory system? We seem to know a lot, continuing the example, about Johnson and his advisers. But we still have not learned much in a more general way about how leaders might structure an advisory process for decision making and with what effects.

What we do know about how presidents structure advisory groups and with what effects we still draw largely from the work of Richard Johnson (1974) and Alexander George (1980b). Indeed, it is in George's study of foreign policymaking that one can find perhaps the clearest attempt to discuss how modern U.S. presidents structure advisory networks and the resulting impact on information processing. There have been some recent attempts to refine the (formalistic, competitive, and collegial) models that Johnson and George both use in their studies (cf. Crabb and Mulcahy 1986; Hermann and Preston 1994; Orbovich and Molnar 1992; Pika 1988), but little empirical research on this topic that lends new insights.

Furthermore, much of the research mentioned here has focused on routine foreign policymaking, not on crisis decision making. Indeed, the applicability of this research for understanding the relationship between structure and process in crises is extremely limited. There is a perception by many in the field that crises are fundamentally different from routine events. Crises are situations characterized by the perceptions of decision makers of (1) a serious threat to national values or interests that may come about as (2) a surprise with (3) relatively little time to respond (see Hermann 1972). Crises are situations that include a high likelihood that force will be used (see Brecher 1978). During these situations, the dominant disciplinary view seems to suggest, decision making is controlled by a few elite leaders and is highly personal, driven by individual perceptions of the situation.[2] Structure may cease to be important during these situations as personalities increase in significance in the policymaking process.

I suggest that this view is inadequate and misses important components of decision making during crises. If crises heighten the importance of a small group of leaders—the "ultimate decision unit" (see Hermann, Hermann, and Hagan 1987; Hermann and Hermann 1989)—as evidence overwhelmingly suggests they do, then the structure and organization of that group ought to continue to have an impact on the way decision making proceeds within those groups during crises. Indeed, if the preceding research is correct in assuming that structure matters, and that the group of top leaders takes on special importance during crises, I would suggest that structure not only *still* matters during crises—*it is a vital component of decision making during crises.*

There are some examples of research that try to make the connection between structure and process in foreign policymaking and focus on crises. One such example is the "bureaucratic politics" approach that is discussed in Brian Ripley's essay (chapter 6) in this volume (Allison 1971; Allison and Halperin 1972; Halperin 1974). Research in this area has focused on how organizational structures and bureaucratic games shape the policymaking process and direct policy outputs or outcomes. Allison (1971) examines these components in American decision making during the October 1962 Cuban missile crisis. For example, Allison demonstrates that the organizational procedures of the navy dictated how the naval blockade of Cuba would proceed, and how these routines had to be overcome by the president when the navy's procedures were seen as counterproductive to Kennedy's political effort in the crisis.

Research within this tradition has extended Allison's method of analysis to different decisions and different national settings, though much of the research within this paradigm has studied noncrisis decisions. Applications include Greenwood's (1975) study of the American decision to use the Multiple Independently-targetable Reentry Vehicle (MIRV) missile technology in its nuclear arsenal, Maoz's (1981) study of the Israeli raid on the Entebbe, Uganda, airport to rescue hostages that had been seized from a hijacked plane, and Vandenbroucke's (1984) study of the 1961 failure at the Bay of Pigs. Levy (1986) explores how organizational routines may contribute to the onset of war. Sigal (1970) uses the perspective to study the Formosa Straits crisis, and Vertzberger (1990) explores the importance of organizational routines in developing countries. Dawisha (1980) discusses the appropriateness and problems of applications of this approach to the Soviet context. Weil (1975) applies the paradigm to decision making in North Vietnam during the war in Vietnam, and Kasza (1987) studies policymaking in Japan, Peru, and Egypt with this approach.[3]

Research on foreign policy structures that points to issues of process has emerged from other quarters as well. In a study that attempts to apply "economic" decision theory to the issues of how structure and process are interrelated in foreign policy, Maoz (1990) discusses the ways that group settings are ripe for manipulation, and explores the implications of this for policy formulation. Maoz draws on earlier work, such as Arrow's theorem of voting, that argues there is not necessarily a straightforward way to translate preferences into outcomes in a group setting. Research in this tradition shows that no decision rule exists for group settings when more than two options are being considered so that individual preferences can be "added up" in a fair and impartial way. The order of debate and voting is critically linked to the decision that is reached. Thus, Maoz attempts to draw attention to the important role played by institutions, decision rules, agendas, as well as individual preferences, in this translation process in foreign policy settings and the potential for the manipulation of them by skilled leaders (cf. Haney, Herzberg, and Wilson 1992).

There has also been some attention to what have come to be called "advocacy" models in the study of policymaking. In a prescriptive article Alexander George presents a view of how leaders of complex organizations can rely on "multiple advocacy" rather than on centralized management for policymaking. This policymaking structure "requires management to create the basis for structured, balanced debate among policy advocates drawn from different parts of the organization" (George 1972, 751). These structures would permit adversarial proceedings or provide for the role of a "devil's advocate" whose job it would be to question others and argue in favor of unpopular viewpoints.

In a more recent and extended treatment Schwenk (1988) elaborates on ways that *policymaking structures* can be established within complex organizations, such as foreign policy organizations, so as to improve the quality of the *processes* of policymaking. The goal of these advocacy frameworks is to develop a set of structures that will allow for a thorough performance of the tasks of decision making and problem solving. The underlying assumption of these models is that some structures are more likely to lead to effective decision making than are others. In other words, they assume that structure does affect process in policymaking and that some structures are better suited for the tasks of policymaking than others. This research clearly has implications for crisis decision making, but the exact nature of those implications remains somewhat unclear as foreign policy crises have not been the subject of much "advocacy" research.

Another line of inquiry that examines the potential relationship between decision structures and the processes of policymaking is the research on "decision units" and their impact on foreign policy behavior (Hermann, Hermann, and Hagan 1987;

Hermann and Hermann 1989). Charles Hermann proposes that changes in decision structure should have an effect on the decision process, which in turn should have an effect on foreign policy behavior (1978, 71). The research strategy employed in this perspective seeks to discover the impact of different "decision units" on foreign policy behavior (Hermann, Hermann, and Hagan 1987). Specifically, research has focused on how different decision units can lead to different types of foreign policy behavior, such as how prone each unit is to use force. Theoretical research has focused on the impact of three different types of ultimate decision units: "predominant leaders," "multiple autonomous actors," and "small groups" (Hermann, Hermann, and Hagan 1987). Empirical support for the theoretical propositions about the different effects of these decision units has been fairly high (see Hermann and Hermann 1989; Kaarbo, Beasley, and Hermann 1990). Note that the decision unit literature has focused on how different ultimate decision units may be related to different types of policy, not on how different units may perform the process of policymaking differently.

One notable example of research that looks to the management of policymaking structures during crises, and the implications of that management for decision-making processes, is Janis's *Crucial Decisions* (1989). Janis tries to develop an understanding of how the management of a policymaking group can eliminate "avoidable errors" in decision making. His goal is to examine management strategies that may lead to "vigilant problem solving." While much of Janis's book examines procedures (and thus may fit better in the discussion of process that follows), in his concluding chapter he presents a number of propositions about how leaders can manage or structure the process of decision making so as to make it more effective.

These efforts to study structure may provide a framework that can allow researchers to examine how the business of policymaking—the gathering and processing of information, providing advice, and performing analysis—proceeds under different management structures during crises. In particular, the three generic models used by Johnson (1974) and George (1980b) may provide a theoretical starting point for exploring the decision-making structures that leaders configure for policymaking and how these structures affect the tasks of decision making. Such an analysis could allow for hybrid models to be explored and could provide a way to start to examine how structure and process are interrelated during crisis situations. In order to better conceptualize what it is that structures may be affecting, we should examine research that has focused on the processes by which decisions are made, especially research on crisis decision-making processes.

■ Foreign Policy Processes

In this context, the term *process* refers to the steps or tasks performed by a group that lead to a decision or policy choice being made, such as conceptualizing goals and objectives, searching for information, and developing contingency plans. Anderson has argued that "at least a few individuals should focus on developing theories which describe the process of policy making in foreign affairs" (1987, 285). His research on "process theory" suggests that policymaking in organizational settings involves deciding among many policy alternatives, relatively few of which are mutually inconsistent, "that are proposed and then simply ignored. They die for what amounts to the lack of a seconding motion" (1987, 297). The picture of process that Anderson presents is one of a loosely coordinated activity that involves a search for goals as much as it does a search for alternatives (1987, 290; cf. 1983). Anderson (1987) concludes that more attention to the decision-making process that occurs in group settings is required.

One tactic for studying the process of policymaking has been the in-depth case study. The goal here is to examine the details of a historical case and from that attention to detail extract lessons about how the process of policymaking works. Comparative case study designs may be employed as well that seek to "trace" the process of decision making and compare it from one case to another (see George 1979a; George and McKeown 1985). Examples of this approach include the comparative research by George and Smoke (1974) on deterrence cases in American foreign policy; by George, Hall, and Simons (1971) on American attempts to use "coercive diplomacy" as an instrument of foreign policy; and the studies of Israeli decision making during the 1967 and 1973 wars by Brecher (1980) and Wagner (1974). Other research on the process of policymaking has also looked to cases as an aid to the process of theory building. Brecher's research on crisis decision making, for example, focuses on how the process of decision making unfolds during different phases, or "periods," of a crisis as part of the International Crisis Behavior Project (ICB): the pre-crisis period, the crisis period, and the post-crisis period (see, e.g., Brecher 1980; Dowty 1984; cf. Brecher and Wilkenfeld 1989).

Probably the most well-known study of the process of decision making is Janis's *Groupthink* (1982). Janis was motivated to explain performance failures, such as the American fiasco at the Bay of Pigs, by examining the internal dynamics or group processes that lead ultimately to group decisions. "Groupthink" is when individuals within "cohesive" groups seek unanimity or concurrence to such an extent that they cease to vigilantly perform the tasks of decision making. Janis hypothesized that the presence of groupthink during the process of decision making might lead to performance or policy failures. As a psychological phenomenon that occurs inside human beings, however, groupthink cannot be directly observed. To cope with this problem, Janis argued that groupthink produces behavioral consequences or symptoms that can be observed. These symptoms include, for example, illusions of invulnerability of the group, stereotyping of "outgroups," and self-appointed "mindguards" who protect the unanimity of the group from dissent.

Janis proposed that the presence of groupthink made it less likely that decision-making groups would perform thoroughly the tasks of decision making; or, in other words, that groupthink made it likely that the decision-making process would include several malfunctions. These malfunctions include:

1. the failure to survey objectives;

2. the failure to survey alternatives;

3. the failure to examine risks of the preferred choice;

4. the failure to reappraise initially rejected alternatives;

5. the failure to search for information;

6. a bias in processing information; and

7. the failure to work out contingency plans (Janis 1982, 175)

Janis proposed that these procedural malfunctions, caused by groupthink, might lead to policy failures.

Problems with groupthink have been discussed in a variety of places (e.g., Longley and Pruitt 1980; Ripley 1988; Whyte 1989). One of the central problems revolves around the issue of group cohesion, which Janis sees as detrimental to effective decision making. What constitutes a "cohesive group"? Making an objective determination about this is difficult. For how long must a group be "cohesive" for the seeds of groupthink to take root? This too is unclear. And why might the same group of people who were victims of groupthink at one point (e.g., the Bay of Pigs) not be victims of it during the deliberations over other issues, even those considered at the same time as the process leading to the fiasco?

There may be serious empirical problems with the groupthink hypothesis as well. If cases exist where groupthink was not present but the decision-making malfunctions were, then groupthink may not be a "necessary condition" for the emergence of decision-making malfunctions. And if cases exist where groupthink is present but the decision making process is carried out in a thorough way,[4] this would suggest that groupthink is not a "sufficient condition" for the emergence of decision-making malfunctions either. If groupthink is neither a necessary nor a sufficient condition for the presence of decision-making malfunctions, then the nature of the causal relationship between them would be quite unclear, though this is an empirical question to which we currently have no real answer.

Finally, there is the problem with determining what is a policy "failure." I know of no completely objective criteria by which to determine whether or not a policy was a "success" or a "failure." Analysts may hold the outcome "up against" the stated objectives of a policy to try to determine this (see, e.g., Herek, Janis, and Huth 1987). Experts may argue about whether a policy was a success or a failure based upon their subjective standards and intuition. And analysts can be clear and explicit about assigning such a value to a policy outcome. Nevertheless, the problem of valuing an outcome remains. What looks like a failure to some can look like a success to others. For example, Eisenhower's policy of not supporting the move by Britain, France, and Israel against Egypt after Nasser nationalized the Suez Canal in 1956 might be seen as a triumph of Eisenhower's anticolonialism or as a failure by Eisenhower to support his allies in their effort against an emerging rival.

In a manner similar to Janis, George (1980b) argues that there are several critical procedural tasks in effective decision making. He argues that decision-making groups must ensure that sufficient information about the situation at hand is obtained and analyzed so that it provides policymakers with an incisive and valid diagnosis of the problem. They must facilitate consideration of all the major values and interests affected by the policy issue at hand. They must assure a search for a relatively wide range of options and a reasonably thorough evaluation of the expected consequences of each option. They must provide for careful consideration of the problems that may arise in implementing the options under consideration. And finally, George asserts that they must remain receptive to indications that current policies are not working out well, and cultivate the ability to learn from experience (1980b, 10).

Drawing on this concept of decision making, George identifies nine common malfunctions of an advisory process. These include, for example, when the president and advisers agree too readily on the nature of the problem facing them and on a response to it; when advisers and advocates take different positions and debate them before the president but their disagreements do not cover the full range of relevant hypotheses and alternative options; when advisers thrash out their own disagreements over policy without the president's knowledge and confront the president with a unanimous recommendation; and when the president is impressed by the consensus among the advisers but fails to ascertain how firm the consensus is, how it was achieved, and whether it was justified (George 1980b, 122–32).

The approaches of Janis and George are quite similar. George's list is not as abstract as Janis's, as George focuses more specifically on U.S. presidents and their advisers, but it incorporates the same conception of decision-making tasks. Indeed, one could extract the generic form of the basic tasks of decision making (the basic processes that must be performed), such as surveying objectives and alternatives, searching for information, assimilating new information, making implementation and contingency plans, and so forth. The Janis and George approaches also share a concentration on decision-making *malfunctions*. That is, both Janis and George are preoccupied with impediments to effective decision making; they focus disproportionate attention on what goes wrong in decision making. While sharing Janis's and George's conceptions of decision making as a series of tasks that groups must perform, and accepting as valid their lists of basic decision-making tasks, I part company with them on their emphasis on malfunctions. If theory about decision-making processes is to be built, it must be built upon a foundation of theoretical and empirical knowledge that addresses what goes right and wrong in organizational decision making, and then focus more closely on how process may be related to structures and outcomes.

In an effort to build upon Janis's earlier work on groupthink and on the research on decision making by Janis and Mann (1977), Herek, Janis, and Huth (1987) use a case survey methodology to try to study the relationship between decision-making process and crisis outcomes in American foreign policy (cf. Williamson 1979). They draw upon multiple case studies of each of nineteen crisis decision-making instances and attempt to "code" whether the malfunctions in decision making described by Janis are present or absent in each crisis. They also have each crisis examined by a specialist to determine whether or not the crisis outcome was a success or a failure for U.S. foreign policy. Finally, Herek and his colleagues examine whether a relationship can be seen to exist between those crises with "high-quality" decision-making processes (those with few or no malfunctions present) and successful outcomes, and those with "low-quality" processes (many malfunctions present) and failed outcomes.[5]

This study merits much attention. First, Herek, Janis, and Huth find support for the notion that the quality of the process of decision making is related to the quality of the outcome, or resolution, of a crisis. They also find that some malfunctions (e.g., failure to reconsider rejected alternatives) occur more regularly than do others (e.g., failure to search for information). They pursue these empirical findings with the aid of the case survey method, essentially using case studies as "data sets" that can be scrutinized and from which additional information can be extracted. Multiple case studies of each crisis are used so as to obtain as full a picture as possible of the decision-making process. Finally, Herek, Janis, and Huth use thresholds to determine the presence or absence of a decision-making malfunction. For example, if the malfunction appears only once, it was perhaps not significant. If, however, it appears three or four times, Herek et al. conclude that there was a significant presence of the malfunction in that instance of decision making.

This combination of factors presents a noteworthy approach to the study of process. Researchers can study process by indicating the decision-making tasks that are to be studied and then establishing reasonable thresholds that cover a range of task performance (this range need not be reserved only for malfunctions but could be extended to cover a full variety of functional as well as malfunctional task performance). The performance of these tasks can be observed in case study accounts of decision making. Not only could process be related to outcome in such a study, as in Herek, Janis, and Huth (1987), but process could also be related to advisory structures in an effort to ascertain how different advisory configurations tend to perform the tasks of decision making.

While research on organizational structures has given relatively little attention to crises, research on process has focused a large amount of scholarly attention on crisis situations (see Holsti 1979, 1989). There are many examples of case studies of "routine," noncrisis policymaking processes, such as Art's study of the TFX aircraft (1968) and Greenwood's analysis of the decision to use MIRV technology on American nuclear missiles (1975). However, efforts to build empirically derived *theory* about policymaking processes, rather than descriptions of particular processes, have tended to focus on decision making during crises rather than on routine policymaking. Still, process theory does not receive the attention that Anderson (1987) encourages in the study of either crises or noncrises. Nor does the process literature tend to look explicitly to structures and institutions as causal influences on process behavior, even though there have been many calls for foreign policy analysts to take the "group" in group decision making more seriously (Gaenslen 1992, 189). Alexander George argues that "information processing will be affected…by the structure, internal processes, and management of [decision making] groups and relationships" (George 1980b, 82). I could not agree more, and I propose that what is needed to help foreign policy analysts bridge the gap between the study of structure on the one hand and the study of process on the other is a conceptualization of politics and decision making that indicates how these issues may be interrelated. I suggest that an institutional perspective may provide one such lens.

■ Bridging Studies of Structure and Process: An Institutional Approach

That foreign policy analysis has largely not developed conceptualizations of, and performed a body of empirical research that focuses on, the relationship between structure and process is perhaps ironic since within political science and related disciplines like sociology and economics increasing attention is being paid to structure and process within the area of overlap between organization theory, institutional theory, and political and social choice (Bacharach 1989; DiMaggio and Powell 1991; Feldman 1993; March and Olsen 1989; Palumbo 1975; Rainey 1984). Within this common ground can be found a renewed emphasis on institutions within political science, economics, law, and public management.

The philosophy that ties these approaches together is the proposition that to understand political decision making it is vital to understand the impact that institutional structures, socialization, norms, expectations, rules, and selection mechanisms have on individual decision makers and thus the process of policymaking; to understand "how social choices are shaped, mediated, and channeled by institutional arrangements" (DiMaggio and Powell 1991, 2). Within political science, research from an institutional perspective has largely focused on the institutions of government (such as studies of the U.S. Congress) and on international regimes within international relations. As I point out later in this chapter, I would argue that foreign policy analysts can draw upon this vision of politics as well.

Definitions of what constitutes an "institution" abound. March and Olsen, for example, define political institutions as "collections of interrelated rules and routines that define appropriate actions in terms of relations between roles and situations" (1989, 160). Young defines them as "recognized practices consisting of easily identifiable roles coupled with collections of rules or conventions governing relations among occupants of these roles" (1986, 107). Keohane argues that the term "institution" may refer to "a general pattern or categorization of activity or to a particular human-constructed arrangement, formally or informally organized, that persists over time" (1988, 383). In an excellent treatment, Kiser and Ostrom state that organizations are composites of participants following rules governing activities and transactions to realize particular outputs (1982, 193). Rules are institutional arrangements. Ostrom defines rules as potentially linguistic entities that refer to prescriptions commonly known and used by a set of participants to order repetitive, interdependent relationships. They specify what actions are required, prohibited, and/or permitted (1986, 5).

In summary, political institutions are sets of rules, constructed by men and women, that set the context for political action. "Institutional structures refer both to the organizational characteristics of groups and to the rules and norms that guide the relationships between actors" (Ikenberry 1988, 223). This conception of an institution can be especially useful to foreign policy analysts because it focuses on both the formal and informal structures used in decision making—an integral part of political decision making. It concentrates attention on the "rules in use" in a decision situation, the rules and norms that are known by members of the group, even if they remain unstated. The existence of the rules of the institution can be inferred from the behavior of members of the institution.

Research by those who share an "institutional perspective" is diverse, and views on what institutions are and how they affect policymaking vary widely. Two characteristics are central to an institutional perspective. First, this approach emphasizes the derivative character of individual behavior. It focuses on how individual action is shaped by institutional settings. This perspective stresses that preferences are not exogenously determined; rather, they are developed through involvement in political activity that is structured by institutional arrangements. Second, in order to be an institution, a set of roles, rules, or behavioral patterns must persist. It is through an iterative process that institutions affect individuals and thus political life.

The most basic feature of an institutional argument, according to Krasner, is that prior institutional choices limit future options: "First, capabilities and preferences, that is, the very nature of the actors, cannot be understood except as part of some larger institutional framework. Second, the possible options available at any given point in time are constrained by available institutional capabilities and these capabilities are themselves a product of choices made during some earlier period" (1988, 72).

Keohane extends this argument by noting that "institutions do not merely reflect the preferences and power of units constituting them; the institutions themselves shape those preferences and that power" (1988, 382). He argues that institutions mediate the types of action that will emerge from a process. If political action is to be the object of study, then the links that exist between observable behaviors and identifiable institutional settings must be explored.

Views on what institutions "do" vary as well. March and Olsen argue that institutions affect the flow of political life. They take as their basic assumption the notion that the organization of political life matters, that institutions "define the framework within which politics takes place" (1989, 18). In a precursor to the new emphasis on institutions, March and Simon argue that the organizational environment in which a decision maker functions "determines what consequences he will anticipate, what ones he will not; what alternatives he will consider, what ones he will ignore" (1958, 139). They argue that these institutional factors cannot be treated as unexplained variables but must be subject to examination themselves if we wish to understand and explain decision making in groups.

Ikenberry argues that institutional structures "serve to mediate the interests and capacities of individuals and groups" (1988, 243). He urges increased research effort on the nature of these "constraining and enabling circumstances" as they impact on political processes. Krasner (1988), drawing on the insights of evolutionary biology and epistemology (e.g., see Gould 1989; Mayr 1982), states that an institutional perspective regards enduring institutional structures as the building blocks of social and political life. The preferences, capabilities, and basic self-identities of individuals are conditioned by these institutional structures; in this sense historical developments are path-dependent. Future decisions and actions, he argues, are constrained and guided by past decisions and arrangements; institutional settings are the genesis of future perceptions, preferences, and political action. In summary, institutional configurations set the context within which individuals operate and decisions are made, an insight which Allison had but, as Ripley points out in his essay (chapter 6) in this volume, which analysts have not known quite what to do with since then; they give incentives and constraints to certain behaviors, and they produce behavioral effects.

An Institutional Perspective in the Analysis of Foreign Policy Crises

It is one thing to suggest that the organization of a policymaking group might have an effect; it is another to be able to specify what type of effects foreign policy structures might have on decision making. Snyder, Bruck, and Sapin (1962a), and other first-generation analysts of foreign policy, had the right idea when they pointed to the potential importance of the organizational context of foreign policymaking. Modern institutional theory may provide a focus that foreign policy analysis has lacked. Building on the insights of the "new institutionalism," foreign policy analysts interested in policymaking during crises should examine the processes or tasks of decision making and explore how these processes may be related to and perhaps generated by the ways that leaders have tried to structure a decision-making group.

Toward this end, studies of structure and process in crisis decision making might begin with the advisory structure models developed by Johnson (1974) and George (1980b) in order to further refine our understanding of the important dimensions of group structure that affect decision-making processes (cf. Crabb and Mulcahy 1986; Hermann and Preston 1994; Orbovich and Molnar 1992; Pika 1988). Such a study would examine the relationship between different policymaking structures and the resultant decision-making behavior, and could be applied to instances of crisis decision making. The goal would be to trace the impact of advisory structures on the performance of the tasks of decision making during crises. An example of this type of research is Haney's (1992) examination of the structures established by Presidents Eisenhower, Johnson, and Nixon during a variety of foreign policy crises and the decision-making processes performed by each group, in which he analyzes the links between different organizational configurations and resulting decision-making processes.

Foreign policy analysts may find it helpful in this endeavor to import concepts from the theory of "agency" in political science and economics.[6] The basic approach of agency theory is that a principal (the president) employs an agent or agents (advisers) to help perform a task (policymaking). However, the preferences and interests of the agent or agents are never in complete accord with those of the principal. The issue then becomes how the principal controls the agents. Much attention in agency theory is paid to how systems of incentives and constraints can work for or against the interests of the principal. They are, in other words, issues of organizational design and configuration. In studying group decision making, foreign policy analysts may well wish to borrow such an emphasis from agency theory to explore the relevant dimensions of organizational design that may have an influence on how members of policymaking groups perform their tasks of providing information, advice, analysis, and policy guidance. This emphasis is consistent with Hult's (1993) argument for a greater focus on "networks" in research. Such an effort would focus on the formal and informal networks of group members, how they are arranged, by whom, what incentives and constraints they are faced with, and what the effects of that structuring are on the process of decision making.

The task ahead for foreign policy analysts working in this area is to develop a more sound base of theoretical and empirical knowledge about (1) the relationship between leaders' styles and the organizational strategies that fit those styles, and about (2) the important dimensions of organizations that make one structure different from another (e.g., centralization, monitoring). We also need (3) a more sound base of abstract theory about how different organizational configurations are related to the process of decision making, and (4) better empirical theory about how these links between structure and process work in practice. Following on this work, researchers should (5) strive toward developing empirically derived and theoretically sound contingent generalizations about the nature of the relationships between structure and process in policymaking. Greater attention to (6) the link between process quality and the success or failure of policies, (i.e., outcomes) is also required. Each of these questions can and should be explored for crisis and noncrisis cases with the goal of developing a better understanding of the relationships between decision-making structures, processes, and ultimately, policy outcomes.

■ Conclusion

In *The Institutional Presidency* (1992) Burke argues that studies of the U.S. presidency need to begin to examine in more depth the nexus between the enduring institutional (structural) features of the presidency and the management strategies and styles of particular presidents, and the implications of each for the other. I argue that a similar bridging exercise is needed within foreign policy analysis for studies of crisis decision making. As I have reviewed here, there is a long tradition of research within universities and governments on the structures of policymaking, though this research has tended to focus on routine policymaking as opposed to crisis decision making. There is also a line of research on the processes by which policy is made, much of which has focused on policymaking processes during crises. What is needed now is an emphasis on explaining the roots of policymaking processes and exploring how these processes may be rooted in the structures within which decision making takes place. I have argued that an institutional perspective may help guide research in this area by highlighting the potential nature of the relationship between structure and process.

What is required in this theory-building effort is a mix of theoretical research that attempts to come to terms with the important dimensions of institutional structure that may affect decision-making processes during crises, and empirical studies of crisis decision making that track the relationship between structure and process. These empirical studies may take a variety of forms—single case studies, small comparative studies that may utilize George's method of structured, focused comparison, or larger-N studies that use a case survey approach. Regardless of the particular approach, researchers need to reinvigorate group decision-making studies with an eye toward building theory that can accumulate over time. Having covered a vast amount of terrain in its first generation that included producing much information and knowledge about each issue of "structure" and "process" in policymaking, the field of foreign policy analysis should, in its second generation, try to fit these two pieces of the puzzle together in ways that further enhance our understanding of foreign policy decision making.

■ Acknowledgments

The author would like to thank Alexander George, Jeanne Hey, John Lovell, Mike McGinnis, Laura Neack, Lin Ostrom, Jim Perry, Leroy Rieselbach, Dina Spechler, Harvey Starr, and an anonymous reviewer of this chapter.

■ Notes

1. See also Burke (1992), Campbell (1986), Crabb and Mulcahy (1986), Henderson (1988), Kessel (1983, 1984), Light (1982), and Porter (1980).

2. See the earlier essays in this volume by Shimko (chapter 5) and Rosati (chapter 4) for a discussion of individual-level approaches.

3. For further discussions of bureaucratic policymaking, see Bendor (1988), Downs (1967), Moe (1989), and Tullock (1987). For comments on and criticisms of Allison's framework for inquiry, see Art (1973), Bendor and Hammond (1992), Caldwell (1977), Freedman (1976), Krasner (1971), Nathan and Oliver (1978), Perlmutter (1974), Steinbruner (1974), Steiner (1977), and Welch (1992).

4. Note that this may be a logical impossibility given the nature of the symptoms of groupthink, which may suggest that a tautological problem exists as well.

5. See also Welch's (1989) criticism of the Herek, Janis, and Huth treatment of the Cuban missile crisis cases, and the rebuttal by Herek, Janis, and Huth (1989); and Haney's (1994) largely confirming note on the Herek, Janis, and Huth process codings of five of their original nineteen cases.

6. See, for example, Arrow 1985; Eisenhardt 1989a; Ferejohn 1987; Harris and Raviv 1978; Pratt and Zeckhauser 1985; Ross 1973; and Shull 1989.

EIGHT

Domestic Political Explanations in the Analysis of Foreign Policy

Joe D. Hagan, WEST VIRGINIA UNIVERSITY

■ Editors' Introduction

In this chapter Joe Hagan provides a comprehensive overview of the linkages between domestic political dynamics and foreign policy behavior. The reader will see that this chapter is considerably longer than other chapters in this book, a necessity given the varied literatures being brought together here. Hagan shares a similar focus with Haney in that both consider the role of institutions in foreign policy behavior. Hagan explicitly considers different institutional responses to domestic political opposition. For example, do authoritarian and democratic regimes respond differently to their opponents? What are the foreign policy implications of those differences? In this way Hagan links the governmental and societal levels of analysis. Hagan not only provides a thorough review of the literature on these questions, but also develops an analytical framework to account for domestic political influences on foreign policy behavior.

In reading this chapter, consider the widely varied influences of domestic political factors on foreign policy behavior. What contingencies are important in explaining these variations? Which domestic variables outweigh others when they compete? Hagan uses many examples to illustrate the effects of domestic political factors on foreign policy; can you think of others that illustrate the concepts introduced here? ■

At the heart of domestic political explanations of foreign policy is the idea that leaders engage in what Putnam (1988) calls "two-level games" or what Tsebelis (1990; also Starr 1991) refers to as "nested games." That is, in explaining government choices in foreign affairs, leaders are viewed as coping simultaneously with the pressures and constraints of their own domestic political systems as well as with those of the international environment. These games are not simply the decision-making dynamics discussed in previous chapters; of concern here is the broader array of autonomous political actors (e.g., factions, parties, and institutions) that influence the regime's daily governing authority and ultimately its long-term hold on office. This balancing of domestic and international concerns in the foreign policy process is not an isolated, aberrant game. Thus, much theoretical research has long argued that the internal political configurations of national governments broadly influence, or modify, their involvement in international affairs. The importance of this insight goes well beyond foreign policy analysis. The implication is that international politics is driven not solely by systemic structures (as posited by realism) but also by the domestic political patterns of at least the major powers.[1]

The purpose of this chapter is to explicate the general logic by which domestic political phenomena are linked to foreign policy. In doing so it draws upon diverse areas of research on this topic that typically have been treated separately. These various core concepts, explanations, and demonstrated foreign policy effects provide the basis for arguing that the linkage between domestic politics and foreign policy is far more *complex* than portrayed by researchers pursuing their own agendas and interests separately. As is discussed in the major portion of this chapter, the relationship is complex because leaders pursue dual domestic political games involving multiple arenas of opposition and, then, respond to that opposition with alternative strategies with divergent foreign policy effects. Furthermore, these games and strategies are pervasive across different types of political systems, although their impact on foreign policy is actually subtle in modifying how leaders respond to international pressures. The chapter closes with an overview of research strategies for incorporating various levels of opposition and contingencies into empirical, particularly cross-national, research on domestic politics and foreign policy.

■ Theoretical Research on Domestic Politics and Foreign Policy

Even though it is often assumed that foreign policy in a dangerous world is, or at least should be, above a nation's internal squabbles, the general significance of domestic politics is a major theme in a wide variety of literatures. These areas of research include U.S. foreign policy, comparative foreign policy analysis, foreign policy making in various specific non-U.S. settings, and recently the development of what Muller and Risse-Kappen (1993) call "complex models of international politics." One goal of this chapter is to bring together the insights of these largely separate areas of research. In doing so, however, it should be kept in mind that none of the four is entirely cohesive. Rather, within each there are separate—if not competing—strands of theoretical logic and research. Juxtaposition of research themes within these four bodies of research, as well as among them, provides the basis for explicating the theoretical logic linking domestic politics to foreign policy.

U.S. Foreign Policy

Political explanations have a long tradition in the study of U.S. foreign policy. The broad significance of domestic political constraints was acknowledged early on by prominent cold war realists such as George Kennan (1951) and Hans Morgenthau (1951), who worried that resurgent isolationism would undercut the country's commitment to an active global role in countering the communist threat.[2] Although a "cold war consensus" giving the president a relatively free hand in countering communism emerged by the early 1950s, domestic politics remained a dominant concern in "national security" studies of the army-navy–air force rivalries over roles, missions, and budgets and related congressional-executive wrangling over military preparedness.[3] Since the Vietnam War, however, domestic politics has been brought into U.S. foreign policy studies in more fundamental ways. First, with the collapse of the cold war consensus after Vietnam and the rise of global economic interdependence, interest was revived in constraints emanating from broader political arenas. Presidents were now viewed as ensnared in a web of constraints imposed by an institutionally jealous Congress, by elite and mass public opinion that was both divided and skeptical, and by a "weak" state apparatus unable to manage the emerging pressures of complex interdependence.[4] Second, the theoretical rigor of the political logic within foreign policy analysis was enhanced by works on "bureaucratic politics" by Allison (1969, 1971) and Halperin (1974), as well as by their critiques and the development of alternative models of the decision-making process.[5] Finally, primarily among historians such as John Lewis Gaddis (1972, 1982), there has emerged a large body of "postrevisionist" research arguing that domestic politics intensified—not diminished—the hard-line, militant cold war policies of the administrations from Truman to Reagan.[6]

Comparative Foreign Policy

Political explanations in this area have been emphasized since the field's inception in the mid-1960s with its call for, among other things, systematic and cross-national analyses of foreign policy. Political phenomena are a major component of Rosenau's (1966) long influential "pre-theory" framework. "Governmental" factors are one of his five general "sources" of foreign policy, and political system properties (accountability and development) are two of the three national characteristics determining the relative importance of the source variables. Conceptualizations of a wider variety of political phenomena are more fully specified in the other major theoretical frameworks proposed by Brecher, Steinberg, and Stein (1969), the Interstate Behavioral Analysis Project (Wilkenfeld et al. 1980), and the Comparative Research on the Events of Nations Project (East, Salmore, and Hermann 1978). Each of these frameworks in its own way focuses on three kinds of phenomena: political system structure (mainly "democratization"), various patterns of political opposition (e.g., regime constraints, linkage mechanisms), and certain shared attributes of the political leadership (e.g., shared images, elite profiles). However, empirical cross-national research has fallen far short of the ambitions of these theoretical frameworks. Most early cross-national studies were limited mainly to political system structure, comparing the foreign policy behavior of "open" and "closed" systems.[7] Far fewer studies attempt to capture the more subtle domestic political phenomena of opposition patterns and leader attributes. The one major exception is the extensive cross-national research into the most extreme manifestation of domestic political instability in the form of mass unrest: the "linkage" between domestic conflict and foreign conflict.[8] Only recent cross-national analyses examine the effects of more routine, organized political opposition within the "regime" as well as from other institutional arenas such as the military, legislature, regional actors, and ruling party factions.[9]

The Politics of Foreign Policy in Non-U.S. Settings

A third area of research consists largely of case studies by country specialists on foreign policy making in various non-U.S. settings. Although initially dismissed by comparative foreign policy researchers as atheoretical and unsystematic, by the 1980s this literature had become more analytic and now offers detailed insights into the precise nature of domestic politics and its influence on foreign policy.[10] Emerging from this scattered literature is a common conclusion that fluid political constraints may or may not exist in any type of political system. Domestic political influences are central to analyses of the foreign policy of the former Soviet Union. Empirical "kremlinological" accounts of politics in the Khrushchev and Brezhnev regimes, and especially case studies of Soviet military intervention, carefully document the actors and debates within the Kremlin as well as their precise impact on foreign policy action.[11] Political explanations also receive widespread attention in the Third World foreign policy literature, as an attempt to depart from idiosyncratic, "great man" explanations of foreign policies (Korany 1986a) and to capture the emerging array of actors and institutions in many of the Third World's political systems.[12] Finally, political influences are emphasized in studies of the Western democracies, most extensively in the case of Japan's factionalized Liberal Democratic Party as well as in coalition governments in a variety of European democracies.[13] That democracies should face opposition is not surprising; what is interesting here is that the level of political constraints, as well as the magnitude of their foreign policy effects, varies substantially among democracies. In fact, taken together, these studies of authoritarian, Third World, and Western democratic systems suggest that it is difficult to generalize about any type of political system and suggest that political effects vary across different issues, situations, and leaders (Hagan 1993, chap. 2).

Domestic Politics and "Complex Models of International Politics"[14]

Most recently, there has been a surge of interest in domestic politics as a supplement to "systemic" explanations in the broader international relations literature—for example, neorealism (Waltz 1979), complex interdependence and cooperation (e.g., Keohane and Nye 1977; Keohane 1984), and global change (Gilpin 1981).[15] Across these topics is a common conclusion: that nations with different domestic political arrangements respond to the constraints of international systemic arrangements with different foreign policy strategies. Research concerned with managing complex interdependence shows that different nations respond to common international economic crises in different ways, which can be traced to domestic coalitions, institutional arrangements, and particularly the strength of the state vis à vis societal actors (e.g., Gourevitch 1986; Katzenstein 1976).[16] Theoretical frameworks also emphasize domestic politics in explaining foreign policy "restructuring" as a response to global change, recognizing that political factors may constrain, prevent, change, or even facilitate foreign policy change (K. Holsti 1982; Goldmann 1988; Hermann 1990).[17] It is, however, the research into the origins of war that has most extensively incorporated domestic political phenomena. Much of this literature examines the "war proneness" of democratic and authoritarian systems, arguing that democracies are less likely to initiate war and to fight each other because they select more moderate leaders and/or because their leaders face greater domestic constraints (e.g., Bueno de Mesquita and Lalman 1992; Doyle 1986; Lake 1992; Russett 1993b).[18] Equally important, although seemingly inconsistent, is research explaining war proneness in terms of more fluid (i.e., nonstructural) political dynamics that may occur in any type of political regime. It shows that domestic political pressures for aggressive and militant foreign policies are found in both democratic and authoritarian systems (e.g., Lamborn 1991; Levy 1988, 1989; Rosecrance and Stein 1993; Snyder 1991). Authoritarian regimes are not the only ones capable of producing leaders who have a hard-line, bellicose orientation to world affairs (Vasquez 1992).[19]

■ The Logic of Domestic Political Explanations of Foreign Policy

The task of this section is to explicate how domestic politics influences foreign policy, and to do so in a way that is well grounded in the theoretical and empirical research. When one examines the literature mentioned in the previous section, it quickly becomes apparent that this is not a simple task. There is no single political perspective used to explain foreign policy. Rather, explanations vary not only in terms of what aspect of foreign policy is to be explained but also with respect to the relevant political arenas and tasks, the alternative political strategies used by leaders to cope with domestic constraints, and the significance of political system structure on foreign policy making. The existing literature offers not a comprehensive theory but rather different pieces of the linkage between domestic politics and foreign policy. The intent here is not to argue in favor of one particular perspective. Rather, my strategy is to attempt a broad synthesis by treating the various themes in the literature as complementary within a broader framework.

All that follows is rooted in the basic notion that foreign policy makers simultaneously cope with the pressures of domestic and international affairs (Putnam 1988; Tsebelis 1990). I elaborate upon the character of these "nested" and "two-level" games by arguing that they are inherently complex in the following ways. First, political leaders as foreign policy makers cope with *dual domestic political imperatives* involving opposition in multiple arenas. Second, the effect of domestic politics is *contingent upon leaders' choices of alternative political strategies* that, in turn, have sharply divergent effects on foreign policy. Third, these dual games and alternative strategies are *pervasive across the different types of political systems* and are not limited to established democracies. Finally, these games and strategies have *subtle effects on foreign policy;* they condition how leaders respond to international pressures but, except in extreme circumstances, are not the sole, or even primary, determinant of foreign policy. This exercise provides the reader with an image of the overall logic of domestic political explanations of foreign policy. Its implication is that any general conception of that relationship must incorporate the complexity inherent in the games and strategies in various national settings.

Dual Domestic Political Games and Multiple Arenas of Opposition

As noted, domestic political explanations of foreign policy rest on the idea that decision makers must simultaneously contend with the pressures of international affairs and domestic politics. What is striking is that different literatures characterize these games in different ways. At one extreme, domestic politics is pictured as the clash of particularistic interests within the well-structured institutional environment of national governments. Take as two examples the intense battles after World War II among the U.S. Navy, Army, and Air Force over defense budgets or certain weapons systems and similar struggles within the "iron triangle" of interest groups, congressional committees, and executive agencies over trade tariffs. At the other extreme are accounts of severe domestic crises in which national leaders aggressively manipulate foreign policy in order to save themselves from being overthrown by domestic opponents. As in the cases of Austria-Hungary, Germany, and Russia before World War II, leaders facing widespread unrest at home used foreign policy as a device for ensuring their personal survival and for preserving the domestic order. While other conceptions fall between these extremes, the point here is that there is not a *single* view of the domestic political setting as it influences foreign policy. Rather, leaders deal with not one, but two, domestic political games: building policy coalitions and retaining political power.

Building policy coalitions. This imperative concerns the leadership's need to build domestic support for any proposed policy initiative. At issue is the task of achieving agreement among at least a subset, or "coalition," of the various actors who formally or informally share the authority to commit the nation's resources and/or implement policy in a sustained manner. Although policymaking often occurs within a single group (e.g., a president and his or her advisers), two conditions may politicize an issue and move it into the broader political arena. The first of these is when decision-making authority is fragmented among autonomous and powerful actors, either because of a power-sharing arrangement between the executive and other institutions (e.g., an autonomous legislature or politicized military) or because of the division of executive authority among separate party factions or multiple parties. Either way, no single group controls the policy process, and a decision requires agreement among multiple actors. The second politicizing condition is the degree to which the actors involved are polarized over the issue itself. In other words, to what extent do the actors involved disagree with each other over the policy's merits? When policy authority is dispersed across politically powerful and contentious actors, the policymaking process becomes a task of building a *coalition* of supporters necessary to gain passage of an initiative. Foreign policy becomes a "political resultant" in the sense that the final decision outcome reflects the political strategies (discussed subsequently) necessary to build agreement to support implementation of the policy.[20]

Coalition building, not surprisingly, is pervasive in the open and pluralist systems of established Western democracies. Although extensive bureaucratic and interest-group activity is common to these complex systems, it differs with respect to the arrangements of national political authority in the American presidential system and the Western European and Japanese parliamentary systems. In the United States, coalition building on major issues ultimately revolves around relations between the Congress and the executive even though the "separation of powers" system provides Congress with the authority (and political autonomy) to veto or restrict major foreign commitments such as waging war, regulating trade, entering into treaties, and spending in foreign and defense policy. When Congress and the presidency are polarized over foreign policy, the impact can be dramatic. Indeed, much of the pre–World War II "underreaction" in U.S. foreign policy can be traced to the failure of international-ist presidents (Wilson and Roosevelt) to gain the support of an isolationist Congress (e.g., Dallek 1977; Stein 1993). In parliamentary systems, in contrast, central author-ity is lodged entirely in a single institution—the cabinet.[21] Where a single party controls the cabinet with a solid parliamentary majority, political constraints are quite minimal and limited largely to bureaucratic politics. However, parliamentary situations become quite problematic when the cabinet is itself politically fragmented by the well-established factions of a single ruling party (as in Japan under the Liberal Democratic Party) and/or by multiple political parties in a coalition cabinet, none of which commands a majority in parliament (e.g., Fourth Republic France, Italian coalitions since World War II, and Israel under Labour and Likud). The deadlocks underlying Fourth Republic France "immobilism" on the Algerian War (Andrews 1962), Japan's reactive posture in foreign policy negotiations (Destler, Fukui, and Sato 1979; Hellmann 1969), and Israel's difficulty in dealing with the occupied terri-tories (Yaniv and Yishai 1981) illustrate the inability of cabinets to agree on even the most pressing policy matters.[22]

Coalition building is not limited to established democracies. Although power in authoritarian systems is conventionally assumed to be controlled by a cohesive political elite, historical and area study research indicates that this is not always the case. Authoritarian regimes such as Nazi Germany and Stalinist Russia had minimal domestic constraints, but others clearly fell short of the monolithic character of "totalitarian" systems (Friedrich and Brzezinski 1956). Political authority in the for-mer Soviet Union, although concentrated in the Kremlin, was significantly dispersed across contending political actors in the two intertwined tiers of that Communist oligarchy: the Central Committee and the Politburo (Roeder 1988). At one level were entrenched bureaucratic and institutional interests represented in the Central Committee, which were polarized over foreign policy into hard-line "security-producer-ideological" and more moderate "consumer-agriculture–public service" groupings (Aspaturian 1966). At another level, ultimate political authority rested in the Politburo, whose authority was, to varying degrees, dispersed among its fifteen or so members that constituted the body. Under both Khrushchev and Brezhnev, achieving a consensus across the tiers of policymaking posed broad constraints on Soviet foreign policy.[23] Other prominent twentieth-century authoritarian regimes—Wilhelmine Germany prior to World War I and militarist Japan in the 1930s—were even more extremely fragmented, or "cartelized," with authority dispersed across separate institutions and groups. Kaiser William II was but one player in an authori-tarian coalition that also included the military, agricultural elites, heavy industry, and democratic elements in the German parliament (Reichstag).[24] Similarly, in 1930s Japan, real control over foreign policy was spread among the imperial court, the army, and the navy, while parties in the Diet were suppressed.[25] In both regimes, despite a hard-line, militant consensus on foreign affairs among these actors, there was still significant debate about the pace and direction of future military expansion (Snyder 1991).

Coalition building is often neglected in analyses of Third World foreign poli-cies, mainly because established institutions and powerful bureaucratic, political, and social groups are assumed to be absent. Although it recognizes many cases where authority is concentrated in the hands of a single "predominant leader," accumulating research points to two general exceptions where power is quite dispersed.[26] First, after several decades of independence, many Third World governments are quite institutionally complex, with entrenched bureaucratic and party interests. This is the case in most larger countries in the Middle East (Korany and Dessouki 1984), Latin America (Lincoln and Ferris 1984), and East Asia, including China (e.g., Barnett 1985; Vertzberger 1984b). Political authority in the Third World is also dispersed in ways that range from well-established collective rule in the royal family in Saudi Arabia (Quandt 1981) to fragmented and unstable regimes in South Korea (Kim 1971), pre-1967 Syria (Bar-Siman-Tov 1983), and Argentina (Levy and Vakili 1990). The second set of exceptions are associated with regimes that appear to be dominated by a single predominant leader but are actually racked by political infighting among contending factions. In these cases the leader is unable or unwilling to act on foreign policy issues until a consensus forms among the actors. Well-documented examples of this situation are the intensely confrontational foreign policies of China under Mao Zedong during the Cultural Revolution (Hinton 1972), Indonesia under Sukarno (Weinstein 1976), and Iran under Khomeini (Stempel 1981). Even though Mao, Sukarno, and Khomeini were uniquely prominent as revolutionary leaders, closer research demonstrates that none of these leaders was politically willing or able to take complete control of foreign policy and, specifically, resolve conflicts among moderate and hard-line leadership factions. Despite each regime's constant flow of intense anti-Western rhetoric in these cases, none was able to take substantively meaningful action to resolve international crises; major foreign policy actions were taken only after power was stabilized and consolidated by one of the government factions.

Retaining political power. Whereas coalition building concerns authority over an immediate policy issue, the longer-term political survival of the ruling group is at the heart of the political imperative of retaining power. One of these goals is political survival. Foreign policy decision makers, acting in their concurrent role as national and political leaders, simultaneously work to maintain and enhance the political base necessary for staying in office. Therefore, when domestic political pressures threaten to evict the leadership from power, foreign policy must be adjusted so that it imposes fewer domestic costs. Certainly not all foreign policy issues become politicized in this manner, but two dynamics combine to suggest that policymakers are likely to be sensitive to the long-term domestic consequences of their foreign policy decisions. One is simply the occurrence of "significant" opposition in the wider environment, that is, competing political groups whose opposition extends beyond specific policy disagreements to a direct challenge for government control. This is most significant when these groups have (or are acquiring) sufficient political resources that indicate they may succeed in the not-too-distant future. The other is a mounting public perception of foreign policy issues as being linked to the overall credibility of the current leadership. For example, confrontation and accommodation with foreign adversaries, respectively, are easily perceived by the public as indicating the government's overall willingness to risk war or its weakness in world affairs. The pressures of political survival are most dramatically illustrated by the crisis leading to World War I, in which the highly vulnerable leaders in most countries feared that *not* going to war would undercut their nationalist credentials and show them to be at their weakest.[27]

The theme of political survival, though not as prominent as coalition policy-making, is found in the various strands of literature on U.S. foreign policy, including core theoretical concepts such as Halperin's (1974) "presidential interest," Mueller's (1971) "presidential popularity," and Hampson's (1988) "divided decision maker." Particularly with the rise of a divided and skeptical public after the failed Vietnam policy, all U.S. presidents appear to have been closely attentive to shifting public opinion on the two broad—and seemingly contradictory—concerns of (1) risking involvement in another war and (2) projecting international weakness suggestive of a decline in U.S. world status (Schneider 1983). Analyses of the logic of Nixon/Ford, Carter, and Reagan/Bush foreign policies explain their alternative "strategies of containment" partly in terms of their alternative ways of managing the media and public opinion. Nor are such interpretations limited to the post-Vietnam period. Presidential survival is a core political theme in postrevisionist analyses of the "origins of the cold war," beginning with the argument that Roosevelt and Truman tailored the emerging cold war confrontation to domestic audiences (Gaddis 1972; Yergin 1977). Even at the height of the cold war, when there was a very wide reservoir of public support for containment, presidents still feared public opinion. For example, research of major episodes such as the Cuban missile crisis (Hampson 1988) and the Vietnam War (Berman 1982; Gelb and Betts 1979) now suggests that Presidents Kennedy and Johnson were preoccupied with the memory of how the "loss of China" destroyed the credibility of the Truman administration and feared conciliation with the communists would lead to the collapse of their own administrations.

Retaining political power is, of course, an important political dynamic in the foreign policies of parliamentary democracies, but as with coalition policymaking the situation reflects their particular institutional arrangements (Waltz 1967). Whereas U.S. presidents are directly elected, prime ministers and the cabinet are selected more indirectly via elections in the Parliament. Although a disciplined and cohesive ruling party can insulate a prime minister from public opinion, a fragmented cabinet severely constrains his or her ability to conduct foreign policy because the defection of any one faction or party can precipitate the government's collapse. If cabinet factions or coalitions are intensely competitive, foreign policy issues tend to be viewed less on their substantive merits than according to their perceived effect on political balances in the cabinet. Indeed, some would argue that the immobilism in the foreign policies of Japan's Liberal Democratic Party (Destler, Fukui, and Sato 1976; Fukui 1977a) or the coalitions of France's Fourth Republic (Andrews 1962) stemmed mainly from the intensely competitive "ministerial merry-go-round" as well as fears of cabinet members' defection and ensuing government collapse.

Like coalition building, the unelected leaders in authoritarian regimes would seem less affected by the task of political survival. Various research suggests that this is not necessarily the case. As portrayed in the historical and war-proneness literature, the leaders of authoritarian political systems in Germany, Russia, and Austria-Hungary were very sensitive to broad domestic political crises (Kennedy

1980; Lamborn 1991; Snyder 1991). During the crisis of 1914, these leaders were probably more preoccupied with the *domestic* political consequences of their decisions than with the international repercussions (e.g., Lebow 1981). Even in the post-Stalinist Soviet Union, no leader could ignore the task of maintaining his nationalist and ideological credentials within the Party and even the broader political system. Constant uncertainty over power sharing in the Politburo meant that any leader could "suddenly find himself removed from office by a political conspiracy of his former political associates" (Schwartz 1975, 177). Not only did this happen to Khrushchev in October 1964, but kremlinological accounts of his leadership as well as those of Brezhnev and Gorbachev reveal a constant game in which each leader sought to consolidate and retain power (Gelman 1984; Linden 1978). Indeed, Valenta (1979) asserts that throughout the 1968 Czechoslovak crisis, Brezhnev remained uncommitted to any particular option and came to support military intervention only to avoid the consequences of being in the Politburo minority on that politically critical issue.

Political survival is a more dominant theme than coalition building in the literature on the politics of foreign policy in Third World countries (e.g., David 1991; Good 1962; Weinstein 1972). A distinctive feature of Third World foreign policy making is the extreme political instability of many regimes, reflective of a persistent crisis of domestic legitimacy and the lack of an institutionalized elite political process. Thus, political survival is pressing because of the extreme distrust among contending players. For example, most accounts of the U.S.-Iranian hostage crisis contend that the policy in Iran was driven mainly by the "fight-to-the-death" attitudes of factions in the revolutionary coalition (Stempel 1981).[28] Even in regimes with an unchallenged predominant leader like Cuba's Castro, Iraq's Hussein, or Syria's Assad, leaders still engage in a continual game of maintaining that centralized power through dealings with support groups as well as the broader public (Hermann 1982; Lawson 1984). It would be a mistake, though, to overgeneralize about Third World political instability. In more established Third World systems, leadership politics largely parallels the processes found in both authoritarian states and advanced industrial democracies. Conflicts among Communist Party factions in Chinese foreign policy since the Cultural Revolution are not terribly different from those of the former Soviet Union (e.g., Barnett 1985). Similarly, competition for power over India's foreign policy does not diverge fundamentally from that in a number of European democracies (Vertzberger 1984b).

Recognition of the twin political games of building policy coalitions and retaining power is important for several reasons. First, both reinforce the point that domestic politics is a widespread and nonaberrant influence on foreign policy. Even if a government is either internally very cohesive or entirely secure in power, it is logically rare that a government would be entirely free of both. Second, recognition of these dual political games suggests that conceptualizations of domestic opposition need to be cast in a way that taps actors in *multiple* arenas of the political system (Hagan 1993). A broad assessment of domestic political influences must consider the constraints of both divisions within the leadership (and its support groups) and those of groups and movements in the wider political environment that threaten its hold on power. Third, and perhaps least obvious, these dual imperatives provide insight into the intensity of constraints faced by foreign policy makers. At one level the constraints of foreign policy choices are particularly severe when strong pressures associated with both games come together and *reinforce* each other.[29] Leaders confronting losses in both games may be unable to act on the issue, even when facing unrelenting international pressures. Post-Vietnam constraints in U.S. foreign policy often bring together the combined pressures of public opinion and congressional opposition. Similarly, extreme deadlock in fragmented parliamentary and authoritarian coalitions often is due to the combined impact of political competition and policy disagreements. However, as shown by Snyder (1991), the strong interaction of these games does not always lead to an inability to act. The combination of coalition building and fears of losing power create "logrolling" dynamics that, in turn, produce an intensely aggressive foreign policy that satisfies the interests of its component groups and their key support groups. It also permits leaders to manipulate foreign policy to fend off outside challenges to their hold on power. These dynamics occurred across a wide range of political settings, including Victorian England, Wilhelmine Germany, 1930s militarist Japan, and both superpowers during much of the cold war, and in all cases contributed to foreign policy aggressiveness and ultimately an overextension of national power.[30]

Alternative Political Strategies and Their Divergent Foreign Policy Effects

This section concerns the *dynamics* by which the games of building policy coalitions and retaining political power influence foreign policy. As with the games themselves, the literature on domestic politics and these foreign policy dynamics is not of a single mind. A substantial body of literature views domestic politics as undercutting a government's ability to take meaningful action in international affairs. Classic illustrations of this are the political constraints on British, French, and U.S. foreign policy in dealing with Fascist aggression in the 1930s. Leaders in these systems had considerable political incentive to avoid another world war. Even when leaders saw war as inevitable, as did U.S. President Roosevelt by 1940, they were precluded from taking forceful action by opposing elements within the government—the isolationist Congress, in FDR's case. Yet, equally often, other literature views domestic politics as propelling governments toward sharply intensified foreign policy confrontations and commitments. Indeed, in the twentieth-century's other world war, domestic politics is widely argued to have contributed to the major powers' failure to stop the drift to war by 1914. By then the governments of almost all the major powers, except Great Britain, faced mounting political crises tied to fragmenting governing authority and the legitimacy of the domestic political order. For the leaders of Germany, France, Russia, and Austria-Hungary going to war was clearly an attractive means for shoring up the domestic political position of each. In fact, these vulnerable leaders feared that backing down in July 1914 would bring about the collapse of their governments, if not the existing domestic order.

The significance of these alternative "pull" and "push" dynamics is that leaders may respond to domestic opposition (at any level) in fundamentally different ways, each of which has sharply different effects on foreign policy. In other words, there is *no single dynamic* by which political opposition affects foreign policy. Instead, leaders use alternative political strategies to respond to opposition in the foreign policy making process. Literatures treating this issue, if taken collectively, suggest the causal linkage between domestic politics and foreign policy reflects one of three general political strategies: "bargaining and controversy avoidance," "legitimization of the regime and its policies," or "insulating" foreign policy from domestic political pressures. As is argued in the following, these alternative responses are key to linking domestic politics to foreign policy.

Accommodation: bargaining and controversy avoidance. In accommodation, decision makers respond to opposition with restraint in foreign policy, as democratic leaders did prior to World War II. In the game of building policy coalitions, accommodation involves bargaining among the players necessary for the ratification and sustained implementation of the decision (Putnam 1988).[31] Compromise among the players is the typical "resultant" of the bargaining process as decision outcomes reflect a choice somewhere between the preferences of the original contenders on the policy (Allison 1971).[32] Where the opposition challenges the leaders' hold on power, accommodation centers on leaders' avoidance of domestically controversial actions that could discredit the overall leadership or upset internal balances within the ruling party (Salmore and Salmore 1978). Leaders seek to contain opposition, and thus retain political power, by avoiding publicly disputed policies and actions that make the country appear weak in international affairs or are closely associated with a widely acknowledged adversary. Whether in response to divisions within the government or opposition in the broader environment, the resulting foreign policy actions are similar. Politics constrains initiatives that are strong in intensity and commitment; in other words, the government engages in low-risk behavior and often avoids changes in policy. In the most extreme scenario, the leadership is deadlocked and unable to take any sort of meaningful action on a foreign policy issue, as occurred between FDR and the Congress right up to Japan's attack on Pearl Harbor.

Accommodation through bargaining and controversy avoidance is a pervasive phenomenon across various political settings but is most typically ascribed to democratic politics.[33] Cold war realists were interested in domestic politics largely because they feared democratic leaders would, as they did in the 1930s, have to accommodate resurgent isolationist or pacifist opinion in a way that would undercut the containment of communist power (Kennan 1951; Morgenthau 1951). Post-Vietnam public opinion research indicates that declining public support does lead U.S. presidents to avoid the use of force (e.g., Mueller 1971) and that polarized opinion precludes stable public support over the long term (e.g., Holsti and Rosenau 1984; Schneider 1983). Even some postrevisionists (e.g., Gaddis 1982), who usually focus on domestic pressures favoring hard-line policies, are careful to acknowledge that certain postwar administrations responded to domestic politics with a "strategy of containment" that, for example, reduced military spending by emphasizing cheaper forms of statecraft (Eisenhower's "New Look") and decreased use of U.S. forces abroad (the "Nixon Doctrine"). Notions of bargaining and controversy avoidance are most often the dominant theme in political analyses of foreign policies of parliamentary democracies with coalitions and/or factionalized ruling parties. Cases of coalition deadlock, such as the inability of Fourth Republic France to extricate itself from Algeria

(Andrews 1962), West German hesitation on early détente initiatives (Hanrieder 1970), and the Netherlands' refusal to deploy cruise missiles (Everts 1985), are traced to very broad compromises within the cabinet and fears that any controversial policy could provoke parliamentary defections. Comparable constraints are found in the dynamics of factional politics in Japanese foreign policy, although these processes are reinforced by strong norms of consensus building in that country's culture (Destler et al. 1976; Fukui 1978). Finally, these dynamics extend to models of foreign policy making outside the senior political leadership and are emphasized for countries with less politicized settings centering around bureaucratic and interest-group politics, such as Great Britain (Wallace 1976; Smith, Smith, and White 1988) and the Scandinavian countries (Sundelius 1982).

Accommodation is not limited to Western democratic politics. Discussions of bargaining and controversy avoidance, albeit within centralized and/or fluid settings, can be found in the theoretical and case study research on the foreign policy of the former Soviet Union and various Third World countries. Analyses of Soviet foreign policy on certain issues or episodes suggest that accommodation was often a central dynamic, particularly on issues provoking the clash of moderate and hard-line institutional and Party actors in the Central Committee (e.g., Aspaturian 1966). Politburo decision making often took the form of political accommodation, most notably the hesitation and delay in that body's reactive and vacillating handling of the 1968 Czechoslovak crisis (Valenta 1979). In fact, one could argue that bargaining and compromise prevailed during the Brezhnev era in Soviet foreign policy, due to the well-institutionalized character of leadership politics (Ross 1980) and Brezhnev's "consensual" style of decision making (Breslauer 1982). Among Third World analyses, accommodation is often similarly downplayed, but there are at least two exceptional situations. The first is literature that points to the institutional complexity of certain well-established political systems, such as the People's Republic of China (Barnett 1985), India (Vertzberger 1984b), and many in Latin America (Lincoln and Ferris 1984). The other Third World exception concerns situations of considerable political instability, which usually lead to legitimization strategies (as noted in the next section), and in which leaders are unable to manipulate the issue aggressively. This is an understudied phenomenon, although Kim's (1971) examination of South Korea's restrained negotiations on the post–World War II peace treaty with Japan is an excellent illustration of a leader's having to accommodate domestic opposition when acting on a volatile foreign policy issue.

Mobilization: legitimization of the regime and its policies. Under mobilization, leaders confront the opposition by asserting their own legitimacy, a strategy taken to the extreme by governments in the July 1914 crisis. Although hoping to deter that opposition, the intended effect is to mobilize new support for the regime and its policies—or, at least, prevent the defection of supporters. This strategy is most often associated with the game of retaining power in which a leadership manipulates foreign policy issues. Leaders seek to enhance the domestic political position of the regime in a number of ways: (1) appealing to nationalism and imperialist themes, or "scapegoating" or "bashing" foreign elements; (2) showing that the leaders have a special capacity and wisdom for maintaining the nation's security and international status; and/or (3) diverting attention away from divisive domestic problems (Levy

1988, 1989; Russett 1990; Snyder 1991). Political legitimization is also a strategy in building policy coalitions. Here, instead of accommodating the positions of adversaries, leaders build coalitions by aggressively selling their policy, often to audiences outside the regime, and thereby increase support for their initiative while discrediting their opponents (George 1980a; Trout 1975). Whatever the political imperative, the effect on foreign policy can be significant: strong, forceful (and typically conflictual) foreign policy actions that cast in the clearest possible light the position and ability of the political leadership. Although often limited to political theater (e.g., threats and promises to act), in the most extreme situations legitimization can drive a nation to commit itself to the use of force or to going to war, as occurred on the road to World War I.

If coalition building is mostly associated with democratic politics, then mobilization via regime and policy legitimization is often linked to authoritarian and especially Third World political systems. In ways that can be traced mainly to the lack of political institutionalization, politics via legitimization strategies is widely emphasized in literature on African, Asian, and especially Middle Eastern foreign policies (e.g., Dawisha 1990). An atmosphere of political instability usually precludes bargaining with opposition that is to be distrusted and unlikely to be accommodated though mutual compromise. Foreign policy is a correspondingly viable means for unifying the public and discrediting domestic adversaries. Although other issues might be divisive, assertions of the nation's independence and status (as well as threats to it) in world affairs play upon one of the few issues that a government can control and about which there is a domestic consensus (Weinstein 1972). Even in highly fragmented regimes, the result can be an extremely hostile and active pattern of foreign policy.[34] Among the more established authoritarian systems, legitimization in the foreign policy process is also a central theme. The political pressures for going to war in Germany, Russia, and Austria-Hungary all reflect the habits of leaders there to manipulate foreign threats and nationalism to channel growing mass participation (Levy 1988, 1989; Snyder 1991). Legitimization dynamics were also prevalent in the former Soviet Union, particularly as a pressure for hard-line, anti-Western policies dating back to Stalin and decisions to intervene in the Third World. In part this reflects the personality of certain leaders. Following Breslauer (1982), political legitimization is the primary strategy for "confrontational" leaders such as Khrushchev (and Yeltsin), whereas accommodation is preferred by the more "consensual" leaders like Brezhnev (and Gorbachev). Yet decisions for intervention in Africa (Valenta 1980b) and the Middle East (Spechler 1987) under the cautious Brezhnev show that he could lean toward assertive action when it provided a means for demonstrating his ideological credentials to critics of détente and other moderate policies toward the West (Gelman 1984).

Though not as widely emphasized as the strategy of accommodation in the U.S. foreign policy literature, political mobilization is a central theme in "postrevisionist" research into the political roots of hard-line, militant cold war policies (e.g., Paterson 1988; Dallek 1983). Trout (1975; Lowi 1967) argues that cold war presidents, including Truman at the advent of the cold war, were predisposed toward more simple and hard-line anti-communist policies because they were attractive to the voting public. Similarly, it is generally accepted that two decades of U.S. intervention in Vietnam was driven, in part, by the desire of successive presidents to demonstrate their foreign policy leadership skills and anti-communist credentials (e.g., Berman 1982; Gelb with Betts 1979). That this represents a broader pattern has been supported by recent empirical studies which show that U.S. presidents are generally more likely to use military force in international crises when they are politically vulnerable, particularly if their approval ratings are declining among their supporters (Ostrom and Job 1986; James and Oneal 1991; Morgan and Bickers 1992). But this is not limited to the United States. Fifth Republic French foreign policy starting with President de Gaulle is a classic case of an active and independent (from NATO) foreign policy designed to unify an otherwise divided public around a new domestic order and policy agenda (Morse 1973). Similarly, one analysis of British foreign policy argues that its military response to the Argentine invasion of the Falkland Islands was motivated, in part, by Prime Minister Thatcher's worries about low opinion ratings (Farrands 1988). Finally, legitimization strategies are not entirely absent from highly constrained settings such as Japan under the Liberal Democratic Party. There is evidence suggesting that "in some cases, [factional politics] can bring new policy initiatives and commitments to the surface" (Destler et al. 1976, 24), namely, when a prime minister believes that pushing a particular issue will enhance his or her faction's political standing.

Insulation: deflecting, suppressing, and overriding opposition. While both of the preceding strategies indicate a strong (though divergent) domestic political impact on foreign policy, it is important to keep in mind another political dynamic: the ability of leaders to insulate a foreign policy issue from domestic politics, even in a situation where significant opposition exists. The essence of this dynamic is that political leaders deflect or reduce domestic constraints on their foreign policy choices. Containing political pressures may involve a number of actions: ignoring opposition challenges, suppressing opponents entirely, or co-opting them with political favors or concessions on other policy issues. Alternatively, when leaders have strong preferences on the foreign policy issue, they are willing to override even strong opponents and hope that domestic controversies may be restricted to acceptable levels.[35] Indeed, if the two world wars correspond to these strategies, the cold war can be treated as a parallel case of avoiding war, partly because Soviet and U.S. leaders were able to keep hard-line and nationalistic domestic political pressures under control.[36]

Much of the U.S. foreign policy literature indicates that leaders can avoid domestic constraints. Some of these stem from critiques of the bureaucratic politics approach by pointing out when political divisions or leaders' sensitivity to them varies. Some of these studies suggest that conflict among contending political players might be contained by the nature of the situation. In crisis situations with immediate, visible threats, political constraints are contained by the contraction of government authority as well as the pressure for leaders to achieve consensus (Paige 1968; Hermann 1972). Other critiques stress that presidents are not passive, constrained actors in the political process but instead can assert their influence to overcome bureaucratic constraints (Perlmutter 1974; Krasner 1971). Analysts argue that a president can set up decision-making groups in a way that permits dissent, or "multiple advocacy," and allows the president to retain autonomy in making the final choice (George 1980a; Hermann 1993). Another strategy is engaging in trade-offs (or payoffs) across separate issues, in which the president and other executive actors gain bureaucratic or Congressional support by making concessions on separate issues, as, for example, in gaining support for arms control agreements (e.g., Johansen 1980) as well as the recent North American Free Trade Agreement. Whatever the strategy, it is important to keep in mind that, even in the face of strong opposition, leaders may insulate foreign policy from domestic pressures.

Non-U.S. cases also provide insight into conditions in which leaders are able to insulate foreign policy from domestic opposition. The research on parliamentary democracies shows that even a highly fragmented cabinet sometimes can get around internal constraints. In analyses of economic issues such as trade negotiations and exchange rate adjustments, Fukui (1978; n.d.) points out that Japan's Liberal Democratic Party factional leaders are willing to insulate certain issues from factional politics.[37] Studies of coalition decision making in Western Europe go even further; although there are numerous cases of these divided cabinets, there also are numerous examples of coalition governments whose members were able to reach meaningful agreements for foreign policy action. Particularly notable here are analyses of the highly "consensual" style of coalition decision making in the Scandinavian countries (Goldmann, Berglund, and Sjostedt 1986; Sundelius n.d.). Comparative studies of Dutch foreign policy show that the deadlock on NATO cruise missiles was not typical of the coalition government's actions on a variety of other issues (see Everts 1985). Additional episodes of Soviet military intervention demonstrate that, at times, Politburo members shared a strong consensus and did not develop policy within a context of political competition. In his analysis of the 1979 invasion of Afghanistan, for example, Valenta (1980b) found few political pressures in the Brezhnev Politburo that he observed in the Czechoslovak and Angola interventions.

These three strategies have considerable implications for research linking domestic politics to foreign policy. Instead of emphasizing one dynamic or the other (as is done in most of the literature), a general theoretical treatment of domestic politics and foreign policy must recognize the possibility of both the *"push"* and the *"pull"* of domestic opposition, as well as the fact that domestic pressure might be effectively contained (Hagan 1993). There is a need to recognize that leaders have choices in dealing with political opposition and that the strategies they employ ultimately tell us much about the effect of opposition on foreign policy. In other words, the linkage between opposition and foreign policy is an inherently *contingent* relationship. Ascertaining the foreign policy effects of opposition thus involves a sequence of two general questions: (1) Does opposition have an impact on foreign policy behavior? (2) If so, how and reflective of which strategy (accommodation or mobilization)?

The Subtle Effects of Domestic Politics on Foreign Policy

This chapter has argued that foreign policy making is an inherently political process, but it is equally important to recognize that domestic political effects on foreign policy are typically rather subtle. These domestic political games and strategies do not alone drive foreign policies but instead usually act as a supplementary influence on how leaders cope with more fundamental constraints from the international environment. A main contribution of research on "complex models of international politics" is the placement of domestic political influences into the context of pressures determined largely by the nation's position in the international system. For example, as Snyder (1991) carefully details, realist analyses are correct in stating that Wilhelmine Germany did face a real security problem of encirclement by powerful adversaries and that 1930s Japan was indeed seriously dependent on foreign sources of natural resources critical to its economy. Domestic politics did not lead leaders to imagine these situations but instead contributed to these leaders' inclinations to overreact to foreign threats and overextend their nation's power. Similarly, the logic of Putnam's (1988) "two-level bargaining" is not that domestic politics defines the economic interests but that domestic constraints affect the extent to which a government can respond to the constraints (and opportunities) of complex interdependence. Change in world politics is dictated mainly by the differential rates of growth in military and economic power (Gilpin 1981; Kennedy 1980). The contribution of foreign policy analyses is to show that domestic politics affects the ability of governments to adapt to change (Skidmore 1994) and the ways they respond to challenges of rising powers (Schweller 1992).

The subtle role of domestic political influences is further illustrated by case analyses of foreign policy decision making. Some of the key studies discussed above are insightful in placing political considerations (debates, public image, etc.) into the broader context of the leadership's consensus about the overall orientation of the nation's foreign relations. Political analyses of the U.S. cold war policies do not dispute an exceptionally strong national consensus on the militant containment of anti-Communism; political pressures instead involved questions of competing military strategies (Gaddis 1982; Gelb and Betts 1979) and the geographic range U.S. commitments (Snyder 1991). The Japanese Liberal Democratic Party factional disputes over how to respond to U.S. economic pressure did not question the party's consensus favoring close U.S.-Japan ties, but rather raised the issue of whether or not concessions should be made to the United States on *that* issue (Destler, Fukui, and Sato 1979). All Soviet leaders in 1968 saw the need to curtail Czechoslovak reforms; the Brezhnev Politburo debated the narrower question of *how* to pressure the Dubcek government, that is, through military force or by economic and political sanctions (Valenta 1979). Even in intensely fragmented Third World regimes, as in Iran during Khomeini's early days and Indonesia prior to Sukarno's overthrow, there was broad agreement that the superpowers were the threat; debates concerned *how much* dependence or contact with the West could be tolerated (Stempel 1981; Weinstein 1976). The collective insight here is that the magnitude of political influences is limited, even from a political decision-making perspective. The leadership's core shared beliefs and interests are the primary motivational basis of the *overall* direction of foreign policy. Domestic political debates and grandstanding typically involve the relatively narrow matters of how policy is to be implemented.

Seen in this context, one should not expect domestic political explanations to account for the general foreign policy goals and the identification of allies and adversaries. Rather, the effects of the domestic political games and strategies discussed throughout this chapter are tied to two more specific dimensions of foreign policy: commitment and risk taking. *Commitment* in foreign policy concerns the allocation of resources internationally or the entering into foreign agreements with other actors—or promises or threats to do either.[38] The foreign policies of the United States and Japan in the twentieth century illustrate the political bases of commitment. In the 1930s isolationism led to the "underextention" of U.S. power in countering recognized threats to interests in East Asia and Europe (Stein 1993). In Japan, army-navy logrolling propelled the expansionist leadership to overextend the country's resources in military actions in China and the Pacific Rim (Snyder 1991). The situation after World War II and throughout the cold war was the reverse: U.S. domestic politics ultimately contributed to an overextension of its power to Vietnam (e.g., Snyder 1991; Paterson 1988), while factional politics within Japan's ruling Liberal Democratic Party created the basis for an unusually reactive and passive foreign policy for a major power (e.g., Calder 1988; Hellmann 1969). The precise effect of domestic politics in these cases centered around the range of international commitments taken.

Risk taking concerns the propensity to initiate action that escalates a confrontation and invites costly foreign retaliation.[39] Analyses cited throughout this chapter consistently suggest that domestic politics affects the likelihood that leaders will use military force in ongoing confrontations. Debate over the level of necessary (and acceptable) risk is at the core of differences between "moderates" and "hard-liners," who must be accommodated in order to authorize the use of force. As illustrated by Soviet military interventions (e.g., Valenta 1979; Anderson 1982), Politburo debates led to compromises invoking economic and diplomatic pressures but not military force (as originally tried in Czechoslovakia) or resulted in decisions not to intervene at all (as in Poland in 1980). Similarly, unstable multiparty coalitions in parliamentary systems avoid risky behavior for fear of parliamentary defections leading to government's collapse. Part of the deadlock in Fourth Republic France's Algerian policy was that any intensification of its war effort would bring about the collapse of the government. Risk-taking propensities are also a primary manifestation of domestic political pressures, which leaders seek to contain by legitimizing the regime and its policies. In the July 1914 crisis the failure of major power leaders to resolve the crisis diplomatically was partially due to their fear that backing down in the crisis would undercut their governments' legitimacy. Expectation of domestic unrest was one factor predisposing German, French, Russian, and Austrian leaders toward finally going to war (Lebow 1981; Snyder 1991). More recently, the escalation of the long Argentine-British dispute over the Falkland Islands can be traced to the fact that both the Galtieri and Thatcher governments expected that a military victory could reverse their political decline at home (Levy and Vakili 1990; Farrands 1988). In these cases, domestic politics did not create the problem or crisis but did contribute to the regimes' propensity to escalate existing tensions through the use of military force and thus risk war.

The theoretical implication here is that the foreign policy effects of domestic political processes should to be viewed in the context of broader international dynamics. The intrinsic significance of domestic political processes is that they "diminish" or "amplify" the propensity to incur commitments and take risks internationally. Where there are strong, sustained pressures for domestic political accommodation, a government is unlikely to respond to systemic dictates. Leaders then reduce commitments and underreact to foreign threats. In contrast, efforts at political legitimization by mobilizing support amplify a leader's predisposition to act. If done in a sustained manner, the result is an overreaction to foreign threats and/or an overextension of the nation's capabilities. In sum, while not determining patterns of conflicts and issues in international affairs, domestic politics is an important influence determining how leaders manage those disputes.

■ Approaches Accounting for Domestic Political Impacts on Foreign Policy

This chapter's purpose is to explicate the core theoretical logic by which domestic politics can be linked to foreign policy. Drawing upon various areas of research on the topic, my argument is that this linkage is inherently complex, with dual domestic political imperatives and contingent upon leaders' choices of alternative political strategies with divergent foreign policy outcomes. Although pervasive across different types of political systems, their effects are subtle in that they modify government commitments and risk-taking propensities in the face of international threats and pressures. While it is hoped that this chapter improves upon earlier depictions of the relationship, it clearly complicates empirical research. Simple research designs comparing basic political systems and asserting a singular effect on foreign policy appear to be inadequate. This is not to say that broad, even cross-national, studies are impossible, but only that they are more complicated. Let me close by briefly identifying three basic approaches for gauging the magnitude and direction of the effects of domestic politics on foreign policy.

The first approach focuses on the *characteristics of opposition,* based on the assumption that leaders are more sensitive to some types of opposition than to others and that their political strategies depend on the opposition's location, strength, and intensity.[40] The "location" of opposition refers to its proximity to the process in which policy and leadership change decisions are made. Three arenas of opposition are (1) divisions within the leadership itself, (2) organized groups operating within (or having access to) state and party institutions, and (3) mass-level activity in the wider political environment.[41] The "strength" of opposition concerns the political resources (votes, military force, etc.) an opposition can use to block policy initiatives or threaten the leadership's hold on power. Opposition "intensity" is the extent to which it challenges the government leadership, and ranges from challenges limited to government policies to those seeking to evict the current leadership, and can even include demands for the entire political system's overthrow. Leaders are more likely to respond to opposition that is close to the centers of power, that controls the greatest amounts of political resources, and that poses the greatest challenge to the domestic political order. It might also be argued that leaders' choice of political strategies depends in part on the character of the opposition they face. For example, accommodation tactics might be employed more often with intraregime opposition that has moderate resources, and whose demands are not extreme. Mobilization strategies are typically used to cope with opposition outside the regime that is extreme in its demands and so strong that it rejects any accommodation with the regime.

A second approach considers *political system structure* based on the assumption that it broadly defines the context in which leaders cope with domestic political opposition. While I argue the imperative of looking at opposition in all types of political systems, structural arrangements remain important. Even though political system structure does not directly account for the presence or absence of opposition, it does shape games of building policy coalitions and competing for power as well as leaders' choice of political strategies. Democratization and institutionalization are two of the most important political system properties. Democratization concerns the extent to which opposition is able to challenge the government's leadership and policies (Dahl 1971). Conventional logic suggests that democratic leaders are more sensitive to opposition they cannot control and are forced to accommodate it in the foreign policy process, while their authoritarian counterparts are more prone to control or manipulate opposition by aggressively legitimizing the regime and its policies.[42] Equally important is political institutionalization, that is, the extent to which political norms and procedures (democratic or authoritarian) are established and accepted as legitimate and constrain the political behavior of the regime and its opponents (Huntington 1968). Leaders and opposition in highly institutionalized systems are willing to accommodate each other because of well-established norms and mutual trust. In contrast, political suppression and legitimacy strategies are more likely in the foreign policy processes of less institutionalized systems, because of distrust among opponents and the absence of political constraints on government coercion.[43]

A third approach considers the *characteristics of the decision setting* as a set of factors mediating the impact of domestic politics on foreign policy. This long-established approach asserts that situational (e.g., Hermann 1972; Snyder, Bruck, and Sapin 1954) and issue area (Art 1973; Zimmerman 1987) factors, along with the political configurations within the regime, influence what type of decision body manages a particular problem.[44] This research tradition is extended by Hermann, Hermann, and Hagan (1987; Hagan, Hermann, and Hermann n.d.) through the concept of the "ultimate decision unit." This concept refers to the decision-making body whose members have the authority and the power to commit national resources to a particular course of action in foreign policy. There are three types of decision units: predominant leader, single group, and a coalition of autonomous groups.[45] The significance of the decision unit scheme is that some of each type of unit are relatively open to outside pressures, while others are closed. Closed decision units are driven by their own internal dynamics and thus are generally unresponsive to and intolerant of broader opposition. These decision units include the highly principled predominant leader who is likely to ignore or suppress opposition, the single group with strong internal loyalty whose decision making is driven by strong group norms creating an atmosphere of "groupthink," and a coalition of autonomous actors without well-established decision rules that creates an atmosphere of extreme internal competition for power within the decision unit. Open decision units are, in contrast, more responsive to the positions of outside opposition, even to the point of attempting to accommodate them. They include pragmatic predominant leaders highly sensitive to actors who might challenge their regime, single groups without strong internal loyalty whose members represent their own constituencies, and coalitions with well-established rules that permit and require incorporation of outside actors and interests.

This concluding sketch hopefully points to the overall logic by which systematic research could take into account the complex, contingent, and pervasive nature of

Figure 8.1
Elements in the Logic of Politicial Explanations of Foreign Policy

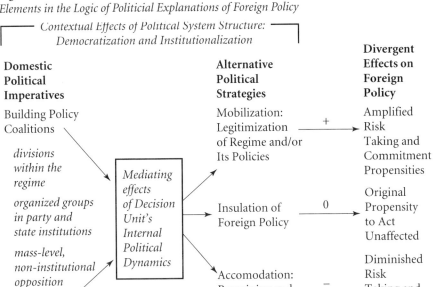

Note: This figure builds on Hagan (1993).

political influences on foreign policy, as outlined in this chapter. This explanatory logic is diagrammed in Figure 8.1. This scheme begins with the idea of dual domestic political imperatives of building policy coalitions and retaining political power that confront leaders coping with the international environment. The pressure of these games stems from the strength and intensity of political constraints, ranging from divisions within the political regime, organized groups in party and state institutions, and mass-level activity such as societal unrest and public opinion. Different levels of opposition are central (but not limited to) the games of coalition building and retaining political power, reflective of their proximity to foreign policy decision makers.

Next, the figure links these political games to foreign policy by way of leaders' choices of political strategies: (1) accommodation through bargaining and controversy avoidance, (2) insulating foreign policy from domestic politics by suppressing, buying off, or overriding opponents, and (3) mobilizing support (and isolating adversaries) by legitimizing the regime and its policies. Two kinds of contingencies likely affect the strategy, or mix of strategies, leaders employ to cope with opposition. The first are "contextual" and concern the conditioning role of political system characteristics, namely, the extent of democratization and institutionalization. The other contingency concerns the "mediating" effects of the relevant type of decision unit and, in particular, the degree to which its internal dynamics predispose its members to be "open" or "closed" to domestic politics. How these contingencies combine to shape leaders' responses to opposition ultimately determines how domestic politics affect foreign policy.

Finally, the political strategies of foreign policy makers, and the contingencies that predispose them to choose one or the other, may ultimately propel foreign policy actions in sharply divergent directions. Accommodation diminishes the government's ability to respond to international pressures or, in the extreme case of political deadlock, immobilizes the government entirely, causing it to grossly underreact to international pressures. In contrast, legitimization strategies amplify the predisposition to act on foreign threats and crises; the result is overreaction to international pressures. Domestic political perspectives that incorporate the complexity and pervasiveness of such effects provide important insights into the ongoing overreaction and underreaction of national governments to the international dynamics of balance of power, interdependence, and change.

■ Acknowledgments

This chapter draws upon several summer seminars at Ohio State University's Mershon Center and especially the contributions of Charles Hermann, Margaret Hermann, Valerie Hudson, and Eric Singer. This debt includes a reading of Charles Hermann's "Political Opposition as Potential Agents of Foreign Policy Change: Developing a Theory." The chapter has also benefited from the substantive ideas and editorial assistance of my research assistant, Deborah Wituski, and the book's editors, particularly Jeanne Hey.

■ Notes

1. The argument presented here should not be seen as posing an alternative to systemic explanations, but conforms with Haggard's (1991) "hegemony" of systemic theories. Except in the most extreme domestic situations (i.e., revolutions or other political convulsions), the role of domestic constraints would be to modify responses to international systemic structures. The primary challenge of research on domestic politics and foreign policy is to show the regularized interconnection between external pressures and internal politics, not to demonstrate that the latter is more important than the former.

2. Similar kinds of concerns have been raised more recently in Destler, Gelb, and Lake (1984). See Almond's (1950) *American People and Foreign Policy* for the most important systematic attempt by a political scientist to gauge isolationist sentiment in U.S. politics at the beginning of the cold war.

3. The literature on interservice rivalries richly describes the contending organizational positions and the compromises over budgets and weapons systems development. See, in particular, Caraley (1966), Davis (1967), Huntington (1961), Schilling, Hammond, and Snyder (1962), and Hammond (1963).

4. Overviews of the political setting of U.S. foreign policy since Vietnam are Nathan and Oliver (1987) and Rosati (1993). On Congress, in particular, see Frank and Weisband (1979), Spanier and Nogee (1981), and Destler (1986). The current major works on public opinion since Vietnam include Holsti and Rosenau (1984), Wittkopf (1990), and Schnieder (1983). Political economy analyses of the U.S. as a "weak" state include Krasner (1978, 1988), Katzenstein (1976), and Ikenberry, Lake, and Mastanduno (1988).

5. The most important of the many critiques of the bureaucratic politics approach are Art (1973), Krasner (1971), Perlmutter (1974), and Bendor and Hammond (1992). Also important are alternative conceptions of the decision-making process concerning "groupthink" (Janis 1982), cognitive processes (Steinbruner 1974), and presidential decision-making styles (George 1980b). For a synthesis of these perspectives, which are typically treated as competing alternatives, see Hermann (1993).

6. The postrevisionist literature represents an attempt to find a middle ground on the question of who was to blame for the cold war, and thus falls between orthodox perspectives (arguing the United States reacted to Soviet aggression) and revisionist perspectives (holding the capitalist U.S. system threatened the Communist bloc). Along with Gaddis's work, key general postrevisionist works include Dallek (1977), Paterson (1988), and Yergin (1977). On U.S. intervention in Vietnam, works by political scientists that employ a parallel logic include Gelb and Betts (1978) and Berman (1982).

7. This was partly because early efforts sought to assess the empirical validity of Rosenau's "genotypes" (e.g., East and Hermann 1974; Moore 1974b), but also because most researchers assumed political constraints on foreign policy could be traced to democratization (e.g., Moore 1974a; Salmore and Salmore 1970; Russett and Monsen 1975). Other studies employ democratization as an intervening variable and find that it conditions the effects of leader personality (Hermann 1980), political opposition (Hagan 1993), and domestic conflict (Wilkenfeld et al. 1980)

8. A very extensive empirical literature examines the cross-national, statistical association between domestic and foreign conflict. See, for example, Wilkenfeld (1973), Hazelwood (1975), and James (1988).

9. See cross-national analyses by Geller (1985) and Hagan (1987, 1993), both of which build on the early empirical work of Salmore and Salmore (1972, 1978).

10. Rosenau (1966) raised this criticism most forcefully as part of his call for a field of comparative foreign policy, but certainly by the 1980s he recognized the theoretical and methodological importance of more recent case study work (Rosenau 1987b).

11. General theoretical frameworks on Soviet foreign policy that stress domestic political factors include Aspaturian (1966), Bialer (1981), Dallin (1981), Simes (1986), and Valenta (1979, chapter 1). Good kremlinological overviews detailing the general political dynamics of the Khrushchev and Brezhnev regimes are, respectively, Linden (1966) and Gelman (1984). Juri Valenta's (1979, 1980a, 1980b, 1984) case studies of Soviet decisions to use military force abroad are the most innovative in detailing the substance of debates and their impact on foreign policy.

12. In addition to Korany (1983, 1986a), important assessments of Third World foreign policy analyses include Weinstein (1972), Clapham (1977), and David (1991). Much of the theoretical work on Third World decision making is, expectedly, regionally specific and covers the Middle East (Korany and Dessouki 1984; Ismael and Ismael 1986; Dawisha 1990), sub-Saharan Africa (Good 1962; Shaw and Aluko 1984), Latin America (Lincoln and Ferris 1984; Muñoz and Tulchin 1984), and Asia (Vertzberger 1984a; Barnett 1985; and Chan 1979). Three excellent analytic cases studies of the politics of foreign policy are Vertzberger's (1984b) analysis of India's 1962 border conflict with China, Weinstein's (1976) examination of Indonesia's confrontation with the West under Sukarno, and Kim's (1971) study of the making of Korea's postwar peace treaty with Japan.

13. Among the Western democracies, the research on the politics of Japanese foreign policy decision making is particularly impressive, led by the research of Haruhiro Fukui. It includes both theoretical overviews of the domestic political actors and processes (Calder 1988; Destler et al. 1976; Fukui 1977a; Hellmann 1969; Hosoya 1976; Ori 1976;

Pempel 1977; Scalapino 1977) and thorough case studies of various types of both security issues (e.g., Fukui 1970, 1977a; Hellmann 1969) and economic issues (e.g., Destler, Fukui, and Sato 1979; Fukui 1978). The work on other advanced democracies is a bit more dispersed but includes analyses of the Netherlands (Everts 1985), the Scandinavian countries (Goldmann, Berglund, and Sjostedt 1986; Sundelius 1982), Israel (Brecher 1972, 1975), and the European powers of Germany, France, and Britain (e.g., Hanrieder and Auton 1980; Hanrieder 1967; Morse 1973; Wallace 1976; Smith, Smith, and White 1988).

14. As noted earlier, the phrase is taken from Muller and Risse-Kappen (1993). Their essay provides a very useful survey of how domestic political phenomena are incorporated into international relations perspectives such as realism and complex interdependence.

15. Careful and precise discussions of how political perspectives can supplement systemic explanations of foreign policy can be found in Snyder (1991), Mastanduno, Lake, and Ikenberry (1989), Putnam (1988), and Siverson and Starr (1994).

16. See Katzenstein (1978) for comparative analyses of statist arrangements in the United States, Japan, and various Western European nations.

17. Cross-national, empirical assessments showing that foreign policy patterns (e.g., alignments) can change as a result of changes in domestic political regimes are Hagan (1989), Moon (1985), and Siverson and Starr (1994).

18. This has spawned a large amount of empirical research demonstrating the absence of war among democracies, even if also finding that they are otherwise as war prone as authoritarian systems (e.g., Chan 1984; Maoz and Abdolali 1989; Maoz and Russett 1993; Schweller 1992; Small and Singer 1976). Dixon (1993) extends the argument to propensity for greater cooperation, while Maoz (1989) links war proneness to the political development with the conclusion that states undergoing radical political change are most likely to enter into foreign conflicts. See also Neack's essay (chapter 13) in this volume.

19. Snyder (1991), for example, argues that the fragmentation of political authority (i.e., cartelization) and resulting bargaining, or "logrolling," among contending hard-line groups contributed to aggressive and overextended foreign policies in Victorian Britain, pre–World War I Germany, 1930s Japan, as well as the Soviet Union and the United States at the height of the cold war. Lamborn (1991) examines political dynamics in Britain, France, and Germany across the two world wars, and his detailed case studies also illustrate general political dynamics common to both authoritarian and democratic systems. Compared with the democracy/war-proneness studies, there have been far fewer studies of these kinds of nonstructural political phenomena, except for Domke (1988), Morgan and Campbell (1991), and Morgan and Schwebach (1992). These literatures are brought together and analyzed in Hagan (1994).

20. Coalition-building processes are also at the core of foreign policy models of domestic structure (e.g., Mastanduno, Lake, and Ikenberry 1989; Lamborn 1991; Risse-Kappen 1991) and of models of single group and coalitional decision units (Allison 1971; Hagan, Hermann, and Hermann n.d.; also Snyder and Diesing 1977). The crisis of authority in the policy process underlies some of the arguments that democracies are less war prone than authoritarian systems with highly centralized governments.

21. Rich comparisons of U.S. and British foreign policy decision-making arrangements are found in Neustadt (1970) and Waltz (1967), and differences between the United States and Japan are overviewed in Destler et al. (1976) and Destler, Fukui, and Sato (1979).

22. Furthermore, the power of bureaucracies and interest groups is enhanced by this extreme fragmentation of leadership authority. Not only does it provide for more

points of access for these particularistic interests, but these actors outside the cabinet also may become important political allies for squabbling central authorities.

23. Thus, for example, even on the critical issue of containing Czechoslovak reforms in the late 1960s, the Brezhnev Politburo was both pressured by the Central Committee and internally divided over the relative merits of military force as opposed to economic and political sanctions. It acted only after eight months of debate and internal wavering (Valenta 1979).

24. For discussions of the fragmentation of political authority in Wilhelmine Germany see Kennedy (1980), Lamborn (1991), and Snyder (1991).

25. Compared to pre–World War I Germany, cartelization appears to have been more fluid, with factionalism within major actors as well as ties with various civilian players. On Japanese foreign policy making in the 1930s, see Fukui (1977b), Hosoya (1976), and Snyder (1991).

26. The concept of the predominant leader is developed by Margaret Hermann in Hermann, Hermann, and Hagan (1987) and in Hagan, Hermann, and Hermann (n.d.). Historical examples are Germany's Bismarck and Hitler and the Soviet Union's Stalin, while contemporary cases are Cuba's Castro, North Korea's Kim Il-Sung, Iraq's Sadaam Hussein, Syria's Assad, as well as the first generation of many African postcolonial rulers.

27. Political survival is pervasive in foreign policy explanations of war (e.g., Levy 1989; Lebow 1981). The task of retaining power is central to the logic of various general foreign policy models (e.g., Hudson, Sims, and Thomas 1993; Salmore and Salmore 1978; Van Belle 1993), particularly the extensive empirical research on the linkage between domestic conflict and foreign conflict (e.g., James 1988; Wilkenfeld 1973).

28. Other well-documented cases of foreign policy making by similarly unstable coalitions include Syria prior to the June 1967 War (Bar-Siman-Tov 1983), Indonesia's confrontation with the West under Sukarno (Weinstein 1976), Argentina's invasion of the Falkland Islands (Levy and Vakili 1990), and China during the Cultural Revolution (Hinton 1972).

29. Risse-Kappen's (1991) model of public opinion and foreign policy effectively combines the dynamics of political survival and coalition building, showing that the latter is constrained in cohesive governments, which are then able to contain the pressures of public opposition.

30. In still other situations the tasks of building policy coalitions and retaining political power may be different, with the result that leaders may be able to act in ways that either game might separately suggest. Leaders, for example, might pursue a publicly unpopular policy because the regime is sufficiently cohesive to carry out its strong preferences, or because one of the critical members of the regime threatens to defect and bring down the regime immediately if it does not act. Another situation is where a severely fragmented regime engages in unexpectedly strong (though often erratic) foreign policy activity. This occurs when deadlocked actors within the regime seek to alter the situation by appealing to political groups outside the regime, often with virulent appeals to public nationalism and other unifying nationalist and ideological themes.

31. Accommodation via bargaining underlies statist approaches in the political economy literature (e.g., Ikenberry, Lake, and Mastanduno 1988; Katzenstein 1976; Krasner 1978) and models of economic policymaking (Destler 1986; Vernon, Spar, and Tobin 1991).

32. Compromise is a central theme in the bureaucratic politics case research on U.S. national security policy, as cited in note 3.

33. Much of the international relations theory on pacific democracies rests upon the idea that domestic politics inhibits foreign policy makers (e.g., Doyle 1986). Lamborn (1991) treats domestic politics as a constraint on the risk propensities of both democratic and authoritarian belligerents.

34. This is true of the additional cases of unstable coalitions, as cited in note 29.

35. This is a critical point in any theory that incorporates domestic political phenomena into a broader theory of foreign policy. Any assessment of domestic political constraints must take into account that these pressures are balanced international imperatives and risks. Frameworks in this direction are developed by Lamborn (1991) and by Hudson, Sims, and Thomas (1993).

36. Nincic (1992), Snyder (1991), and Russett (1990) suggest that these dynamics can be contained by democratic systems before they provoke major wars or irreversible overextension of power.

37. These issues were then handled by senior ministerial bureaucrats, although it is important to note that these actors too were divided on the issue and unable to act much more effectively.

38. This definition is broadly based on Callahan (1982). Discussions of overextended commitments in international affairs are found in Snyder (1991) and Kennedy (1987), while Stein (1993) develops the theme of underextension.

39. The concept of risk taking in foreign policy is developed in Bueno de Mesquita (1981) and Lamborn (1991).

40. The articulation of the logic of this approach draws upon Hermann (1987b).

41. See Hagan (1993) for a complete discussion of the conceptualization and operationalization of organized opposition in terms of the following three properties. Mass-level opposition is the focus of cross-national analyses of domestic and foreign conflict (e.g., Wilkenfeld 1973; James 1988).

42. Of course, the importance of democratic constraints is demonstrated by the extensive literature that shows that democracies rarely fight wars with each other, although they are as war prone as authoritarian systems when fighting nondemocracies. See the literature cited in the first section of this chapter as well as the more extended discussion in Hagan (1994).

43. Several studies point to the importance of institutionalization as a broad foreign policy influence. Snyder's (1991) analysis of five cases of cartelized regimes shows that these pressures were contained in relatively institutionalized systems (mid-eighteenth-century Britain and the U.S. and U.S.S.R. during the cold war) but were not contained in less institutionalized systems (pre–World War I Germany and Japan in the 1930s). Maoz (1989) finds that newly established polities (both democratic and authoritarian) created through revolutionary processes are more prone to international disputes, as compared with more established systems undergoing evolutionary change. Hagan's analysis (1993) finds political influences on foreign policy are most pronounced for regimes in moderately institutionalized political systems, whose leaders have neither the power to suppress opposition nor the norms of consensus building to work with them. Finally, across the case study literature of the politics of foreign policy in non-U.S. settings, the contextual effects of institutionalization would seem as important as those of democratization (Hagan 1993, chapter 2).

44. It is widely accepted, for example, that in "crisis" situations policymaking becomes concentrated at the highest levels of government and debate is minimized by the pressures of high threat, short decision-making time, and surprise. Others argue that "redistributive" (Lowi 1967) and "institutionally grounded" (Art 1973) issues involve a greater

dispersion of authority and more intense conflict than do others of a less "zero-sum" nature.

45. Formal definitions of the three decision units are as follows. A predominant leader is a single individual with the authority to commit, irreversibly, national resources in response to a problem. A single group is an entity of two or more people who interact directly with all other members and who collectively are able to reach a decision without consulting outside entities (e.g., cabinets, juntas, and politburos). A coalition of autonomous groups has two or more politically autonomous groups (e.g., parties, institutions/bureaucracies), none of which alone has the ability to commit national resources without the support of all or some of the other actors. See Hagan (1993, 218–23) for a full discussion of adapting the decision-units approach to understanding how leaders respond to domestic opposition in foreign policy.

NINE

Event Data in Foreign Policy Analysis

Philip A. Schrodt, University of Kansas

■ Editors' Introduction

In this chapter Philip Schrodt reviews the development and use of event data to study foreign policy. Schrodt shows how the use of event data to study (usually) interstate behavior has been a part of the study of foreign policy from the beginnings of the field in the 1960s and continues to be important in the second generation of foreign policy analysis. He also discusses how new developments in theories, concepts, and technologies have changed how event data are generated, stored, and used; and how the questions addressed with event data have changed with the field's development. Schrodt discusses data sets that focus on actors (e.g., Great Britain, Iraq, the PLO, the UN) and others that focus on episodes (e.g., wars, crises, negotiation). These event data sets have provided the evidence of foreign policy for many who focus their research on the interaction among actors in world politics. Schrodt argues that in the second generation of foreign policy analysis, those using event data are trying to keep pace not just with technological innovations but also with conceptual changes as those in the field try to understand more complex processes and include more and different actors in the data sets.

Questions the reader should focus on when reading this chapter include the following: What are event data? What different types of event data are there? What types of foreign policy questions can be addressed with event data? What are some of the shortcomings of this approach to studying foreign policy? How are the changes in world politics and technology changing this methodology? And what types of interesting foreign problems can you think of that may be able to be studied with this type of method? ■

Foreign policy analysis developed at about the same time as the behavioral approach in political science. The objective of the behavioralists was to study political behavior using systematically measured variables, statistical techniques, and unambiguously stated hypotheses. In some areas of political science, the behavioralist studies used measurement techniques that had been developed earlier. For example, researchers attempting to model elections found that the traditional questions asked of potential voters in survey research—party affiliation, whether they had voted before, who they were planning to vote for, and so forth—provided a useful foundation for their studies. While the statistical methodologies and survey methods used in contemporary voting research are substantially more sophisticated than the voting surveys of the 1920s and 1930s, the basic measurement instrument—the public opinion survey—is the same.

No equivalent data existed in the field of foreign policy analysis. Traditional studies of foreign policy primarily used narrative sources such as documents, histories, and memoirs, and there was no way to directly analyze these in a statistical framework. This disjuncture necessitated the development of new methods for generating data. A variety of these methods have been discussed in the other chapters of this volume; this chapter will focus on one of the most commonly used measurement techniques of foreign policy behavior, event data.

The basis of many studies of foreign policy is the fundamental question "Who did what to whom?" For example, during the Nixon administration (1969–74), the United States and the Soviet Union had a relaxation of diplomatic tensions known as the *détente* period. This was reflected in a variety of foreign policy actions, including arms control agreements, a decrease in hostile rhetoric, increased trade, and increased cooperation in resolving disputes. A decision maker living during this period would have a general perception that the hostility between the two superpowers had decreased. This perception would be based on a general pattern of cooperative interaction, rather than on a single incident.

Event data are a formal method of measuring the phenomena that contribute to foreign policy perceptions. Event data are generated by examining thousands of newspaper reports on the day-to-day interactions of nation-states and assigning each reported interaction a numerical score or a categorical code. For example, if two countries sign a trade agreement, that interaction might be assigned a numerical score

Figure 9.1
U.S. Actions Toward the Soviet Union, 1948–78

Source: COPDAB scores in Goldstein and Freeman (1990, 162).

of +5, whereas if the two countries broke off diplomatic relations, that would be assigned a numerical score of -8. When these reports are averaged over time, they provide a rough indication of the level of cooperation and conflict between the two states.

Figure 9.1 shows the actions that the United States directed toward the Soviet Union for the period 1948–78 as measured by the Conflict and Peace Data Bank (COPDAB) event data set collected by the late Edward Azar (1980, 1982). In the COPDAB coding scheme, negative numbers indicate conflictual behavior; positive numbers indicate cooperation. COPDAB is based on the *New York Times* and a variety of regional newspaper sources; the data cover the period 1948–78.

The COPDAB time series shows three general periods. The early cold war (1948–62) is characterized by uniformly negative relations, though these are more stable in the late 1950s than in the early 1950s. A partial "thaw" occurs in 1962–70 following the Cuban missile crisis, with the relationship being neutral. Finally, the 1970–78 period shows the rise and fall of the détente policy. Other event data sets covering the 1980s record the "new cold war" of the early Reagan period followed by the improved relations that occur when Gorbachev comes to power in the USSR (see Goldstein and Freeman 1990).

The event data record of U.S.-Soviet interactions corresponds closely to the patterns one would expect from a historical study. Moreover, the event data can also be used to fine-tune that chronology. For example, while Nixon clearly intended to implement a détente policy from the beginning of his administration in 1969, there was continued disagreement between the United States and Soviet Union over U.S. involvement in Vietnam, the 1968 Soviet invasion of Czechoslovakia, and other issues, so the interaction pattern is not actually positive until 1971. Positive interactions peak about the time of Nixon's resignation in 1974; the event data scores then decline during the two years of the Ford administration and return to post–Cuban missile crisis levels by 1976.

Figure 9.2 shows another example of the use of event data to chart the evolution of a complex international interaction, the Palestinian *intifada* (uprising) that

Figure 9.2
Israeli-Palestinian Interactions, 1982–92

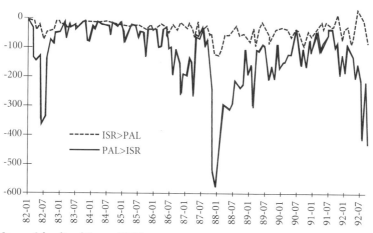

Source: Schrodt and Gerner (1994).

began in December 1987. This chart is based on the coding of news stories on Israeli-Palestinian interactions reported by the Reuters international news agency. These reports were automatically coded by a specialized computer program into the World Events Interaction Survey (WEIS) event data categories developed by Charles McClelland (1976). The categorical WEIS events were then converted to a monthly numerical score using a scale devised by Goldstein (1992); as in Figure 9.1, negative scores indicate conflict and positive scores indicate cooperation.

This time series shows the pattern of interactions—largely uses of force—in considerable detail. The initial increase in conflictual activity in 1982–83 corresponds to Israel's invasion of Lebanon, which was initially directed against Palestine Liberation Organization forces. The invasion is followed by a period of five years of relative quiet, though a separate series of event data on Israel's interactions with *Lebanon* during this period shows a great deal of conflict as opposition to Israeli forces shifts from the PLO to various Lebanese groups. The *intifada* begins abruptly in December 1987 and then gradually declines over the next five years, though there is another upsurge in violence following the election of a Labor government in Israel in the summer of 1992.

As with the case of the U.S.-Soviet interactions, this time series gives a more exact measure of the patterns of events over time. For example, while the *intifada* follows a lull in conflict during the summer of 1987, the event data also show a general increase in conflict beginning about eighteen months earlier. This increase may have been a precursor to the larger uprising (see Schrodt and Gerner 1994).

As these two figures illustrate, event data can be used to summarize the overall relationship between two countries over time. The patterns shown by event data usually correspond to the narrative summaries of the interactions found in historical sources, but unlike narrative accounts, event data can be subjected to statistical analysis. As a consequence, event data are frequently used to study foreign policy outcomes and some characteristics of the international environment within which foreign policy decisions occur.

■ Creating Event Data

The creation of event data is basically a process of *content analysis* (see Krippendorff 1980; Weber 1990) and involves three steps. First, a source or sources of news about political interactions is identified. This could be an internationally oriented newspaper such as the *New York Times,* a set of regional newspapers and news magazines, a news summary such as *Facts on File* or *Deadline Data on World Affairs,* or a news wire service such as Reuters or the Associated Press. As will be discussed later, the choice of the event source can have a substantial effect on the number and type of events reported.

Second, a coding system is developed, or a researcher may decide to use an existing coding system such as WEIS or COPDAB. The coding system specifies what types of political interactions constitute an "event," identifies the political actors that will be coded (for example, whether nonstate actors such as international organizations and guerrilla movements will be included in the data set), specifies the categories of events and their codes, and specifies any information to be coded in addition to the basic event. For example, the COPDAB data set codes a general "issue area"—whether an action is primarily military, economic, diplomatic, or one of five other types of relationship. WEIS, in contrast, codes for specific "issue arenas" such as the Vietnam War, Arab-Israeli conflict, and SALT negotiations.

In a project using human coders, these coding rules are collected into a manual used to train coders; these manuals are often fifty or more pages in length and deal with a variety of contingencies that coders may encounter. The third stage involves training coders so that a news story will be assigned the same codes irrespective of the individual coding it. Coders in event data projects generated in universities are typically graduate students or advanced undergraduates in political science. The training stage is frequently quite time-consuming, but with sufficient training, most projects train coders to the point where two coders will assign the same code to a news report in 85 to 90 percent of the cases (see Burgess and Lawton 1972). In a project dealing with a relatively short period—for example the 1990–91 Persian Gulf crisis—a single researcher may do all of the coding to ensure that a single coding standard is used.

In a machine-coding project, coding rules are implemented in a computer program, usually using extensive dictionaries that identify actors and events and then associate these with specific codes (see Gerner et al. 1994; Lehnert and Sundheim 1991). These dictionaries are typically developed by coding a large number of test sentences from the actual data and adding the appropriate vocabulary when the machine makes an error.

When these three tasks have been completed, coding can be done. Generating a large human-coded data set such as WEIS or COPDAB takes a number of years, during which time intercoder reliability must be maintained despite the turnover in the coders. Machine coding is much faster—a computer program can code hundreds of events per minute—but machine coding is restricted to simple event categories and cannot extract more complicated types of information from a story.

Table 9.1 shows a sample of the lead sentences of reports on the Reuters news wire that preceded Iraq's invasion of Kuwait in August 1990.[1] Generally each lead corresponds to a single event, though some sentences generate multiple events. For example, the report "July 23, 1990: Iraqi newspapers denounced Kuwait's foreign minister as a U.S. agent Monday" corresponds to an event in the WEIS event coding scheme: the WEIS category 122 is defined as "Denounce; denigrate; abuse." In this event Iraq is the *source* of the action and Kuwait is the *target*. Together, these generate the event record "900723 IRQ KUW 122" where "900723" is the date of the event, IRQ is a standard code for Iraq, KUW is the code for Kuwait, and 122 is the WEIS category. Table 9.2 shows the Reuters stories converted to WEIS events.

Event data analysis relies on a large number of events to produce meaningful patterns of interaction. The information provided by any single event is very limited; single events are also affected by erroneous reports and coding errors. However, important events trigger other interactions throughout the system. For example, while Iraq's invasion of Kuwait by itself generates only a single event with WEIS code 223—military force—the invasion triggers an avalanche of additional activity throughout the international system as states and international organizations denounce, approve, or comment, so the crisis is very prominent in the event record.

Table 9.1 Reuters Chronology of 1990 Iraq-Kuwait Crisis

July 17, 1990: RESURGENT IRAQ SENDS SHOCK WAVES THROUGH GULF ARAB STATES

Iraq President Saddam Hussein launched an attack on Kuwait and the United Arab Emirates (UAE) Tuesday, charging they had conspired with the United States to depress world oil prices through overproduction.

July 23, 1990: IRAQ STEPS UP GULF CRISIS WITH ATTACK ON KUWAITI MINISTER

Iraqi newspapers denounced Kuwait's foreign minister as a U.S. agent Monday, pouring oil on the flames of a Persian Gulf crisis Arab leaders are struggling to stifle with a flurry of diplomacy.

July 24, 1990: IRAQ WANTS GULF ARAB AID DONORS TO WRITE OFF WAR CREDITS

Debt-burdened Iraq's conflict with Kuwait is partly aimed at persuading Gulf Arab creditors to write off billions of dollars lent during the war with Iran, Gulf-based bankers and diplomats said.

July 24, 1990: IRAQ, TROOPS MASSED IN GULF, DEMANDS $25 OPEC OIL PRICE

Iraq's oil minister hit the OPEC cartel Tuesday with a demand that it must choke supplies until petroleum prices soar to $25 a barrel.

July 25, 1990: IRAQ TELLS EGYPT IT WILL NOT ATTACK KUWAIT

Iraq has given Egypt assurances that it would not attack Kuwait in their current dispute over oil and territory, Arab diplomats said Wednesday.

July 27, 1990: IRAQ WARNS IT WON'T BACK DOWN IN TALKS WITH KUWAIT

Iraq made clear Friday it would take an uncompromising stand at conciliation talks with Kuwait, saying its Persian Gulf neighbor must respond to Baghdad's "legitimate rights" and repair the economic damage it caused.

July 31, 1990: IRAQ INCREASES TROOP LEVELS ON KUWAIT BORDER

Iraq has concentrated nearly 100,000 troops close to the Kuwaiti border, more than triple the number reported a week ago, the Washington Post said in its Tuesday editions.

August 1, 1990: CRISIS TALKS IN JEDDAH BETWEEN IRAQ AND KUWAIT COLLAPSE

Talks on defusing an explosive crisis in the Gulf collapsed Wednesday when Kuwait refused to give in to Iraqi demands for money and territory, a Kuwaiti official said.

August 2, 1990: IRAQ INVADES KUWAIT, OIL PRICES SOAR AS WAR HITS PERSIAN GULF

Iraq invaded Kuwait, ousted its leaders and set up a pro-Baghdad government Thursday in a lightning pre-dawn strike that sent oil prices soaring and world leaders scrambling to douse the flames of war in the strategic Persian Gulf.

Source: Reuters.

Table 9.2 WEIS Coding of 1990 Iraq-Kuwait Crisis

Date	Source	Target	WEIS Code	Type of Action
900717	IRQ	KUW	121	CHARGE
900717	IRQ	UAE	121	CHARGE
900723	IRQ	KUW	122	DENOUNCE
900724	IRQ	ARB	150	DEMAND
900724	IRQ	OPC	150	DEMAND
900725	IRQ	EGY	054	ASSURE
900727	IRQ	KUW	160	WARN
900731	IRQ	KUW	182	MOBILIZATION
900801	KUW	IRQ	112	REFUSE
900802	IRQ	KUW	223	MILITARY FORCE

■ The History of Event Data in Foreign Policy Analysis

Event data were originally developed by Charles McClelland in the early 1960s as a bridge between the traditional approach of diplomatic history and the new quantitative analysis of international politics advocated in the behavioral approach.[2] McClelland reasoned that history could be decomposed into a sequence of discrete events such as consultations, threats, promises, acts of violence, and so forth. Event data formed a link between the then-prevalent general systems theories of international behavior and the textual histories which provided an empirical basis for understanding that behavior. According to McClelland,

> International conduct, expressed in terms of event data, is the chief dependent variable of international relations research.... It is interesting that a starting point is provided as readily by the ordering principle of classical diplomatic history as by the basic concepts of general system analysis. Thus, we may assert that the prime intellectual task in the study of international relations is...to account for the relations among components of the international system by...tracing recurring processes within these components, by noting systematically the structure and processes of exchange among the components, and by explaining, finally, the linkages of within-component and between-component phenomena. Obviously the classical definition of diplomatic history is less ponderous and more literary than the general system definition of the task but both...carry about the same information and involve nearly the same range of choices of inquiry and analysis (1970, 6).

During the 1960s and 1970s, several event data collections were assembled. The COPDAB (Azar 1980, 1982; Azar and Sloan 1975) and WEIS (McClelland 1976) data sets attempt to code all interactions by all states and some nonstate actors such as the United Nations and various national liberation movements; the COPDAB and WEIS coding schemes have subsequently been used in a number of other data sets. A variety of domestic and international event data were also collected in the context of more general data sets such as Rummel's "Dimensionality of Nations" collection (Rummel 1972a), the *World Handbook* (Taylor and Hudson 1972), and various internal conflict data sets collected by Gurr (1974); these usually focus on a limited set of actions such as uses of force, domestic violence, or changes of government. The

Comparative Research on the Events of Nations (CREON) data set (Hermann et al. 1973), which is specifically designed for the analysis of foreign policy, was also developed during this period.

For a period in the late 1970s and early 1980s, event data were collected by United States governmental agencies such as the Department of State, the Department of Defense, and various intelligence agencies (see Andriole and Hopple 1984; Daly and Andriole 1980; Hopple 1984; Hopple, Andriole, and Freedy 1984; Laurance 1990), and by private political consulting firms such as CACI Inc. The Department of State experimented with coding event data for a small set of states in 1971 in its Foreign Relations Indicator Project (FRIP) (see Lanphier 1975). The Pentagon's Defense Advanced Research Project Agency (DARPA) sponsored a large-scale project in the 1970s to develop event data models for crisis forecasting and management, and in the early years of the Reagan administration a major event data collection and analysis effort was undertaken by the National Security Council staff in the White House.

These efforts apparently had little long-term impact on the formulation of foreign policy, though many of these event data sets are now available in the archives of the Inter-University Consortium for Political and Social Research at the University of Michigan and are used in research.[3] Laurance (1990) analyzes the reasons for the limited impact of event data on policy, which include the failure to coordinate the event data projects with the analysts and policymakers who were supposed to use the data, the absence of guidelines on how event data could be used with traditional, nonstatistical sources of information, and the absence of user-friendly analytical tools.

Event data collection experienced a hiatus in the mid-1980s, though the COPDAB and WEIS data continued to be refined, other data sets such as CREON were used in research, and some new data sets focusing on international crises—notably Leng's Behavioral Correlates of War (BCOW) (Leng 1987) and Sherman's SHERFACS (Sherman and Neack 1993)—were developed during this time. Large-scale event data efforts were revived in the early 1990s in the second phase of the National Science Foundation's Data Development in International Relations project (DDIR), directed by Dina Zinnes and Richard Merritt (see Merritt, Muncaster, and Zinnes 1993). Rather than simply extending the work of the 1970s, DDIR emphasized the development of new approaches, with particular emphasis on exploiting the computing power available in personal computers and using machine-readable news sources.

■ Event Data Sets

Event data sets fall into two general categories. Actor-oriented data sets record all interactions between a set of actors for a specific period of time, for example the Middle East 1949–69. Episode-oriented sets look at the events involved in a specific historical incident, usually an international crisis or use of force.

Actor-Oriented Data Sets

WEIS. The WEIS coding scheme classifies events into sixty-three specific categories; these are organized into twenty-two general categories such as "Consult,"

"Reward," "Protest," and "Force" (see Table 9.3). The general categories form a very rough cooperation-conflict continuum. WEIS coding was the de facto standard used by the U.S. government–sponsored projects during the 1970s, and consequently a number of the data sets in the ICPSR use the WEIS scheme.

The WEIS data set available at the ICPSR covers only eleven years (1966–77) and contains only about ninety thousand events; the source text is the *New York Times*. Data after 1977 have continued to be coded by McClelland and several of his students (e.g., Rodney Tomlinson at the U.S. Naval Academy), but the full series is not available in the public domain at the present time. DDIR has sponsored the development of a machine-coding system for WEIS (Gerner et al. 1994), which could facilitate the generation of WEIS-coded data in the future.

Because most common statistical routines, such as regression analysis, use numerical rather than categorical data, WEIS events are often averaged into numerical scores before being analyzed. Vincent (1979) and Goldstein (1992) provide two such scales that assign numbers on a cooperation-conflict continuum to each WEIS category; Figure 9.2 was produced using Goldstein's scale. WEIS codes can also be translated into the COPDAB scale, though one cannot translate from COPDAB to WEIS because COPDAB makes fewer distinctions in the type of event.

COPDAB. The COPDAB data set is substantially larger in size and scope than WEIS, with about 350,000 international events for the period 1948–78. COPDAB uses a number of different news sources rather than depending solely on the *New York Times;* in particular, it uses a variety of regional sources to cover events outside of North America and Europe.[4] In contrast to the categories in WEIS, COPDAB uses an ordered coding scheme that goes from 1 to 16 (see Table 9.4) supplemented by a numerical cooperation-conflict intensity scale developed by Azar and Sloan (1975).

Table 9.3 Examples of WEIS Event Codes

11. REJECT

111	Turn down proposal, reject protest demand, threat
112	Refuse, oppose, refuse to allow

12. ACCUSE

121	Charge, criticize, blame, disapprove
122	Denounce, denigrate, abuse

13. PROTEST

131	Make complaint (not formal)
132	Make formal complaint or protest

17. THREATEN

171	Threat without specific negative sanctions
172	Threat with specific nonmilitary negative sanctions
173	Threat with force specified
174	Ultimatum: threat with negative sanctions and time limit specified

18. DEMONSTRATE

181	Nonmilitary demonstration, walk out on
182	Armed force mobilization, exercise, and/or display

Source: McClelland (1976).

Table 9.4 Examples of COPDAB Event Codes

09	Nation A expressed mild disaffection toward B's policies, objectives, goals, behaviors with A's government objection to these protestations; A's communiqué or note dissatisfied with B's policies in third party.
10	Nation A engages in verbal threats, warnings, demands and accusations against B; verbal, hostile behavior.
11	Nation A increases its military capabilities and politicoeconomic resources to counter Nation B's actions or the latter's contemplated actions; A places sanctions on B or hinders B's movement in waterways or on land and attempts to cause economic problems for B.

Source: Azar and Sloan (1975).

COPDAB coding also classifies an event into one of eight types—for example symbolic, political, military, economic, or cultural.

Under DDIR sponsorship, a group at the University of Maryland directed by Gurr and Davies is extending the COPDAB data set from 1990 to the present (Davies and McDaniel 1993). Their project, the Global Event Data System (GEDS), is based on the COPDAB framework but uses a much richer data format that preserves much of the original text reporting the event; GEDS also codes a number of internal political actors, particularly ethnic groups.

CREON. The Comparative Research on the Events of Nations data set (East, Salmore, and Hermann 1978; Hermann et al. 1973) is specifically designed for the study of foreign policy interactions. Its basic event coding scheme is similar to that of WEIS, but CREON in addition codes over 150 variables dealing with the context of the event, related actions, and internal decision-making processes. Unlike WEIS and COPDAB, CREON does not code all interactions during a period of time: instead, it covers a random sample of time periods during 1959–68 and a stratified sample of thirty-six nation-states, which contains a disproportionate number of developed and English-speaking countries. The purpose of CREON is to study the foreign policy *process,* rather than foreign policy output. In practice this means that CREON is better suited than WEIS or COPDAB to studying the linkages between the foreign policy decision-making environment and foreign policy outputs for specific decisions, but it cannot be used to study policy outputs over a continuous period of time or for countries not in the sample.

Other actor-oriented event data sets. While WEIS, COPDAB, and CREON are the largest actor-oriented data sets, a variety of smaller sets exist. As noted earlier, the ICPSR has several regionally specific, WEIS-coded data sets dating from the 1970s, and additional regional data sets are being collected at the present time. The South Africa Event Data set (SAFED) (van Wyk and Radloff 1993) is a WEIS-coded collection focusing on southern Africa for the period 1977–88; it has unusually dense coverage of nonstate actors such as guerrilla movements. Ashley (1980) assembled a data set focusing only on the interactions of the superpowers—the United States, Soviet Union, and People's Republic of China—for 1950–72; this contains about fifteen thousand events and is coded with a COPDAB-like scale.

Episode-Oriented Data Sets

BCOW. The Behavioral Correlates of War data set (Leng 1987) codes a sample of 38 major international crises over the period 1816–1975. Roughly half of these crises culminated in war and the other half were resolved without war. Most of the crises (31 out of 38) are in the twentieth century; about one-third (12) are post–World War II; and many of the crises preceding the two world wars are included in the sample. The BCOW event codes are an expanded version of the WEIS scheme, containing about one hundred categories and differentiating more clearly between verbal, economic, and military behavior. Leng (1993b) contains an extensive analysis of this data set.

BCOW uses multiple sources of information, including newspaper accounts, diplomatic histories, and chronologies (Leng 1987, 1). The number of events in each crisis range from 120 events in the 1889–90 British-Portugal crisis in southern Africa to 2,352 events in the 1956 Suez crisis. The ICPSR data set is accompanied by a very extensive coding manual that would allow a researcher to code additional crises in a manner consistent with the original data; it also includes some specialized software that can be used to analyze the data.

CASCON. The Computer-Aided System for the Analysis of Local Conflicts system (CASCON) codes the characteristics of sixty-six internal and international conflicts during the post–World War II period. The analytical framework is based on a study by Bloomfield and Leiss (1969) and is organized around six predefined conflict phases ranging from the issues leading to the initiation of the dispute to the resolution of the dispute. CASCON codes 540 "factors" for each crisis; some of these describe specific types of events; others describe contextual characteristics of the crisis such as whether the parties to the conflict are dependent on outside aid.

Table 9.5 Examples of BCOW Event Codes

Military Actions (sample from a total of 36 categories)
11212 International Peacekeeping Force
11333 Alert
21143 Change in Combat Force Level
31133 Fortify Occupied Territory

Diplomatic Actions (sample from a total of 35 categories)
12121 Negotiate
12362 Declare Neutrality
12213 Punish or Restrict Foreign Nationals
32151 Grant Independence to Colony

Economic Actions (sample from a total of 20 categories)
13121 Economic Negotiation
23121 Sell or Trade
23231 Pay for Goods or Services

Unofficial Actions (sample from a total of 11 categories)
14251 Proforeign Demonstration
14213 Antiforeign Demonstration
14152 Hostage Taking

Source: Leng (1987).

The current version of the data set, CASCON III (Bloomfield and Moulton 1989), is an integrated "decision support system" designed to help decision makers compare current crises with the historical data on the sixty-six CASCON crises; the system runs on a personal computer. The CASCON III system contains the conflict data set, a variety of analytical tools that can be used to compare conflicts, and a sub-system for entering new cases into the database. An earlier version of the data set, containing only fifty-two cases during the 1945–69 period and without the analytical software, is available from the ICPSR.

SHERFACS. The SHERFACS data set (Sherman and Neack 1993) codes over seven hundred international disputes and almost one thousand domestic disputes in the 1945–84 period. It combines several different coding schemes, including COPDAB event codes, the CASCON crisis phase structure, and a variety of conflict management variables originally used in the Butterworth (1976) data set in crisis mediation. SHERFACS is particularly strong on coding nonstate actors such as ethnic groups, transnational actors such as intergovernmental organizations, and nonnational actors such as multinational corporations.

An early version of SHERFACS is available from the ICPSR (Alker and Sherman 1982, 1986); the current version is being completed as part of the DDIR project. While SHERFACS is not part of an integrated software system like CASCON, Unseld and Mallery (1992; cf. Mallery n.d.) have been developing specialized software for analyzing the data and deriving general rules from it. This software is based on artificial intelligence techniques and could be generalized to work with other types of event data.

Other episode-oriented event data sets. As noted earlier, several other data collections available from the ICPSR such as *The World Handbook* contain some limited amounts of event data. Another example is the PRINCE Project data set (Coplin, O'Leary, and Shapiro n.d.). This data set was originally collected in conjunction with a computer simulation project and contains a small set of event data dealing with political issue positions for the period January 1, 1972, to June 30, 1972. Other data sets have been collected for the study of a specific crisis: for example, Lebovic (1993) coded events during the period prior to the 1991 Gulf War (August 2, 1990, to January 16, 1991) in order to analyze the impact of foreign policy "momentum" in that crisis.

■ Applications

Event data have been used in a variety of studies in foreign policy analysis. This section will briefly discuss five applications that illustrate some of the different analytical techniques employing event data.

Reciprocity in Superpower Interactions

In an extensive analysis reported in their book *Three-Way Street,* Goldstein and Freeman (1990) combine three event data sets—WEIS, COPDAB, and Ashley's superpower data—to create a time series of interactions between the United States, the Soviet Union, and the People's Republic of China, extending from 1948 to 1986.

These data are analyzed using a statistical technique called *vector autoregression,* which assesses the effects of a change in one variable in the system on other variables. The study is important in two respects. First, the forty-year time series clearly displays the major shifts in the relationships between three major powers, such as the cold war of the 1950s between the United States and the Soviet Union, the détente period of the early 1970s, and the Reagan-Brezhnev "New Cold War" of the early 1980s. Similarly, the effects of the Cultural Revolution and the Nixon rapprochement with China can be seen in the U.S.-Chinese relationship.

Goldstein and Freeman's statistical findings show that most of the interactions between the superpowers were reciprocal, that is, each state received interactions from other superpowers similar to those it projected to them. This pattern of reciprocity had been predicted by a number of theories, and more generally the study of reciprocal behavior has been a major focus of event data research.[5] The study also showed a great deal of inertia in the superpower relationships: the level of cooperation or conflict was maintained about the same level from year to year, changing only slowly.

Political Influence in Arms Transfers

Schrodt (1983) studies the effects of the international sale of weapons on international behavior using event data. One key concern in this arms transfer research is the "arms and influence" relationship: does the supplier of weapons gain political influence over the recipient? The study uses data from the Stockholm International Peace Research Institute (SIPRI) on weapons sales from the United States and the Soviet Union to a number of Middle Eastern countries. The COPDAB data set is used to measure cooperative and conflictual behavior between the supplier and the recipient. The statistical technique used was cross-correlation: the correlation between the level of sales and the cooperative or conflictual behavior at times before and after the arms transfer.

Figure 9.3
Cross-correlation of Arms Transfers and International
Cooperation from Recipient to Supplier

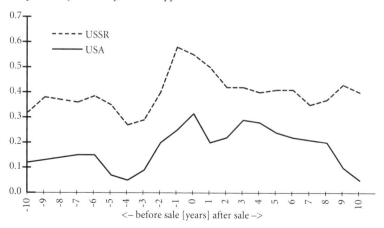

This technique was successful in demonstrating a number of features of the arms and influence relationship. As expected, there was no significant influence prior to the transfer except during the one or two years prior to the transfer when it was probably being negotiated, but the data showed statistically significant cooperation lasting for about five years after the transfer. The contrast between the United States and the Soviet Union was even more interesting. As expected, the cooperation of recipients with the Soviet Union was considerably higher than that with the United States: the Soviet Union gained more cooperation, in the short term, from its recipients. However, in the longer term, after about five years the Soviet Union also had significantly increased *conflict* with its recipients, whereas arms transfers did not significantly change conflictual behavior toward the United States. This result for the Soviet Union had been anticipated in some of the nonstatistical literature (cf. Pierre 1982, 81–82), where the tendency of the Soviet Union to alienate its arms recipients was known informally as the "Ugly Russian Problem."

Interdependence of International Interactions

Schrodt and Mintz (1988) use the COPDAB data set to study interactions between six Middle Eastern states: Jordan, Syria, Saudi Arabia, Kuwait, Iraq, and Iran, during the period 1948–78. The study looked at the probability that an interaction between one pair of nations—for example, Syria to Iran—would trigger other interactions, for example, Iran to Syria or Saudi Arabia to Iraq.

The study reached a number of conclusions—for example, we found that interactions almost always increase, rather than decrease, the probability of other interactions. However, in retrospect our most interesting finding was the prominent role of Kuwait: "When some interaction occurs with Kuwait, this interaction disproportionately sets off other interactions in the system. This initially seems counterintuitive because Kuwait is the least powerful of the states we are studying, though that status may be the *reason* Kuwait is so important. If this characteristic holds generally, we may find that minor powers are more important in determining interaction interdependence than major powers" (Schrodt and Mintz 1988, 227–28). This was written in 1984, six years before the 1990–91 Iraq-Kuwait crisis. The importance of Kuwait was deduced exclusively from the event data itself, rather than from a traditional political analysis.

Decision-Making Units and Foreign Policy

Margaret Hermann and Charles Hermann (1989) use the CREON data set to study the effect that the type of foreign policy decision-making unit has on the character of foreign policy. The types of decision-making units studied are "predominant leader," "single group," and "multiple autonomous actors." The nation-states in the CREON data set are coded into these categories according to an explicit set of coding rules; in many cases the category varies due to changes in governments and in some countries (e.g., Switzerland) differs depending on the foreign policy issue. The CREON event data provided the dependent variable, foreign policy behavior, which was coded for affect, commitment, and the choice of instruments of statecraft; the study also controlled for whether the unit was self-contained or could be influenced externally.

The results of the study are clearest on the issue of affect, where Hermann and Hermann report: "The single group decision units engaged in the most extreme behavior of the three types, evidencing the most conflictual behavior. Multiple autonomous actors were the least conflictual, with predominant leaders in between....Also as hypothesized, self-contained decision units (a control variable) were significantly more conflictual—that is, more extreme in their behavior—than the externally influenceable units" (1989, 380). In the areas of commitment and choice of instruments, the results are more complex, with interaction effects between the type of decision unit and the control variables. For example, "predominant leaders in self-contained units (the insensitive leaders) use more economic and military instruments of statecraft than those in the externally influenceable units (the sensitive leaders)" (1989, 382).

Influence Strategies in Militarized Interstate Conflicts

Leng (1993a) uses the BCOW data to study the relationship between the bargaining strategies employed by states in a dispute and the outcome of the dispute. Starting with the forty crises in BCOW and eliminating those crises where no negotiations preceded war, Leng classifies the influence strategies used by seventy parties to the crises into three categories, using the events recorded in the BCOW data set:[6]

Bullying: the actor employs increasingly severe negative inducements until the other side complies with its demands;

Reciprocating: Tit-for-Tat responses to the actions of the other side, along with occasional unilateral cooperative initiatives;

Trial-and-Error: the actor simply adjusts its choice of inducements based on the target's response to the preceding influence attempt;...inducements that produce

Figure 9.4
Influence Strategies and Dispute Outcomes

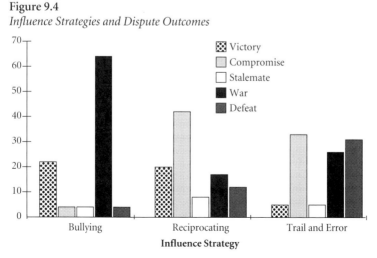

Source: Author, based on Leng (1993a).

positive responses are repeated and inducements that produce negative responses are changed. (1993a, 5)

Figure 9.4 shows the relationship with the strategies used and the crisis outcomes. As Leng observes:

The comparison between escalating coercive bullying strategies and reciprocating strategies is particularly striking. Escalating bullying strategies leads to war or submission in 69% of the cases, and to a victory or compromise in 27% of the cases; whereas reciprocating influence strategies leads to a victory or compromise in 64% of the cases, and to war or submission in 28% of the cases. When bullying strategies are successful, they do tend to result in diplomatic victories (23%), rather than compromises (4%), but reciprocating strategies also achieve diplomatic victories in 20% of the cases…along with compromises 44% of the time. (1993a, 6)

The trial-and-error strategy is intermediate between the other two strategies, producing more war and less compromise than the reciprocating strategy but less war and more compromise than the bullying strategy. Leng's results reinforce the theoretical results of Axelrod (1984) and a number of other researchers on the value of tit-for-tat strategies in conflict situations.

■ Problems with Event Data

Event data, like any data used in social research, contain errors due to their source, coding techniques, and other factors. The advantages and disadvantages of event data have been extensively studied and discussed; the field is nothing if not introspective.[7] The following is a brief survey of these issues.

Coding Systems

Reflecting the cold war environment in which they were first developed, the existing coding systems, particularly WEIS and COPDAB, focus primarily on military and diplomatic interactions between nation-states. They provide considerably less detail on economic interactions, newer issues such as refugees, multilateral operations and environmental regulation, and nonstate actors such as international organizations and subnational groups.[8] This is not a problem if one is primarily interested in diplomatic and military interactions between nation-states, but many contemporary studies have a broader focus.

Because of the substantial expense involved with the human coding of events, little experimentation has been done with the implications of alternative coding schemes, and the idiosyncrasies of the existing codes have been frozen into place. For example, WEIS has separate codes for a "Warning" and "Threat," though these are often synonymous, and it has only three categories for the use of force, whereas BCOW recognizes about twenty.

Despite its popularity in statistical studies, the conflict-cooperation continuum used by COPDAB and the scaled transformations of WEIS is problematic because there is considerable evidence that conflict and cooperation are *independent* dimensions in international behavior. Nations that have extensive cooperation, for example, in trade or alliances, also tend to have greater conflict than nations that are mutually isolated.

Most and Starr (1984) have identified the general empirical problem of "foreign policy substitutability": different actions in foreign policy may have the same general effect. For example, Israel and the Palestine Liberation Organization agreed to mutual recognition in 1993 following secret talks mediated in Norway and a public ceremony at the White House, but one could as easily imagine a different set of circumstances where the recognition occurred after secret talks at the United Nations and a public ceremony in Egypt. Depending on the theoretical issue being discussed, these two scenarios might or might not be considered equivalent. The effect of an event data coding scheme is to define a set of equivalent foreign policy actions and assign them identical codes, but the same set of codes may not work equally well for all theoretical questions.

In all likelihood, there will be greater experimentation with new coding systems in the future, particularly as machine-coding systems are developed. The reports of the early event data efforts by researchers such as McClelland and Azar show they had no intention of freezing into place a single standard for event coding; instead they expected that their coding schemes would be refined through experience and further theoretical developments. As the cost of coding drops, such experimentation and refinement should be possible.

Source Bias

One of the most widely studied problems in event data collection is the editorial and coverage bias introduced by the journalistic sources. One of the earliest systematic studies of this problem was performed by Doran, Pendley, and Antunes (1973), who found a dramatically higher level of reported violence in Latin America if they used regional sources rather than international sources. Azar found only a 10 percent overlap between events reported in the *New York Times* and the *Middle East Journal,* with the latter more likely to report cooperative events (Azar and Ben-Dak 1975, 4). Hoggard (1974) generally found only 10 to 20 percent overlap between the *New York Times Index* and regional sources. Gerner et al. (1994) report a similar low level of overlap when comparing Reuters to two specialized regional sources.

The interactions of some 180 nation-states are necessarily complex, and it is unlikely that any event data set will capture more than a small percentage of all political activities. However, some events, such as the outbreak of war, are more important than others in determining international behavior, and the likelihood of missing an event is probably inversely proportional to its importance: the more important an event, the more likely it will be reported.

Researchers have taken two different approaches to this problem. Some projects, such as COPDAB, SAFED, and BCOW, have used multiple sources to try to capture as many events as possible. This effort is still limited by the time and resources available to the project, but as a greater number of machine-readable sources become available, the costs of coding from multiple sources has decreased. Other projects, such as WEIS, CREON, and GEDS, have relied on a single source—the *New York Times, Deadline Data,* and Reuters, respectively—under the assumption that by maintaining a consistent source the *changes* in the patterns of interaction will be more evident.

Additional Variables

All event data sets have in common the use of a basic "<date> <source> <target> <event>" format, but they differ substantially in whether additional information is coded. WEIS codes only the simple format and an optional "arena" code; COPDAB adds an "issue type" code (e.g., diplomatic, military, economic). BCOW and GEDS, in contrast, add dozens of additional variables; SHERFACS and CREON contain hundreds of factors.

Most of this additional information could be categorized as providing "context" for the event. For example, what subnational decision unit was responsible for the event? What other events were related to it; what other actors were involved? If the event occurs during a crisis, is it part of an escalation or de-escalation? What is the underlying intent of the event, if that can be inferred? In some of the data sets, particularly those dealing with crises, this context, rather than the pattern of discrete events, is the primary focus of the data collection.

The motivation behind adding contextual information to an event record is clear: human decision makers perceive events in a very context-rich manner. Human associative memory provides decision makers with immediate linkages to other events, provides a means of inferring motive, and so forth. However, whether one can *systematically* analyze contextual information is an open issue—after all, if one really wants context, one should be reading the original text sources and not bothering with event data in the first place. Most of the existing applications of event data have not used the contextual information and instead have focused on very crude aggregate measures such as moving averages, though this is changing as more sophisticated analytical tools, such as those used with CASCON and SHERFACS, are developed.

■ Future of Event Data

While the concept of event data is nearly three decades old, the approach has just entered its second generation. Most of the event data research efforts to date have been based on concepts and techniques little changed since 1970. However, fundamental changes in the information-processing capabilities available to researchers now make possible analytical techniques that were impossible when event data were first developed. Inexpensive personal computers have already passed the speed and mass-storage capacities of university mainframes available in the 1970s and are rapidly approaching the capacities of supercomputers available in the 1980s. At the same time, many of the sources traditionally used for event data coding have become available in machine-readable form. Consequently, the past may be a poor guide to the future, and what was practically impossible a decade ago may be trivial a decade from now. The impact of increased computing power is most clearly reflected in machine coding and new analytical methods.

Machine Coding

The human coding of event data is slow and expensive. Laurance (1990) estimated that DARPA spent approximately $1 million on a variety of event data projects in the period 1967–73 (equivalent to about $3.5 million in 1993 dollars). While there has been occasional public funding of event data research since that time—for example, the National Security Council support for WEIS in the early 1980s and the $380,000 in NSF funds to DDIR in the early 1990s—these amounts have not been sufficient to systematically maintain existing data sets, much less experiment with new data or coding schemes.

Machine-readable texts dealing with political events and the availability of low-cost personal computers capable of automated coding are changing this situation. Over the past five years, a number of newspapers have become available on CD-ROM, as has *Facts on File*. These newspapers, as well as news wire services such as Reuters, United Press International, Agence France Press, and a number of regional news wires are also available on commercial data services such as NEXIS and Dialog. These sources allow the possibility of having a computer do the event data coding rather than using human coders. This dramatically reduces the cost of generating the data and should therefore encourage experimentation with new coding schemes.

Over the past three years a group at the University of Kansas has been developing, with DDIR funding, a machine-coding system called the Kansas Event Data System (KEDS) (see Gerner et al. 1994). KEDS does some simple linguistic parsing of the news reports—for example, it identifies the political actors, recognizes compound nouns and compound verb phrases, and determines the referents of pronouns—and then employs a large set of verb patterns to determine the appropriate WEIS event code. KEDS can take Reuters news wire reports as input and generate a WEIS event data set as output with no human intervention. KEDS-generated data appear to track political events quite well, and statistical analyses using KEDS data do not appear to differ systematically from the results obtained with human-coded data (Schrodt and Gerner 1994).

Machine coding has limitations when compared with human coding: KEDS could not handle a complex event coding scheme such as that used in BCOW, SHER-FACS, or GEDS; it fails to correctly code some complex sentences, and it cannot handle situations whose interpretation requires complex background information. Development of the verb pattern and actor dictionaries for KEDS also required an extensive investment of labor. On the other hand, machine coding can be considerably more sophisticated than KEDS. Lehnert and Sundheim (1991) report on a series of artificial intelligence projects that extract a complex set of data from news wire reports. These methods are still experimental but suggest that in the future software may be available to handle coding schemes considerably more complex than WEIS.

New Analytical Techniques

Event data are very different from the data used in most statistical studies in the social sciences (see Schrodt 1994). The conventional statistical repertoire of the social sciences has almost no techniques explicitly adapted to this type of data and, as Achen (1987) points out, there has been virtually no original statistical work to fill these gaps. To date most of the effort in event data analysis has been devoted to carefully constructing and implementing coding schemes rather than systematically exploring what one can do with the data once they have been collected.

McClelland originally envisioned event data as being analyzed as patterns of discrete events.[9] These efforts were unsuccessful, and after some years of work with event data focusing on several crises, McClelland concluded:

> It proved relatively easy to discern event patterns and sequences intuitively. We found we could follow the successions of action and response in flow diagram form. Stages of crisis and the linkage of event types to temporary *status quo* situations also were amenable to investigation. We were defeated, however, in the attempt to categorize and measure event sequences. This was an early expectation that was disappointed by the data which showed too few significant sequences to support quantitative or systematic treatment. (McClelland 1970, 33)

With the perspective of two decades of hindsight, the information-processing technology and sequence analysis techniques available to McClelland were woefully inadequate. McClelland writes of analyzing hundreds or at most thousands of events; a contemporary event data researcher has available hundreds of thousands of events and would be capable of working with millions.

While many studies of event data still use relatively simple methods, in recent years a variety of more complex techniques have been proposed. Some of these are based on advanced statistical methods such as vector autoregression (Goldstein and Freeman 1990), Poisson regression (King 1989), and event history analysis (Allison 1984). Another set of techniques for event data analysis is found in the computational modeling literature derived from research in artificial intelligence (Hudson 1991; Unseld and Mallery 1992); techniques designed to study molecular sequences (Sankoff and Kruskal 1983) have inspired some other methods; and some computation methods are being designed specifically to analyze sequences of social and political events (Heise 1988; Schrodt 1990). Most of these new methods require substantial amounts of computing power and would have been impractical a decade ago, so in the future it may be possible to do considerably more systematic analysis with event data than was possible in the past.

■ Conclusion

The event data approach demonstrates that it is possible to systematically code a very large number of individual foreign policy interactions and then use that information to test general hypotheses about foreign policy behavior using statistical techniques. These hypotheses may deal with national-level characteristics (Hermann and Hermann 1989); the effectiveness of specific strategies (Schrodt 1983; Leng 1993b); patterns of interaction within a subsystem (Goldstein and Freeman 1990; Schrodt and Mintz 1988; van Wyk and Radloff 1993); or patterns in a type of behavior such as crisis behavior (Sherman and Neack 1993).

The existence of an assortment of event data sets in public archives such as the ICPSR simplifies and systematizes the measurement of many characteristics of interest to analysts of foreign policy behavior. Event data provide a means of controlling, for example, for the effect of the U.S.-Soviet détente in studying the foreign policy of the United States or the effects of the Camp David agreements on the foreign policy of Israel. While event data are imperfect indicators, they are still likely to provide a better measure than alternatives such as assuming the détente period coincided with the Nixon administration or that the Camp David agreements had an immediate impact. The behaviors measured by event data may also be at the core of a study: this is particularly true for CREON and the episode-oriented data sets.

The early work in event data analysis was confined to methods that by contemporary standards were slow, laborious, and oftentimes of dubious statistical value. The quantum leap in information-processing capability in the past decade has clearly opened the way for a distinct second generation of event data analysis where machine-assisted coding replaces human coding, computer-intensive sequence analysis methods replace descriptive statistics and contingency tables, and analytical software designed to work with specific data sets—currently seen with BCOW, CAS-CON and SHERFACS—supplements the use of standard statistical packages. The implications of this change for the field of foreign policy analysis are as yet unclear, but they are potentially profound.

■ Acknowledgments

My thanks to Harold Guetzkow for providing an extensive collection of early WEIS memoranda, to Deborah J. Gerner and Juliet Kaarbo for helpful suggestions on the empirical literature, and to the editors of this volume for their comments on an earlier draft.

■ Notes

1. The Reuters reports were downloaded from the NEXIS data service. The full set of reports is considerably more extensive, particularly during the week prior to the invasion.

2. There is a fairly substantial paper trail in the development of event data sets, in particular, Azar, Brody, and McClelland (1972) provide a series of papers coming out of Azar's Michigan State event data conferences in 1969, 1970, and 1971; Burgess and Lawton (1972) also cover this period. The early theoretical development of WEIS is thoroughly discussed in a series of papers by McClelland (1967a, 1967b, 1968a, 1968b, 1969, 1970); Azar's early development of COPDAB is also fairly well documented (e.g., Azar and Ben-Dak 1975; Azar et al. 1972; Azar and Sloan 1975).

3. The ICPSR has about two dozen international event data sets; most universities with graduate programs are members of the ICPSR and have access to its archives. Some of the more recent data sets discussed below—for example, SAFED, GEDS, CASCON III, and SHERFACS—are not presently at the ICPSR; they usually can be obtained from the individual researchers.

4. Because WEIS and COPDAB are based on different sources, they do not have a high degree of overlap; *International Studies Quarterly* (1983) contains two analyses of this along with a commentary by McClelland.

5. See, e.g., Richardson, Kegley, and Agnew (1981), Ward (1982), Dixon (1986), Goldstein (1991), and van Wyk and Radloff (1993).

6. Leng also identifies two additional cases where a party used an "appeasement" strategy (both resulted in defeat) and two cases where a party used a "stonewalling" strategy (both resulted in war).

7. See, for example, Andriole and Hopple (1984), Azar and Ben-Dak (1975), Brody (1972), Burgess and Lawton (1972), Gaddis (1987), *International Studies Quarterly* (1983), Laurance (1990), McGowan et al. (1988), Merritt, Muncaster, and Zinnes (1993), Munton (1978), Peterson (1975), Rosenau (1974), and Sigler, Field, and Adelman (1972).

8. Some of the nonstate actors active in the 1970s are coded (e.g., the United Nations, the Irish Republican Army, and the Palestine Liberation Organization), but the bulk of the interactions in the data sets involve nation-states.

9. Azar, in contrast, saw event data fundamentally in terms of numerical measures; see, for example, Azar and Ben-Dak (1975). Nonetheless, virtually all event coding schemes other than COPDAB and its derivatives (e.g., GEDS) use categorical coding.

TEN

The Politics of Identity
and Gendered Nationalism

V. Spike Peterson, University of Arizona

■ Editors' Introduction

In the following chapter, V. Spike Peterson presents a feminist analysis of the nature of nationalism and the implications of this for states' foreign policies. Peterson's discussion, in the first instance, involves the notion of "problematicizing," or putting issues into a particular framework for analysis. She problematicizes the issue of nationalism as a core focus of states' foreign policies that takes us beyond the state-level evaluations of societal groups and governmental institutions of the preceding chapters. Specifically, she contends that national culture and the derivative political identities and institutions should be understood as male-gendered phenomena.

This chapter offers a fascinating comparison to the previous chapters by Joe Hagan (chapter 8) and Philip Schrodt (chapter 9) in that all three speak to similar issues but from widely different analytical starting points. Moreover, the starting assumptions and frameworks of the Hagan and Schrodt chapters are fairly typical to foreign policy analysis, whereas it is rare, if not completely impossible, to find a foreign policy volume that includes a discussion written from a feminist viewpoint. Feminist scholars have made considerable impact in the last decade or so on how analysts are rethinking international relations theory, however, and so we turned to international relations theorists when we sought to include a feminist voice in this volume. Thus, Peterson's analysis is not as explicitly linked to foreign policy process or behavior as are other chapters in this volume, but it clearly speaks to foreign policy issues in a broad sense. This chapter, along with those by John Rothgeb (chapter 3), Laura Neack (chapter 13), and Karen Mingst (chapter 14), represent some of the many ways in which international relations theory has long contributed to our understanding of foreign policy making and behavior.

When reading this chapter, the reader may find it useful to try to categorize the activities of different nations in terms of the masculine-feminine dichotomies Peterson explores. Are there countries that exhibit traditional "masculine" characteristics and behavior (belligerence, fierce independence, self-interested actions over community interests)? Are there countries that exhibit traditional "feminine" characteristics and behavior (pacificity, passivity, cooperative problem solving, mediation)? After reading this chapter and that by Laura Neack (chapter 13), try to make the argument that "middle powers" are countries that have charted a gender-neutral foreign policy path. ■

In international theory—neorealism in particular—nations and nationalisms register as a key area of empirical neglect and theoretical infertility....Despite the manifest salience of the "national factor" in some extraordinary recent transformations of our global political landscape, we have yet to see a serious disciplinary effort to reconsider nationalism in light of contemporary transformations. (Lapid 1991, 1–2)

The trouble is this. Our conception of what the field is subtly shapes what we study and where and how we look for relevant information and ideas. That is, a conception is a kind of map for directing our attention and distributing our efforts, and using the wrong map can lead us into a swamp instead of taking us to higher ground. (Morgan 1987, 2)

This chapter explores the politics of identity and the problematics of nationalism through a gender-sensitive lens. It argues that gender is a structural feature of the terrain we call world politics, shaping what we study and how we study it. Mapping practices[1] conventionally employed in international relations fail to "see" and therefore do not analyze this pervasive ordering principle. As a consequence, our conventional maps are not simply limited but actually misleading.

Gender refers not to anatomical or biological distinctions but to the social construction, which is always culturally specific, of masculine and feminine as hierarchical and oppositional categories. Symbols, theories, practices, institutions, and, of course, individuals are gendered, meaning that their characteristics can be associated with, or construed as manifestations of, masculinity or femininity. A gender-sensitive lens enables us to see how gender hierarchy shapes our ways of thinking, knowing, and doing, and therefore has patterned consequences that are relevant to the study and conduct of foreign policy.[2]

■ Gender and Second-Generation Analysis

Until recently, gender was "invisible" (Halliday 1988) as a substantive topic or category of analysis in international relations. It is included in this book because in the past decade gender has emerged as an empirical and theoretical dimension of international relations.[3] As the various contributions to this volume make clear, the second generation of foreign policy analysis is distinguished by a shift toward explanatory frameworks that address the complex interaction of multiple (multisource, multilevel) variables. These include personal beliefs, sociocultural metaphors, cognitive maps, economic dynamics, institutional arrangements, political hierarchies, ecological constraints, and globalization processes. Second-generation analysts understand that monocausal or reductionist models pay too high a price in explanatory power for elegance in abstract form. They argue instead that the interdependence of events, people, and institutions in today's world requires that our explanatory frameworks address the mutual interaction of multiple variables and the complexity this entails.

In particular, the discipline's conventional dichotomies—domestic-international, order-anarchy, peace-war, internal-external, agent-structure, realism-idealism—are recognized as misleading simplifications. The either-or conception of the field that these dichotomies impose turns out to be the "wrong map" for addressing today's needs. In reality, interstate relations share some of the characteristics of domestic politics, peace exhibits some of the features of war, agents and structures are mutually constituted, and realists employ mapping practices associated with idealists. Rather than addressing the overlap, categorical oppositions lock us into binary thinking that is static (unable to acknowledge or address change), stunted (unable to envision alternatives), and oversimplified (unable to accommodate the complexities of social reality).[4]

What we require instead are mapping practices that enable us to perceive and interpret events *in relation*—to embed them in context so that we have the most accurate and adequate "map" of multidimensional variables. In short, thinking relationally means greater attention to *contextualizing* the belief systems, events, people, and institutions we study. In this regard, and in light of today's integration-disintegration dynamics, perhaps the most important lesson of the past decade is the necessity of understanding processes of change *and* continuity. As James Rosenau noted in support of adopting the term *postinternational politics,* "It clearly suggests the decline of long-standing systemic patterns without at the same time indicating where the changes may be leading. It suggests flux and transition even as it implies the presence and functioning of stable structures" (Rosenau 1989, 3).

The shift to second-generation perspectives is a consequence of two *interacting* processes: changes in the "real world" and changes in the conceptual maps we use to think about, act within, and understand "reality." For example, as the number of states in the system increased and transnational actors assumed new importance, analysts developed new models of state interaction and revised state-centric theories to accommodate the role of nonstate agents. But it is also true that conceptual filters—like self-fulfilling prophecies—have concrete effects. While the number of nonstate actors increased, theoretical developments both within and outside of the discipline, spurred largely by critiques of positivist orthodoxy, engendered an openness to new approaches and a plurality of perspectives that better enabled analysts to "see" and theorize the presence of multiple agents in the international system. Second-generation insights result from this reciprocal interaction of "real-world" events that both produce and are produced by changes in our mental maps.

Similarly, gender has gained currency as a consequence of both empirical and conceptual developments. As a substantive topic, gender becomes visible when we examine how women are situated differently than men as a consequence of gendered practices and institutions. The stark reality of gender hierarchy is captured in the United Nations finding that although women constitute one-half of the world's population and perform two-thirds of the world's work hours, they receive only one-tenth of the world's income and own less than 1 percent of the world's property. Women constitute a disproportionately high number of single parents, illiterates, and refugees and a disproportionately low number of elite decision makers in governments, militaries, corporations, the media, and religious and educational institutions.[5] Dimensions of the past decade that have increased our awareness of the gender-differentiated effects of world politics include greater visibility of women in the paid labor force, the centrality of women's roles in economic development, the politicization of reproductive rights, the United Nations Decade of Women, the feminization of poverty, the plight of women as war victims and refugees, the impact of feminist struggles, and the gradual expansion of women into positions of decision-making power.

As a category of analysis, gender becomes visible when we examine how constructions of masculinity and femininity filter how we think, how we order reality, how we claim to know what is true, and therefore how we understand and explain the social world. Due to the reciprocal interaction between concrete realities and conceptual frameworks, when we use a gender-sensitive lens not only the "what" of international relations but "how" we think about it is different. Specifically, we see the extent and structure of gender inequality, the patterns situating women *and* men in regard to global dynamics,[6] the significance of gender in shaping how we think about world politics, and how international processes themselves shape gendered thought and practice. In the past decade, awareness of and developments in feminist theorizing have been shaped by the growth of women's studies programs, extensive gender-differentiated research, the interdisciplinary development of feminist schools of thought, debates on the intersection of race, class, gender, and other social hierarchies, and the flourishing of postpositivist and critical theories of knowledge production that share feminist critiques of science, instrumentalist rationality, and binary logic.

In sum, second-generation approaches emphasize multidimensional perspectives that analyze objects *in relation,* that is, in context. Insofar as specifying a context is an unlimited process, the challenge for foreign policy analysts then becomes discerning which relationships or dimensions are the most pertinent in any particular case. Moreover, it is extremely difficult to surrender our dependence on the simplification afforded by mutually exclusive, oppositional categories provided by traditional Western practices. A gender-sensitive lens does not overcome but addresses these challenges. It also illuminates them in unexpected ways, not least of which is to reveal how gender produces and is produced by oppositional—either-or—wor(l)ds. Most relevant to this chapter, a gender-sensitive lens enables us to perceive, interpret, and begin to analyze the dichotomy of masculine and feminine in international politics and how it is relevant to foreign policy analysis.

■ Gender as a Lens on Social Relations

International relations is dominated by men who engage in and study stereotypically masculine (and not apparently sexual) activities: war, diplomacy, high politics, foreign policy analysis, and macroeconomic management. Through traditional lenses, the absence of women, femininity, and sexuality was considered "proof" that the field was gender-neutral. This is like claiming the paucity of African Americans in positions of power proves that racism is *not* relevant! On the contrary, the patterned *absence* of women and that which is associated with femininity is not an accident and clearly not random. It can be explained only by reference to gendered maps and practices that position men and women differently and structure international relations as a "man's world." If we ask, "Why are the women absent?" or "What are they doing while men engage in masculine activities?" we begin to see how gender structures the power relations of the world we study.

Why Are the Women Absent?

In large part women are absent from decision making in international relations for the same reasons they are underrepresented in all of society's powerful institutions: they lack the encouragement, opportunities, training, role models, credentials, self-image, contacts, and resources that facilitate access to positions of societal power.[7] But the dynamics are exacerbated in politics and international relations, where the stereotype of femininity—being passive, dependent, emotional, weak, noncompetitive, irrational, domestic, and so forth—continues to work forcefully against women demanding and all of us supporting the presence of women in positions of power and leadership, especially when those positions involve the use of force (McGlen and Sarkees 1993, 37).

The point here is that, as a dichotomy, masculinity and femininity are constructed as mutually exclusive. To the extent that a man displays emotionality, "softheadedness," passivity, and so on, he is likely to be identified as nonmasculine, which is to say, feminine. Insofar as a woman is stereotypically assumed to be feminine and femininity is stereotypically assumed inappropriate for leadership and the exercise of power, women can participate in politics only to the extent that they become "like men."[8] Stated differently, as long as our mapping filters position women exclusively in the home (or in the bedroom), they will appear "out of place" in political office.

What Are They Doing While the Men Engage in Masculine Activities?

Gender stereotypes structure not only expectations but also practices and institutions. In this instance their effects are compounded by the dichotomy of public and private and its naturalization (depoliticization) of politics as an exclusively masculine activity.[9] For millennia, women and that which is associated with femininity have been conceptually and empirically excluded from identification with public sphere activities: the rights and duties of citizenship, collective decision making, power wielding, military action, political leadership, and foreign policy analysis.

In the context of early state formation, the gendered division of public and private was established in Athenian texts and practice. Its influence has been felt throughout the centuries, but especially in the similar context of state formation in modern Europe: once again, women were denied the stature of autonomous personhood that was required for citizenship. They were relegated instead to an increasingly subordinated private sphere of affect, necessity, and inequality, where their provision of services enabled male heads-of-household to participate in the public sphere. The point here is that private-sphere activities were not peripheral or accidental; they were the basis upon which public-sphere activities depended.

The gendered significance of separating public and private spheres gained additional force as industrialization processes shifted production outside of the home. In this context women were denied not only political but also economic autonomy. In the same period, science (a public-sphere activity) and the positivist, instrumental, and dualistic thinking it celebrated were gaining in prominence. The rise of science marked a transformation not only in "ways of knowing" but also in gender relations and gender symbolism, a transformation in "ways of being" as suggested by reconfigured identities and new metaphors. As in Athens, scientific reasoning was explicitly constructed as male and explicitly promoted as superior to and *exclusive* of that which was marked as female/nature/feminine (Lloyd 1984; Merchant 1980; Peterson 1992c; Schiebinger 1989). The rational spirit that was required for science, capitalism, and liberalism discriminated against women both materially (as evidenced in witch persecutions and the professionalization of medicine that excluded women and eliminated sources of their authority) and symbolically (the enduring and insidious identification of woman/feminine with the denigrated qualities of objectified nature, necessity, and irrationality). By the twentieth century, the dichotomy of masculine-feminine "mapped onto" a litany of dualisms that fundamentally structure Western thought and practice: mind-body, culture-nature, objective-subjective, reason-affect, public-private, order-anarchy, modern-primitive, production-reproduction.

In sum, European state formation involved gendered processes of exploitative accumulation, centralization of political authority, consolidation and maintenance of coercive power, (re)constitution of individual and collective identities, and ideological legitimation. More than any other, the public-private dichotomy captures how gendered divisions of power, violence, labor, and resources favored men at the expense of women. The dichotomy privileges male identity (the objective scientist, rational actor, economic man) and masculine activities (creating knowledge, power wielding, military activities, market competition) over female identity and activities associated with the family and household reproduction. To appreciate how these gender developments shape international relations, we must first examine how international relations is shaped by the dichotomy of public and private.

■ Public and Private in International Relations

First, the separation of public-private informs the disciplinary definition of international relations as the study of relations between states. Insofar as the state is equated with the public sphere, which is masculine, then the abstraction employed so pervasively in international relations—the state—carries a masculine identity, in fact mimics the identity of rational actor/political man. Because the public/state is masculine and categorically separate from the private sphere and femininity/women's activities, international relations treats the latter as irrelevant: the discipline is definitively about relations between, not within, states. What goes on within the state—domestic politics from an international relations perspective—is deemed to be of a different order than and therefore not analogous to international politics.

One effect of this construction is explanatory frameworks in international relations that exclude all reference to activities associated with the private sphere:

subsistence maintenance, affective relations, identity formation, socialization, biological and social reproduction. Yet these activities are in fact how the world's social relations come into being and are sustained and sometimes contested and altered: they are the core of continuity and change. Their effect on macrostructures is indirect—therefore difficult to "trace" on conventional maps—but pervasive and ultimately definitive. Thus, they are pertinent factors in a contextual analysis of foreign policy, as suggested by the discussion of nationalism to follow.

A second effect is to render invisible the gendered divisions of labor, power, violence, and resources that enable and sustain social relations generally and the activities of statesmen specifically. To the extent that the public-private dichotomy is naturalized (taken for granted, as a given rather than a historical construction), the power relations at work, that is, the politics of denying the *interdependence* of public and private are obscured. That which is associated with the private sphere is denied the status of being political in the important sense of being contingent (not given), contestable (not fixed), and of collective interest (not simply personal). In reality, treating domestic violence as a private matter is an expression of particular power relations and is thus profoundly political. Identifying activities with the private not only trivializes them (by denying them the more valued status of being political) but also naturalizes them (by treating them as outside the sphere of contingent, contestable, and collective arrangements). Finally, this division lends authority and legitimacy to divisions of labor that position women outside of political leadership, military activities, macroeconomic management, and foreign policy analysis. The corollary is that women are not only denied access to valued and more powerful masculine activities but are assigned to specific roles and images required to enable, support, and legitimate men's activities: men lead because women are apolitical, men work because women are dependents, men go to war because women need protection.

Yet a third effect of the standard separation of domestic and international politics is the assumption, pervasive in politics and international relations, that male experience and perspective represent human experience and perspective. Modern political theory, its models of human nature, the foundational myths of international relations (Hobbes's state of nature, Rousseau's stag hunt), and the central constructs it employs (the state, rational actor, national security) are abstractions from exclusively male (and especially elite male) experience.[10] The point is not that these accounts are "false" in themselves (although this also warrants examination) but that their claim to universality—to represent the *human* condition and its most pertinent problematics—is empirically and conceptually erroneous. These androcentric (male-as-norm) accounts distort our understanding of actual social relations by excluding all but elite male experience and by failing to embed that experience in context, that is, in relation to other relevant dimensions. Because these distortions occur in the discipline's foundations, the inaccuracies they introduce permeate and have consequences throughout the discipline. Again, although their effects on foreign policy analysis are indirect they are by no means irrelevant.

The public-private dichotomy also structures our perceptual mapping of external relations. Notions of progress, reason, civil society, certainty, and politics in the classical sense—all associated with masculinity and the public sphere—are deemed inapplicable outside of the state. Categorically distinguished from relations within states, anarchy, irrationality, disorder, uncertainty, and the absence of civil norms—frequently associated with femininity—characterize the interactions between states. In this version, stereotypes of femininity characterize relations outside of the state—the anarchic realm that statesmen aspire to impose order on. Rendered as a dichotomy, definitive differences are emphasized and the interdependence of states and the international system is not acknowledged.

One effect of this construction is the projection of different—public versus private—moralities onto external relations. Principles of justice, fairness, and progress that characterize civil society are deemed inappropriate and even dangerous where conditions of anarchy, uncertainty, irrationality, and brute force ostensibly prevail. It is a commonplace assertion that actions undertaken to "protect national interests" are evaluated by different moral criteria than those applied to actions within civil society. Insofar as internal and external relations do exhibit patterned differences, the application of different moral criteria may be appropriate. But construing the moralities as a dichotomy of anarchy/"anything goes" versus order/"morality prevails" effectively denies the continuity between internal and external relations and excuses us from more discriminating assessments of when—if ever—might makes right (Kaldor 1991).

Similarly, a categorical separation of public and private is at work when we identify "us" and "them" for purposes of applying moral criteria. What matters here is who gets counted as insiders and outsiders: normative commitments are extended to those we identify with and accept as inside the group but do not necessarily apply to those who are different enough to be considered outside of the group, its norms, and traditions. This is especially clear when coercive activities, that would be reprehensible if perpetrated against group members, are undertaken against "others" and justified by reference to their being outside of the normative community. Nationalism is important here because "the nation...marks the limits of belonging, the border of the moral community, beyond which organized violence becomes thinkable" (Pettman 1992, 4).

In sum, there are three aspects of the public-private dichotomy that, in varying combinations, shape the practice and especially the conceptual maps of international relations. Because it is a dichotomy so fundamental to Western political philosophy, the public-private structures multiple dimensions of international relations (as suggested earlier) yet is so taken for granted that we rarely reflect on the consequences of employing this mapping device. Because the dichotomy is historically, empirically, and conceptually gendered, its deployment in international relations reproduces and naturalizes multiple gendered effects, yet these are rendered so "invisible" that we engage in virtually no self-reflection on the distortions—and discriminations—this institutionalizes. Because the public-private division is constituted as a dichotomy of mutually exclusive domains, whenever it is at work it reproduces and reinforces oppositional separations—of internal-external, domestic-international, production-reproduction, us-them—at the expense of recognizing how these categories are, in reality, interdependent.

■ Nationalism and International Relations

> *No single political doctrine has so profoundly shaped the mind and face of the modern world as has nationalism....The epochal political events of the last 200 years...all have their origins in the collective drive toward self-identity that we call nationalism. Nationalism is primarily a political phenomenon, but its effects are pervasive. (Gleason 1991, 213)*

In spite of its potency in the modern world of nation-states, nationalism is notoriously difficult to define. As Alexander Motyl points out, "Nationalism, like *revolution, state, class, modernity, development* and most other weighty social science terms, is...an 'essentially contested concept'...(resonating) with a number of different meanings" (Motyl 1992, citing Connolly 1974). Typically, the term *state* refers to the territorially based, political-legal organization of a social order while the term *nation* refers to the socioculturally based cohesion or collective identification of a group. Nationalism is most frequently used in two related senses: first, as allegiance to and promotion of a particular community or nation and its interests; second, as belief in the desirability of coterminous political and cultural communities. The latter is captured in Gellner's definition of nationalism as "primarily a political principle, which holds that the political and the national unit should be congruent...[It] is a theory of political legitimacy, which requires that ethnic boundaries should not cut across political ones" (Gellner 1983, 1). Succinctly capturing both the cultural and political—or ethnic and territorial—dimensions, Gleason condenses the meaning of nationalism to "politicized ethnicity" (Gleason 1991, 221).

Nationalism promotes a sense of identity, it "tells us who we are and who we like and who we don't like" (William Wallace, quoted in Frankel 1990, 16). Most significant for foreign policy analysis, it is a potent force because it is the identity for which people are willing to kill others and to die themselves. By determining who constitutes "us" and "them," insider and outsider, friend and foe, nationalism significantly shapes who the world's political actors are and the forms in which they interact. When nationalist struggles are militarized they become flash points—or enduring conflicts—that pose foreign policy challenges.

Nations and nationalism are thus central to international relations. To the extent that states and nations do coincide, the discipline's ubiquitous references to the state are also references to the nation and vice versa. In Mayhall's words, "Nationalism has become structurally embodied in all parts of the world, as the basis of the modern state" (1990, 152). Similarly, the objective of foreign policy decision makers is to identify strategies that promote the *national* interest—they thus act on behalf of a particular community or nation.[11] In these accounts nationalism is central to international relations because states are equated with nations.

Of course, the interplay of nationalist behaviors and how nations and nationalism are employed in our mapping practices is much more complicated. To begin with, contemporary scholars frequently bemoan our failure to adequately theorize "the state," "nation," and "nationalism," in spite of their centrality to the discipline (Lapid 1991). The problems are compounded by developments in today's world, where states and sovereignty are in transition and nationalism appears in a variety of forms that may or may not resemble state-based power. On top of these difficulties, the ideal fusion of cultural and territorial coincidence in one "nation-state" (exemplified by Japan) is the exception, not the rule. Among the world's states in 1972, only twelve (9.1 percent) so qualified (Connor 1972, 320), and ethnic revivals in the past two decades suggest that discrepancies between community and territory are increasing.

Analysts are hampered in addressing these developments to the extent that state-centric approaches continue to dominate the conceptual maps of international relations.[12] When a model of states as unitary, rational actors pursuing the national interest is adopted, a number of questions regarding agency and the formation of group objectives cannot be asked. Rather, state-centric models take nation-state political identity as given; they fail to problematize and therefore do not analyze questions of who in fact is acting and in the name, interests, and objectives of what group. They also neglect nonstate agents, whose numbers and significance are increasing. Whatever their utility in earlier studies, state-centric models are far from adequate in the context of today's changing states, proliferating actors, and competing nationalisms.

■ Political Identity

In this chapter I employ the concept of political identity as a way of referring to identification with a particular group—whether that group is bounded by ethnicity, culture, territory, or shared purpose—and actions on behalf of that group as they influence and are influenced by power relations. Political identities associated with subnational, international, or transnational groups take a variety of forms (social movements, religious communities, military alliances) but typically do not seek a territorially bounded political status. Nationalism is then the territorially based subset of political identity that takes one of two related forms: state-led (assimilation of all within a state to the state's preferred cultural forms) and state-seeking (mobilization of group identification in pursuit of recognition as an independent state). As Charles Tilly points out, "state-led nationalism stimulates state-seeking nationalism" as the homogenizing project of the former threatens the viability of nonstate identities; to ensure the latter, subgroups seek the sovereignty afforded by state status—and if successful, tend to impose their own homogenizing project (Tilly 1992, 709).[13]

The political identity framework permits a useful expansion of mapping tools. It preserves the role of state-centric agency but situates that agency in relation to, rather than at the expense of, other expressions of collective agency. Not only state-led nationalism but ethnic revivals, Islamic fundamentalism, Third World feminism, and mobilization in support of global identities are accommodated within this frame. The latter is especially significant in light of globalization processes that increasingly shape world politics but are not easily accommodated in conventional, state-centric accounts. To meet these challenges we must nurture some notion of "global citizenship" even as we continue to identify with nation-states.

Using this framework, foreign policy decisions and actions remain and are understood as expressions of state-centric political identity. But to generate appropriate, effective decisions and actions, foreign policy analysts must consider their own interests in relation to multiple other—complementary, competing, and contradictory—expressions of political identity. How is German unification related to alliance dynamics and the European Community's political agenda? What politics and whose identities are involved in representing Arab states as maniacally fundamentalist? How do competing loyalties in South Africa prevent stability in the entire region? How does identification with Western capitalism shape global divisions of labor, trade, aid, and military policies? Through a political identity framework, a variety of apparently disparate actors and events can be seen in relation and thereby contextualized.

This framework is consistent with the growing sense—fueled by scholarly research and global realities—that politics is not only about power but also about communities: how humans interact, acquire identities, and engage in the reproduction and transformation of power relations. In a study of continuity and change, we must ask how authority, in particular the authority to engage in organized violence, is legitimated. A political identity approach permits us to ask that and the following questions: What are the causes of particular group/community configurations? Who are their participants and leaders? How do they create and reproduce "identity" and "difference"? What are their objectives? How are they related to other groups, identities, objectives? What are their implications for understanding world politics generally and the analysis of foreign policy specifically?

■ Gendered Nationalism

Nationalism has always been problematic from the vantage point of conflict between nations: sameness within the state is purchased at the price of institutionalizing difference—and, too often, conflict—among states. But nationalism has also been problematic from the vantage point of those within the nation who share least in elite privilege and political representation, especially those whose identity is at odds with the projected image of national unity (Corrigan and Sayer 1985). Whether understood in terms of "imagining" (Anderson 1991) or "inventing" (Gellner 1983) a national identity, or in terms of privileging a particular "natural" community (Smith 1991), the promotion of uniformity—by persuasive and coercive means—threatens some more than others. How particular individuals and subgroups are situated in relation to the homogenizing project will depend on a variety of historical factors: there are no essential or predetermined "givens" in how race, class, ethnicity, gender, and so forth are linked to nationalist projects. It is possible, however, to identify *historical* patterns as a step toward developing useful conceptual maps, especially as we venture into relatively uncharted terrain.[14]

Drawing upon but altering the framework introduced by Yuval-Davis and Anthias (1989), I identify five gender-differentiated dimensions or ways in which women have typically been situated in relation to nationalist processes: as biological reproducers of group members; as social reproducers of group members and cultural forms; as signifiers of group differences; as participants in political identity struggles; and as societal members generally. How these dimensions relate to nationalism will be clearer if we first consider the dynamics—and problematics!—of group identity formation and how groups achieve continuity through time.

As noted earlier, in spite of its significance in modern history, nationalism remains poorly understood and insufficiently studied. Jill Vickers argues that "this difficulty of understanding nationalism as a form of self-identification and of group organization reflects the profound difficulty that male-stream thought, in general, has had in understanding the public manifestations of the process of identity construction" (Vickers 1990, 480). The dilemma is this: Once we move beyond the biological parameters of females bearing and breast-feeding infants, how are groups—and the social relations they entail—formed and reproduced?

Vickers argues that patriarchal social relations can be interpreted as *one* way of "constructing enduring forms of social organization, group cohesion and identity" (Vickers 1990, 483).[15] Insofar as men seek group affiliation and continuity, they attempt to control women's sexual reproduction and to institutionalize social relations that engender loyalties to a male-defined group extending beyond the mother-infant bond. Lacking an immediate biological connection, men appropriate an abstract concept of the blood tie and employ it to promote bonding among males and group identity based on male-defined needs.

Implementation of this strategy involves a "battle of the cradle" over women's sexual reproduction and a "battle of the nursery" over identities and loyalties (Vickers 1990, 485). To the extent that women are excluded from the definition of group interests and compelled to comply with male-defined needs, their freedom and autonomy are limited. So excluded, women are at the same time denied the status of "personhood" attached to group decision makers (in the modern state, this is institutionalized through the public-private dichotomy). In sum, the coherence and continuity of the group—and the gender hierarchy it imposes—is "maintained and secured only by limiting the autonomy, freedom of choice and social adulthood of the group's physical and social reproducers" (Vickers 1990, 482).

What this analysis points out is that reproduction is the most political—power-laden and potent—of activities. Conventionally ignored as a dimension of the ostensibly apolitical private sphere, the power relations of reproduction fundamentally condition who "we" are and how groups/nations align themselves in cooperative, competing, and complementary ways. On this view gender relations are a crucial, not peripheral, dimension of the states and nations that constitute world politics.

Women as Biological Reproducers of Group Members

The battle of the cradle is about regulating under what conditions, when, how many, and whose children women will bear. The forms it takes are historically specific, shaped by socioreligious norms, technological developments, economic pressures, and political priorities. Pronatalist policies may include restriction of contraceptive knowledge and techniques, denial of access to abortions, and provision of material rewards for bearing children. From Sparta, where a mother "reared her sons to be sacrificed on the alter of civic necessity" (Elshtain 1992, 142), to South Africa, where white women were exhorted to bear "babies for Botha" (McClintock 1991, 110–11), women have been admonished to fulfill their "duty" by bearing sons to fight for and daughters to care for the motherland.

Population control works both ways. To limit the size of "undesirable" groups, immigration controls, expulsion, sterilization, and even extermination have been—

and are being—practiced. Women's bodies are often used as a battleground of men's wars. In Bosnia, systematic rape and sexual enslavement not only violate countless Muslim women but sabotage the underpinnings and therefore continuity of community. These are not epiphenomena of war or displays of innate male aggression: they are politically driven strategies in the context of group conflict.

Women as Social Reproducers of Group Members and Cultural Forms

The battle of the nursery is about ensuring that children are bred in culturally appropriate ways. This may involve the regulation—through religious dogma, legislation, social norms, and coercion—of sexual liaisons so that religious, ethnic, class, and citizenship boundaries are maintained. By enforcing legislation regarding marriage, child custody, and property and citizenship inheritance, the state controls the reproduction of membership claims. For example, under British nationality laws until 1948, a British woman was deemed an "alien" if she married a non-British subject, and until 1981 she could not pass on her nationality (in her own right) to children born abroad (Klug 1989, 21–22).[16]

The battle of the nursery also involves the ideological reproduction of group members. Under patriarchal relations, women are the primary socializers of children, both within the family and in elementary schools. They are largely responsible for inculcating beliefs, behaviors, and loyalties that are culturally appropriate and ensure intergenerational continuity. This cultural transmission includes learning the "mother tongue," as well as the group's symbols, rituals, divisions of labor, and worldviews. Research indicates that from an early age, children are aware of and identify specifically with a "homeland." Robert Coles studied the "political life of children" on five continents and concluded that everywhere "nationalism works its way into just about every corner of the mind's life," fostering children's recognition of their nation's flag, music, slogans, history, and who counts as "us" and "them" (Coles 1986, 60, 63, as quoted in Elshtain 1992, 149).

Because of their assigned roles in social reproduction, women are often stereotyped as "cultural carriers." When minority groups feel threatened, they may increase the isolation of "their" women from exposure to other groups or the legislative reach of the state. In Lebanon, for example, competing indigenous groups insist that marriage, divorce, adoption, inheritance, and so forth, are "personal" matters under the exclusive control of the community rather than subject to central authorities. In cases where the state promotes a more progressive agenda than patriarchal communities, this kind of agreement among men to "leave each other's women alone" may be at the expense of women gaining formal rights. If the private sphere constitutes the "inner sanctum" of group identity and reproduction, nationalist men have an incentive to oppose those who would either interfere with it or encourage women's movements outside of it (Kandiyoti 1991a).

Woman as Signifiers of Group Differences

As biological and social reproducers, it is women's capacities and activities that are "privatized" in the name of male-defined groups. But women also serve as symbolic markers of the nation and of the group's cultural identity. Shared images, symbols, rituals, myths, and a "mother tongue" play essential roles in the reproduction of social groups that are based on abstract bonds between men. Men appropriate the model of human reproductive ties, but their distancing from reproductive activities forces them to privilege "imagined" relations wherein "identity, loyalty and cohesion centre around male bonds to other men" (Vickers 1990, 484). In this context the symbolic realm is elevated to strategic importance: symbols become what's worth fighting—even dying—for and cultural metaphors become weapons in the war. The metaphors of nation-as-woman and woman-as-nation suggest how women—as bodies and cultural repositories—become the battleground of group struggles.

The personification of nature-as-female transmutes easily to nation-as-woman, where the motherland is a woman's body and as such is ever in danger of violation—by "foreign" males. To defend her frontiers and her honor requires relentless vigilance and the sacrifice of countless citizen-warriors (Elshtain 1992). Nation-as-woman expresses a spatial, embodied femaleness: the land's fecundity, upon which the people depend, must be protected by defending the body/nation's boundaries against invasion and violation. But nation-as-woman is also a temporal metaphor: the rape of the body/nation not only violates frontiers but disrupts—by planting alien seed or destroying reproductive viability—the maintenance of the community through time. Also implicit in the patriarchal metaphor is a tacit agreement that men who cannot defend their woman/nation against rape have lost their "claim" to that body, that land.

Clearly, the nation/woman is being denied agency. Rather, "she" is man's possession, and like other enabling vessels (boats, planes) is valued as a means for achieving male-defined ends: the sovereign/man drives the ship of state. Thus, the motherland is female but the state and its citizen-warriors are male and must prove (its) their political manhood through conflict: "The state is free that can defend itself, gain the recognition of others, and shore up an acknowledged identity" (Elshtain 1992, 143). In Cynthia Enloe's words, "If a state is a vertical creature of authority, a nation is a horizontal creature of identity" (Enloe 1990, 46). Significantly, this horizontal identity is one of *fraternal* bonding: the sexism of language (which privileges masculine gender; Penelope 1990) and the sexism of liberal "democracy" (which institutionalizes patriarchal citizenship; Pateman 1988) converge in the slogan "liberty, fraternity, equality." Excluded intentionally from the public domain, women are not agents in their own right but instruments for the realization of male-defined agendas.

Woman-as-nation signifies the boundaries of group identity, marking its difference from alien "others." Assigned responsibility for reproducing the group through time, women are singled out as "custodians of cultural particularisms" and "the symbolic repository of group identity" (Kandiyoti 1991a, 434). Because symbols of cultural authenticity are jealously guarded, actual women face a variety of pressures to conform to idealized models of behavior. In Jan Jindy Pettman's words,

> Women's use in symbolically marking the boundary of the group makes them particularly susceptible to control in strategies to maintain and defend the boundaries. Here women's movements and bodies are policed, in terms of their sexuality, fertility, and relations with "others," especially with other men. This suggests why (some) men attach such political significance to women's "outward

attire and sexual purity," seeing women as their possessions, as those responsible for the transmission of culture and through it political identity; and also as those most vulnerable to abuse, violation or seduction by "other" men. (1992, 5–6)

We observe a variation of this manipulation in colonial contexts, where foreign intervention is justified by reference to a "civilizing mission" that involves the "rescue" of oppressed indigenous women! The most efficient and successful domination is that which persuades the dominated of their inferiority. To legitimate their global domination of "others," Europeans drew upon notions of bourgeois respectability: "'decent and correct' manners and morals, as well as the proper attitude toward sexuality" (Mosse 1985, 1). Sexual practices at variance with Victorian codes of feminine respectability were singled out as demonstrating the "backwardness" of indigenous peoples. Lacking respectability, these peoples had no claim to respect and the equality of relations it entails: foreign domination is then not only justified but re-presented as a project of liberation. Similarly, during the Gulf War the "oppression" of Arab women (veiled, confined, unable to drive cars) was contrasted with the "independence" of U.S. women (armed, at large, able to drive tanks), thus suggesting a "civilizing" tone to the war against Iraq.[17]

Women as Participants in Political Identity Struggles

In reality, women are not only symbols, and their activities extend well beyond the private sphere. In contrast to the stereotype of women as passive and peace-loving, women have throughout history supported and participated in conflicts involving their communities. They have provided essential support in their servicing roles (feeding, clothing, and nursing combatants), worked in underground movements, passed information and weapons, organized their communities for military action, taken up arms themselves, and occasionally led troops into battle (Peterson and Runyan, chapter 4). Yet the significance of their contributions remains "hidden" and therefore unanalyzed in conventional accounts.

For reasons alluded to earlier, women have historically been denied public-sphere activities: they rarely appear in combatant or leadership roles and in the arena of high politics. Because conventional accounts of war focus on these activities, it is not surprising that women appear only as "an off-stage chorus to a basically male drama" (Enloe 1987, 529). Contemporary analysts continue to understand war as a "basically male drama," but they recognize that battlefield action is only the tip of the iceberg. Leadership personalities, production capabilities, popular sentiments, communication technologies, historical animosities, political alignments, diplomatic protocols, media politics, and normative principles are some of the multiple variables upon which battlefield outcomes depend. There is no fixed pattern in how gender shapes the most pertinent variables and their interaction in a specific case. But our knowledge of the iceberg is inaccurate and therefore inadequate unless we "see" how gender is at work and undertake systematic study of its effects.

Women as Societal Members Generally

This category extends our mapping of gender beyond the immediate context of nationalist struggles. It reminds us that women are not homogeneous or typically united. Social hierarchies—racism, classism, ageism, heterosexism, ablism, an so forth—structuring any particular society are interactive: racism is not independent of but mutually shapes expressions of sexism (Mohanty, Russo, and Torres 1991). As a consequence, allegiance to particular causes may complement, coexist with, or contradict allegiance to other group objectives. How and to what extent feminist and nationalist projects converge depends on contextual specifics. Kumari Jayawardena found that at the end of the nineteenth and beginning of the twentieth centuries, feminism was compatible with the modernizing dynamic of anti-imperialist national liberation movements in Asia and a number of other colonized countries (Jayawardena 1986). In contrast, Val Moghadam examines contemporary movements and finds that "feminists and nationalists view each other with suspicion, if not hostility, and nationalism is no longer assumed to be a progressive force for change" (Moghadam 1994, 4 in ms.). She argues that nationalism has been recast from a secular, modernizing project to one that emphasizes "the nation as an extended family writ large" or "a religious entity"; "women become the revered objects of the collective act of redemption, and the role models for the new nationalist, patriarchal family" (Moghadam 1994, 4–5 in ms.). In this context women face a variety of pressures to support nationalist objectives even, or especially, when these conflict with feminist objectives.

Women are situated differently than men (and differently among themselves) in regard to divisions of power, violence, labor, and resources. In the context of nationalism, these various locations shape the allegiance various women, or women in concert, will have toward group identity and objectives. How the tradeoffs are played out may have international consequences. For example, Denmark's initial rejection of the Mastricht Treaty—a "no" vote that threatened to undermine Community solidarity—was significantly shaped by gender issues. Danish feminists campaigned against the treaty because work and welfare provisions in the Community structure are less progressive than those obtaining already in Denmark (True 1993, 84). Different tradeoffs pertained in the United Kingdom. There, lack of equal-opportunity legislation meant that British women had a political interest in seeing their country's adoption of more progressive Community policies, even though this represented a loss of traditional sovereignty (Walby 1992, 95).

These examples remind us that there is no "given" or automatic relationship between women's interests and national interests. But they also demonstrate that gender is a pervasive feature of the territory—world politics—we are attempting to map when we examine foreign policy.

■ Conclusion

The whole study of states is today being reconfigured,....[N]ew attention is being given to the salience of the forces of nationalism in all their modern manifestations, at the same time that more fundamental questions are being asked about the international order. (Graubard 1993, vii)

World politics is entering a new phase in which...the dominating source of conflict will be cultural...[as] the principal conflicts of global politics will occur between nations and... will dominate global politics. (Huntington 1993, 22)

Second-generation analysts recognize the necessity of multidimensional, multilevel frameworks that enable us to contextualize and think relationally. The field's earlier simplifications—expressed especially in traditional dichotomies—provide not only limited but actually misleading "maps." Gender is a structural feature of social reality—including international relations—and as such must be "put on the map," systematically studied, and its symbolic and material effects incorporated in our production of contextual, relational accounts. This chapter's examination of political identity in general and nationalism in particular reveals both how traditional maps distort "reality" (they are the "wrong" map) and how gender-sensitive analyses improve our mapping practices (they provide better directions to "higher ground").

In particular, the gendered dichotomy of public-private structures the study and practice of international relations and foreign policy. One important consequence is the discipline's neglect of activities associated with the private sphere. The latter include individual and group identity formation, cultural socialization, and social reproduction: the maintenance of social relationships and meeting of basic needs upon which world politics ultimately depends. When we neglect reproductive processes we easily lapse into reifying our constructs rather than understanding them in historical context. When we ignore these activities we fail to contextualize sources of group compliance, cooperation, and conflict that directly affect international relations when expressed as nationalistic foreign policy behaviors.

Many analysts believe that nationalism is the single most important source of conflict in today's world. By establishing cultural boundaries that determine insider and outsider, friend and foe, nationalism shapes who the world's political actors are and at what level of hostility they interact. These are preeminently foreign policy concerns.

As the identity people are willing to kill and to die for, nationalism demands our best mapping techniques. Foreign policy analysts cannot afford to rely on partial and distorted accounts, especially in the face of mounting nationalist struggles. Traditional analyses of geopolitical conditions and international economics are necessary but not sufficient guides to effective foreign policy in today's world. We must understand as well how group identities are formed, how cultural loyalties are reproduced, and how nationalist movements in support of those identities and loyalties affect the foreign policy making of existing states.

A gender-sensitive analysis improves our map of nationalism. It illuminates the processes of identity formation, cultural reproduction, and political allegiance that are key to understanding collective identities and their political effects. It also informs our understanding of domination dynamics. In patriarchal societies (currently the norm worldwide), group coherence and continuity is achieved through denial of equality within the group. The battles of the cradle and the nursery are at the expense of women's autonomy internally and mutually respectful relations externally. As the inequality that is most naturalized, and therefore used to justify multiple hierarchies, gender hierarchy is central to the construction and reproduction of asymmetrical social relations. The exclusivity and domination "faces" of nationalism typify such asymmetrical relations.

In short, the gender hierarchy of masculine over feminine and the nationalist domination of insiders over outsiders are doubly linked. As described earlier, nationalism is gendered in terms of how the *construction* of group identity (allegiance to "us" versus "them") depends upon divisions of masculinity and femininity. In this sense the process itself presupposes gendered social relations. Nationalism is also gendered in terms of how the *naturalization* of domination ("us" at the expense of "them") depends upon the prior naturalization of men/masculinity over women/femininity. In this sense, taking domination as natural obscures its historical context and disables our knowledge of and attempts to transform hierarchical relations.

The point of gender-sensitive analyses is not that gender is always the primary or *most* salient dimension of a particular context. But it is consistently at work, making a difference, and, in the context of nationalism and the foreign policy challenges it poses, may be the difference we most need to see—and move beyond. As such, gender-sensitive analyses complement and expand upon our understanding of the many state-level sources of foreign policy.

■ NOTES

1. "Mapping" is similar to "modeling" in that both are ways of representing complex phenomena. Mapping differs from modeling, however, in that mapping is conceptually a more active process in which differences between things are clearly presented to the one drawing or following the map.

2. In this chapter *gender hierarchy* and *patriarchy* both refer to systems of power that privilege men and that which is associated with masculinity over women and that which is associated with femininity. *Androcentrism* refers to male-centered orientations that privilege men's ways of being and knowing as the norm or standard for all people, thus eclipsing alternative perspectives. *Masculinism*, like sexism, is an orientation that justifies and "naturalizes" gender hierarchy by not questioning the elevation of ways of being and knowing associated with masculinity over those associated with femininity. *Feminism* is an orientation that views gender as a fundamental ordering principle in today's world, values women's diverse ways of being and knowing, and promotes the transformation of gender and related hierarchies.

   Gender-sensitive research both "deconstructs" androcentric (male-as-norm) accounts (by locating "invisible" women and incorporating women's experiences and perspectives in the study of humankind) and "reconstructs" them (by rethinking fundamental relationships of knowledge, power, and community and developing feminist epistemologies). See, for example, Butler and Scott (1992); Hekman (1990); Mohanty, Russo, and Torres (1991); Nicholson (1990). On the basis of this research, many contemporary feminist scholars argue that "all of social life is gendered" (Nelson 1989, 4), and allegedly "gender-neutral" accounts distort our understanding by obscuring the significance of gender.

3. In the 1970s, gender-sensitive research documented the centrality of women as agents in economic development processes, bringing a host of new issues to the attention of development planners and theorists. Feminist scholars have since produced studies in virtually all of the discipline's conventional areas. For literature reviews see Alexandre (1989); Sylvester (1992–92). On feminist-international relations generally see D'Amico and Beckman (1995); Enloe (1990); Peterson (1992a); Peterson and Runyan (1993); Pettman (1991); Sylvester (1994); Tetreault (1994); Tickner (1992); *Alternatives* (1993); *Fletcher Forum* (1993).

4. As applied to international relations, I expand this critique of dichotomies and the shift from oppositional to relational thinking it entails in Peterson (1992d); also Peterson and Runyan (1993), chapter 2.

5. On the extent of pattern of global gender inequalities see, for example, Peterson and Runyan (1993); Rhoodie (1989); Schmiltroch (1991); United Nations (1991); Vickers (1991).

6. In the stereotypical form of either-or dichotomies, constructions of masculinity are not independent of but depend upon opposing constructions of femininity. Due to this zero-sum interdependence, when we study patterns in women's lives we also learn about men's lives and therefore generate a more accurate and comprehensive "map" of social reality.

7. Research in support of this generalization is extensive. In regard to political elites see, for example, Lips (1991); Randall (1987); Staudt (1989); for an overview see Peterson and Runyan (1993), chapter 3.

8. "Iron Lady" Margaret Thatcher is the classic example. Although the dynamics appear to change as women achieve a "critical mass" in elite decision-making, at present the generalization holds and is confirmed in studies of women in foreign policy (Crapol 1992; McGlen and Sarkees 1993).

9. In this discussion, public refers to government, market, and civil relations, and private refers to household and family relations. The gender-differentiated effects of the public-private dichotomy and state formation have been studied extensively by feminist scholars. The argumentation in this section draws especially on Peterson (1992c); Runyan and Peterson (1991); Eisenstein (1981); Elshtain (1981); Grant (1991); Nicholson (1986); Pateman (1988).

10. The following is only a sampling of the extensive research in these areas: Brown (1988); Clark and Lange (1979); Di Stefano (1991); Hartsock (1983); Okin (1979); Pateman (1989); Saxonhouse (1985).

11. Due to its association with the manipulation of mass emotions, nationalism is readily observed in others but rarely acknowledged in ourselves. When citizens are incited to wave the flag, support the troops, cheer on their state's military depredations, and believe that God is on their side, it is no less nationalist in the United States than it is in Iraq (Motyl 1992).

12. See essay by Bruce Moon (chapter 11) in this volume.

13. Gleason (1991, 223–28) identifies these aspects of nationalism as three "faces": liberation (the self-determination associated positively with nationalism), exclusivity (the promotion of group uniformity and "difference" from "others"), and domination (the negative effects of suppressing difference within the group and/or domination of "outsiders" in the name of the group). The liberation aspect is usually associated with the democratic potential (or claims) of nationalist movements (as in Eastern Europe; for a critique see Mayhall [1993]) but all three aspects are integral to nationalism, and the domination dynamic cannot simply be ignored. While space does not permit elaboration here, the coexistence of all three aspects has important implications for "rethinking the contemporary relation between sovereignty and democracy" (Connolly 1991, 215), that is, whether today's state-based democracies are undermined by the lack of global democracy. This suggests an additional sense in which nationalism is key to contemporary world politics.

14. For an overview of the literature on state making, political identity, feminism, and nationalism, see Peterson (1993); also Mayhall (1993); True (1993). To the extent that states have historically institutionalized class, gender, and race/ethnic hierarchies, state-led or state-seeking nationalisms are problematic from the perspective of struggling against these hierarchies. On critiques of the state see citations in note 9 and Afshar (1987); Burstyn (1983); Connell (1990); Kandiyoti (1991b).

15. With Vickers (1990), I emphasize that the development of gender hierarchy was neither "necessary" nor "inevitable" but represents one among numerous possibilities. Like states, racism, and nationalism, gender hierarchy is a complex, contingent, historical development. Approaches that reduce these developments to "nature" inevitably sustain—by their naturalizing, that is, depoliticizing effects—the phenomena they purport to explain and in effect promote the hierarchical relations characteristic of states, racism, nationalism, and sexism.

16. As states assume ever greater responsibility for provision of basic needs, claims to citizenship assume ever greater significance, determining not only one's obligations but also one's rights—to work, stable residency, legal protections, and educational and welfare benefits. See Jones (1990); Lister (1993); Yuval-Davis (1991).

17. The principle of gender equality was not an objective but a pawn in these conflicts: European colonizers oppressed women at home and abroad, and the United States was ostensibly defending Kuwait, where women cannot even vote. Enloe argues that these apparent contradictions make sense if viewed as strategies not of liberation but of justification: legitimating the domination by some men over "other" men and their communities (Enloe 1990, 49).

ELEVEN

The State in Foreign
and Domestic Policy

Bruce E. Moon, LEHIGH UNIVERSITY

■ Editors' Introduction

*In this chapter Bruce Moon introduces two critical concepts tradition-
ally neglected in foreign policy analysis: the state and
core-periphery relations. Moon deconstructs the term state according
to its usage in a variety of theories. Specifically, he demonstrates
that realist conceptions of the state as a body seeking to protect the
"national interest" may explain the international behavior of
wealthy states in the "core" but fail to account for foreign policy in
the world's less-developed countries in the "periphery." Moon adds
to the theoretical and conceptual elements required in a theory of
foreign policy and in so doing contributes to the bigger theoretical
umbrella that second-generation scholars deem necessary. This
chapter also establishes a basic understanding of political dynamics
in Third World societies and therefore sets the context for Jeanne
Hey's chapter that follows.*

*In reevaluating the state as a fundamental and static unit of
analysis, Moon parts company with many realist scholars. In reading this chapter, consider the following questions: Is the theoretical
concept of a unitary state more useful for analyzing the foreign policies of some states than others? How has the emphasis on the
state influenced scholars' view of foreign policy making and limited
the scope of their inquiry? What peripheral states can you think of
that do not conform with traditional views of the state and behave
in ways inconsistent with what first-generation foreign policy analysts might have expected?* ■

We have been reminded repeatedly in recent years that the concept of the state is fundamental to theorizing about policy behavior (Benjamin and Duvall 1985; Caporaso
1988; Krasner 1984; Skocpol 1985). Yet the scholarly analysis of foreign policy has
been handicapped by a rather crude conception of the state. This essay suggests that
this conception could be enriched by borrowing from the better-developed theories
of the state current in studies of comparative domestic policy.

After reviewing the conceptions of the state implicit in realism and contrasting them with alternative theories, I will argue the following five points: First, the modern state is motivated by rather different goals than those suggested by realist. analysis. Second, the state faces major constraints that limit its ability to pursue even those realist ambitions it may possess. Third, for these reasons, conventional accounts rooted in realist images of the state are prone to misunderstand the foreign policy of many nations. Fourth, some attributes of state behavior not easily addressed by current foreign policy theory flow naturally from political economy conceptions of the state. Finally, this alternative vision is particularly necessary in order to understand foreign policy outside the core of economically and politically developed nations of Europe and North America.

■ The State in Realist Thought

Foreign policy behavior cannot be understood without an appreciation of the goals and priorities, the internal and external constraints, and the perceptions and expectations that guide state action. Thus, any theory of foreign policy behavior must contain within it a theory of the state, however unconscious or incomplete.

The realist conception of foreign policy, which underlies most contemporary international relations theory, is rooted in assumptions about the foreign policy of nations that constitute an implicit theory of the state. The heart of the realist state is captured in Morgenthau's famous declaration that the central foreign policy goal of every nation is to achieve "the national interest defined in terms of power." Such a formulation has its strengths. Its simple form and universal scope are admirably suited to the central task of realism: "to bring order and meaning to a mass of phenomena which without it would remain disconnected and unintelligible" (Morgenthau 1967, 3). Realism has been generally successful on these terms: the historical record of the Eurocentric international system of the modern era can be interpreted as a struggle among states for power. Furthermore, this simplifying assumption concerning the motivations of states encourages the analyst to shift theoretical attention away from questions about why nations behave as they do toward challenging and promising questions about the causes and consequences of interactions among states. This emphasis upon system-level phenomena has bequeathed international relations a rich theoretical literature on interaction patterns, power balancing, system polarity, deterrence, spheres of influence, and much more.

Up until now these strengths—the ability to interpret a relatively narrow range of international affairs in a plausible, consistent, coherent way and to encourage creative theoretical elaboration—have insulated realism's conceptual foundation from sustained and explicit scrutiny (Halliday 1988b). Realism has avoided more stringent empirical tests because most realists are not sanguine about the possibility of *any* theory having the capacity to yield precise predictions. Moreover, realism's success in dealing with politicomilitary interactions among stable and homogeneous developed nations was sufficient in an era dominated by this Eurocentric "high politics" vision of international relations.

However, this essay suggests that realism fares less well the further it is removed from the Eurocentric core and the national security issue area where it was born, especially when it is held to the higher standard of predicting precise behavior. This is so simply because the implicit assumptions concerning the nature of the state upon which realism is built are less plausible outside the core and less relevant outside national security issues. Closer examination will show that the significance of "the national interest defined in terms of power" lies as much in what it excludes from the calculus of states as in what motivations it attributes to them. Realism focuses upon the state's outward behavior but largely ignores its origins, its composition, and its relations with civil society. As a result, the realist state has an ironically unrealistic essence.

■ Alternative Theories of the State

At the same time that studies of international politics have relied upon an *implicit* conception of the state, scholarship *explicitly* focused on the nature of the state has blossomed in recent analyses of comparative domestic politics. Two claims common to this literature contrast with realist assumptions. First, the state is complex and multifaceted in origin, in function, and in behavior (Lentner 1984; Rosenau 1988). Like any multidimensional object, the state exposes different faces to observers viewing it from different perspectives. Each face of the state highlighted by these theories suggests foreign policy behavior somewhat different from that implied by a realist state that seeks the "national interest defined in terms of power." Second, the variation among historical origins and contemporary environments guarantees that state forms, functions, attributes, and behaviors will exhibit enormous variation across cases (Skocpol 1985; O'Donnell 1980). This discussion identifies the foreign policy behavior consistent with the types of states most often found outside the core.

Alternative conceptions of the state are rooted in political economy analyses of the structure of society, economy, and polity. Though these state theories, unlike realism, are not principally oriented toward foreign policy, they do provide a framework for probing the determinants of foreign policy behavior, especially among noncore states. They also encourage the integration of comparative politics and international relations by postulating foreign and domestic policies as expressions of similar structural imperatives.

The "instrumentalist" view associated with Milliband (1969) offers the most dramatic denial of the realist conception of the state as an autonomous actor. Milliband rejects the realist premise that the linkage between the state and the society it represents may be safely ignored in policy analysis. Far from being largely unconstrained by domestic factors, the instrumentalist portrays the agenda of state goals and the broad strategy for meeting them as a direct reflection of the nature of the society itself. Milliband's conception of advanced industrial society emphasizes the existence of a ruling class composed of economic elites who dominate both the state and the society that spawns it. The resulting view that the state is an instrument of one class is exemplified by the famous quotation from *The Communist Manifesto*: "The executive of the modern state is but a committee for managing the common affairs of the whole bourgeoisie." Thus, the instrumentalist position portrays a very different motivation for a state's foreign policy than that assumed by the realist dictum of "national interest defined in terms of power."

Critics of instrumentalism point out that democratic institutions and other corporatist or pluralist arrangements constitute major challenges to the power of the dominant economic class. However, this objection holds with much less force outside the core of developed democratic nations. Less-developed countries are marked by much greater disparities in political influence and economic welfare across classes, while countervailing institutional power is largely absent. Thus, instrumentalist theory, though originally constructed with reference to advanced industrial societies, is probably more helpful in understanding the noncore state.[1] While theoretical and empirical challenges have led most theorists to reject instrumentalism in its pure form, three elements of it are found in other state theories.

First, the economic role of the state and the centrality of economic considerations for state policy are far greater than is recognized in most realist analyses. While the economic role of the state had not been totally ignored in earlier non-Marxist literature (Resnick 1986), structural theories in the neo-Marxist vein, discussed subsequently, have developed this theme most effectively.

Second, the social origins of state personnel guarantee that the interests of rich and powerful groups will be furthered by state policies. The best-known empirical studies of the methods by which this political influence is exerted are those of Domhoff (1967, 1969, 1978) in the United States, but a variety of radical non-Marxist theorists have contributed as well (Mills 1959; Shoup and Minter 1977; McGowan and Walker 1981; Frieden 1977).

Third, the state plays a major role as an instrument of social control, especially as a means of ideological legitimation of the existing order. Defending the legitimacy of the basic social structure is made more difficult by lower material achievement, greater levels of inequality, and poorer government performance. Thus, though best known through the writing of Gramsci and Offe on relatively developed states, this motivation for foreign policy is probably more prevalent among noncore states.

Structural views emphasize the role of the state in providing necessary functions for the maintenance of a capitalist system. In these functions the state is constrained not so much by the direct policymaking role of economic elites as by the structural dependence of the state on the process of capital accumulation that creates wealth. This process, controlled largely by economic elites, is indispensable not only because most broad social goals depend upon it but also because the state itself can be sustained only by the revenue it generates. Thus, from a somewhat different perspective, structural views would derive an expectation similar to instrumentalism: state policy owes more to the assumptions, views, and priorities of upper classes than to other elements of society.

Still, while the state must bias its policies toward the interests of the wealthy and powerful, the state cannot simply mirror the policy preferences of elites, in part because they vary and in part because slavish devotion to the interests of particular elites may well undermine the interests of the class as a whole. That is, the state must be partially *autonomous* of the very class it most represents.

Moreover, the state must be *seen* to be autonomous because its perceived legitimacy lies precisely in public acceptance of the proposition that the state operates as an honest broker among conflicting domestic groups in representing the nation as a whole. With respect to foreign policy, this means that realism's "national interest" interpretation of state goals must be widely shared. Failure to maintain the legitimacy of the state undermines not only the authority of the state itself but threatens the legitimacy of the system as a whole. The result is social instability and, most often, the violent suppression of dissent. The structural perspective sees foreign policy outside the core dominated by these twin structural imperatives of capital accumulation and legitimation, not by "national interest defined in terms of power."

A set of alternative views that ascribe markedly greater autonomy to the state has gained increasing currency in recent years among both neo-Marxist and more traditional analysts. The source of that autonomy is identified less with the necessity of maintaining the socioeconomic system than with the tendency of state policy to give first priority to defending the state itself. Such a priority is driven by the interests of a state conceived as a class-for-itself, made up of personnel who have shifted loyalty and identification to the state and away from the social class from which they have come.[2] Thus, goals more frequently derive from the interests of the relatively autonomous state and its personnel than from either the interests of the dominant class or the needs of the system as a whole (Caporaso 1982). Unlike the realist assumption that the state pursues the *national* interest defined as power relative to *external* actors, this view postulates a state pursuing its *own* interests defined as power relative to other *internal* actors.

One expression of this conception is the growing interest in what has been called a "statist" approach, which strongly rejects structural explanations because they imply that all states face similar pressures and behave in similar ways (Krasner 1984). Instead, this approach emphasizes the need for attention to the historical processes that have generated any particular state. Recent currents in neo-Marxist theory also have emphasized variations in the nature, role, and behavior of the state—even in relatively similar settings (Therborn 1986). To be sure, differences between states—indeed, the extent to which the state is an important category across different nations—has always been at least a minor theme in state analyses (Nettl 1968), but theories with a structural flavor tend to emphasize structurally mandated similarities and deemphasize historically induced uniqueness.

Each of these conceptions of the state point to goals that must be considered in foreign policy analyses. The realist tradition argues for the primacy of the maintenance of sovereignty, territorial integrity, and power vis-à-vis other external actors. Conventionally, foreign policy is also seen to promote broad societal values (Lentner 1984), especially emphasizing the achievement of economic prosperity conceived in aggregate terms. The Weberian tradition and its contemporary "statist" derivatives also draw our attention to the goals of maintaining the state itself as the preeminent intranational actor (Tilly 1975) and protecting the government personnel who control the state. Structuralist theory posits as primary the maintenance of capital accumulation and the perceived legitimacy of both the system and the role of the state within it.

Foreign policy can be best understood as the product of these partially competing goals, each of which reflects one face of the complex makeup of the contemporary state. The relative emphasis placed on each is largely a consequence of the character of the particular state and the environment in which it functions.

Most state theories acknowledge differences between the types of states typically found outside the core and those of Europe that initially spawned realist theory. While elements of similarity exist *across* these two groups and differences can be seen *within* both of them, some generalizations are possible. For example, the behavior of the noncore state is much less likely to approximate that associated with the realist vision because it often pursues markedly different goals and priorities. Further, even when goals are similar, they may be pursued in very different policy arenas. For example, legitimation and capital accumulation may be met by domestic policy in the core, but they are more likely to be pursued in the foreign policy realm by the noncore state. Thus, despite the danger of overgeneralization, the next three sections utilize the distinction between core and noncore state as a device to illustrate some of the variations that affect foreign policy behavior.

■ The Origins of the Peripheral State

The differences between the types of states found in the core and periphery derive from both their different origins and their distinctive environments. The colonial heritage common to the peripheral state combines with the poorly developed economic and political capacities of most Third World nations to yield a state-society relationship with important implications for policy behavior.

Unlike the organically created European state, with few exceptions the peripheral state was imposed from outside under conditions of colonialism. As Tilly observes, "The later the state-making experience...the less likely...internal processes...are to provide an adequate explanation of the formation, survival, or growth of a state" (1975, 46). The consequences of this distinction for the relationship between state and society are multiple.

First, if the state is not deeply rooted in the social, cultural, and political identity of the nation, one prominent explanation for foreign policy behavior is undermined. Why should state personnel choose to maximize the national interest rather than some other set of goals? A key linchpin in the usual argument involves an implicit acceptance of a Hegelian conception of the state "which embodies the notions of community, public purposes,...and the common good" (Lentner 1984, 370). Particularly during early statehood, however, there seems little reason to accept this characterization of the peripheral state or to anticipate the behavior that would follow from it. Government officials are not likely to be representative of the populace nor dependent for their status on domestic political institutions. There is neither a tradition of public service nor a set of precedents to guide and constrain claims to the national interest. In sum, a state that is foreign in origin may pursue goals very different from those of a state more deeply rooted in indigenous cultural, social, and political ideas.

While one certainly cannot be precise about the policy direction that will result, it seems likely that state personnel will identify less with the nation than with the state—and thus pursue goals more relevant to the latter than the former. As development proceeds, of course, connections between state and society usually grow, but the gap is likely to remain wider in the periphery than in the core. Of course, the process of the state becoming more deeply rooted in the domestic society does not imply that state policy will come to resemble realist prescriptions. Indeed, in the absence of pluralist mechanisms, behavior consistent with an instrumentalist perspective seems at least as likely.

Second, maintaining legitimacy is a persistent challenge for a state with such an ambiguous identity. For many newly formed states in fluid environments, the *juridical* component of "stateness" dominates the *empirical* component: a state exists when external legitimators *say* it exists, not when it establishes empirically its capacity to control a territory or to represent a nation (Jackson and Rosberg 1982). Thus, official recognition by outside powers has been highly prized during times of civil war, decolonization, and legal ambiguity, not least during the chaos following the breakup of the former Soviet Union. At such times, state policy must be differential to the juridical judgment of external sources or risk loss of recognition as a sovereign actor. At the same time, the state cannot undermine the internal perception that sovereignty—an important basis for legitimacy—is being vigorously exercised. There is much at stake in this balancing act, since an internal perception of illegitimacy threatens both social stability and the direct interests of state personnel.

While all states must be concerned with legitimacy, of course, the specific challenges vary greatly in degree and in kind. The widely accepted legitimacy of the state in developed nations derives from a number of sources often not available to non-core states: a long tradition of democratic representation and resulting compliance, the material performance of the system, and a low incidence of social instability. The most serious challenge occurs where the state must play an active role in nation building. It is difficult to establish the legitimacy of a state when the very nation it is said to embody is itself suspect. The postcolonial state in most of Africa, for example, inherited political boundaries that were arbitrary with respect to preexisting notions of nationhood. In parts of the former Soviet Union, groups clash over boundaries drawn around either ethnic populations or previous political units.

In such a setting, the state frequently will look to foreign policy to meet this legitimation function. Even in core nations, of course, the nature of foreign policy makes it a haven for symbolic action. There are few unequivocal measures of success or failure, and public judgment is likely to rest with the rationale offered in defense of policy goals rather than with the resultant outcomes. That is, performance standards are low or nonexistent. Policy is relatively easy to manipulate, and issues with only one plausible pole of opinion abound (e.g., no one is opposed to peace, military strength, or national security). By contrast, domestic problems are often a hopeless muddle of contradictory goals and competing interests, technically difficult problems, and sharply bounded possibilities.

Foreign policy enables the state to portray itself as the embodiment of nationalist pride. Nettl (1971, 88) notes that less-developed countries seek "self-definition, integration and even domestic viability by emphasizing their international role." Thus, he concludes that they are an "extra-societal form of state, which constitutes and defines itself primarily through its foreign relations." Legitimating appeals come in a variety of forms, often emphasizing an external enemy against whom the state is seen as a unifying force. This may help to explain the disquieting frequency of conflict among nations whose poverty would seem—to outsiders—a more appropriate target for scarce resources than the military establishment. At first glance such willful sacrifice of "national interest" might appear to result from the irrationality of leadership. It is instructive, however, that from an explicit state perspective the choice may lie between ruinous external conflict and an even more debilitating collapse of domestic authority. The outcome may be no less tragic, but it is explicable as a virulent pathology associated with the legitimation problems of the peripheral state. Its treatment, unlike its symptoms, is internal.

Alternative attempts to build state legitimacy through foreign policy consensus involve ideological appeals that give much of Third World foreign policy its strident rhetorical tone and limited substantive content. Examples include the appeal to pan-Africanism, support for the Palestinian cause, and opposition to colonialism and apartheid. This is not to say, of course, that such efforts are either insincere or inappropriate. To the contrary, to command wide support such legitimation appeals must tap and mobilize existing consensus rather than create it artificially. It does appear, however, that many such efforts are largely ineffectual with respect to classical realist goals of peace, prosperity, and power but are directly relevant to the motivations ascribed to the state by alternative theories.

More controversial initiatives, such as the New International Economic Order (NIEO), are also interpretable as originating as much in the imperatives of an internally vulnerable state as in the pursuit of the prosperity and external power components of national interest. To be sure, such policies are probably overdetermined—any one explanation from the available set would be sufficient to predict NIEO support. But the angle provided by Krasner's (1985) exposition of the domestic weakness of the Third World state does shed light on particular features of the NIEO proposals. He argues that the evident antiliberal character of NIEO is rooted in a strong preference for authority-based rather than market-based modes of allocation. Not only does this approach tend to strengthen Third World actors in dealing with the First World—the ostensible rationale—it also enlarges the legitimate economic role of the Third World state, thereby strengthening it in dealing with internal actors. Combined with the legitimation benefits associated with fostering Third World solidarity and challenging such unpopular actors as the United States and the International Monetary Fund, the domestic needs of the noncore state would make a compelling case for NIEO even if there were no external consequences at all.

Third, while legitimation difficulties plague many noncore states, that is not the only source of internal weakness which motivates foreign policy action. Government personnel are more precariously situated in both the Third World and Eastern Europe than in the core. Even if legitimacy claims can be sustained on behalf of the state, the ruling regime must also beat back the challenge from competitors for the mantle of state power. Political opposition and especially the military present a constant threat to coup. The threat often can be met more effectively in the foreign policy sphere than in the domestic policy sphere. Because the support of external powers is usually critical (though often controversial), bilateral relations often are more rooted in domestic political contests than in realpolitik calculations. (Of course, it is equally clear that external actors—aid givers, for example—are often as motivated by a desire to strengthen the state and/or the ruling regime as they are by concern with the nation.) Also, insofar as the military is frequently decisive in domestic political conflicts, no aspect of defense policy or military budgeting can be seen as purely, perhaps even primarily, a foreign policy issue.

In short, the variation in the locus of challenges faced by different states ought to be reflected in the theories used to explain their respective foreign policy behavior. The primacy afforded power vis-à-vis other nations by realism stems from the perception that the greatest threat to national interest lies in the vulnerability of state sovereignty to the military power of other states. For the noncore state, the greatest vulnerability to state sovereignty often arises from the precarious domestic position of the state and the ruling regime. The principle that follows is that the state will act to maximize its power toward other internal actors. This may sometimes require the sacrifice of more traditional realist goals, such as when the dependent state acquiesces to diminished policy latitude in exchange for the wherewithal to maintain internal power (e.g., foreign economic and military aid).

■ The Economic Role of the Peripheral State

Another distinctive characteristic of the peripheral state stems from its introduction rather early in the developmental process. In much of the colonial world the state preceded the rise of a powerful capitalist class, while elsewhere, especially in Eastern Europe, the state forcibly displaced it. As a consequence, the state became a more direct economic actor, often assuming the entrepreneurial role played by private capital in the core. It retains that presence in the economy of both the Third World and the postsocialist nations today. A World Bank study (1988) indicates that public sector investment, for example, constitutes nearly half of total investment among developing countries. Capital spending in the public sector is a much higher percentage of GNP among developing countries, especially those in the middle-income range. The incidence of state-owned enterprises in the periphery—capital outlays are typically between 5 and 7 percent of GNP—is also markedly higher than in the core. Wage expenditures by government are a higher percentage of GNP among middle-income countries than among developed nations. Of course, the greater centralization of planning that is a well-known characteristic of development in the Third World assumed a commanding presence in the state socialist regimes. In short, the noncore state is a dominant economic actor whose role goes far beyond the core state's function of maintaining the institutional structure required to allow capital accumulation to occur in the private sector. The consequences are multiple.

First, as a major employer, the state frequently has interests identical to those of private capital. This reinforces the structurally induced affinity of the state for the policy positions held by business as opposed to workers or consumers. As a result, the possibility of such a state achieving legitimacy as an arbiter of class conflict wanes; the state acts not only as a visible ally of capital but as a business with direct participation in the production process. Consequently, the drive for legitimacy must be directed elsewhere, often toward the foreign policy realm.

A second consequence is that the economic arena will become a more central priority of state policy while economic considerations will come to dominate other goals, especially in the foreign policy realm. The fusion of the public and private sector magnifies the pressure on the government since it blurs further the distinction between government performance and macroeconomic outcomes. With system legitimacy and government stability hanging in the balance, the state emphasis on economic policy is virtually assured. While many aspects of the state and its relation to civil society have changed in Eastern Europe, this economic primacy has not.

Of course, the role of the state only accentuates a tendency already inherent in the prominence of economic problems outside the core. Economic growth is such a key prerequisite to so many other goals in a poor nation, all policy is ultimately constrained by the imperatives of capital accumulation. This is seen vividly in government budget allocations. The share of the budget devoted to economic services is two and a half times larger in developing than developed nations. Most dramatically, 56 percent of the government budget in industrial countries is in the social sector, while the comparable figures for middle-income and low-income nations are 34 percent and 8 percent, respectively (IMF 1987). Because of both similar imperatives in the two spheres and the efforts of the development bureaucracy to secure additional instruments in pursuit of their goals, it would be surprising if these different priorities in domestic policy did not carry over to foreign policy as well. Indeed, given that capital accumulation in a penetrated economy requires a state to be active in the foreign policy sphere (a point discussed in greater detail later), for many peripheral states the chief goal of foreign policy is to lay the groundwork for successful development policy. This usually implies the maintenance or expansion of external economic flows.

A third consequence for foreign policy requires an appreciation of the extraordinary transformation of relations among classes and elites that is implied by the presence of an economically active state imposed from without on a less-developed nation. As O'Donnell puts it, "...Instead of the state being...some sort of reflection of civil society, it was, to a large extent on the contrary, the state apparatus that shaped the basic features of our societies" (1980, 717). The state shapes society principally by controlling opportunities for wealth creation and power accumulation. That is, "contrary to the classic capitalist patterns..., an emerging dominant class did not shape the political power embodied by the state...[instead] the domestically dominant class has been the child of the state apparatus."[3] Two results would seem to follow.

First, the shift of elite identification and allegiance to the state required by statist conceptions should be greatly eased. A policy bias toward state interests, as opposed to national or class interests, would thus seem likely. Second, in an environment where the state is at least as important a determinant of material success as the market, rent-seeking behavior concentrated on control of the state is a rational response. Such competition will be especially fierce, thereby adding to pressures on the government and elevating the priority attached to protection of the existing government from domestic challenge.

Finally, neither the class structure nor the institutional patterns in the periphery are comparable to those that influence the core state to seek the "national interest." For example, greater inequality in educational opportunities gives state personnel a class bias that better fits the instrumentalist than the pluralist perspective. Further, the representational mechanisms that introduce nonelite constraints on state behavior are weak or absent outside the core.

In short, the nature of state-society relations in most of the periphery affords greater plausibility to the foreign policy predictions derived from some theories of the state than others. This consideration favors either the state-for-itself prediction of behavior designed principally to protect the state from domestic competitors or the instrumentalist perspective in which the state supports the interests of the capitalist class. The structuralist view of promoting capital accumulation and maintaining legitimacy also fares well, with the proviso that, as we see later, a state can arise that is neither structurally dependent on internal capital nor pressed by a powerful class which enforces that goal. Such a state could be quite indifferent to economic development and capital accumulation, though one or the other is usually posited as a universal goal. It would appear that "the national interest defined in terms of power" is more likely to be a goal complimentary to one of the above than to be a primary motivation. The case for the pluralist vision of a state maximizing aggregate welfare is not obvious.

■ State Reaction to Foreign Penetration

An even stronger link between domestic state goals and foreign policy is rooted in the dependence of the national economy on trade and various capital flows. The importance of these transactions is too well known to require extensive treatment, but the role of the state in maintaining them has been less fully appreciated. Because the domestic economy is so deeply rooted in the external economy, much of the state's activity in sustaining the conditions necessary for capital accumulation carry it into the foreign policy realm. For example, while core states may seek to increase investment through manipulating macroeconomic policy, the source of marginal investment in the periphery is primarily external. While productivity increases might be sought through deregulation or shifting incentives in the core, the issue in the periphery involves technology transfer. Demand management is a domestic problem in the core but a foreign policy issue in the periphery.

Many of these functions can be performed only by the state, especially when foreign actors are specifically involved. For example, negotiations with the IMF and foreign banks over loans and debt rescheduling, with multinational corporations over investment incentives, and with foreign governments over aid terms all tend to expand the already large role of the state in economic planning. Among low-income countries (excluding China and India), for example, net official development assistance averages 9 percent of GNP. External public debt among lower-middle-income countries exceeds 50 percent of GNP. The sheer size of these public flows not only elevates the prominence of the state and makes foreign actors significant players in the domestic economy but also erodes the distinction between domestic and foreign policy.

In this environment the maintenance or expansion of external economic flows becomes a primary proximate goal pursued in the foreign policy realm. When it became necessary to reassure powerful external actors concerning economic stability during the cold war period, for example, East-West alignments and anti-Left rhetoric were frequently used as litmus tests. Most analysts assumed that the result would be greater efforts to please Western capital sources. While often true, the domestic vulnerability of the state usually requires that other reactions also be considered, including attempts to play off other donors, to achieve collective self-reliance, and to seek structural reform of international regimes.

Of course, the noncore state relies on the external world for goals other than capital accumulation. External sources of military support (training, personnel, equipment) may be necessary for regime survival, for example, while economic aid increases the resources available specifically to the state as well as to the nation more generally.

More broadly, however, the state is itself as structurally dependent upon these flows as is the economy. This is especially significant in economies marked by an export enclave such as mining or plantation agriculture. Just as substantial inflows of capital go directly to the state (e.g., aid and loans), tax revenues are heavily derived from external transactions. While there are marked differences among nations, on average the state in low-income countries derives more than 28 percent of its revenues from taxes on international transactions (chiefly trade), while the comparable figure for the industrial market economies is about 1 percent. While nontax revenues constitute 9 percent of total income for industrial states, elsewhere the figure is between 20 and 30 percent.

As the state becomes structurally dependent upon the foreign sector, its range of interests narrows correspondingly. While it accepts the mission of assuring the social stability necessary to sustain that sector, its operations are not as complex as those of a state facing a better-developed class structure and more interests to balance, more conflict to mediate, and more goals to pursue. In short, it need not be so attentive to the broad social goals suggested by Hegelian conceptions or the definition of economic prosperity imposed by pluralist mechanisms in the core.

It is likely, however, that the well-known volatility of the peripheral economy coupled with the state's structural dependence upon it will incline the state toward arrangements that strengthen the state. One example is the hostility toward market-oriented modes of allocation and the preference toward authority-based ones visible in NIEO proposals (Krasner 1985). Another is the markedly more regulated character of foreign trade outside the core, an issue that has frequently pitted a dependent country against a more liberal dominant one. As Bates (1981) makes clear, these arrangements also involve tradeoffs between the power of the state and such other goals as growth and equity. It is instructive that such conflicts have not succeeded in substantially affecting the state-centric character of most development in the Third World, though some change is apparent over the last decade.

■ Conclusion

In sum, the character of the state and the nature of the policy environment in which it functions produce distinctive foreign policy behavior. Thus, foreign policy outside the core is more likely to be a tool to achieve domestic goals than a means to the outcomes emphasized by realism. In particular, the special circumstances of both Eastern Europe and the more traditional Third World make foreign policy an indispensable tool for meeting state imperatives: capital accumulation, state legitimacy, social stability, and government maintenance.

These differences in goals and constraints are likely to lead realist analysts to misjudge foreign policy outside the core. Because peripheral states possess few of the capabilities classically associated with power politics—military power, political influence, economic resources—it is often thought that their foreign policy activity will be similarly limited. One might well assume that their diminished capacity to influence the outcomes of international politics together with their less immediate concern with issues rather remote from them should dampen their willingness to expend scarce resources on foreign policy.

To the contrary, peripheral states are very active in foreign policy. It is true, of course, that their behavior patterns are somewhat different—they are more attuned to the low politics of economic matters than to military geopolitics, for example. But this pattern is not as strong as might be expected from the limited ability of the Third World state to *win* in the issues of high politics. The inability to achieve realist goals does not diminish the imperatives associated with the other faces of the noncore state. Legitimacy, for example, flows from *opposition* to imperialism, not from its defeat.

In short, though foreign policy may be inconsequential from the standpoint of achieving realist goals, it remains absolutely critical for the goals of the noncore state. Moreover, foreign policy position taking will be both more important and markedly more contentious than commentators have sometimes supposed. Far from being an arena in which autonomous elites can afford to respond to external actors, foreign policy is a critical component of the political program of the government and frequently a key foundation of the state itself.

As a consequence of its centrality and political importance, foreign policy is less prone to external influence than theory might otherwise suggest. In particular, noncore states are frequently more intransigent than acquiescent in dealing with great powers and international institutions. This is not because they obstinately refuse to acknowledge the realities of international power but because they understand too well the realities of *intra*-national power. An overly compliant state loses domestic legitimacy. More than that, there is often a direct goal tradeoff. IMF agreements, for example, typically require cuts in state spending that accentuate problems of state legitimacy and regime security by undermining the ability of the state to present itself as protector of the poor and mediator of class conflict. Similarly, the anti-Western rhetoric espoused by many UN member states that has so dramatically affected attitudes in the United States toward the UN is difficult to eliminate. It is neither idle nor irrational but a structurally necessary element that helps to hold together the total policy package that sustains the government.

In sum, the state that acts in international politics is the same state whose attributes are such a central part of our study of comparative politics. Recognizing this linkage will improve our understanding of both.

■ Notes

1. In the poorest nations, however, the inchoate class structure does not include a fully developed capitalist class capable of controlling the state. Within this structure the state is usually dominated by a traditional landowning class.

2. This shift should be most pronounced in those economies in which the state controls the chief means to acquisition of wealth.

3. Of course, there is considerable variation within the European experience. The state has played a larger role in shaping modern France, for example, than this argument acknowledges. Still, the distinction is justified both by the origins of the state—largely internal in one case but largely external in the other—and by the degree to which the state dominated development processes.

TWELVE

Foreign Policy in Dependent States

Jeanne A. K. Hey, MIAMI UNIVERSITY

■ Editors' Introduction

In this chapter Jeanne Hey introduces a series of theories of "dependent foreign policy" relating to economically dependent, usually Third World states. Hey illustrates the flaws in the conventional wisdom that "dependencies," those states that are economically dependent on a core state, align their foreign policies with those of the core. She argues that theory in this area must account not only for dependent foreign policy outcomes, but also processes, i.e. how foreign policy is generated, as was explained by Patrick Haney (chapter 7). This chapter reveals that dependent states have a very rich foreign policy repertoire, a finding that was too rarely acknowledged in first-generation research. This chapter also speaks to the following chapter by Laura Neack on linking state types with foreign policy behavior.

In reading this chapter, consider the following questions: What is the direct or indirect impact of economic dependence on foreign policy? In addition to those countries discussed in this chapter (Jamaica, Ecuador, Mexico), what other examples can you think of that illustrate the models of dependent foreign policy? Do you expect that the end of the cold war will have an influence on the United States' ability to influence its dependencies' foreign policy? Finally, how does Hey's discussion bridge with Moon's analysis of the state, particularly as it applies to Third World countries? ■

Many students of the foreign policy of Third World, dependent, and small states have lamented the fact that most theoretical models in foreign policy analysis have been developed to explain the behavior of the First, and to a lesser extent, the Second Worlds. Too often the foreign policy of weak states is viewed as the manifestation of those states' inferior position within the international system. Their leaders are left to react to global events and to resign themselves to an ineffective position in world affairs. According to this position, their low status on the global ladder overwhelms other explanatory factors of their foreign policy (Cammack et al. 1988, chapter 7; Handel 1990, 261).

Increasingly, empirical research informed by a growing sophistication within foreign policy analysis demonstrates that Third World foreign policy processes are as complex as those in the rest of the world. This is not to say that Third World foreign policy content and processes do not differ from those in the "developed" world. Current models designed to explain developed states' foreign policies may require modification to explain weak state behavior. But the image that weak states' foreign policies are designed by single, usually dictatorial, leaders who have few options but to respond to global events determined by others is disappearing within foreign policy analysis. Former Costa Rican President Oscar Arias's development of a successful peace plan for war-torn Central America is but one example of a Third World leader's creative diplomacy in a policy area considered by many as superpower territory. Foreign policy in weak states, as in all states, is of course conditioned by the international environment. Providing more than a gross explanation of foreign policy requires careful and detailed analysis of domestic political conditions and processes in Third World states just as it does in the "developed" world.

This chapter focuses on patterns of conduct and explanatory factors within a particular subgroup of Third World states: those with dependent economies. A discussion of the definitions of dependent states is followed by an examination of the methodologies employed in dependent foreign policy analysis and the findings generated by research in this area. The chapter concludes with an elaboration of four models of dependent foreign policy behavior.

■ What Is a Dependent State?

Defining dependence is critical to the study of dependent foreign policy. Overlapping literatures treat the foreign policies of "small," "Third World," "weak," and "dependent" states. The aforementioned assumption, namely that these are nonplayers on the global scene, too frequently has been attached to all of these. "Small" typically refers to those countries that are either small in physical size or population (Vellut 1967, 254–56). Both the Netherlands and Dominica are small states, but they have drastically different histories and foreign policies. A state's smallness does not necessarily indicate that it is weak, dependent, or a member of the Third World.

The Encyclopedia of the Third World defines the "Third World" "as the politically nonaligned and economically developing and less industrialized nations of the world" (Kurian 1992, ix). The definition is surprising, as most Third World states are indeed aligned either with a superpower or with regional allies. Similarly, many non–Third World states, most notably those of Eastern Europe, are in early stages of development while the newly industrialized members of the Third World are quite industrialized. *The Encyclopedia's* definition presents the Third World in an abstract form and ignores the political and economic realities of the modern international system. More typically, the "Third World" is distinguished from the advanced industrialized Western democracies of the First World as well as from the Soviet Union and its East European allies of the now-defunct Second World (Buzan 1991, 432; Wolf-Phillips 1987). Although the Third World thus defined is diverse in both political and economic systems, the noncapitalist members such as Cuba or North Korea rarely receive much attention within the group. Third World states are generally considered those with free-market economies and integrated into the global capitalist system. Recently added to this classification scheme is the "Fourth World," used to distinguish the chronically poor from those developing countries showing some economic promise. This addition is encouraged by the World Bank's four-tiered classification, which differentiates "low-income economies" from "lower middle-income economies" (Wolf-Phillips 1987, 1313–14). In 1992 the former's members ranged from Mozambique, with a GNP per capita of $80, to Egypt, with a GNP per capita of $600. The latter's members ranged from Bolivia with a GNP per capita of $630 to Iran with a GNP per capita of $2,490. This scheme is based solely on GNP per capita and interestingly places many traditionally Third World states with the Second World in its "higher middle-income economies" category. Kuwait, another Third Worlder, is at the top of the World Bank's entire global income scale (World Bank 1992, 218–19).

"Small" and "Third World" are thus typically defined with objective measures such as geographic size and GNP per capita, measures that may not capture the characteristics of these states that make them interesting to foreign policy analysts. An alternative conceptualization is that of "weak states," which implies that power is relative. Weakness is meaningful only when compared with strength. Singer refers to wealth, organization, and status as the components of power that weak states lack. He adds that *perception* is also critical, that is, that other global actors perceive that a particular state is powerless (Rothgeb 1993, 29; Singer 1972, chapters 1, 2). Conversely, Handel discourages relying on a single set of variables to measure state power in the global system. Weak states, he argues, "form the largest class of states and have the most diverse membership—facts which make it still more difficult to assign them any common denominator other than their overall relative weakness" (Handel 1990, 30). As the dimensions of power are multifarious, the defining characteristics of weakness (or strength) need to be flexible.

Much of the literature on small, Third World, and weak states is marked by an "I know one when I see it" understanding of classification. Theorists spend little time arguing over definitions of the terms and instead focus on the role of weak states in the international political system. Indeed, "weak" states are often defined by their position in the international system—those that because of any number of factors (their poor capabilities, their neocolonial status, their internal chaos, and so forth) are relegated to noninfluential players or pawns in the global system. This concern with weak states' status in international affairs, as opposed to elements of their global *behavior,* demonstrates more interest in international relations than in foreign policy. In other words, classifying weak states according to their international rank emphasizes the unlikelihood that they will be influential actors on the world stage, rather than the policies they develop to meet their goals. Indeed, clear definitions may not be critical to a student of international politics concerned with global or regional patterns of conduct. However, the student of foreign policy analysis, in explaining the foreign policy behavior of a particular type of state, must be very careful with definitions. The defining elements of weakness may be critical contributing factors to a foreign policy explanation.

Clearly the terms discussed here are frequently related. The colonial legacy shared by most Third World states can generate economic dependence and weakness in the international system. Small states often suffer from limited resource bases that make them weak. Despite the interrelatedness of the concepts, we should not assume that Third World necessarily implies weak, small, or dependent. It is in this respect that *dependence* gains potency as an analytical concept in foreign policy analysis. It refers to a specific relationship between a state and its economic partners that is hypothesized as important in understanding that state's foreign policy behavior.

Dependence can manifest itself culturally, politically, and economically. The most easily measured and arguably the most important of the three, *economic dependence*, receives the vast majority of attention in dependent foreign policy studies. It is important to distinguish between dependence and dependency (or dependencia). Many scholars, some of them working within dependency theory, agree with James Caporaso who argues that dependence is the pattern of external reliance of nation-states on one another, while dependency involves a more complex set of relations centering on the incorporation of less developed, less homogeneous societies into the global division of labor (Armstrong 1981, 402; see also Duvall 1978; Menkhaus and Kegley 1988, 319; and Richardson 1981, 88).

As Caporaso explains, dependency differs from dependence in the sense that dependency is a contextual situation defined by both domestic and international variables that frequently defy attempts to quantify them. That dependency thus defined resists quantification and therefore empirical analysis is a major source for criticism of dependency theory. It is also the principal reason why foreign policy analysts (with the notable exception of Bruce Moon [1983, 1985]) choose to study the more readily measured dependence.

What exactly constitutes dependence? According to Neil Richardson, "Dependence refers to a distinctively asymmetrical situation in which one country is significantly reliant on another even as the second country no more than slightly depends on the first" (Richardson 1981, 88). Richardson's efforts to delineate and measure dependence have been particularly meticulous. He explains that three features must characterize the economy of the "first," or dependent, state but not that of the second. First, the dependent state's economic relations with the "second," or core, state must be exclusive, that is, the former cannot share similar relations with other states. Second, the availability of substitute economic partners must be low, making it difficult for the dependent state to diversify its economic relations or choose new partners. Finally, the relationship must be important to the entire economy of the dependent state. Economic aid, for example, can be a measure of dependence only if that aid constitutes a significant part of the recipient's economy (Armstrong 1981; Richardson 1981, 91–92).

The most common indicators used to identify dependent states are the economic benefits they secure from trade, foreign aid, and direct foreign investment from the core country. Trade is the most popular and has been most strongly correlated with dependent foreign policy behavior (Menkhaus and Kegley 1988; Ray 1981; Richardson 1976; Richardson and Kegley 1980). Foreign economic and military assistance has been frequently studied as a means to coerce foreign policy alignment (Kegley and Hook 1991; Moon 1985; Rai 1980; Wittkopf 1973). A few studies compare the effects of trade dependence and aid dependence on the foreign policy behavior of dependent states and arrive at competing conclusions (see, e.g.,

Menkhaus and Kegley 1988; Roeder 1985). Studies linking foreign investment with foreign policy behavior usually consider the role of the multinational corporation as an intervening agent operating in the interests of the host country (Richardson 1978; Rothgeb 1987, 1989). Richardson (1978) combines these three measurements to identify a list of states dependent on the United States. Indeed, with a few notable exceptions (e.g., Keohane 1966; Menkhaus and Kegley 1988; Ray 1981; Roeder 1985), most empirical studies examine the relationship between the United States and its dependencies. The emphasis on the United States reflects the availability of data as well as the fact that theories of core-periphery relations, from which many dependent foreign policy hypotheses are developed, have been developed largely within the context of understanding relations between the United States and its dependencies.

The set of "dependent" states, as identified by these indicators, overlaps heavily with the Third World, weak states, and, to a lesser extent, small states. The overlap is functional in that it allows studies of dependent foreign policy to inform theory in these other areas. This does not mean that we can become lax in our definitions of dependence or that we can assume that a dependent state is also a weak state, a small state, or a member of the Third World. It remains essential that clear defining criteria be employed in choosing dependent cases, as it may be those same criteria (e.g., trade, aid, and investment dependence) that most influence foreign policy behavior.

■ Methodology in Dependent Foreign Policy

The essential question posed in dependent foreign policy research is whether economic dependence leads to foreign policy compliance. Do dependent states implement the foreign policy preferences of their principal trade/aid/investment partner? Two principal methodologies dominate attempts to address the issue.

Case Studies

The first principal methodology is case studies, ranging from examinations of individual regimes or states to considerations of foreign policy behavior within or across regions. Rarely do case studies of individual states or regimes focus specifically on the relationship between dependence and foreign policy behavior. Rather, most seek a comprehensive analysis of the foreign policy process within which an understanding of the dependence–foreign policy relationship can be found (see, e.g., Corkill and Cubitt 1988, chapter 5; Hunter 1992, chapter 5; Korany 1986b; St. John 1992; Ward 1992; Wright 1992). Edited volumes on the foreign policy dynamics of different *regions* within the Third World also contribute indirectly to theory in dependent foreign policy. However, chapters in such volumes generally do not address specifically the relationship between dependence and foreign policy. Instead, they typically focus on regional foreign policy patterns and the peculiarities of specific countries' international behavior (Braveboy-Wagner 1989; Ferris and Lincoln 1981; Lincoln and Ferris 1984; Muñoz and Tulchin 1984; Okolo and Wright 1990).

That few case studies have systematically contributed to the dependent foreign policy literature does not indicate the methodology's weakness. Rather, too few scholars of dependent foreign policy have used case studies for theory building in this area. Those who have done so have contributed significantly. For example, William Biddle and John Stephens (1989) examined the relationship between dependence and foreign policy in the first Manley administration in Jamaica. They demonstrated that the negative effects of dependent development led Jamaicans to favor a Third World–oriented foreign policy and to challenge U.S. global and regional dominance. Similarly, Kenneth Menkhaus and Charles Kegley (1988) employed a case study of Somalia to investigate the foreign policy effects of a state's economic dependence on a number of trading partners. They found that Somalia complied most with its most important trading partner, Saudi Arabia, but also maintained strong relationships with many others such as the United States, the Soviet Union, and Italy. Hey and Kuzma (1993) demonstrated that Costa Rican and Mexican economic dependence on the United States did not prevent these middle American states from developing Central American peace plans hostile to U.S. interests as defined by the Reagan administration. Hey (1993) examined a series of cases of Ecuadoran foreign policy to explore the explanatory capacity of different dependent foreign policy theories.

Case studies are a promising avenue for expanding understanding of dependent foreign policy. As is discussed later, the links between economic dependence and foreign policy behavior and process are multidimensional, complex, and varied. Data needed to capture this relationship in quantitative analyses are not available for many poor, dependent states. Case studies allow for in-depth examinations of dependence and foreign policy behavior. Furthermore, a growing body of research on conducting and using case studies in a systematic and comparative fashion makes this methodology increasingly attractive to foreign policy scholars in general, and particularly to those studying the dependent world (Eisenhardt 1989b; George 1979a; George and McKeown 1985; Gerner 1992a; Lijphart 1975; Ragin 1987).

UN Voting and Quantitative Analysis

The second dominant methodology is statistical analysis of aggregate data, which typically examines the foreign policy behavior of a number of dependent states. Most common are studies inquiring whether economic dependence correlates with foreign policy compliance. Measurement of these concepts is a key part of these studies. Economic dependence is operationalized with a variety of indicators measuring trade, aid, and investment dependence (Duvall 1978; Menkhaus and Kegley 1988; Richardson 1981). These data are readily available from a number of sources—the International Monetary Fund (IMF), World Bank, and United Nations among the most commonly used.

More difficult is the measurement of a dependent state's compliance with the foreign policy wishes of the dominant economic partner. Despite a few noble efforts at finding sophisticated measures of this complex concept (DeRouen and Mintz 1991, 27–32; Richardson 1981), the vast majority of scholars working within this tradition employ UN voting data to capture compliance. The most common measure is the degree to which a dependent state votes with its dominant economic partner in the UN General Assembly. Lijphart (1963), Richardson (1976), Wittkopf (1973), Rai (1980), Richardson (1978), Richardson and Kegley (1980), Armstrong (1981), Ray (1981), Moon (1983, 1985), Roeder (1985), Menkhaus and Kegley (1988), Christian and Dokhanchi (1991), and Kegley and Hook (1991) all use some indicator of UN voting agreement between the peripheral and the core states as a measure of foreign policy compliance. The overwhelming majority of these authors focus specifically on the United States and its dependencies' voting records. In recognition that pressure to vote with the core is more likely applied in those areas salient to the core state, Wittkopf (1973), Richardson (1978), Richardson and Kegley (1980), Ray (1981), and Roeder (1985) also selectively examine "cold war" votes, those on which the United States and the Soviet Union voted in opposition to each other.

Very few researchers in this area have relied on other types of data to measure compliance. Notable among them are Rothgeb (1987, 1989), who uses indicators of conflict and cooperation based on the COPDAB event data set, and Armstrong (1981), who compares the UN General Assembly–based results with those based on the Dimensions of Interaction event data set.[1] Interestingly, Armstrong's findings from the event data set, arguably containing richer indicators of compliance, reveal lower degrees of compliance than those based solely on UN votes (Armstrong 1981, 417).

UN General Assembly voting data, when used to measure foreign policy compliance, have provided the basis for a number of important advances in understanding dependent foreign policy. Using these data, the researcher can examine many cases, compare them cross-nationally and subject them to time-series tests. Large-N analyses of UN voting are also helpful in demonstrating trends in dependent states' foreign policy behavior. For example, Richardson and Kegley's longitudinal analysis of the foreign policy behavior of U.S. dependencies demonstrates declining levels of compliance in the 1950–73 period (Richardson and Kegley 1980). Quantitative cross-national studies also facilitate comparing the foreign policy effects of different types of dependence (trade, aid, investment; see Armstrong 1981; Roeder 1985). Finally, these types of studies generate significant questions to be addressed with other methodologies. For example, with respect to Richardson and Kegley's just-mentioned finding, were declining UN agreement rates a function of the United States' decreasing interest in the UN as a global forum? Or do they reflect a real loss of Washington's ability to link economic dependence with foreign policy compliance (Richardson and Kegley 1980, 216–17)? Responses to these questions are best addressed by scholars of regional foreign policies, international organizations, and U.S. foreign policy.

While quantitative research has been an invaluable contributor to understanding in this field, a number of important drawbacks of UN votes as a measure of compliance should be mentioned. First, UN voting behavior is not foreign policy. As a proxy for foreign policy, it is arguably weak. A state's voting behavior in the UN is a mere fraction of the composite of its foreign policy behavior. Second, compliance presupposes influence or power on the part of the core state to force its dependencies to do what they otherwise would not. A dependent state is compliant only if it implements a policy not in accordance with its own preferences (Ray 1981, 113; Richardson 1981, 89–90). However, UN voting data provide no information on a dependent state's preference. Similarly, as Ray (1981, 113–14) points out, a vote against the core state may not necessarily indicate foreign policy defiance, as the core may be willing to allow its dependencies to "blow off steam" from time to time in the UN General Assembly. These concerns are almost universally acknowledged, but cast aside, by those who argue that UN voting is an appropriate measure of foreign policy behavior. Richardson (1978, 130), Ray (1981, 114), and Roeder (1985, 197) all cite Karl Deutsch's assertion that influence and compliance are best captured with observations of "a repetitive class of similar outcomes, such as votes in the United Nations Assembly" (Deutsch 1968, 24–25). Indeed, the vast majority of researchers relying on UN votes devote a section or paragraph to eschewing the concerns of those wary of UN votes as a measure of compliance.

These scholars' defensiveness betrays their anxiety about the validity of UN votes as a measure of foreign policy behavior. The principal concern here, and a third critique of UN voting, is that UN votes are not only a small part of the whole of foreign policy behavior, but that a regime's UN voting record may *not* reflect that government's overall foreign policy orientation or behavior. An important article by Tomlin (1985) demonstrates that states often vote and operate in regional blocs in the UN. Their behavior outside of the UN, however, does not correspond to their behavior within. Regional cohesion that may appear quite strong in the UN may be absent or weak in bilateral and multilateral relations occurring at home.

A fourth and final critique is that UN votes do not allow the researcher to look into the policymaking process. Foreign policy analysts in general have been as concerned with foreign policy decision-making process as with foreign policy outcome. Indeed, many foreign policy researchers are more interested in process than in outcome. With the exception of Bruce Moon (1983, 1985), who creatively applies statistical techniques using UN voting data to procedural questions about dependent foreign policy, few scholars working with aggregate data are able to use those data to provide insights into the foreign policy process. Instead, the process question receives little attention or is addressed with speculation and qualitative assessments at the end of the research presentation (see, e.g., Menkhaus and Kegley 1988, 341). As mentioned earlier, it is appropriate that quantitative analyses generate questions in need of qualitative methods. Nonetheless, the failure to address directly the process dimension of dependent foreign policy conveys the false impression that dependent states' foreign policy processes are less complex than those of their nondependent neighbors.

Students of dependent foreign policy should employ both qualitative and quantitative methods. The two should not compete as the most appropriate methodology in this field. Rather, researchers engaged in cross-national studies with aggregate-level data should take more seriously the questionable validity of UN votes as measures of foreign policy compliance (Russett 1970, 431). They should also explicitly identify questions emanating from their findings that are best addressed with more qualitative research. Case studies should be conducted in a rigorous manner, addressing the relationship between dependence and foreign policy behavior, and with particular attention paid to the generalizability of findings. Case studies should also be designed to examine and clarify the intricate foreign policy processes behind the aggregate trends exposed in quantitative longitudinal studies.

■ Dependent Foreign Policy Process and Outcomes

Does economic dependence lead to foreign policy compliance? If it does, what is the process behind a dependent state's decision to implement a compliant foreign policy?

Studies in dependent foreign policy address these questions and arrive at many, sometimes conflicting, conclusions.

It is useful at this point to report the results of the quantitative analyses discussed previously. When considered as an entire body of research, quantitative analyses of dependent foreign policy behavior overwhelmingly conclude that the relationship between dependence and foreign policy compliance is very weak, if existent at all. Some studies find a positive correlation, while others find a negative relationship or none at all. Wittkopf (1973) discovers an association between U.S. foreign aid and dependents' compliance but recommends caution in interpreting the results. Neil Richardson, an important pioneer in this field, finds that U.S. dependencies vote with the United States in the UN, but the relationship between dependence and compliance is nonlinear, that is, the most dependent states do not comply with the greatest frequency (Richardson 1976, 1978). Ray (1981) and Roeder (1985) find that Eastern Europe had significant degrees of compliance with the Soviet Union. Other studies of states dependent on the United States, however, reveal little evidence for the dependence-compliance hypothesis. Rai (1980), Richardson and Kegley (1980), Armstrong (1981), Moon (1983, 1985), and Menkhaus and Kegley (1988) all report very weak results. Richardson and Kegley (1980) show that compliance with the United States is in decline. More recently, Kegley and Hook (1991) demonstrate that even when the Reagan administration specifically developed a policy linking dependent states' UN voting behavior to U.S. foreign aid disbursements, U.S. dependencies failed to comply.

It is not particularly surprising that this weak empirical record has not deterred political scientists from continuing to scrutinize the relationship between dependence and foreign policy behavior. Most remain convinced that a relationship exists but that it is highly complex and may occur outside the venue of the UN. In order to examine the many dimensions of dependent states' behavior in the international realm, it is useful to consider both the *content and process* of dependent foreign policy. Doing so reveals a number of different foreign policy manifestations of dependence.

The following discussion is arranged according to the content of foreign policy behavior. Do dependent states develop foreign policies in alignment with the core's preferences? The first section deals with those that do, while the second considers those that do not. Each section discusses the processes behind either pro-core or anti-core dependent foreign policies.

Pro-Core Foreign Policies

A dependent state's development of a pro-core foreign policy[2] is not necessarily the product of the dependent relationship. As mentioned previously, the dependent state may share the foreign policy preferences of the core and implement pro-core policies without ever considering the economic or political consequences. The critical procedural question that must be asked about pro-core foreign policies, then, is whether a pro-core foreign policy was somehow coerced or otherwise pressured from actors outside of the dependent state.

If the policy was developed from within and not subject to external pressure, the policy cannot be categorized as compliant. This does not indicate that there is no relationship between dependence and foreign policy behavior, however. Bruce Moon's research (1983, 1985) has contributed greatly to our understanding of the development of pro-core foreign policies outside of a framework of compliance. Moon looks to dependency theory to explain consistently pro-core behavior by U.S. dependencies and concludes that *consensus* among elites in periphery and core leads to foreign policy alignment. Dependency theorists, most frequently in reference to Latin America, explain that peripheral states' economies are controlled by a class of economic elites whose financial interests are directly linked with those of foreign investors. In addition to material ties, the peripheral elites share ideological views on politics and economy with elites in the core. In many cases the peripheral elites are educated in the core. This confluence of interests, background, and opinions leads to agreement between peripheral and core leaders (who are part of the dominant economic class) on many issues, including foreign policy. Thus, foreign policy alignment is *consensual,* not compliant. Pro-core foreign policies are nonetheless a product of dependence, according to this view. The marriage of interests and ideologies is inextricably tied to the dependent relationship between periphery and core. This relationship favors the core and a small elite in the periphery but inhibits real peripheral development and an equitable distribution of wealth (Amin 1974; Cardoso and Faletto 1979; dos Santos 1970; Moon 1983, 1985).

A clear empirical example of consensus occurred in Ecuador in 1984 when, shortly after his inauguration, President León Febres Cordero signed a foreign investment agreement with the United States. Ecuador allowed the Overseas Private Investment Corporation (OPIC), a U.S. government agency, to operate in Ecuador. OPIC grants risk insurance to U.S. investors abroad but requires that local laws be favorable to investors and that any disputes between investors and the host country be arbitrated internationally. Although these restrictions were inconsistent with current Ecuadoran practices, Febres Cordero went ahead. This is an example of consensus because the Ecuadoran president, a strongly pro-U.S. free marketeer, was not pressured into signing this agreement against his wishes. Instead, he fully agreed with canceling restrictions on foreign investments and implemented a policy that was consistent not only with his own views but with those of the Reagan administration as well (Hey 1992, 1993).

Moon's work is somewhat unique in its attempt to develop hypotheses from dependency theory and to test them with rigorous, quantitative empirical analysis. Much more common among studies of pro-core foreign policies are those testing the popular hypotheses of *compliance.* Compliance assumes an affirmative answer to the question of whether pro-core policies are a response to some external pressure on dependent foreign policy makers. Compliance theorists, whose work is discussed earlier, formulate their hypotheses within the realist tradition of international relations and anticipate that dependent states will develop foreign policy within the context of their asymmetrical economic relationships. Economic instruments from the core (trade, aid, investment, credit) and foreign policy behavior from the periphery are seen as bargaining chips within the hegemon-client relationship. Dependent states comply with the foreign policy wishes of the core in exchange for economic rewards or to avoid economic punishments. Implicit in the compliance notion is that the dependent state would prefer not to implement pro-core policies. Richardson explains that the dependent state's "support may be grudging, but it may be necessary because the dominant state has asymmetric control, especially in the long-run, over the costs and benefits to be derived from their economic relations" (1978, 64). Because of weak empirical evidence, the compliance or bargaining model of dependent foreign policy has recently lost support among foreign policy researchers (DeRouen and Mintz 1991, 44–45). This is not to say that numerous examples of compliance cannot be found within the current international system. One recent example of compliance is the United States' forgiving Egypt's $7 billion arms debt in exchange for its support of the coalition fighting Iraq in the Gulf War (Gilsenan 1992, 228). This example illustrates the direct linkage between an economic carrot or stick (forgiveness of debt) and Third World foreign policy behavior (agreeing to join the coalition) that compliance expects. Nonetheless, compliance is but one of a set of explanations for dependent foreign policy behavior. Consensus is another explanation of pro-core foreign policies.

Anti-Core Foreign Policies

One might initially conclude that an anti-core policy is evidence that no relationship exists between dependence and foreign policy, or that anti-core behavior is an exhibition of an independent foreign policy. Indeed, true foreign policy independence, defined as a policymaking process influenced in no way by a state's dependent status, is certainly possible (Hey 1993). However, a more plausible explanation for most anti-core policies is that they are related to dependence in one of two ways.

First, anti-core behavior may be a hostile reaction to the state's dependence. This is known as *counterdependence* and is described by Marshall Singer as a "psychological state of individuals or groups in the process of altering a relationship from one in which they felt dependent and/or inferior, to one in which they feel equal. It is often an angry 'lashing out' to redefine an existing relationship. In psychological studies it is used synonymously with the word 'rebellion'" (1972, 42).

Counterdependence in the foreign policy realm is the manifestation of dependent leaders' frustration with their countries' dependent situations. It is an attempt to use foreign policy as a means to counteract dependence and to achieve greater independence. In an excellent study of counterdependence (though they do not use the term), Biddle and Stephens describe former Jamaican Prime Minister Michael Manley's anti–United States behavior as a "direct product of the negative and contradictory aspects of dependent development itself" (1989, 412). Prior to Manley's assuming power in 1972, the United States played a large role in Jamaica's "decision" to adopt a development plan that brought uneven economic growth and an increasingly inequitable distribution of wealth. This situation caused resentment among Jamaican voters, who then elected Manley, a democratic socialist committed to breaking ties with the United States and fostering stronger bonds with the Third World. Hey (1992, 1993) describes Ecuador's policy on Latin American debt as a second example of counterdependence. Ecuadoran President Osvaldo Hurtado (1981–84), reacting to indebted Latin America's very weak bargaining position with international creditors, invited all regional leaders to the Latin American Economic Conference, held in Quito, Ecuador, in 1984. Hurtado purposefully invited no leaders from the United States and other creditor governments and devoted the meetings to the development of a regional debt strategy that would improve Latin America's negotiating position vis-à-vis creditors. The resulting conference policy was a direct manifestation of Hurtado's frustration with Latin America's dependence on creditors in the core.

A second process by which an anti-core foreign policy develops reflects dependent leaders' use of foreign policy to mollify domestic opposition to dependence. The *compensation* model of dependent foreign policy is common among studies of Mexican foreign policy. Though few of these studies speak directly to the dependence–foreign policy relationship, they have much to contribute to an understanding of dependent foreign policy. Mexican foreign policy makers have consistently implemented anti–United States policies, especially in the diplomatic realm. Scholars agree that an anti–United States position is necessary for the ruling "revolutionary" PRI[3] party to maintain its internal legitimacy despite strong economic ties with the very nonrevolutionary United States. Former Mexican President Miguel de la Madrid's participation in the Contadora Peace Plan for Central America, against U.S. wishes, is an example of compliance (Castañeda 1985, 88; Ferris 1984, 214, 222; Grabendorff 1978; 1984, 86; Hey and Kuzma 1993; Pellicer 1981, 91; 1985, 85).

Examining compensation takes us directly into the domestic political situation of a dependent state and is an ideal representation of what Rosenau (1969a) labeled "linkage politics."[4] As Kegley and Hook (1991, 308) state in their explanation of the compliance model's poor performance, dependent states' policies are "driven more powerfully by interests other than by the economic threat of a hegemon." In the Mexican case, the other interests relate to the PRI's level of support from popular sectors. It is important to make clear here that the Mexican domestic displeasure with the PRI is explained as a direct product of Mexican economic dependence on the United States. Thus, dependence has led indirectly to an anti-core foreign policy. The intervening variable is public opinion in the dependent state.

■ Conclusion

The four explanations or models described here—consensus, compliance, counterdependence, compensation—most likely do not exhaust the possible manifestations of dependence on foreign policy behavior. They nonetheless provide a point of departure for theorizing about (and then examining) the specific links between economic dependence and foreign policy. As the empirical record demonstrates, there is no unidimensional relationship that expresses itself consistently over time. Instead, the association between the two concepts is complex and subject to influences at the individual, domestic, and international levels of analysis.

Future research should continue to examine the dependence–foreign policy relationship exhibited in the recent past. No consistent patterns are yet evident. Recent global changes also present new challenges for scholars working in this field. In the post–cold war era, the degree to which dependent states remain constrained by their relationship with core states assumes particular importance. If dependent states' foreign policy alignment was sought by the superpowers to improve the latter's strategic position in the bipolar world, will compliance lose its allure now that bipolarity is ended? Also, now that cold war issues are less important, what issues will become the most salient to core leaders? Has the end of the cold war provided dependent states with a new opportunity to achieve independent foreign policies? Alternatively, will the end of the cold war provide core states with more energy and resources to devote to keeping their dependencies "in line"? These new questions should be added to the agendas of foreign policy scholars studying dependent states.

■ Acknowledgments

I would like to thank Laura Neack, Patrick J. Haney, and Michael Snarr for their comments on an earlier draft of this paper, which was presented at the 1993 meetings of the International Studies Association in Acapulco.

■ Notes

1. See the chapter by Philip Schrodt (chapter 9) in this volume on the use of event data in foreign policy analysis.

2. The term *core* here refers specifically to the state on which the dependent state is economically dependent. For example, for most of Latin America, the critical core state is the United States. In most political economy discussions of international relations, *core* refers to the advanced capitalist states that dominate the global economy. In this discussion the term refers to that country or those countries with explicit economic ties to the dependent state in question.

3. PRI is the Spanish acronym for Institutional Revolutionary Party.

4. See chapters by Joe Hagan (chapter 8), Karen Mingst (chapter 14), and Bruce Moon (chapter 11) in this volume for discussions of domestic political forces in foreign policy and linkage politics.

THIRTEEN

Linking State Type with Foreign Policy Behavior

Laura Neack, MIAMI UNIVERSITY

■ Editors' Introduction

In this chapter Laura Neack explores some of the ways in which analysts have considered whether states exhibit certain foreign policy behaviors because of the "types" of states they are. This chapter continues a general theme pursued by the first generation as well as by Joe Hagan (chapter 8), Bruce Moon (chapter 11), and Jeanne Hey (chapter 12) in this volume. Neack spends most of this chapter considering two relatively new and popular lines of research on state type and foreign policy behavior—the "pacific" democracies theory and middle power theory—both of which draw heavily upon international relations theory. Neack suggests that these lines of inquiry demonstrate a changing orientation of scholars toward contextualized analyses of state type and foreign policy behavior, a marked departure from the first-generation desire to construct universal theories on this linkage. This chapter speaks directly to the issues of political reasoning and the implications of politicized assumptions that are raised earlier by John Rothgeb and V. Spike Peterson.

When reading this chapter, consider how much countries are influenced by their image when constructing foreign policies. For instance, as the remaining superpower and the "winner" of the cold war, can the United States disengage from an activist foreign policy and stay home, or does this contradict the expectations associated with being a world leader? What internal and external dynamics feed the growth of a particular state image? What does it take for countries to get out from under their perceived images and roles? Finally, recall the task posed at the end of the chapter by V. Spike Peterson: Are middle powers states that follow a gender-neutral foreign policy? If so, is this because of the state type (middle power) or because of other reasons (more women in national office, for instance)? ■

Analysts commonly assert that certain types of states act in patterned, predictable ways, that the foreign policy of the state is somehow linked to the kind of state it is. For instance, consider this statement:

> The point has been made before, and is repeated in the country studies, that it is very much in the interests of middle powers, particularly those dependent upon trade, to contribute to the development of international trade, financial, and monetary regimes which would negotiate and enforce common rules and standards. (Pratt 1989, 194)

Or, consider this statement:

> Theoretically, I always found the argument fairly convincing that democratic governments are more concerned with the avoidance of war than are other governments. (Weede 1984, 652)

These statements link state type with more or less specific foreign policy behaviors. Such proposed relationships often serve as the theoretical frameworks guiding foreign policy research. Sometimes these expected relationships even guide individual and collective decision making, serving as explanation or justification for particular foreign policy behaviors.

In this chapter I discuss three research efforts that link state type and foreign policy behavior. I begin with a brief discussion of a first-generation effort to link "ideal nation-types" with foreign policy behavior at the aggregate level. Then I consider one current variant on this line of inquiry, which I label "pacific democracies" research. Finally, I discuss "middle power theory" research, a line of research that, among the three discussed, is the most successful at establishing a credible linkage between state type and foreign policy behavior. The success of middle power research can be attributed both to the intellectual origins of middle power theory and to the rich, contextualized nature of the theory itself.

■ Nation-Types and Foreign Policy Behavior

The formal comparative study of "ideal nation-types" and foreign policy behavior was initiated largely by James Rosenau in his "pre-theory" of foreign policy (1966). Rosenau hypothesized that three national attribute indicators—physical size, level of economic development (as in developed or underdeveloped), and nature of the political system (open and democratic or authoritarian and closed)—are associated somehow with differences in states' foreign policy making processes and in their foreign policy behaviors. He combined these three national attributes into the following eight "ideal nation-types," and offered examples of states that fit into each category:

1. Large, developed, open: United States

2. Large, developed, closed: Soviet Union

3. Large, underdeveloped, open: India

4. Large, underdeveloped, closed: China

5. Small, developed, open: Netherlands

6. Small, developed, closed: Czechoslovakia

7. Small, underdeveloped, open: Kenya

8. Small, underdeveloped, closed: Ghana

Rosenau did not suggest the types of foreign policy behaviors that might be associated with these nation-types. Indeed, his primary focus in the "pre-theory" article was to develop a typology for ranking variables from five levels of analysis according to the relative importance of each in the foreign policy making process of the eight nation-types. Thus, for instance, for large, developed, open countries, he proposed this ranking of variables: role, societal, governmental, systemic, individual. For large, underdeveloped, closed countries, he proposed this ranking: individual, role, governmental, systemic, societal. Rosenau left it to other scholars to explore the relative importance of these variables in the foreign policy making process of the different nation-types, just as he left it to others to discover the types of foreign policy behaviors that might be associated with the ideal nation-types.

The purpose of the "pre-theory" article was to sound a call to action (research) for foreign policy scholars. With Rosenau's "pre-theoretic" musings as launching pads, scholars could begin a systematic search for pieces of knowledge that could be used both for grounding future research efforts as well as for building generalized theory around which the scientific study of comparative foreign policy could coalesce. Rosenau's ideal nation-types would facilitate this activity in the following way: "The concept of nation-type makes it unnecessary to examine individual nations in considering the certain types of foreign policy activity. To this extent, we can move away from analysis of discrete objects and concentrate on classes of objects and the different patterns of foreign policy associated with each" (East and Hermann 1974, 272). Thus, ideal nation-types were conceived as useful tools for facilitating the development of general statements linking state type and foreign policy behavior. These general statements, or laws, in turn, would help both academics and statespersons better understand and predict the "real stuff" of states' foreign policies.

While Rosenau was issuing his "pre-theory" call, other researchers (e.g., Rummel 1969, 1972a) were finding statistical evidence to support the proposition that physical size, economic development, and political orientation *were* significant in explaining the variation in states' foreign policy behaviors (East and Hermann 1974; Hermann and Peacock 1987). With this evidence accumulating, foreign policy scholars began to try to measure the association between these national attributes, the derivative nation-types, and *specific* foreign policy behaviors.

One research effort in this vein was conducted by Maurice East and Charles Hermann. East and Hermann (1974) used the Comparative Research on the Events of Nations (CREON)[1] data set to test twenty-seven bivariate hypotheses linking size, economic development, and political accountability with nine foreign policy behavior measures. One of their objectives was to determine whether any one of the three national attributes could explain some of the observable variation in states' foreign policy behaviors. They also measured the interactive effect of four combinations of the three national attributes on the foreign policy measures. The interactive combinations were: size x development, size x accountability, development x accountability, and size x development x accountability. This last interactive combination between all three national attributes was a direct test of Rosenau's ideal nation-types. The foreign policy behaviors examined included verbal events, diplomatic events, military events, and cooperative events, among others.

East and Hermann found that some of the national attributes seemed to be strongly associated with foreign policy behaviors. Of the single indicators, East and Hermann concluded that physical size best accounted for foreign policy behavior. The next most important indicator was political accountability, especially in conjunction with economic development (1974, 299). Conversely, they were unable to find much support for Rosenau's ideal nation-types. According to East and Hermann:

> The conception of eight distinct nation-types based upon the interaction of the three dichotomized attributes appears unjustified as a means of explaining foreign policy behavior. Admittedly, this conclusion rests upon the examination of only 33 countries and nine classifications of foreign policy behavior. But the findings take on more significance because they confirm the analysis by Salmore (1972) who used a different sample of nations, a different set of foreign policy measures, and a different collection of data. (1974, 300)

Although Rosenau's ideal nation-types were not supported by East and Hermann's research, nor by other efforts, the notion that nation-types could be identified as engaging in particular foreign policy behaviors was not put to rest. International relations textbooks, such as Bruce Russett and Harvey Starr's *World Politics: The Menu for Choice* (1992), typically discuss Rosenau's nation-types and "pre-theory" before any discussion about different types of states manifesting different foreign policy behaviors. Further, empirical quantitative research aimed at measuring the association between Rosenau's three national attribute indicators as well as other selected indicators and specific foreign policy behaviors continued throughout the first generation. For instance, East (1973) and Rudolph Rummel (1979) continued this line of research using various event data sets. Much of the work was inconclusive and heavily dependent upon how the nation-types being studied were delineated (Neack 1991). One of the more successful and enduring research lines deriving from this tradition is the "pacific democracies" research that spans both generations in the study of foreign policy.

■ Pacific Democracies

A popular variant on the search for empirical evidence linking certain foreign policy behaviors with ideal nation-types is found in the "pacific democracies" literature (see Chan 1984; Morgan 1992; Russett 1993b; Weede 1984, 1992). This research finds its intellectual roots in Kant's proposition that democracies are peace-loving countries (Gleditsch 1992; Morgan 1992). According to the first version of the pacific democracies theory, appearing in international relations and foreign policy scholarship during the 1970s, democratic states are less likely to go to war than nondemocratic states. In its later version this theory proposes that democracies do not fight other democracies (Gleditsch 1992; Weede 1992). If this is true empirically, democratic states would have an interest in promoting and deepening democratization around the world both to protect themselves and to promote international peace (Gleditsch 1992; Rummel 1979; Russett 1993a).

Research on pacific democracies differs from the first-generation scholarship on ideal nation-types in that the pacific democracies research is well grounded in theory. The ideal nation-type research was largely atheoretical and deductive, with most of the research efforts adopting Rosenau's "pre-theory" nation-types without much consideration of the selection of Rosenau's three indicators nor of Rosenau's contention that the three indicators worked interactively.

There is, however, considerable theoretical foundation for pacific democracies research (Morgan 1992). Indeed, there are two different theoretical accountings of why democracies are supposedly more pacific than nondemocracies. The first explanation focuses on the culture of democracies. The cultural explanation is that "liberal democracies are more peace loving than other states because of the norms regarding appropriate methods of conflict resolution that develop within society" (Morgan 1992, 198). That is, peaceful conflict resolution techniques learned in domestic politics are mapped onto foreign relations. The second theoretical explanation focuses on the structure of democracies. The structural explanation is that "some institutional arrangements produce greater impediments to decisions for war than do other arrangements" (Morgan 1992, 199). Leaders of democracies are restrained by other officeholders and voters in the types of activities they may attempt abroad, especially violent and hostile activities. Both explanations command considerable support among scholars, with some of the more recent scholarship being conducted by devotees of one or the other explanation aimed at proving their own theory and disproving the other.

This flurry of activity aimed at accumulating evidence for one or the other theoretical accounting suggests that the pacific democracies theory is not a theory as much as a law. That is, the considerable debate on the proper explanation for why democracies are more pacific suggests that democracies have been *proven* to be more pacific than nondemocracies. However, the jury is still very much out on this issue. Much of the research on pacific democracies "has sought to reconcile the monadic level findings that democracies are as war prone as other states with the dyadic level findings that democracies do not fight one another" (Morgan 1992, 198).[2] That is, the empirical results are mixed on pacific democracies. "First, there is little difference in the war involvement of democracies and other regimes. Second, war or military conflict is extremely rare among democracies" (Weede 1992, 377). These results could be rephrased: democracies are just as likely to go to war as are nondemocracies (with both going to war fairly infrequently), but the target of the warfare differs from democracies to nondemocracies.

We can only draw this rather unenlightening conclusion from the research, however, by disregarding the substantial analytical discrepancies between and within research efforts. The research on pacific democracies is marked by inconsistent research designs, including the use of restrictive as well as elastic definitions of what is meant by "democracy" and "war." Another troubling aspect of this research line is that the claim that "democracies don't fight each other" disregards aggregate-level and case evidence that directly contradicts the claim.

Consider the conceptual inaccuracies found in the work of one of the strongest proponents of the pacific democracies theory. The proposition that "freedom inhibits violence" of any sort has been most loudly advanced as well as confused by Rudolph Rummel (1979). As described by Erich Weede: "On the one hand, Rummel (1979, 292) argues: 'The more libertarian a state, the less it tends to be involved in violence.' On the other hand, he argues on the very same page: 'I do not expect that there will be a correlation between libertarianism and the frequency of involvement in war or violence'" (Weede 1984, 650).

Clearly Rummel's comments reflect some tension between what he believes *ought* to be true and what quantitative analysis will reveal. He had reason to be pessimistic about the latter; many analysts have noted the contradictory and confusing empirical evidence resulting from quantitative attempts to prove the peaceful democracies claim. Melvin Small and J. David Singer concluded after one such study: "It may be true that freely elected governments rarely fought one another; but they did become involved in quite a few wars, and not always as defenseless victims of a dictator's aggression. Governments that are not freely elected have no monopoly on unnecessary and aggressive wars" (1976, 68).

Further, Steve Chan (1984) and Weede (1984) present evidence that suggests that the claim that democracies don't fight each other is true only for a relatively short period of time, historically speaking. Weede examined war and conflict in the 1960s and 1970s and concluded that democracies did not fight other democracies only in the period of the late 1970s (1984, 656–57). Chan examined wars from 1816 to 1980 and concluded that there was a *positive* association between democracies and war from 1916 to 1973; that is, democracies were more war prone than nondemocracies. Chan found that Rummel's assertion about democracies held true only from 1973 to 1980 (1984, 642).

Indeed, despite the fact that Chan's study is now a decade old, no study has been able to dispute his most telling criticism—that research on the pacific democracies notion yields different results because of the different analytical choices made by the analysts. Similarly, Weede has recently concluded that, "all findings depend on the context of the study—i.e., on assumptions about causes of war and about how to combine them.... The crucial question is whether the theoretic assumptions behind the research design and the fairly simple calculations are meaningful" (1992, 382).

Nils Petter Gleditsch echoed this conclusion when he stated that the pacific democracies studies "seemed to be based, on the one hand, on raw empiricism ... and, on the other, on airy philosophical principles" (1992, 373). The whole range of quantitative research on pacific democracies is criticized by Gleditsch for being too simplistic: "In the midst of regression analyses, factor analyses, and numerous other multivariate techniques, the idea that *one variable* alone is a sufficient (but not necessary) condition for a state of peace in the sense of non-war seems ridiculously naive" (Gleditsch 1992, 371).

The evidence from case studies also directly contradicts the "peace-loving democracies" as well as the "democracies don't fight each other" claims (e.g., Chan 1984; Forsythe 1992; Weede 1984, 1992). For example, David Forsythe's intensive case studies on intervention provide evidence that some democracies do use violence against other democracies: "The USA has repeatedly acted covertly, sometimes with threat or use of force, against political regimes that were not only elected but which could be accurately termed partially or basically democratic. In political and somewhat hyperbolic terms, there was a war between the USA and these elected governments" (1992, 392). Forsythe adds that U.S. interventionism in the domestic affairs of non-Western democratic countries[3] is generally excused by the claim that "the political regimes targeted by US covert action, especially forcible action, did not meet the threshold conditions for complete liberalism" (1992, 393). That is, the United States does not use violence against other democracies, since the targets of U.S. interventionism have not been democracies in the truest—read "Western"—sense.

Forsythe's study is important for more than its refutation of the "democracies don't fight each other" assertion; it demonstrates the contextual nature of the foreign policy decision-making process. In order to excuse away intervention in these democratic states, the United States (and the scholars who serve as national apologists) can offer as justification its own *perception* of the target states (as less than democratic), as well as its own *perception* of what would happen around the globe if it did *not* intervene in the affairs of the target states (the "domino theory").[4]

Another problem with the pacific democracies claim, one that is related to the problem of explaining away intervention in non-Western states' affairs, is that its proponents ignore the role that Western democracies have played in perpetuating and exacerbating civil and interstate conflicts and wars since World War II. Beyond disregarding interventionism and other coercive and violent tools of statecraft, pacific democracies advocates limit their study to "the presence or absence of war rather than the process of 'war-making.' The latter concern expands the scope of judgment to include actions preceding or following a war, including the spread of weapons and military technology which might facilitate wars...in the first place" (Latham 1993, 147).

A commonly noted feature of the international order since World War II is rapid militarization and the predominant role of advanced industrialized countries (and the former Soviet Union) in contributing to this phenomenon. For example, according to Stockholm International Peace Research Institute (SIPRI) estimates, the top ten arms exporters of conventional weapons to developing countries over the years 1987 to 1991, ranked from largest to smallest were: (1) the Soviet Union, (2) the United States, (3) France, (4) China, (5) the United Kingdom, (6) the Federal Republic of Germany, (7) Brazil, (8) the Netherlands, (9) Italy, and (10) Czechoslovakia (SIPRI 1992, 272). Admittedly, a substantial amount of this arms trade, but not all of it, can be attributed to the cold war. Moreover, since the collapse of the Soviet Union, the United States now accounts for 50 percent of the arms trade in the world. On the face of it, this seems inconsistent with the idea of enlarging the circle of democracies to better ensure a peaceful world. A similarly troubling finding is that the most active UN peacekeeping states are also among the world's largest arms exporters (Neack 1994). Pacific democracies theorists rarely, if ever, address this apparent inconsistency.

This has not been lost on Robert Latham in his criticisms of the pacific democracies theory: "Islands of liberal democratic peace have not only waged war on non-democracies, they have also been responsible for—and are uniquely successful at generating—high levels of global militarization and have contributed significantly to militarization in, and conflict among, non-democratic states, conditions that can help undermine the successful spread of liberal democracy in the long-term" (1993, 139). Latham contends that pacific democracies theorists have conveniently over-looked "important ways in which military force and international liberal relations are intertwined" (1993, 140). Latham suggests that these two phenomena are linked in two broad ways. The first involves the macro construction of the post–World War II liberal economic order that absolutely depended upon the continued presence of either a single military hegemon (the United States) or a collective military hegemon (NATO). Latham contends that the West never required that other countries be liberal democracies, just that they be committed to the liberal economic order and stand with the Western states against the Communist world's challenge to that order. The "common denominator" or thread holding members of the liberal economic order together would be Western and Western-linked *military* alliances. Thus, we can explain Western support for nondemocratic regimes such as those in Saudi Arabia and Kuwait.

The second broad way in which military force and international liberal relations are intertwined involves the more immediate contributions that liberal democracies have made to continued armed conflict in many developing states. One of these contributions is the West's role in global militarization discussed previously. Other contributions made by the West involve the "evolution" of warfare techniques, including dramatic advancements in weapons systems and technologies, the creation of the modern air force, the development of the military-industrial complex, and even—as begun in the 1840s relationship between the United Kingdom and France—the arms race (Latham 1993, 152). Again, pacific democracies theorists ignore the many ways in which the "pacific democracies" do not contribute to peace in the world but instead ensure the transfers of more and more deadly weapons and modes of warfare.

Beyond this major failure of the pacific democracies theory (if the theory can withstand yet another problem), the whole body of pacific democracies research may be built on little more than fantasy. As Weede has noted, "War is an inherently infrequent event. The probability of war between any randomly chosen pair (or dyad) of nations within a decade or two is very close to zero. And it is difficult to demonstrate that some condition, like both states being democracies, will reduce some likelihood which is already very close to zero, even in its absence" (1992, 377).

Indeed, with Weede's caution in mind, Gleditsch offers a list of reasons why the pacific democracies theory ought to be "thrown on the scrap-heap of history" (1992, 373). Gleditsch contends that this theory is a political outgrowth of the cold war (1992, 373–74). If democracies are more peaceful, it would then serve the purposes of democracies and the world to *force* states to democratize in the Western style. Thus, the pacific democracies theory could be used as a justification for armed intervention—conveniently enough, used against nondemocratic or "unstable" democratic states that were leaning toward the Soviet Union. This echoes the conclusion drawn by Forsythe (1992) discussed previously. According to Gleditsch, this politicized use of the pacific democracies theory was apparent in a related phenomenon: "The debate about imperialism in the 1970s focused, unsurprisingly, more on the war-mongering nature of several democracies than on their peacefulness (1992,

374). Gleditsch suggests further that the Western rhetoric in the Persian Gulf War of 1991 seemed to derive from an "imperative" to act to ensure a world made in the Western image or at least made for Western purposes.

The perpetuation of the pacific democracies discussion into the post–cold war period does seem to reflect some of the self-congratulatory mood apparent in the West, particularly in the United States. This ongoing celebration of Western-style democracy and the theory of the pacific democracies seems to ignore the international context in which analysts first found evidence to support this theory and the international context in which analysts continue to perpetuate it (now as a "law" of international relations, according to Maoz and Russett [1992, 246]). Western democracies stopped waging war against other Western democracies because together they successfully created a postwar international system in which they would all stand to benefit. As John Rothgeb points out in this volume (chapter 4), this was the spoil of war that fell to the victors. Moreover, Rothgeb concludes, the international order these Western democracies constructed and maintained was one in which Western democracies could put aside the costly old tools of foreign policy—violent foreign policy behaviors—in their relations with one another. These tools could be discarded because the Western democracies had effectively eliminated their mutual territorial insecurities. With this context in mind, it does not seem particularly surprising that analysts have found that "democracies don't fight each other." Indeed, it is only surprising that some analysts have treated this "finding" with such surprise.

From the perspective of the study of foreign policy, pacific democracies research is an example of second-generation foreign policy analysis that builds upon and leaves behind first-generation work. The tie-in to the first generation is obvious; the departure occurs in two ways. First, this research eschews efforts to delineate all possible combinations of ideal nation-types and their foreign policies, and instead seeks to demonstrate empirically and understand a simple hypothesized bivariate relationship. The narrower focus can be attributed to the theoretical foundation of the pacific democracies research, a foundation generally found absent in the first-generation ideal nation-type research. Second, discrepancies in the reported findings of pacific democracies research that result from analytical choices are openly discussed in the literature. Indeed, the work on pacific democracies self-consciously admits to methodological biases and arguments between theoretical traditions.

Both of the research efforts discussed here have the same flaw, however; both contend that the relationship between state type and certain foreign policy behaviors exists in a contextual vacuum. But there are some important contextual variables that ought to be included in any analysis of foreign policy behavior: the nature of the international system, countries' perceptions of opportunities and dangers in that system, and national self-perceptions. That the nature of the international system would somehow affect the foreign policy choices of states no matter their type and/or national attributes seems intuitive and is a fundamental tenet of international relations theory (e.g., Gourevitch 1978; Holbraad 1984; Mares 1988; Waltz 1959). That national self-perception (of the country's mission, of its international responsibilities, of its historical legacies, and so on) and the country's perception of the opportunities and dangers present in the international system would have an effect on foreign policy behavior also seems intuitive and is frequently supported by the literature (e.g., Hey [chapter 12] in this volume; Karns and Mingst 1987; Papadakis and Starr 1987).

In an assessment of the foreign policy literature that links state type with foreign policy behavior, Deborah Gerner (1992b) suggests that this research could be improved by using the environmental model proposed by Papadakis and Starr (1987). The model is described as follows:

> The state is an entity in an environment, and the environment may be divided into different levels with different sets of variables characterizing each level. The environment defines the context within which a state may act, but how the state *actually acts* or deals with its environment depends upon a number of factors: the set of opportunities that the characteristics of the sub-environments "objectively" provide the state, how the state perceives its environment, its willingness to take a particular course of action, and so on. (Papadakis and Starr 1987, 416, as quoted in Gerner 1992b, 165)

I agree with Gerner's suggestion and see it as a call to action for second-generation foreign policy scholars in much the same way as Rosenau's "pre-theory" called to first-generation scholars. The type of foreign policy behavior in which a state engages is a function of the state's perception of its "type" and the roles it perceives as being associated with that type, along with its perceived opportunities and constraints, both of which derive from the domestic and international contexts. Furthermore, these different factors are probably interdependent, such that variations in one can transform the natures of the others. The "middle power" theory proposed primarily by Canadian, Australian, and Scandinavian scholars implicitly embodies this complex model; thus it serves as a good illustration of the direction in which foreign policy scholars should turn.

■ Middle Powers

It should be noted from the outset that "middle power theory" is not a theoretical framework nor a methodological approach developed by scholars attempting to link state type and foreign policy behavior. Middle power theory was developed by statespersons to describe the status, international role, and foreign policy behaviors of their states (Hawes 1984; Holmes 1982; MacKay 1969). Middle power scholars have adopted the idea of the middle power from these statespersons and have spun a considerable literature upon it. Middle power theory is discussed in this chapter because it is a richly contextual, multifaceted "theory" that can serve as an example for other second-generation attempts to explore the linkages between state type and foreign policy behavior.

Middle powers are states that commit their relative affluence, managerial skills, and international prestige to the preservation of the international order and peace (Cooper, Higgott, and Nossal 1993; Holmes 1982; Krause, DeWitt, and Knight 1990; MacKay 1969; Puchala and Coate 1989).[5] They help to maintain the international order through international coalition building, by serving as international mediators and "go-betweens," and through international conflict management and resolution activities, such as UN peacekeeping. Middle powers perform these international activities because of an idealistic imperative that they associate with being a middle power. The imperative is that middle powers have the moral responsibility and collective ability to protect the international order from those who would challenge it when the greater powers will not and the lesser powers cannot (Hawes 1984; MacKay 1969; Puchala and Coate 1989).

In common usage, the "middle powers" are Canada and Australia, *some* of the Western European countries, especially the Netherlands, Norway and Sweden, and sometimes *some* of the "regional" powers such as Brazil, Mexico, Algeria, and India (Higgott and Cooper 1990; Holbraad 1984; Krause, DeWitt, and Knight 1990; Mares 1988; Pratt 1989). Unfortunately, the ambiguity in this statement about who the middle powers are reflects the lack of a systematic, widely accepted definition of "middle power" in the general study of international relations and the specific study of foreign policy (Cooper, Higgott, and Nossal 1993; Neack 1991, 1993). Often, "middle power" in any given analysis is defined to fit the state or activity under discussion. This is a stumbling point for many discussions of middle power behavior, but one that cannot be adequately addressed within this chapter. What is important to note here is that most discussions of middle powers in international politics are idiographic discussions of the foreign policies of self-identified middle powers (Neack 1991, 1992).

The view of the middle power as international peacekeeper, mediator, and coalition builder got started by a single state trying to secure for itself a position in the post–World War II international system. During the Dumbarton Oaks discussions over the shape of the United Nations, Canadian Prime Minister King requested that Canada be given a special status in the new UN. This status would reflect the capacities of Canada as well as its responsibility to the international system. According to King,

> The simple division of the world between great powers and the rest is unreal and even dangerous. The great powers are called by that name simply because they possess great power. The other states of the world possess power and therefore, the capacity to use it for the maintenance of peace.... In determining what states should be represented on the [Security] council with the great powers, it is, I believe, necessary to apply the functional idea. Those countries which have most to contribute to the maintenance of the peace of the world should be most frequently selected. (as quoted in MacKay 1969, 134)

What King wanted was a special middle power status codified into the UN. Canada was joined in this effort by Australia, another self-identified middle power. Of course, this attempt to codify middle power status was not successful.[6] Thus, "middle power" became essentially a self-elected post for many states.

Despite the fact that middle powers "elected" themselves to this post (and thus presumably could just as easily deny the label), the middle powers have internalized their self-assumed responsibility for preserving the international order. They take on certain international roles *because* the roles are seen to be those of a middle power (Cooper, Higgott, and Nossal 1993; Doxey 1989; Hawes 1984; Pratt 1989). This sounds tautological and in many respects it is, yet it also is quite relevant to our understanding of middle powers and their foreign policy behavior (although difficult to establish empirically). Self-perception and role perception are key parts of

Papadakis and Starr's "environmental model" mentioned earlier: "The concept of environment, or 'milieu,' includes all phenomena to which the environed unit's activities may be related, including the psychological or perceptual environment" (Papadakis and Starr 1987, 415).

Unfortunately, perhaps, for the middle powers, this middle power psychology can sometimes bind them into behaviors they would rather forego. For example, recall that middle powers perceive themselves to be international coalition builders and that they also perceive themselves to be the states most responsible for protecting the international order, particularly as embodied in the UN system. These two imperatives combined and severely limited any independent action by Canada and Australia during the months leading up to the 1991 Persian Gulf War. As the United States maneuvered the UN and its member states into backing the multilateral use of military force to compel Iraq to vacate Kuwait, Canada and Australia found themselves stuck (Cooper, Higgott, and Nossal 1993). Canadian and Australian involvement in the Gulf War resulted from these states' inability to maintain in the abstract their images as good coalition members and supporters of the UN without in actuality having to play the parts as defined in this instance.[7]

Perception goes beyond what the middle power imagines as its own international role; it is also important to understand how the middle power perceives the international environment and its opportunities and dangers. Papadakis and Starr add this element to their discussion of the environmental model: "In this environmental model, foreign policy derives from a state's capacity to act and its willingness to avail itself of particular opportunities. However, a state's capacity to act is not derived simply from its material resources, but rather by its relationship with all aspects of its environment, both tangible and relational" (1987, 415).

Higgott and Cooper (1990) and later Cooper, Higgott, and Nossal (1993) provide an example of this interplay of middle power role imperative and perceived opportunities in the international environment when they discuss the efforts of Canada and Australia in putting together the "Cairns Group," a group of middle powers that came together to promote negotiations on agricultural trade issues within the Uruguay Round on the General Agreement on Trade and Tariffs (GATT). Canada and Australia helped organize the Cairns Group because they perceived an international leadership vacuum on agricultural issues and because they perceived themselves as being well suited as middle powers to help the international community work through these issues. Thus, the opportunity created by the perceived leadership vacuum blended with the internationalist imperative of the middle power to cause Canada and Australia to engage in international coalition building and mediation.

Thus, the "theory" of middle powers in international politics employs contextual analysis; that is, the theory informs us that a middle power's behavior will be geared toward its perception of the operative context. This theory's origins and intellectual development also reflect the political context in which these scholars have worked. Middle power "scholarship" began with the memoirs and philosophizing of the middle power statespersons who first proposed the idea of the middle power (Hawes 1984, 3). These statespersons so dominated the national debate on the role of their states in world affairs that middle power societies internalized the identity (Hawes 1984). Within this national identity, academics began to describe the ways in which their states acted like middle powers. These scholars were and are deeply integrated into their societies and serve to reinforce the national middle power self-perception through their work.[8]

A great deal of the scholarship on middle powers has been atheoretical and descriptive (Hawes 1984; e.g., Holmes 1982). Indeed, middle power scholarship was and is methodologically unsophisticated in the dominant Western social scientific sense. This is not to suggest that middle power scholarship fails to contribute to a theoretical understanding of middle powers; "scientific" research is not the only way in which we can contribute to the growth of knowledge in a field. Our theoretical understanding of the self-perception, international perception, and foreign policy behavior of middle powers has been shaped by a dialogue conducted within the middle power countries between statespersons and scholars. Within this dialogue, the country's role and behavior as a middle power are constantly reevaluated and reexamined for inconsistencies as well as for possibilities for evolutionary change (Hawes 1984). As a result, middle power foreign policy behavior tends to be highly consistent with the standards and expectations set forth in middle power theory. Thus, middle power foreign policy behavior is fairly predictable, having been shaped by a complicated milieu of perceptions, expectations, and reactions.

Thus, although middle power theory was not developed through any standardly accepted social scientific models, it is a theory that contributes to our understanding of the foreign policy orientation and behavior of the middle powers. Middle power theory, by virtue of its unscholarly origins and internalization by the middle power societies, is a multifaceted approach to analyzing foreign policy that fits the baseline criteria desired of any theory—it contains high explanatory and predictive value.

■ Conclusion

What we learn from this brief examination of some of the research on state type and foreign policy behavior is that our understanding of the linkages between state type and behavior is enhanced when we adopt a multifaceted, contextual model. We also can conclude that atheoretical "objective" social scientific inquiry can leave us with unidimensional, largely unconvincing images of reality (and, as ever, its "objectivity" is questionable). A different approach to theory development, such as that illustrated by middle power theory, might lead us to theories of state type and foreign policy behavior that actually reflect reality in its great complexity. The task for second-generation scholars, then, is to develop new hypotheses in which the impact of the interaction between context and state type on foreign policy behaviors is clearly considered. Further, the work of first-generation scholars need not be discarded; instead, second-generation scholars can attempt to recast the old theories linking state type and foreign policy behavior in light of the relevant operative contexts.

■ Acknowledgments

I wish to thank Roger Knudson, Jeanne Hey, and Pat Haney for comments and suggestions on earlier drafts of this chapter.

■ Notes

1. See the chapter by Philip Schrodt (chapter 9) in this volume for a detailed discussion of this and other event data sets.

2. "Monadic-level findings" refers to evidence accumulated from the study of one country's foreign policy behavior, typically longitudinally (over time). "Dyadic-level findings" refers to evidence accumulated from studying pairs of states and their foreign policy behaviors toward each other.

3. Forsythe reviews U.S. intervention in Iran in 1953, Guatemala in 1954, Indonesia in 1955, Brazil during the 1960s, Chile in 1973, and Nicaragua during the 1980s.

4. See Keith Shimko's essay (chapter 5) in this volume for a discussion of the use of the "domino theory" and other metaphors in foreign policy making.

5. The use of "middle power" in this chapter derives from the primarily idealist and transnationalist literatures on Canada, Australia, and the Scandinavian countries. There are studies from other theoretical traditions that use the phrase "middle power"; these are not considered in this chapter. See Neack (1991) for an extensive discussion of the various literatures on "middle powers" and "middle states."

6. Holbraad (1984) has suggested that other states had political reasons for not backing the middle powers. The greater powers saw the middle power claim as a challenge "from below." The smaller powers resisted because they "saw no special advantage in recognizing an intermediate class of powers, since it implied a relegation of themselves to a level of status and influence even lower than the one they occupied together with the secondary powers in a simple division between great powers and others" (Holbraad 1984, 64).

7. For this idea I am indebted to the members of my foreign policy seminar at Miami University in the summer of 1993. For a detailed discussion of Canadian and Australian "followership" in the Gulf conflict of 1991, see Cooper, Higgott, and Nossal (1993).

8. This brings to mind an experience I had at a scholarly conference in 1989, at which I presented a paper on the conflict management activities of "middle states." Before I discussed these activities, I discussed the statistical method by which I arrived at my listing of great, middle, and small states. Canada, it turned out, was in the list of great states. A Canadian scholar stood up and complimented the research and then said that despite my sound methodology I should put Canada *back* into the middle state list because "we *know* Canada *is* a middle state."

FOURTEEN

Uncovering the Missing Links: Linkage Actors and Their Strategies In Foreign Policy Analysis

Karen A. Mingst, University of Kentucky

■ Editors' Introduction

In the following chapter Karen Mingst takes us beyond the largely state-centric approach to foreign policy analysis that has dominated the field. Mingst examines the internal/domestic and external/international sources of foreign policy making by specifically focusing on the substate and trans-state actors that operate across countries' boundaries as well as across multiple levels of analysis. Earlier chapters by Joe Hagan (chapter 8), Philip Schrodt (chapter 9), Bruce Moon (chapter 11) and Laura Neack (chapter 13) allude to, but do not explicitly focus upon, some of these nonstate actors. Mingst's typology of foreign policy actors and their operating strategies helps us understand that other entities have "foreign policies" that influence and are influenced by states' foreign policies. Although this chapter derives from established theoretical traditions in the study of international relations and despite an early call in the first generation of foreign policy analysis to study linkage actors, its inclusion in this volume marks one of the "newer," multileveled lines of research in the study of foreign policy.

When reading this chapter, consider the following questions: How may linkage actors create conflicts between states? How may linkage actors encourage cooperation between states? Think back to John Rothgeb's chapter (chapter 3) and consider the roles that linkage actors have played in eliminating the possibility of war between Western states. How may linkage actors bridge the differences between Western and non-Western states? Why do you think most foreign policy analyses treat linkage actors as entities to be acted upon or through, but never as independent actors in their own right? ■

It was James Rosenau writing in the late 1960s who urged first-generation foreign policy scholars to examine the interpenetration between domestic political systems and foreign policy behaviors. This clarion call came with some suggestive concepts—

the need to examine linkage politics or an interpenetrated system. But the reality is that most scholars continued to emphasize either international *or* domestic factors. And early on, Rosenau explicated the problem that has continued to plague the field:

> To identify factors is not to trace their influence. To uncover processes that affect external behavior is not to explain how and why they are operative under certain circumstances and not under others. To recognize that foreign policy is shaped by internal as well as external factors is not to comprehend how the two intermix or to indicate the conditions under which one predominates over the other. And in these respects progress has been very slow indeed. (Rosenau 1966, 31)

Even as recently as 1988, the historian Christopher Thorne confirmed Rosenau's premonition: "Contemporary historians of American foreign relations, however, have generally invested more energy in debating the relative primacy of internal and external than in articulating their connectedness" (1988, 125). Second-generation foreign policy scholars have recently been intellectually reinvigorated by Robert Putnam's (1988) formulation of the linkage problem. Putnam describes the linkage as a two-level game. The metaphor posits that domestic interest groups pressure the government to adopt specific policies and forge coalitions, while internationally, governments not only must satisfy domestic constituencies but must react to behaviors of other national actors as well. What makes the game unusually complex is that "moves that are rational for a player at one board…may be impolitic for that same player at the other board" (Putnam 1988, 434). Neither a "second image" explanation (domestic causes and international effects) nor a "second image reversed" explanation (international causes and domestic effects) are sufficient. What is needed is an explanation of "how the domestic politics of several countries became entangled via an international negotiation" (Putnam 1988, 430). The strength of Putnam's analysis is that it focuses on interaction between the two-level game.

Taking up Rosenau's first-generation challenge to focus on the interaction variables, invigorated by Putnam's notion of entanglement between the domestic and international level, this chapter has three objectives. First, I review the literature on domestic and international linkages beginning from Rosenau's seminal work, as well as work from the theories of functionalism, complex interdependence, and state/society relations. Second, drawing on this rich literature that addresses bits and parcels of the linkage problem, I propose a typology of linkage actors, both governmental and nongovernmental, with appropriate examples. Third, I identify different linkage strategies employed by the various actors. Having specified the actors and strategies, students of foreign policy analysis are better able to make the connections, the linkages between domestic politics and international relations.

■ Approaches to Linking Domestic and International Factors

The dominance of the realist paradigm in the study of international relations in the 1950s and 1960s made it understandable that domestic and international factors were treated as analytically separate. Political realism is, after all, predicated on the dual assumptions that the state is a unitary actor and that international politics and domestic politics are two separate spheres of activity, utterly independent of each other. Thus, the political processes within each of the domains are fundamentally different. Neither interconnections, interpenetration, nor even linkages between the two domains are acknowledged, much less appreciated.

Challenges to the dominant realist paradigm came indirectly in the 1950s with the rediscovery of functionalist theory. Building on the work of David Mitrany in *A Working Peace System* (1966), functionalists contend that the distinctions between the construct of the state and the international system need to break down. In fact, the territorial state, so central in realist theory, is by functionalist accounts an inefficient, largely outdated unit. The functions of the state should be undertaken by nonpolitical elites, scientific and technical personnel whose commitment to resolving "the problem" (transnational nonpolitical problems) takes precedent over allegiance to the state. As these elites perform specific functions in collaboration with other similarly situated transnational elites, cooperative works will "spill over" into other more controversial domains. Spillover is the feedback between the domestic and international developments. In the long term, habits of cooperation develop, ultimately both sustaining the enterprise *and* undermining the state system. In functionalism, then, the interconnectedness between domestic politics and the international system comes through a specific type of transnational technical actor and the process occurs through spillover to other issue areas.

The aspiration of the founders of the European Community to go "beyond the nation-state" is the embodiment of functionalist thinking. The European Commission, where supposedly nonpoliticized individuals represent communitywide rather than national interests, is the principal organ between the state and the community system. So functionalism and its empirical referent the European Community have provided one type of linkage actor, as well as having alerted theorists to the possible connections between the two systems.

Rosenau goes further in proposing two concepts that connect domestic and international systems. First, Rosenau introduced the idea of a penetrated political system, "where nonmembers of a national society participate directly and authoritatively, through actions taken jointly with the society's members, in either the allocation of its values or the mobilization of support on behalf of its goals" (Rosenau 1966, 65). In these systems the political processes differ both from those found within a national political system and from those in the international system. Face-to-face interactions between nonmembers of the society and societal members are extensive. Second, Rosenau proposed linkage politics as the process within a penetrated system. Linkage was defined as "any recurrent sequence of behavior that originates in one system and is reacted to in another" (Rosenau 1969, 44). Essential to this definition in its original formulation is the idea that a single reaction does not constitute a linkage; only sequences of behavior are of interest, behaviors that cross boundaries between systems. Some linkages may be fused—"a sequence in which an input fosters an output in such a way that they cannot meaningfully be analyzed separately" (Rosenau 1969b, 49). Yet empirical researchers were slow to pick up and utilize these concepts, despite the important and suggestive dimensions being tapped.

In 1972 the publication of Robert O. Keohane and Joseph S. Nye's book *Power and Interdependence* provided an additional challenge to the realist paradigm.[1] The complex interdependence perspective posits that there are other actors important in international politics, although the state may continue to be *the* most critical; that states may not necessarily act as units—subgovernmental actors and different societal actors may have different and sometimes conflicting foreign policy agendas than the central government; that military security issues do not necessarily dominate the political agenda, other issues are of increasing salience; that international governmental organizations are not the inconsequential actors that the realists believed. So the interdependence view identifies not only a new suite of actors, subnational actors, and revitalized international organizations but also new political processes—transgovernmental policy coordination, transnational coalition building, regimes, agenda setting (Keohane and Nye 1989). Additional valuable contributions of the perspective are the two measures introduced to evaluate the amount that a state reacts to or can thwart the external environment. A state is sensitive to external factors when there are costly effects imposed from outside before policies are altered to try to change the situation, whereas a vulnerable state is liable to suffer costs imposed by external events even after policies have been altered (Keohane and Nye 1989, 13). With these concepts, researchers are able to begin to measure the relative impact of the international system on domestic politics.

Complex interdependence does challenge the realist position: the nation-state is disaggregated; political processes that cross the boundaries between the international system and the domestic system are identified; and the boundary separating international and domestic politics becomes more fluid. But as the authors themselves admit (Keohane and Nye 1989, 256), the impact of international relations on domestic politics ("second image reversed") is ignored in complex interdependence. Furthermore, "What researchers must now do is to link a process-oriented version of systemic theory closely with an analysis of domestic politics" (Keohane and Nye 1989, 260).

Finally, throughout the 1980s, the literature on foreign economic decision making has contributed to thinking about the interconnectedness of domestic and international political systems. Peter Katzenstein delineated the importance of domestic factors in foreign economic policy: "Content and consistency of foreign economic policies result as much from the constraints of domestic structures as from the functional logic inherent in international effects" (1976, 45). What Katzenstein was reacting to was a literature that attributed determinants of foreign economic policy to international power structure and bargaining of societal factors (pluralism). He argued strongly, "The joint impact of international effects and domestic structures thus condition government policy" (1976, 19). National decision makers must be concerned *simultaneously* with domestic and international pressures.

Later work by both Gourevitch (1986) and Rogowski (1989) supported Katzenstein's theory about the domestic-international linkage. For Rogowski (1989) the international economic environment, specifically changes in international trade, triggers changes in domestic politics and hence policy choice; for Gourevitch (1986), international economic crises lead to policy debates and controversy, then new domestic policies emerge.

Thus, gradually, the state-international dichotomy posited by political realists has been challenged by quite different theoretical traditions. Each has suggested that the distinction between state and international systems has been eroded by transnational actors, processes, and the appearance of new issues. The time is ripe for exploring these transnational factors, starting with a typology of linkage actors, one drawn from diverse theoretical traditions.

■ Typology of Linkage Actors

The erosion of the state as unitary actor has not led to a diminution of governmental actors. In fact, the proposed typology of linkage actors prominently includes both governmental and nongovernmental actors. Table 14.1 identifies the relevant actors.

Governmental *negotiators* are the first type of linkage actor. Recently, scholars have realized that international negotiations provide an important venue from which to think about the interaction between domestic and international structures and processes. One variant is introduced in the work of Putnam (1988), who identifies Level I as bargaining between international negotiators and Level II as discussion within each group of constituents about whether to ratify Level I agreements. Level I and II bargaining is linked through an iterative process. The key variable is the size of the "win-set." The win-set for Level II constituency is the set of all possible Level I agreements that would win, that is, gain a majority among constituents. The larger the win-sets, the more likely the Level I agreement. The *size* of the win-set depends primarily on the distribution, preferences, and possible coalitions among Level II constituents (Putnam 1988, 437, 440, 442). While the chief negotiator is the formal link between Level I and Level II, the negotiator may have individual interests; however, under pressure, the allegiance of the negotiator belongs to the domestic level (Putnam 1988, 456). Thus, what Putnam does for the international negotiator as actor is to provide a linkage concept—win-sets—between Level I international bargaining and Level II domestic constituencies.

Mayer also puts key emphasis on the international negotiating situation, which he describes as, "an internal-external bargaining process in which the parties to the external bargain, i.e., nations, are not unitary actors but rather are composed of domestic factions which share power but which differ in their interests. Domestic factions negotiate internally over what positions will be taken by their party in the

Table 14.1 Linkage Actors

Governmental	Non-Governmental
Negotiators	Actors in Second-Track Diplomacy
International Governmental Organizations	Nongovernmental Organizations
International Courts	
Transgovernmental Coalitions	
Epistemic Communities	

external negotiation" (1992, 794–95). Using game-theoretic language, he identifies the bargaining set as the set of physically possible outcomes that are considered optimal improvements on the no-agreement alternative. But Mayer suggests a different concept that links the domestic and international—the side-payment. Side-payments allow domestic factions to compensate one another, thus permitting opportunities to reexamine the international bargain—a bargain previously blocked by domestic factions (Mayer 1992, 806–7).

Like Putnam and Mayer, game theorists are linking domestic and international arenas through negotiations. McGinnis and Williams (1993) relax the assumption of autonomous state actors and focus on strategic action at the individual (or group) level, while Friman (1993) examines the negotiator's tactics of both side-payments and issue redefinition. And Schoppa (1993) focuses on synergistic strategies for negotiators, arguing that approaches focusing on neither the system level nor the domestic level explains outcomes.

Thus, international negotiators are one type of linkage actor; win-sets, side-payments, and issue redefinition allow them to negotiate at both the international and the domestic level *simultaneously*.[2] This is an innovative approach to foreign policy analysis.

International governmental organizations (IGOs) have always been acknowledged as actors by political realists, but their importance has been minimized. If, indeed, the issue of military security remained dominant on the international agenda, then a tertiary role for IGOs is neither surprising nor unreasonable, particularly in the post–World War II cold war environment. In the United Nations, security issues are the prerogative of the Security Council and the veto guarantees that the five Great Powers must agree among themselves before any unified action is taken. However, the end of the cold war has resulted in the demand for stronger and permanent peacekeeping and peacemaking mechanisms. And these demands have resulted in intervention directly into the security affairs of member states, even without their consent. Somalia and Bosnia, under the guise of "humanitarian intervention," may be serving as important precedents, with the United Nations serving a key linkage function.[3]

If IGOs are viewed more broadly as actors in other issue areas, then their role of linkage actor is even more apparent (Karns and Mingst 1990). Keohane and Nye have suggested such a broad view: "In a world of multiple issues imperfectly linked, in which coalitions are formed transnationally and transgovernmentally, the potential role of international institutions in political bargaining is greatly increased. In particular, they help set the international agenda, and act as catalysts for coalition-formation and as arenas for political initiatives and linkage by weak states" (1989, 35).

The International Monetary Fund (IMF) and, to a lesser extent, the International Bank for Reconstruction and Development (World Bank or IBRD) have exercised key roles in this regard. The IMF plays an increasingly key role in less-developed countries plagued by persistent deficits. Expanding from its short-term loan function, the IMF provides longer-term loans, as well as an "international stamp of approval" for both multilateral and bilateral lenders and private banks. Such loans are increasingly dependent on high conditionality, with the IMF requiring that a country design a specific set of measures approved and monitored by them in order to eliminate fundamental economic problems before loans are granted. The country may be required to make both internal adjustments (following deflationary fiscal and monetary policies) and external adjustments (eliminating import controls and exchange restrictions and valuing its currency). Once a strategy is negotiated, the IMF monitors the adjustment programs and interprets whether performance criteria have been met.

As the IMF performs this function penetrating directly national economic policy, it has been the subject of intense criticism especially in Latin America and Africa. Critics charge the institution with providing too little aid, at too high interest rates, only slightly below market rates. Vehement criticisms have arisen also against the content and timing of the conditionality imposed. IGOs become controversial when states are mandated to follow specific policies by international institutions when such policies are politically unpopular. This example confirms the conclusion that Karns and Mingst offered: "As integral components of the contemporary international system, as both influencers and instruments, IGOs have generated unique patterns of interpenetration between the domestic and systemic sources of foreign policy" (1987, 473).

International courts are a third type of linkage actor, although the International Court of Justice does not play such a role. The European Court of Justice (ECJ) provides an example of a regional court that serves as a direct linkage between domestic political and legal systems and the greater European community.

The founders of the European Court never envisaged such an extensive role for the court. Until 1963 the Treaty of Rome depended entirely on the actions of national legislatures; the unitary states enforced the international treaty. But by 1965 the balance began to change as the "skin" of the state began to peel away. First, a citizen of a community country could ask a national court to invalidate any provision of domestic law found in conflict with provisions of the treaty. Second, by 1975 a citizen could seek invalidation of a national law found to be in conflict with self-executing provisions of community "directives" issued by the European Community Council of Ministers. Third, by 1990 community citizens could ask national courts to interpret national legislation consistently with community legislation, if there was undue delay in passing the directive on the part of national legislatures (Burley and Mattli 1993, 42). Community citizens have direct access not only to their national legal systems but to a community-based one as well.

In addition, one specific provision within the Treaty of Rome has provided the foundation for the interpenetration of the court into domestic legal systems. Article 177 of the treaty authorizes the court to issue "preliminary rulings" involving interpretations of community law arising in national courts. Lower national courts could refer questions for such judgments at their discretion. Although largely unanticipated, it has been through the Article 177 procedure that the links between the court and subnational actors, including private litigants, lawyers, and lower courts, have been forged (Burley and Mattli 1993, 58). What this has done is remove the ECJ from litigating direct conflicts between member states or even between the European Commission and member states. According to Burley and Mattli (1993, 72), Article 177 has thus shifted the "vanguard of community law enforcement" to cases involving primarily private parties.

Transgovernmental coalitions are a fourth type of linkage actor. Such coalitions arise when the state is no longer acting as a unit and when political agendas broaden into many different issue areas. Bureaucracies in different states, like the ministries of transportation, trade, or agriculture, find that they need to deal with each other directly, rather than indirectly through the foreign ministry. One former American official put it thus, "It is a central fact of foreign relations that business is carried on by the separate departments with their counterpart bureaucracies abroad, through a variety of informal as well as formal connections" (reported in Keohane and Nye 1974, 42–43). This is particularly true when there is no central policy or where strikingly different interests are at stake.

The coordination forged by the major economic powers in order to bargain over issues of the New International Economic Order with the Third World countries is an excellent example of effective use of transgovernmental coalitions. On the issue of debt relief and the establishment of the Common Fund, "hard-liners" were typically located in the finance and economic ministries of the United States, Japan, Great Britain, and France, while the "soft-liners" were those in the foreign affairs and foreign aid bureaus. Members of these ministries found it useful to forge transgovernmental coalitions with counterparts in ministries sharing similar views. Four separate transgovernmental coalitions formed. One, composed of finance ministry officials, acted to resist pressures for concessions on the issue of debt relief in both Third World countries and from their own foreign ministry and foreign aid agencies. The foreign ministry and foreign aid coalitions were successful in forging concessions on the part of the developed countries on the Common Fund. As Crane concludes, "The coalitions may therefore have prepared the way for some incremental change in the international economic order. Their actions also helped to diminish overt tensions in North-South relations" (1984, 427).

Linkage actors may also be nongovernmental agents. *Individuals participating in track-two diplomacy* represent a fifth type of linkage actor. Track-two diplomacy utilizes individuals outside of governments to engage in the task of conflict resolution. Montville (1987, 7–8) delineates three processes of track-two diplomacy. First, unofficial individuals from different international groups meet in a small problem-solving workshop in order to develop personal relationships and an understanding of the shared problem from the perspective of others. Second, these individuals seek to influence public opinion in constituent states, which, in the words of Montville, "consists of reducing the sense of victimhood of the parties and rehumanizing the image of the adversary" (1987, 7–8). If successful, political leaders will find a "safer" climate in which to undertake negotiations. Third, individuals engage in cooperative enterprises, usually but not necessarily economic in nature, which "provide incentives, institutional support, and continuity to the political and psychological process" (Montville 1987, 8). Not all track-two endeavors involve each of these stages, but the essential elements of the process revolve around its informality, its unofficial nature, and its long-term commitment to build up trust among parties.

Two examples confirm the success of track-two diplomacy. In the spring of 1993, Eritrea signed a declaration of independence, seceding from Ethiopia after years of both low- and high-intensity conflict. The foundation for the agreement was negotiated in numerous informal meetings in Atlanta and elsewhere between the affected parties and former U.S. President Jimmy Carter acting through the Carter Center's International Negotiation Network at Emory University. In the fall of 1993 the startling framework for reconciliation between Israel and the Palestine Liberation Organization was negotiated through track-two informal mechanisms—facilitated by the wife of the Norwegian foreign minister with parties meeting informally in the foreign minister's Oslo house, building up trust in an informal atmosphere.

Nongovernmental organizations (NGOs) are a sixth type of linkage actor. Such organizations are typically divided into two categories—multinational corporations (MNCs), or for-profit organizations, and not-for-profit groups. There is a vast literature on the first type, with numerous studies examining the MNCs as agent, linking the international capitalist system and developed countries with the dependent, less-developed countries (Evans 1979; Moran 1985) or the state with international markets. In each the emphasis is on how MNC elites "operating at the intersection of domestic and international systems, must respond to conflicting demands" (Golich 1992, 901).

Less studied are the nonprofit NGOs, yet this group has grown exponentially over the past two decades. They are engaged in a wide variety of activities at the local, national, transnational, and international level; they function in all the various issue areas, perhaps most notably in human rights, humanitarian, and environmental issues. They work together with subnational groups, with IGOs, and with other NGOs in what are often described as interorganizational networks. For example, environmental NGOs have been critical actors in mobilizing the mass publics toward environmental protection—saving the whales, labeling "green" products in Europe and Canada, working with IGOs like the United Nations Environmental Programme, running parallel NGO conferences to foster networking at both global environmental conferences in Stockholm, 1972, and Rio, 1992 (the International Forum of NGOs and Social Movements), and helping to implement both local and national legislation, as well as international treaties (Mingst 1993).

NGOs may have some advantages over other types of actors. As Caldwell delineates: "In both the forming and execution of international policy they [NGOs] may act more rapidly and directly, and with less risk to national sensitivities than can the official intergovernmental agencies" (1984, 264). Others, likewise, have pointed to the strengths of NGOs: they are usually politically independent from any sovereign state; they have developed processes for data collection; they can participate at all levels from policy and decision making to implementation. If the purpose of NGOs, then, is to influence state behavior, they have a number of different approaches at their disposal to penetrate the state, by initiating formal, legally binding action, by pressuring authorities to impose state sanctions, by carrying out independent investigations, and by linking issues in ways that force compliance on at least some. Thus, NGOs are versatile, and increasingly powerful, linkage actors.

A seventh type of linkage actor is the *epistemic community*. Individual experts, technical specialists according to the functionalists, experts from both NGOs and IGOs, along with their counterparts in state and substate agencies may well form part of an epistemic community. As Haas describes: "An epistemic community is a network of professionals with recognized expertise and competence in a particular domain and an authoritative claim to policy-relevant knowledge within that domain or issue-area"

(1992, 3). They have: (1) "a shared set of normative and principled beliefs," (2) "shared causal beliefs," which serve as the basis for elucidating the multiple linkages between possible policy actions and desired outcomes," (3) "shared notions of validity," and (4) "a set of common practices associated with a set of problems to which their professional competence is directed." Members of such transnational knowledge communities play key roles in influencing both state and international secretariat behavior.

The United Nations Environmental Programme's Mediterranean Action Plan has relied on epistemic communities. After 1972, individual experts were invited to meetings in a professional nonofficial capacity. Meetings bound the experts in the process, meaning that UNEP administrators relied on the epistemic community for getting the data to establish the monitoring program and to modify it in accord with the data received. These individuals also became active in the domestic bargaining process, fostering learning among governmental elites. As Haas summarizes: "The transnational alliance between the ecological epistemic community and national marine scientists led governments to define their interests, so that they accepted a collective program that was increasingly comprehensive and complied with such arrangements domestically" (1990, 188). In this case the influence of the epistemic communities is largely an elite-driven process, with many of the issues falling under the purview of a small group (Haas 1990, 163).

Seven different actors have the potential to link domestic polity and the international system. Each of these has been woefully neglected by political realists who view domestic politics and international politics as separate spheres of activity. These actors have traditionally not been emphasized by the first-generation foreign policy analysis community, yet they are increasingly critical and are able to employ specific strategies for exerting influence. I turn next to an examination of these linkage strategies.

■ Linkage Strategies

Four different strategies are utilized by these linkage actors. The strategies include the following: the power approach, the technocratic approach, coalition building, and grass-roots mobilization.[4] Not all actors are able to employ all strategies; some actors are especially suited to a particular strategy. Whether the respective actors are able to use successfully these strategies clearly depends not only on specific characteristics of the actor but also on both the domestic and the international context of the situation.

In the *power approach*, linkage actors attempt to target top decision makers in either domestic political systems or the international system through direct intermediation. These actors utilize personal contacts and persuasion tactics, sometimes circumventing normal governmental channels. This is a highly risky strategy; success by a linkage actor is apt to lead to sweeping and critical outcomes; failure can lead to a diminution of the actor's long-term influence and a loss of legitimacy.

The IMF's imposition of conditionality on loans is an excellent example of the power approach. Member teams from the IGO are sent to specific countries to meet with high-level governmental officials in order to hammer out an "acceptable" economic plan. Should the government accept the agreement, then public and private loans will flow to the country. Should the government not agree, or should the government fail to implement the agreed-upon strategy, then funds are withheld. The risks are high for both parties—the government risks both loss of international funds and loss of control (and face) with respect to domestic economic policy; the IMF risks its reputation, as well as jeopardizing the support of Western donor countries.

Several UN officials, international negotiators, have utilized a power approach, negotiating with the highest-level officials. In early 1986 Diego Cordovez, an assistant to UN Secretary-General Perez de Cuellar, used the influence and power of his office to mediate an accord on the Afghan conflict, negotiating ways in which the UN could facilitate the withdrawal of Soviet forces. And in 1987 Secretary General Perez de Cuellar himself, after a decade of delicate negotiations, reconciled the views of the five members of the Security Council, which paved the way for Security Council Resolution 598—a UN-supervised cease-fire between Iran and Iraq. Top-level negotiators exercised direct power instruments to forge settlements between domestic actors and the international community.

In the *technocratic approach,* various actors including IGOs, NGOs, epistemic communities, and international courts, acting individually or collectively, use knowledge of procedural mechanisms as well as the legal system. Such actors learn how both the domestic system and the international system operate. They then use this knowledge to link the two systems, often in order to achieve specific objectives, to warn of policy trends, to intervene administratively, or to institute litigation. The technocratic approach operates most effectively when IGOs, NGOs, epistemic communities, and international courts rely on linkages with subunit constituencies.

NGOs, for example, can initiate formal legal proceedings against states to try to force compliance with international norms. An interesting example emerged from the 1972 Marine Mammal Protection Act (MMPA), U.S. legislation passed to reduce incidental kill or serious injury of marine mammals coincident with commercial fishing. Specifically the legislation was designed to mitigate the problem of tuna fishermen encircling dolphins with a "purse-seine" net to capture the tuna below, often harming the dolphins in the process. In June 1990 the Earth Island Institute, an NGO, brought suit in U.S. District Court to compel the executive branch to comply with the MMPA. The court enjoined the executive from permitting tuna imports into the United States from the offending countries (Wirth 1992). Mexico then challenged the tuna import ban under the international trade organization (General Agreement on Trade and Tariffs, or GATT). GATT's three-member panel concluded that the United States had not proven that import restrictions were aimed at conservation or that other measures were not available. They suggested that unilateral trade measures designed to protect resources outside of a state's jurisdiction conflict with GATT's trade principles. GATT was more generally calling into question other treaties that depend on trade restrictions for enforcement, including the ozone, endangered species, and hazardous waste treaties. This example illustrates how an NGO tried to utilize the domestic legal system but was challenged by an IGO (GATT) technical ruling framed in terms of a different issue.

Another way that an NGO may use a technical strategy is by trying to change the structure of an IGO. The International Whaling Commission was originally composed of the United States, Japan, and the Soviet Union, each a whaling or former whaling power. Early policies established quotas, effectively legitimizing whaling. Few NGOs played any role. In the late 1970s, NGO participation increased; they worked to convince more states—nonwhaling states—to join. With increased numbers of nonwhaling members, it would be possible to attain the three-fourths state majority necessary to pass a proposed moratorium on whaling (Birnie 1984). Changing the structure of the IGO through both expanding membership and enhanced participation by more NGOs—both technical changes—changed the international policy.

In the *coalition-building approach,* linkage actors utilize domestic actors to build coalitions, forging domestic policy consensus as a basis for generating transnational coalitions. The process of coalition building includes linking issues, penetrating social networks, and linking groups across national borders. Transgovernmental coalitions, track-two diplomats, and international negotiators are well positioned to employ this strategy.

Transgovernmental coalitions have occurred in a number of issue areas under complex interdependence, although such coalitions are not always easy to identify. In the area of oceans policy, a number of transgovernmental coalitions have emerged with varying saliency at different times. Such coalitions include the following: (1) between navies of different countries (e.g., the U.S. and Indonesia navy with respect to the issue of the Strait of Malacca); (2) among the fisheries ministries responsible in a number of states; (3) among the ministries charged with oceanographic scientific research, to name a few. Keohane and Nye summarize the general impact of transgovernmental coalitions:

> The various "clubs" of delegates with similar functional interests in fishing, navies, oil, mining, and so forth that were established as part of the informal conference diplomacy set up regular channels of communication that cut across and created tension within the already fragmented national positions. Many of the smaller and poorer states had simpler positions, which were thus less affected by these transgovernmental contacts. In large-scale conference diplomacy, transgovernmental contacts helped the small and poor to penetrate the large and strong more than vice versa. (1989, 116)

Transgovernmental coalitions are certainly more viable and noteworthy in large pluralist democracies, creating the possibility of a variety of linkages with the international system actors, where in smaller unitary states such linkages are less easily forged.

In *grass-roots mobilization,* linkage actors try to build widespread public involvement in several countries. Appeals to the grass roots may occur through direct action, even confrontational "outrageous acts," or through an appeal to an ideology. Tactics may include letter writing, campaign contributions, and personal contacts. Track-two diplomats and NGOs are well suited to utilizing this technique.

Mobilizing the grass roots is a core strategy of track-two diplomats—a technique that has been used as a prelude to IGO action. For example, there was extensive grass-roots organization that occurred simultaneously with the development of the European Coal and Steel Community—particularly Franco-German reconciliation after World War II. As Montville describes it: "Tens of thousands of French and German academics, businessmen, journalists, politicians, artists, schoolchildren, and young people participated in collaborative exchanges in their areas of interest. Activities included language instruction, summer camps, and joint performances of theater and music groups. All this activity literally and figuratively signified the reintegration of the two peoples on a positive, human psychological level" (1991, 264).

An example of NGO grass-roots mobilization came during the 1990 London meetings of governments and NGOs concerning revision of the 1987 Montreal Protocol on Substances that Deplete the Ozone Layer. A number of NGOs were critical of UN Environmental Programme Secretary General Mostafa Tolba for not advocating more stringent regulations on ozone-destroying chemicals. Among the groups, Friends of the Earth International, Greenpeace International, and the Natural Resources Defense Council held press conferences and circulated brochures to the public, media, and officials complaining of weak regulations. The precise strategy pursued varied—Friends of the Earth approaching the matter analytically and Greenpeace staging a confrontational theatrical happening—but the intent was the same: to focus concern on strengthening the Montreal Protocol (Benedict 1991, 165–66). By publicizing inadequacies, NGOs force discussion both within and between states in international forums.

Foreign policy analysis is a bridging discipline. These approaches—the power, the technocratic, coalition building, and grass roots—are the strategies which the various actors have at their disposal in order to build the bridges between states and their subunits, and the international system. Yet each linking actor may use a variety of strategies depending on the situation. MNCs, for example, often employ a power approach, followed by technocratic procedures, while other NGOs rely on techniques other than the power approach. The strategic choice made by each actor is conditioned by the goal to be achieved, the issue at stake, and a cost-benefit assessment of each strategy.

■ The Challenges for Second Generation Scholars and Students

Students of foreign policy see and experience the intimate linkages between domestic politics and international policy in their daily lives. The task for second-generation scholars is clear: to return to Rosenau's call for examining the linkages, to focus on the interaction variables and entanglements between international and domestic systems. This chapter represents an important step in the bridging activity by identifying key concepts, describing different kinds of actors, and elucidating strategies. Now, however, the need to move in these directions is more than academic. With the end of the cold war, the waves of democratization, and the deepening of interdependence, these linkage actors have become all the more important to world politics and to a state's foreign policy making.

■ NOTES

1. Keohane and Nye first published the book in 1972; however, the edition cited below is the second, republished in 1989. In a sequel essay to that volume, the authors soften their argument to say that complex interdependence did not challenge political realism but just added a new dimension to it.

2. These ideas are explored and elaborated in a series of case studies in Evans, Jacobson, and Putnam, eds. (1993).

3. For recent articles on peacekeeping, see Goulding (1993) and Higgins (1993).

4. Moon (1988) delineates these categories, with reference to the strategies employed by transnational lobbyists.

FIFTEEN

Epilogue: Reflections on Foreign Policy Theory Building

Charles F. Hermann, MERSHON CENTER,
THE OHIO STATE UNIVERSITY

■ Editors' Introduction

Charles Hermann here brings us back to the central concern of both generations of foreign policy scholars: building theory that can help us to explain and forecast *foreign policy. Within the context of this central concern, he critiques the second-generation scholarship presented in this book and considers the progress that has been made in foreign policy analysis, pointing to the spaces in which a third generation of scholarship might fruitfully arise. His perspective on this is unique and interesting given his standing as one of the premier foreign policy scholars. More importantly and more generally, he uses his chapter to help remind us that foreign policy scholarship must reflect the realities of—and the changes within—the international system. In this he brings us back to some of the issues raised by John Rothgeb in his context-setting chapter (chapter 3). Rothgeb suggested the ways in which World War II changed aspects of the international system perhaps permanently, changes that require us to look at the foreign policies of different groups of states in different ways. Similarly, Hermann asks us to consider the ways in which the end of the cold war has changed international politics, necessitating a change in the types of questions we must ask about foreign policy. He reminds us that our pursuit of theory in foreign policy will always be subject to revision by real-world changes in international politics and suggests that our task is to construct theories that can be flexible enough to accommodate such changes. Hermann also issues a warning to foreign policy analysts that we must get moving on this, lest we be left behind in the "tidal wave of change sweeping over world affairs."*

When reading this chapter, consider the following issues: What questions about the "new world order" (the post–cold war world) can be addressed within the context of the present scholarship? What questions cannot be adequately addressed using any of the frameworks established here? Given Hermann's views on change in the international system, can we ever build theories or laws if the international context can change in such fundamental ways as to leave our starting assumptions ungrounded? If you were to construct a new "conversational space" for a third generation of foreign policy scholarship, what issues would you include for discussion? ■

■ Predicting the End of the Cold War

Why didn't someone predict the ending of the cold war? Diplomatic historian John Gaddis poses exactly this question in a recent provocative essay (1992/93). Gaddis reviews the efforts of three groups of international relations theorists whose approaches he labels as behavioral, structural, and evolutionary. He finds each group's theoretical perspective flawed in ways that made the task unlikely to be achievable. In fact, Gaddis concludes that no member of any group forecasted the end of the cold war with recognizable accuracy.

In the spirit of the American late-night television talk show host, David Letterman, one might make a list of the "five best reasons" why no one predicted the particular ending of the cold war. A partial list might look like this:

1. We don't do predictions (see an astrologist, the CIA, or a futurist).

2. Policymakers blew it too. Why expect scholars to have done better?

3. No one seriously asked the question.

4. Systematic forecasting of discrete social phenomena is not possible.

5. We had the wrong theories.

We Don't Do Predictions

Gaddis goes to some length in his review to identify scholars in each of his clusters who claimed that forecasting, if not prediction, was an important purpose of developing theory about international relations. Yet it is remarkable how uncommon are theory-based predictions in the study of foreign policy and international relations. Certainly prescriptive essays occasionally advance a dire picture of future developments if the advocated course is not followed. (Example: If North Korea is allowed to develop nuclear weapons, Japan also will become a nuclear power.) Moreover, systematic forecasts are somewhat more likely in world affairs when they can draw on theory and data outside of the domain of international politics, such as actuarial or demographic data. (Example: Major change will occur in China after the present leadership dies; or the AIDS epidemic will drastically alter the population of Africa in the next decade.) Such forecasting contrasts sharply with the silence of scholars drawing on theories of international relations. Indeed in his review, Gaddis often has to extrapolate from hypotheses and arguments of international relations scholars to formulate their assumed interpretation about the cold war. It is probably fair to say that most academic researchers dealing with foreign policy and international relations do not undertake their studies with the purpose of being able to make an informed forecast about some phenomenon at its conclusion.[1]

Policymakers Blew It, Too

In general, that seems to be true. The way the cold war ended seems to have caught almost everyone by surprise. In contrast to academic scholars, various agencies in the U.S. government and in other governments are given the task of making forecasts about certain kinds of events. Groups in the Departments of Defense, State, and Treasury, and, of course, the Central Intelligence Agency are quite accustomed to making forecasts. Often these are of a short-term nature, but when it comes to determining what weapons to acquire and how to configure future forces, there is a requirement for long-term forecasting of the international strategic environment. It is certainly a case of "cold tea for hard times," however, to conclude that theories and insights from experiences of the policy community used by government analysts did no better than those of scholars.

No One Asked the Question

The primary concern of most researchers—academics or policy analysts—was whether the cold war would turn hot. The future-oriented question that received extensive attention was the possible conditions that might trigger war between the United States and the Soviet Union or their respective allies. Studies were frequent of the circumstances leading to deterrence failure, crisis escalation, or the accidental unintended outbreak of war. Such inquires were not necessarily driven by the question: Is this the most likely way the cold war will end? Instead, in the spirit of worst-case analysis, escalation represented the class of outcomes that were widely regarded as the most disastrous—the most costly—and, therefore, the ones that we should strive to understand so that preventive steps could be taken.

Systematic Forecasts Are Not of Discrete Events

A distinction needs to be drawn between predictions and forecasts. In a rigorous definition, prediction is understood to specify the exact conditions that will always yield a specified outcome (if, and only if, A occurs, then B occurs). Few would claim that theory-based statements about future human social occurrences can take that form. A forecast, demonstrated in everyday life by weather prognostications made by meteorologists, is grounded in probability thinking. Even when formal probability reasoning is not engaged, a forecast is stated in terms of the conditions that make a particular class of occurrences more or less likely rather than the specification of the necessary and sufficient conditions. Thinking in terms of likelihoods (forecasts) establishes a different context than predictions.

Forecasts suggest that on some occasions one outcome will occur, while in others it will not, even though all the occasions have the same prior specified conditions. In other words, forecasts require one to be able to imagine a range of outcomes. If one conceptualizes a historical event in all its particulars as unique, then a "forecast" of that exact set of historical circumstances is not a reasonable expectation. Instead, we must generalize to a class of events (e.g., elections, wars, trade agreements) in which various specific outcomes can be grouped. Thus, a forecast of the ending of the Soviet-American cold war would require us to define it as one instance of a class of phenomenon that occur repeatedly. If one can imagine repeating the same sequence of significant events leading to the end of the cold war multiple times—in much the same way as Margaret Hermann and I did in the simulation of the outbreak of World War I (Hermann and Hermann 1967)—would it end every time with the largely peaceful collapse of the Soviet empire and the regime itself? More likely, there would be a range of outcomes—sometimes a coup d'état, sometimes a civil war, sometimes an external war, sometimes a revolution, and so forth. It might be that in the class of all possible international system–transforming events, as in the simulation of such occurrences, the peaceful implosion of one of the major powers is an extremely unlikely event. If so, analysts might not be harshly criticized for failing to forecast an event whose likelihood was remote.

We Had the Wrong Theories

In evaluating why the nature of the cold war's conclusion was not anticipated, all the previous arguments (and some others as well) deserve review. But the question of wrong or inadequate theories is particularly intriguing to consider at the conclusion of a book on conceptualizations and theory development in foreign policy. Inadequate theories, together with methodological constraints, lie at the heart of John Gaddis's (1992/93) critique as well. Most of the theories that Gaddis evaluated with reference to the ending of the cold war are broad and inclusive in scope. For the most part they were not constructed to explain or forecast the conclusion or transformation of bipolar international systems. Most people would probably accept the argument that it is far more difficult—at least at this point in human intellectual development—to construct either accurate explanations or forecasts from a general, all-purpose, time-insensitive theory of collective political actions than one tailored to account for a specific type of occurrence in a defined set of historical conditions.

General international theories can be critiqued on other grounds as well. Gaddis effectively argues that several of them lack adequate treatment of dynamics and change. There is a general lack of attention to dynamic processes and to the conditions that precipitate significant change as opposed to stability. "It is … the case that we tend to bias our historical and our theoretical analyses too much toward continuity … we rarely find a way to introduce discontinuities into theory or attempt to determine what causes them to happen" (Gaddis 1992/93, 52).

Furthermore, international relations theories also can be seen as deficient for their failure to give adequate attention to domestic politics and the internal factors within countries that may powerfully shape their role in international affairs. From the vantage point of hindsight it is difficult to interpret the end of the cold war without examining the internal conditions within the Soviet Union—the ruptured economy, the political alienation, and erosion of the will of state officials, and so forth. In brief, the major international relations theories available to Gaddis were deficient exactly in the area of primary concern to foreign policy analysts. This deserves further consideration. It is the contention of this essay that as scholars reflect on the end of the cold war, they increasingly recognize that international relations theories must introduce domestic considerations from within nations. This realization gives additional significance to theoretical work on foreign policy analysis that has concentrated on domestic factors.

■ Challenges to Theory Development from the Ending of the Cold War

The termination of the cold war has released an avalanche of criticism of the ability of existing theories to explain its ending. If most scholars have not been concerned about the predictive capabilities of their theories, they have raised questions about their explanatory power. The prevailing theories of international politics—realism or its more recent formulations known as neorealism or structural realism—have been primary targets. Using these theories is it possible to explain the dramatic changes in Soviet foreign policy in the late 1980s under Gorbachev (i.e., accepting the zero-option in INF, unilateral troop withdrawals, asymmetrical cuts in strategic arms agreements, declining to use force to protect East European regimes, etc.)? Furthermore, can they explain the cautious response of the West to these initiatives? A variety of scholars conclude that these theories at best are indeterminant; taken alone they cannot account for the timing or the direction of the changes. Although scholars differ in their proposed amendments or alternative theoretical concepts that should be added, those examining the issue agree that it is necessary to take into account the internal structures and processes in the societies involved. As Risse-Kappen observes: "To understand the revolution in Soviet foreign policy and the various Western responses to it which together brought the cold war to an end, one cannot ignore domestic politics and leadership beliefs" (1994, 193).

Realists themselves have always acknowledged a modest role for domestic factors. Thus Waltz notes that domestic factors affect foreign policy but that the international system's "pressures of competition weigh more heavily than ideological preferences or internal pressures" (1986, 329). More recently, readers may find a slightly more generous tone in Waltz's recurrent references, written after the collapse of the Soviet Union, to the constraints and opportunities that the changing international structure affords certain states, but he notes whether and when they respond to these shifting conditions depends upon their policy choices. He concludes that "foreign-policy behavior can be explained only by a conjunction of external and internal conditions" (Waltz 1993, 79).

In the context of this shifting intellectual emphasis one finds major new works such as *Myth of Empire* (Snyder 1991) that seeks to explain why great powers often tend to overextend their international ambitions to the point where their costs outstrip any gains. To explain the five cases he examines, Snyder primarily draws upon theories of domestic politics in which narrow interests capture government policy for their own benefit—while disguising their purpose in "myths of empire" propaganda to the general public that must assume the costs. Snyder's work triggers criticism from structural realists who contend he has gone too far and given inadequate attention to systemic factors. Thus in his review, Zakaria writes "He [Snyder] should have begun by separating the systemic causes of state behavior from the domestic ones" (1992, 196–97).

It is not only in the critiques of structural realism's explanations that one finds greater attention given to the integration of international structure and domestic politics. The ending of the cold war has underscored two other related developments. First, there is now a greater interest in explaining cooperative behavior rather than the earlier more exclusive attention given to the causes of hostilities and war. Second—and linked in some important respects to the first—there is a greater concern with international economic activity. Clearly both these areas of intellectual inquiry were well established during the cold war, but its demise has pushed them more directly into the center of the theoretical concerns of international relations theorists.

Studies of international cooperation took as their point of departure the nature of the interaction among independent international actors. Thus, Axelrod's (1984) major initiative considered alternative strategies that one negotiating party might pursue to reward or punish its counterpart, while also signaling a desire to continue cooperation rather than engage in a prolonged cycle of reciprocal defections. Putnam's (1988) metaphor of the two-level game expanded thinking about cooperation by suggesting that each international negotiator struggles to reach an agreement (cooperation) while balancing the requirements of their domestic constituents with those of the other international actor. Thus the negotiators are engaged in two connected "games," one domestic and the other international. Success or cooperation is determined by being able to settle on an agreement that is in the "win-set" of the players at both levels. In other words, Putnam seeks to explain international cooperation as the function of both international and domestic factors. A subsequent series of case studies (Evans, Jacobson, and Putnam 1993) designed to probe the plausibility and range of two-level game phenomena affirmed not only the potential explanatory importance of both domestic and international political considerations but also the distinctive role that governmental leaders play in integrating the forces from those two levels: "The image of the state leaders as 'Janus-faced,' forced to balance domestic and international concerns, stands at the core of the integrative approach, making it 'state centric,' not in the realist sense of emphasizing nation-states as units but in the sense of seeing chief executives, and state bureaucracies more generally, as actors whose aims cannot be reduced to reflections of domestic constituent pressure" (Evans 1993, 401–2).

These case studies of domestic factors in international negotiation also provide insight into some of the post–cold war changes that might flow from the altered mix of issue areas. For many countries after the cold war, foreign economic issues may displace security matters as the domain most frequently engaging vital interests. If this is so, distinctions between most security-type issues and those that are primarily economic become important. Thus, for example, Evans suggests that "territorial conflicts between long-term military adversaries are least likely to evoke complex domestic divisions," but, by contrast, "bargains about trade, investment, and labor flows may evoke bitter distributional contention" (1993, 424–25). He proposes that such differences in the domestic dynamics of security and economic issues may alter the structure of international negotiations. Cooperative agreements may be more likely for economic matters if multiple issues are linked, permitting synergistic strategies on which tradeoffs between the parties permits everyone to win on some issues while accepting losses on others.

Such an argument rests on two broad assumptions—first, that the end of the cold war may change the mix of economic and security issues that figure centrally in the international concerns of some nations and, second, that economic and security issues often invoke different kinds of domestic political dynamics that in turn affect the process of international agreements. For our purposes, the argument—which certainly requires further exploration—illustrates yet another way in which the end of the cold war is changing both international affairs and scholarship about it. Such changes underscore the importance of constructing explanations that integrate domestic factors with international phenomena.

Even in the theoretical explanation of security issues, and most particularly studies of the sources of international war, there is new interest in introducing domestic considerations. Two recent attempts to consider how domestic factors contribute to the explanation of war were undertaken by Levy (1989) and Schweller (1992). Schweller contributes to what has become a major area of recent international scholarship, the possible relationship between regime type and the engagement in interstate war. With the waning of the cold war, the world has experienced what Huntington (1991) has described as a third wave of experimentation with democratic forms of government in countries that previously had experienced authoritarian rule. Associated with this international development has been a renewed interest in the relationship between democracies and war, reformulated as the hypothesis that democracies are less likely to fight wars with other democracies. As one of the authors in this volume notes, the hypothesis weakens when the dependent variable, interstate war, is stretched to suggest democracies pursue a more pacific form of foreign policy generally, but in its narrower form the empirical results are intriguing. The general research interest in democracy and war further highlights the renewed interest in seeking to understand international behavior at least in part by reference to internal features of countries.

Russett (1982) anticipated this need to pay more attention to domestic factors in explanations of international phenomena when more than a decade ago he reviewed the accumulated quantitative research in two areas that had generated substantial inquiry. In the literature on both arms races and dependency, he concluded that studies were more likely to find significant relationships between the international phenomena examined if the researchers introduced domestic factors as mediating variables. "The implications of this will not necessarily please 'realists,' and they will be more satisfying to students of comparative foreign policy than to students of international systems" (Russett 1982, 12). His conclusions explain the reasons for this observation. "We do find generalizations and regularities, but they are complex, interactive, heavily conditioned. Clearly they show the importance of detailed country-specific knowledge" (Russett 1982, 19).

More recently, Zakaria has suggested that the scope and specific accuracy one seeks from theory may influence the extent to which domestic factors need to be taken into account. "The parsimony of systemic theory is useful for some purposes, but more accurate theories are far more useful for many other purposes. Domestic politics explanations can be more useful in explaining events, trends, and policies that are too specific to be addressed by a grand theory of international politics" (Zakaria 1992, 198).

■ A New Round of Foreign Policy Theory Development

It would be unfair to say that the contributors to this volume are oblivious to the international developments that have rocked the study of international politics. They are certainly aware of the changes that have led a number of scholars and analysts who previously concentrated almost exclusively on international structures and processes to reexamine the predictive and explanatory power of their theories and to look anew at the dynamics within countries. The specific reference point for this volume, however, is neither the actual collapse of the cold war nor the repercussions it has triggered among theory-oriented scholars of international politics. It is nevertheless useful to ask whether the recent work in foreign policy reflected in this volume can help fill the intellectual gap now emerging in international politics. To that end, it is important to review the efforts represented by this volume on their own terms.

For the most part the point of departure for the editors and contributors is the earlier work of a group of primarily American foreign policy theorists who collectively identified themselves as "comparative foreign policy" scholars. The collection of review essays and advocacy pieces that constitute this volume seek to correct, extend, or revise these earlier undertakings. What must not be overlooked is the major commitment these authors share with their predecessors. The common property is a commitment to promote a theory-driven field of foreign policy that is empirically grounded. Although the purpose of such theory is largely unexpressed in these pages, one of the editors concludes her own essay by referring to "the baseline criteria of any theory … high explanatory and predictive value" (Neack, chapter 13 in this volume). There is a further shared position that theory must be substantiated by (the editors' introduction states "informed by") systematic empirical analysis. Furthermore, Moon in his chapter (chapter 11) refers to the need for a "stringent empirical test," and Schrodt's entire chapter (chapter 9) is devoted to developments in one kind of empirical data. But a commitment to methodological openness constrains any consensus among the contributors on the test procedures for determining the fit between theory and the reality it is intended to explain or forecast.[2] Equally noteworthy and reasonable is the willingness to persist with a theory because of the absence of an alternative explanation, even when repeated empirical analysis by one set of procedures fails to confirm its expectations. Thus Hey's chapter (chapter 12) shows how dependency hypotheses should not be dismissed despite unimpressive results from earlier quantitative studies. Regardless of their reservations about the adequacy of any particular methods for establishing goodness of fit between a theory and aspects of actual foreign policy activity, these scholars share with earlier investigators an insistence on empirical grounding of theory.

Beyond this shared foundation, it is tempting to summarize in pop journalism fashion the differences the contributors perceive between themselves and the earlier comparative foreign policy analysis:

What's out

Hegemony of positivism

Realism[3]

General or grand theory

Parsimony

What's in

Multilevel, multicausal explanations

Contextuality

Middle-range theories

Bridging to other fields

Behind the slogans and shorthand phrases, of course, are real issues that bear significantly on the attempts to contribute to an understanding of foreign policy. For that reason, a closer examination of the current direction of theory construction is essential.

Multilevel, Multicausal Explanations

The careful reader will have noted that the chapters in this volume follow a rough sequence introducing different levels and kinds of explanation. They begin with an overview of the international system (Rothgeb) and then move back to the individual decision maker (Rosati and Shimko), the group, bureaucracy, and institution (Ripley and Haney), political organization or opposition (Hagan), the state (Moon and Neack), and society (Peterson). Each of these chapters offers an inventory of potential explanatory variables, competing hypotheses, or alternative theories. Thus, the reader interested in explanatory variables can consider the different techniques of comparison—including analogies and metaphors—that humans use to interpret new, unfamiliar situations (Shimko) or alternative ways women and roles have been specified in nationalist movements (Peterson). Competing empirical hypotheses are advanced by Neack on democratic states and war, while Hey offers different hypotheses about the expected foreign policy behavior of dependent states. Rosati reviews alternative theories of cognitive processes; Moon focuses on alternative theories of the state.

There can be little doubt about the varied and rich menu of multilevel conceptual products introduced in this volume. It is the next step that is so daunting. How are variables, hypotheses, or even theories from different analytical levels to be integrated into more complete explanations? This is not a new problem in the study of foreign policy. Rosenau (1966) in his pre-theories essay sought to do it by a kind of reductionism, that is, he argued that the relative importance (potency) of different levels of explanation would vary depending on the type of nation-state. Different levels of explanation could be reduced to a primary one depending on the nation-type. Wilkenfeld and his associates (1980) attempted to integrate variables from multiple levels to explain foreign policy behavior using a statistical process (partial least squares mode). Alker and Bennett (1977) sought a multilevel foreign policy synthesis through a computer simulation using a complex set of contingency decision rules. It is easy to see that none of these efforts were entirely satisfactory. The contributors of this volume appear to be on very solid ground in arguing that adequate theories of foreign policy must in all likelihood integrate multiple, interrelated sources of explanation drawn from different levels of analysis. Of course, one might ask whether the requirements of theory might depend upon what is to be explained or forecasted. More on that point later.

Contextuality

The phrase "contextuality" captures ideas expressed in various ways in this volume, for example, cultural sensitivity, gender sensitivity, contingency analysis, issue and domain specification. The argument is that our explanations must be bounded and qualified. (This is exactly the point made by Russett in 1982.) Presumably, these applicable conditions must be specified by the researcher. I might have titled this section "Farewell Ceteris Paribus" because a large portion of social science research has involved the exploration of hypotheses in which investigators consciously prefaced the stipulated relationship with the caveat "other things being equal." Of course, the difficulty is that in human affairs, all other things beyond their stated relationship are almost never equal at all times and places. The researchers examining an ad hoc hypothesis without stipulating the boundary conditions, the appropriate context, the externalities to which the relationship is sensitive can arguably be said to be engaged in intellectually irresponsible behavior. The contributors seem justified in criticizing much earlier empirical research—including, particularly, that studying comparative foreign policy—for devoting so much effort to the examination of ad hoc hypotheses devoid of any specification of context.

It is possible to read this entire book as a series of candidates for boundary setting, qualifying, or mediating variables. Readers are encouraged to recognize differences among kinds of situations (e.g., crisis versus noncrisis), international systems, actors (including nonstate actors), actor strategies, political opposition, states, bureaucratic cultures, and so on. There can be little doubt that such distinctions—and many others—can be critical in certain policy explanations. We are discovering, for example, that when women are responsible for designing international population control policies and practices, their approach is different from that favored when men dominated population policy. A hypothesis about the effects of micro financial loans to aspiring individual entrepreneurs would at least in some cultures yield different results if controlled for gender. (Women are more successful.) In other words, as Peterson argues, in some areas women approach international problems and behave differently from men. In this example, as in all other matters concerning sensitivity to context, the challenge is to determine which contextual properties must be considered and when.

In his chapter Ripley states, "A model helps an analyst interpret a complex real-world phenomenon (such as foreign policy decision making), identify the most important features, and understand how those features are interrelated." As with a model, a theory or a set of hypotheses must be selective in specifying the included components. It must select from all possible elements in the environment, which ones are likely to impinge in a substantial way on the examined relationships. Individual researchers and teams of researchers should be implored to be more contextually sensitive in their studies, but in all likelihood we will continue to depend on a community of scholars to help each other out. Others, who approach a problem from different perspectives, can test amendments to earlier work to see if the results are stable or are altered by the introduction of different variables. The chapters by Moon and Hey in this volume are two examples of exactly that process.

Middle-Range Theories

What should it be? Broad, all-encompassing theories? Micro, extremely restricted theories? Middle-range theories? This scope requirement for theory development is rather more difficult to specify. In one way it might be interpreted as a vague reaction to earlier efforts to develop theories of foreign policy activity that claimed—explicitly or implicitly—to have universal applicability. The argument might be that since those efforts seem to have offered rather poor explanations, we should be more modest in our aspirations. This could be regarded as simply another statement of the need for greater attention to contextuality.

Another way to interpret the call for middle-range theories is to be more specific about the kind of activity to be explained, that is, the dependent variables. Long ago I engaged in a critique of theoretical efforts in foreign policy for being remarkably vague about what was to be explained (C. Hermann 1978b). Except for a substantial body of research on the causes of war that includes scholarship from foreign policy, international politics, and other numerous fields, studies of foreign policy often neglect to specify the kind of foreign policy to be explained—military interventions, trade agreements, sanctions, scientific cooperation on joint projects, diplomatic recognition, peacekeeping initiatives, and so on.[4] Seldom are these or any of hundreds of alternative ways of characterizing foreign policy activity incorporated into theoretical efforts. The event data effort (whose resurgence is well described in this volume by Schrodt) was undertaken in part to develop measurable ways to characterize different kinds of foreign policy activity. Sadly, the marriage between the empirically grounded indicators of foreign policy behavior and efforts at constructing foreign policy theories has been extremely slow to occur. Certainly, there is absolutely no requirement that the dependent variables of any foreign policy theory must be specified in terms of concepts that can be operationalized as events. Far from it. That, however, does not eliminate the necessity for theorists to make clear what is to be explained. By doing so the theorist moves a considerable way down the path toward establishing the scope of the theoretical effort. An attempt to explain pacifist activity of all international actors certainly is a broader-ranging theory than one limited to understanding interstate wars, which in turn is broader than one concerned only with wars between global powers. Thus the breath of coverage included in the dependent variable can be used to create middle-level theory.

Several efforts in this volume explore hypotheses with specified kinds of foreign policy as the dependent variable. Neack in her chapter takes a critical look at the considerable research activity going on around the hypothesis that democracies are less likely to engage in war with one another. Hey contends that one polity's dependency on another can result in one of several specified kinds of foreign policy behavior (e.g., compliance). Moving from hypotheses to more inclusive theories that designate certain behaviors, we have the example of Rosati's account of the cognitive revolution involving a shift from cognitive consistency theories to social cognition and schema theories. These developments in cognitive theory suggest, among other things, how belief systems affect us as individual problem solvers. The implication for those who wish to explain the decision making of foreign policy leaders is clear and exciting. But Rosati cautions that results from empirical studies attributing certain foreign policy behaviors (presumably what we wish to understand) to different belief structures is quite mixed. In his conclusions Rosati proposes that differences in the type of situation (e.g., whether the problem is familiar or the degree of uncertainty) may affect the power of schema theory to account for behavior. That is an example of the contextual sensitivity noted previously.

These illustrations do not exhaust the current efforts to define theoretical scope by specifying the type of behavior to be explained. Unfortunately, however, they remain the exceptions rather than the rule. As in the past, we witness too many efforts that proclaim another variable or class of variables that will improve our ability to explain undifferentiated "foreign policy." Theory, particularly the specification of middle-range theory, demands more. Those of us concerned with theoretical development in foreign policy must do more to stipulate the foreign policy problem, puzzle, or behavior we seek to explain and how proposed variables contribute to it.

Bridging to Other Fields

The idea that the field of foreign policy is a conceptual bridge can be quite instructive. Within the discipline of political science, the need to make connections between comparative politics (the study of politics within countries) and international politics (the study of politics among countries) seems as obvious as it is neglected. Rosenau (1969b), among others, has stressed the desirability of a "linkage politics" that conceives of foreign policy as the bridge between domestic and international politics.[5] In her chapter, devoted far more to breaking new conceptual ground than reviewing ongoing research, Mingst picks up Rosenau's challenge by suggesting a typology of actors that creates a bridge between internal and external constituencies. She also describes the various strategies available to them. (Her chapter is an open invitation for someone to specify the conditions that might indicate when different actors might pursue alternative strategies.)

The editors are not far from the mark, in my judgment, in suggesting earlier foreign policy research borrowed the approach of comparative politics (i.e., a focus on cross-national studies and the use of comparative methods) but incorporated remarkably little of the substantive domain. Hagan's chapter vividly demonstrates the potential gain to be made in foreign policy by working more directly with the concepts and variables of domestic politics. He hints at the possible use of coalition theory, which for some puzzling reason has not yet attracted strong interest in foreign policy. Peterson's discussion of nationalism and Neack's examination of the classification of states also draw on work in comparative politics and underscore the field's importance to foreign policy.

Bridging, or more precisely borrowing, from other domains is not limited to other fields in political science. The reader finds both Moon and Hey drawing on political economy, Ripley and Haney using organizational and institutional concepts, Gerner and Schrodt introducing artificial intelligence and information theory, Rosati and Shimko working with material from cognitive psychology. Looking at this book one could almost characterize foreign policy analysts as a band of intellectual thieves stealing ideas from almost everyone!

It is perhaps notable that this volume includes only one chapter devoted directly to possible insights from the study of the international system.[6] Rothgeb's thesis that at least two parallel international systems are emerging and that the dominant foreign policy behaviors in each are quite different suggests the importance of looking more carefully in this direction for an understanding foreign policy. Many of the international politics scholars whose work was noted at the outset of this chapter are looking to domestic factors to condition their international explanations. It is a wonder that foreign policy analysts, from their different perspectives, do not more often look to international factors to condition their expectations about foreign policy.

■ Conclusions: Theory Trek, the Next Generation

In their introduction to this volume the editors note that earlier scholarship on building foreign policy theory was influenced by the cold war and other aspects of the international environment (e.g., the number of new nations that emerged in the 1960s and the associated concern with economic development). The ending of the cold war is one of the most profound changes in international affairs in the twentieth century. It will influence future scholarship.

In the first part of this chapter I have suggested that scholars concerned with theories about the international system appear to be engaged in serious reexamination of their work as a result of the cold war collapse. Interestingly, theoretical inquiry in foreign policy—at least as reflected in this volume—has not yet given much attention to the implications of this systemic transformation for their undertakings. The major exception is Rothgeb's chapter, and, of course, his subject is the international system.

As in the past, it seems likely that future scholarship of foreign policy analysts will address the changes in the worlds they study. This seems particularly so since the recent changes have resulted to a significant degree from domestic factors within countries and their effects on the foreign policies nations have pursued. (At least that is one of the conclusions from international relations theorists, as I interpreted them, at the beginning of this chapter.) My guess is that the impact on foreign policy theory of the cold war's end and the surge in economic issues will occur long before another scholarly generation appears. How might these international developments affect some of the themes and emphases about theory captured in this book?

Certainly one likely result is more incorporation of change and dynamics in theories of foreign policy. Concern for when and how policies might change is not a central theme in the contributions to this volume. In fact, the editors include a footnote in their introductory chapter acknowledging change is not one of the subjects that is included. But their concern with specifying context and incorporating variables from multiple levels invites attention to time and the effects of the dynamic interplay of variables on policy. Yet more direct treatment seems essential, not just as a separate chapter on when states and other actors change direction but as an integral part of any theoretical formulation.

It is noteworthy that one of the late Karl Deutsch's most direct efforts to contribute to foreign policy theory, *The Nerves of Government* (1966), sought to deal with change. Somewhat later Steinbruner (1974) took a different approach to cybernetics to address some of the same issues. Neither study seems to have served as a springboard for much continuing effort. Perhaps the time has arrived to revisit the concerns that drove their initiatives.

I have argued that theory-inclined scholars of international politics have rediscovered domestic politics. Their interest in incorporating variables and theories about politics within countries may well be reciprocated as foreign policy analysts come to grips with the post–cold war world. After all, we have observed the strong disposition of contemporary foreign policy analysts to bridge and borrow. To make this connection, however, those of us in foreign policy scholarship will be required to accept one critical assumption. We already treat it as a central feature of our daily accounts of foreign policy, and it energizes our classroom discussions and conversations with colleagues, but we do not incorporate it as a major feature in most theories of foreign policy.

The assumption is simply that foreign policy is extremely responsive to the actions and statements of other international actors. Of course! This, after all, is the core of international politics. Conceptually the central position of interaction or exchange in international relations theory may be an obstacle for foreign policy analysts. There may be a tendency to think that if we examine the interaction of actors we are dealing with international politics, not foreign policy.

How does one create an interactive theory that takes the perspective of an actor in the system, rather than that of the system itself, while at the same time taking into account that the actor is constantly responding to perceived external feedback to its prior actions, new initiatives of others, differing situations, and shifts in the international structure? We must address the question. This must be done while including in the theory the internal dynamics that the contributors to this volume effectively illustrate. I think this is parallel to the question that some international relations theorists are approaching from the opposite direction as they review their theories after the cold war. The press for better explanations is likely to push foreign policy analysts in a similar manner.

In this regard it is instructive that Schrodt includes in his chapter a quote from Charles McClelland, the early pioneer in event data, that includes the observation: "We were defeated, however, in the attempt to categorize and measure event *sequences*" (italics added). McClelland is acknowledging the great difficulty of creating reliable and valid chains of action and reaction—the essence of foreign policy as a sequence of exchanges. This underscores what may be a more difficult problem in both theory and data for foreign policy than for international relations theory. Foreign policy theorists are more likely to want to understand differentiated kinds of near-term interaction (e.g., the responses to a specific kind of move) rather than patterns of interaction that develop over extended periods of time. Although the task may be difficult, the requirement may be the key to better explanations and forecasts.[7]

The question posed by John Gaddis with which this chapter began illustrates another way in which future theory in foreign policy may evolve. Gaddis's question about prediction emerged from what was, for him, a puzzle. He observed all the interest in theory in international politics as compared to the modest attention it receives in history. He puzzled over the question of whether more attention to theory makes for better predictions. Similar questions or puzzles seem to drive much of the theoretical work of our international relations colleagues. Thus, Snyder (1991) asks why major powers so often seem to engage in destructive overextension. Waltz (1993) asks, if economic issues become more predominant in the post–cold war, will the international system be less competitive? Questions, puzzles, or problems seem less often to motivate theoretical efforts in foreign policy analysis. If they are asked, the questions are remarkably unfocused and are seldom followed with a thesis or hypothesis as a possible answer. Too often, I believe, we still are only advocating the addition of new explanatory variables to the list of sources for undifferentiated foreign policy.

But the major changes occurring in world affairs are likely to stimulate the formulation of questions and puzzles in foreign policy as in international relations. Furthermore, the commitment to middle-level theory expressed repeatedly in this volume may be promoted by concentrating theoretical efforts on the treatment of puzzles and problems that lead to well-formulated questions. We can limit the focus of a theory by designating specific foreign policy activity and by sharpening the research question it is intended to answer.

This book has suggested some emerging patterns or trends among those who have joined the effort to construct theories of foreign policy. I have observed that a tidal wave of change in world affairs is sweeping over all of us. As we react to our evolving international environment, it will shape our thinking and interact with some of the theoretical patterns captured in this volume. These changes may stimulate additional, new, exciting efforts to explain and forecast the foreign policies of international actors.

■ Notes

1. In fact, description, prescription, and explanation of singular policy occurrences are most often the purpose of foreign policy analyses rather than theoretically driven work from which more general explanations and forecasts might be derived.

2. I suspect there might be disagreement among the contributors to this volume on the nature of appropriate empirical evidence and how it should be related to theory. Clearly the opposite side of the coin for the advocated new methodological openness is a lack of consensus among different foreign policy analysts on how theories are to be substantiated.

3. Realism and structural realism are the objects of repeated reference and critique in this volume. What is remarkable is the virtual absence of any attention to rational choice theory as an alternative conceptual approach to foreign policy and international relations. The important ongoing work in this area is almost totally ignored. One example of how developments in this area are affecting theoretical work in foreign policy is provided by Bendor and Hammond (1992).

4. There are articles and books devoted to these and other kinds of foreign policy activity, but few are directly concerned with the development of a theory that explains when and why they occur.

5. Recognition of the need to connect comparative and international politics is not new. A conference devoted to this topic at Northwestern University resulted in Farrell's (1966) volume in which Rosenau's "pre–theories" essay appeared.

6. Admittedly, several contributors touch on features of the international system and might have developed its characteristics further in fuller studies, but Rothgeb is the only one presently to explore its impact directly.

7. Efforts to study reciprocity in both foreign policy and international relations have resulted in some recent attempts to identify action-reaction sequences, but success at capturing specific chains of interaction among actors, particularly those involving more than two countries, has still been elusive. For some efforts with event data, see Hermann (1984), Goldstein and Freeman (1990), and Leng (1993a).

► BIBLIOGRAPHY

Abbott, Michael H. 1988. *US Army Involvement in Counterdrug Operations: A Matter of Politics or National Security?* Carlisle Barracks, PA: U.S. Army War College.

Abelson, Robert P., Elliot Aronson, William J. McGuire, Theodore M. Newcomb, Milton J. Rosenberg, and Percy H. Tannenbaum, eds. 1968. *Theories of Cognitive Consistency: A Source Book.* Chicago: Rand McNally.

Achen, Christopher. 1987. Statistical Models for Event Data: A Review of Errors-in-Variables Theory. Presented at the Data Development in International Relations Conference on Event Data, Columbus, Ohio.

Addo, Herb. 1974. "The Structural Basis for International Communication." *Papers of the Peace Science Society* 23:81–100.

Afshar, Haleh, ed. 1987. *Women, State, and Ideology: Studies from Africa and Asia.* Albany: State University of New York Press.

Alexandre, Laurien. 1989. "Genderizing International Studies: Revisioning Concepts and Curriculum." *International Studies Notes* 14:5–8.

Alker, Hayward J., and James P. Bennett. 1977. "When National Security Policies Breed Collective Insecurity." In *Problems of World Modeling*, ed. Karl W. Deutsch, L. J. Edinger, Roy C. Macrielis, and Richard L. Merritt. Cambridge, Mass.: Ballinger.

Alker, Hayward J., James P. Bennett, and Dwain Mefford. 1980. "Generalized Precedent Logics for Resolving Security Dilemmas." *International Interactions* 7:165–200.

Alker, Hayward J., and Cheryl Christensen. 1972. "From Causal Modeling to Artificial Intelligence: The Evolving of a UN Peace-Making Simulation." In *Experimentation and Simulation in Political Science*, ed. J. A. LaPonce and P. Smoker. Toronto: University of Toronto Press.

Alker, Hayward J., and W. Greenberg. 1976. "On Simulating Collective Security Regime Alternatives." In *Thought and Action in Foreign Policy*, ed. M. Bonham and M. Shapiro. Basel: Birkhauser Verlag.

Alker, Hayward R., Jr., and Frank L. Sherman. 1986. *International Conflict Episodes, 1945–1979.* (ICPSR 8303) Ann Arbor, Mich.: Inter-University Consortium for Political and Social Research.

———. 1982. "Collective Security Seeking Practices since 1945." In *Managing International Crises*, ed. Daniel Frei. Beverly Hills, Calif.: Sage.

Allison, Graham T. 1971. *Essence of Decision: Explaining the Cuban Missile Crisis.* Boston: Little, Brown.

———. 1969. "Conceptual Models and the Cuban Missile Crisis." *American Political Science Review* 3:689–718.

Allison, Graham T., and Morton H. Halperin. 1972. "Bureaucratic Politics: A Paradigm and Some Policy Implications. *World Politics* 24 (supplement): 40–79. Reprinted in *Theory and Policy in International Relations*, ed. Raymond Tanter and Richard H. Ullman. Princeton, N.J.: Princeton University Press.

Allison, Graham T., and Peter L. Szanton. 1976. *Remaking Foreign Policy: The Organizational Connection.* New York: Basic Books.

Allison, Paul D. 1984. *Event History Analysis: Regression for Longitudinal Event Data.* Beverly Hills, Calif.: Sage.

Allport, Gordon W. 1931. "What Is a Trait of Personality?" *Journal of Abnormal and Social Psychology* 25:368–72.

Almond, Gabriel A. 1950. *The American People and Foreign Policy.* New York: Praeger.

Alternatives. 1993. "Special Issue: Feminists Write International Relations." 18.

Amin, Samir. 1974. *Accumulation on a World Scale.* New York: Monthly Review Press.

Anderson, Benedict. 1991. *Imagined Communities.* 2d ed. London: Verso.

Anderson, Paul A. 1987. "What Do Decision Makers Do When They Make a Foreign Policy Decision? The Implications for the Comparative Study of Foreign Policy." In *New Directions in the Study of Foreign Policy,* ed. Charles F. Hermann, Charles W. Kegley, Jr., and James N. Rosenau. Winchester, Mass.: Unwin Hyman.

———. 1983. "Decision Making by Objection and the Cuban Missile Crisis." *Administrative Science Quarterly* 28:201–22.

———. 1981. "Justifications and Precedents as Constraints in Foreign Policy Decision-Making." *American Journal of Political Science* 25:738–61.

Anderson, Paul A., and Stuart Thorson. 1982. "Artificial Intelligence Based Simulations of Foreign Policy Decision-Making." *Behavioral Science* 27:176–93.

Anderson, Richard D., Jr. 1982. "Soviet Decision Making in Poland." *Problems of Communism* 31:21–36.

Andrews, William G. 1962. *French Politics and Algeria: The Process of Policy Formation, 1954–1962.* New York: Appleton-Century-Crofts.

Andriole, Stephen J., and Gerald W. Hopple. 1984. "The Rise and Fall of Events Data: From Basic Research to Applied Use in the U.S. Department of Defense." *International Interactions* 11:293–309.

Armstrong, Adrienne. 1981. "The Political Consequences of Economic Dependence." *Journal of Conflict Resolution* 25:401–28.

Arrow, Kenneth J. 1985. "The Economics of Agency." In *Principals and Agents: The Structure of Business,* ed. John W. Pratt and Richard J. Zeckhauser. Boston: Harvard Business School Press.

Art, Robert J. 1973. "Bureaucratic Politics and American Foreign Policy: A Critique." *Policy Sciences* 4:467–90.

———. 1968. *The TFX Decision: McNamara and the Military.* Boston: Little, Brown.

Ashley, Richard K. 1980. *The Political Economy of War and Peace.* London: Frances Pinter.

Aspaturian, Vernon. 1966. "Internal Politics and Foreign Policy in the Soviet System." In *Approaches to Comparative and International Politics,* ed. R. Barry Farrell. Evanston, Ill.: Northwestern University Press.

Axelrod, Robert. 1984. *The Evolution of Cooperation.* New York: Basic Books.

———. 1976a. "The Analysis of Cognitive Maps." In *The Structure of Decision,* ed. Robert Axelrod. Princeton, N.J.: Princeton University Press.

————. 1973. "Schema Theory: An Information Processing Model of Perception and Cognition." *American Political Science Review* 67:1248–66.

————. 1972. *Framework for a General Theory of Cognition and Choice.* Berkeley, Calif.: Institute for International Studies.

————, ed. 1976b. *Structure of Decision: The Cognitive Maps of Political Elites.* Princeton, N.J.: Princeton University Press.

Azar, Edward E. 1982. *The Codebook of the Conflict and Peace Data Bank (COPDAB).* College Park, Md.: Center for International Development, University of Maryland.

————. 1980. "The Conflict and Peace Data Bank (COPDAB) Project." *Journal of Conflict Resolution* 24:143–52.

Azar, Edward E., and Joseph Ben-Dak, eds. 1975. *Theory and Practice of Events Research.* New York: Gordon and Breach.

Azar, Edward E., Richard A. Brody, and Charles A. McClelland. 1972. *International Events Interaction Analysis: Some Research Considerations.* Beverly Hills, Calif.: Sage.

Azar, Edward E., Stanley H. Cohen, Thomas O. Jukam, and James McCormick. 1972. "Making and Measuring the International Event as a Unit of Analysis." In *International Events Interaction Analysis: Some Research Considerations,* ed. Edward E. Azar, Richard A. Brody, and Charles A. McClelland. Beverly Hills, Calif.: Sage.

Azar, Edward E., R. D. McLaurin, Thomas Havener, Craig Murphy, Thomas Sloan, and Charles H. Wagner. 1977. "A System for Forecasting Strategic Crises: Findings and Speculations about Conflict in the Middle East." *International Interactions* 3:193–222.

Azar, Edward E., and Thomas Sloan. 1975. *Dimensions of Interaction.* Pittsburgh: University Center for International Studies, University of Pittsburgh.

Azar, Edward E., and Chung-In Moon, eds. 1988. *National Security in the Third World: The Management of Internal and External Threats.* College Park, Md.: Center for International Development and Conflict Management.

Bacharach, Samuel B. 1989. "Organizational Theories: Some Criteria for Evalution." *Academy of Management Review* 14:496–515.

Balassa, Bela. 1982. *Development Strategies in Semi-Industrial Countries.* Baltimore: Johns Hopkins University Press.

Ball, Desmond J. 1974. "The Blind Men and the Elephant: A Critique of Bureaucratic Politics." *Australian Outlook* 28:71–92.

Barnet, Richard J. 1971. *The Roots of War.* Baltimore: Pelican Books.

Barnet, Richard J., and Ronald E. Muller. 1974. *Global Reach.* New York: Simon and Schuster.

Barnett, A. Doak. 1985. *The Making of Foreign Policy in China: Structure and Process.* Boulder, Colo.: Westview.

Barner-Barry, Carol, and Robert Rosenwein. 1985. *Psychological Perspectives on Politics.* Englewood Cliffs, N.J.: Prentice-Hall.

Baron, Robert A., and Donn Byrne. 1981. *Social Psychology: Understanding Human Interaction*. Boston: Allyn and Bacon.

Barrett, David M. 1988. "The Mythology Surrounding Lyndon Johnson, His Advisers, and the 1965 Decision to Escalate the Vietnam War." *Political Science Quarterly* 103:637–63.

Bates, Robert H. 1981. *Markets and States in Tropical Africa*. Berkeley, Calif.: University of California Press.

Bar-Siman-Tov, Yaacov. 1983. *Linkage Politics in the Middle East: Syria between Domestic and External Conflict, 1961–1970*. Boulder, Colo.: Westview.

Bem, Daryl J. 1970. *Beliefs, Attitudes, and Human Affairs*. Belmont, Calif.: Brooks/Cole.

Ben-Zvi, Abraham. 1978. "The Outbreak and Termination of the Pacific War: A Juxtaposition of American Preconceptions." *Journal of Peace Research* 15:33–49.

———. 1976–77. "Misperceiving the Role of Perception: A Critique." *Jerusalem Journal of International Relations* 11:74–93.

———. 1975. "American Preconceptions and Policies toward Japan, 1940–1941." *International Studies Quarterly* 19:228–48.

Bendor, Jonathan. 1988. "Review Article: Formal Models of Bureaucracy." *British Journal of Political Science* 18:353–95.

Bendor, Jonathan, and Thomas H. Hammond. 1992. "Rethinking Allison's Models." *American Political Science Review* 86:301–22.

Benedict, Richard Elliot. 1991. *Ozone Diplomacy: New Directions in Safeguarding the Planet*. Cambridge, Mass.: Harvard University Press.

Benfer, Robert A., Edward E. Brent, Jr., and Louanna Furbee. 1991. *Expert Systems*. Newbury Park, Calif.: Sage.

Benjamin, Roger, and Raymond Duvall. 1985. "The Capitalist State in Context." In *The Democratic State*, ed. Roger Benjamin and Stephen Elkin. Lawrence: University Press of Kansas.

Bennett, Jane. 1987. *Unthinking Faith and Enlightenment*. New York and London: New York University Press.

Bennett, W. Lance, and Martha S. Feldman. 1981. *Reconstructing Reality in the Courtroom: Justice and Judgment in American Culture*. New Brunswick, N.J.: Rutgers University Press.

Benveniste, Guy. 1977. *The Politics of Expertise*. 2d ed. San Fransisco: Boyd and Fraser.

Berke, Richard. 1989. "Panel Said to Seek New Military Role in Fighting Drugs." *New York Times*, July 2.

Berman, Larry. 1989. *Lyndon Johnson's War: The Road to Stalemate in Vietnam*. New York: Norton.

———. 1982. *Planning a Tragedy: The Americanization of the War in Vietnam*. New York: Norton.

Bernards, Neal, ed. 1990. *War on Drugs: Opposing Viewpoints*. San Diego: Greenhaven Press.

Best, James J. 1988a. "Presidential Learning." *Congress and the Presidency* 15:25–48.

———. 1988b. "Who Talked to the President When? A Study of Lyndon B. Johnson." *Political Science Quarterly* 103:531–45.

Best, James J., and Kim DesRoches. 1991. Learning from Crises: An Empirical Analysis of Crisis Situations in the Kennedy and Johnson Administrations. Presented at the annual meeting of the Midwest Political Science Association, Chicago.

Bettenhausen, B., and J. Murninghan, 1985. "The Emergence of Norms in Competitive Decision-Making Groups." *Administrative Science Quarterly* 30:350–72.

Betts, Richard K. 1978. "Analysis, War, and Decision: Why Intelligence Failures Are Inevitable." *World Politics* 30:61–89.

Bialer, Seweryn. 1981. "Soviet Foreign Policy: Sources, Perceptions, Trends." In *The Domestic Context of Soviet Foreign Policy,* ed. Seweryn Bialer. Boulder, Colo.: Westview.

Biddle, William Jesse, and John D. Stephens. 1989. "Dependent Development and Foreign Policy: The Case of Jamaica." *International Studies Quarterly* 33:411–34.

Birnie, Patricia. 1984. "The International Organization of Whales." *Denver Journal of International Law and Policy* 13:309–33.

Blainey, Geoffrey. 1988. *The Causes of War.* New York: Free Press.

Blasier, Cole. 1976. *The Hovering Giant: U.S. Responses to Revolutionary Change in Latin America.* Pittsburgh: University of Pittsburgh Press.

Bloomfield, Lincoln P., and Amelia C. Leiss. 1969. *Controlling Small Wars.* New York: Knopf.

Bloomfield, Lincoln P., and Allen Moulton. 1989. *CASCON III: Computer-Aided System for Analysis of Local Conflicts.* Cambridge, Mass.: MIT Center for International Studies.

Boardman, Anthony E., and Aidan R. Vining. 1989. "Ownership and Performance in Competitive Environments." *Journal of Law and Economics* 32:1–33.

Bock, Joseph G. 1987. *The White House and the National Security Assistant: Friendship and Friction at the Water's Edge.* New York: Greenwood.

Bonham, G. Matthew, Daniel Heradstveit, O. Narvesen, and Michael J. Shapiro. 1978. "A Cognitive Model of Decision-Making: Application to Norwegian Oil Policy." *Cooperation and Conflict* 13:93–108.

Bonham, G. Matthew, and Michael Shapiro. 1976. "Exploration of the Unexpected: The Syrian Intervention in Jordan in 1970." In *The Structure of Decision,* ed. Robert Axelrod. Princeton, N.J.: Princeton University Press.

———, eds. 1977. *Thought and Action in Foreign Policy.* Basek and Stuttgart: Birkhauser Verlag.

Bonham, G. Matthew, Michael J. Shapiro, and Thomas L. Trumble. 1979. "The October War: Changes in Cognitive Orientation toward the Middle East Conflict." *International Studies Quarterly* 23:3–44.

Boulding, Kenneth E. 1959. "National Images and International Systems." *Journal of Conflict Resolution* 3:120–31.

———. 1956. *The Image: Knowledge in Life and Society.* Ann Arbor: University of Michigan Press.

Braveboy-Wagner, Jacqueline A. 1989. *Caribbean in World Affairs: The Foreign Policies of the English-Speaking States.* Boulder, Colo.: Westview.

Braybrooke, David, and Charles E. Lindblom. 1963. *A Strategy of Decision: Policy Evaluation as a Social Process.* New York: Free Press.

Brecher, Michael. 1980. *Decisions in Crisis.* Berkeley: University of California Press.

————. 1978. "A Theoretical Approach to International Crisis Behavior." *Jerusalem Journal of International Relations* 3:5–24.

————. 1977. "Toward a Theory of International Crisis Behavior." *International Studies Quarterly* 21:39–74.

————. 1975. *Decisions in Israel's Foreign Policy.* New Haven, Conn.: Yale University Press.

————. 1972. *The Foreign Policy System of Israel: Settings, Images, Process.* New Haven, Conn.: Yale University Press.

Brecher, Michael, with Benjamin Geist. 1980. *Decisions in Crisis: Israel, 1967 and 1973.* Berkeley: University of California Press.

Brecher, Michael, Blema Steinberg, and Janice Stein. 1969. "A Framework for Research on Foreign Policy Behavior." *Journal of Conflict Resolution* 8:75–101.

Brecher, Michael, and Jonathan Wilkenfeld. 1989. *Crisis, Conflict, and Instability.* New York: Pergamon.

Breslauer, George W. 1982. *Khrushchev and Brezhnev as Leaders: Building Authority in Soviet Politics.* Boston: Allen and Unwin.

Broad, Robin. 1988. *Unequal Alliance.* Berkeley: University of California Press.

Brodie, Bernard. 1978. "The Development of Nuclear Strategy." *International Security* 2:65–83.

Brody, Richard A. 1972. "International Events: Problems in Measurement and Analysis." In *International Events Interaction Analysis: Some Research Considerations,* ed. Edward E. Azar, Richard A. Brody, and Charles A. McClelland. Beverly Hills, Calif.: Sage.

Bronfenbrenner, U. 1961. "The Mirror-Image in Soviet-American Relations: A Social Psychologist's Report." *Journal of Social Issues* 17:45–56.

Brooke, James. 1990. "U.S. Will Arm Peru to Fight Leftists in New Drug Push." *New York Times,* April 22.

Brown, Seyom. 1983. *The Faces of Power: Constancy and Change in United States Foreign Policy from Truman to Reagan.* New York: Columbia University Press.

Brown, Wendy. 1988. *Manhood and Politics.* Totowa, N.J.: Rowman and Littlefield.

Bueno de Mesquita, Bruce. 1981. *The War Trap.* New Haven, Conn.: Yale University Press.

Bueno de Mesquita, Bruce, and David Lalman. 1992. *War and Reason: Domestic and International Imperatives.* New Haven, Conn.: Yale University Press.

Bull, Hedley. 1977. *The Anarchical Society.* New York: Columbia University Press.

Bundy, McGeorge. 1988. *Danger and Survival.* New York: Random House.

Burgess, Philip M., and Raymond W. Lawton. 1972. *Indicators of International Behavior: An Assessment of Events Data Research.* Beverly Hills, Calif.: Sage.

Burke, John P. 1992. *The Institutional Presidency.* Baltimore: Johns Hopkins University Press.

———. 1984. "Responsibilities of Presidents and Advisers." *Journal of Politics* 46:818–45.

Burke, John P., and Fred I. Greenstein. 1989. *How Presidents Test Reality.* New York: Russell Sage Foundation.

Burley, Anne-Marie, and Walter Mattli. 1993. "Europe before the Court: A Political Theory of Legal Integration." *International Organization* 47:41–76.

Burstyn, Varda. 1983. "Masculine Dominance and the State." In *The Socialist Register,* ed. R. Miliband and J. Saville. London: Merlin Press.

Butler, Judith, and Joan W. Scott, eds. 1992. *Feminists Theorize the Political.* New York and London: Routledge.

Butterworth, Robert Lyle. 1976. *Managing Interstate Conflict, 1945–74: Data with Synopses.* Pittsburgh: University Center for International Studies.

Buzan, Barry. 1991. "New Patterns of Global Security in the Twenty-first Century." *International Affairs* 67:431–51.

———. 1984. "Economic Structure and International Security: The Limits of the Liberal Case." *International Organization* 38:597–634.

Calder, Bobby J., and Michael Ross. 1973. *Attitudes and Behavior.* Morristown, N.J.: General Learning Press.

Calder, Kent E. 1988. "Japanese Foreign Economic Policy Formation: Explaining the Reactive State." *World Politics* 40:517–41.

Caldwell, Dan. 1977. "Bureaucratic Foreign Policy-Making." *American Behavioral Scientist* 21:87–110.

Caldwell, Lynton Keith. 1984. *International Environmental Policy: Emergence and Dimensions.* Durham, N.C.: Duke University Press.

Callahan, Patrick. 1982. "Commitment." In *Describing Foreign Policy Behavior,* ed. Patrick Callahan, Linda P. Brady, and Margaret G. Hermann. Beverly Hills, Calif.: Sage.

Campbell, Colin. 1986. *Managing the Presidency: Carter, Reagan, and the Search for Executive Harmony.* Pittsburgh: University of Pittsburgh Press.

Caporaso, James A. 1988. "Introduction to a Special Issue on the State in Comparative and International Perspective." *Comparative Political Studies* 21:3–12.

———. 1982. "The State's Role in Third World Economic Growth." *Annals of the American Academy of Political and Social Science* 459(January):103–11.

———. 1978. "Dependence, Dependency, and Power in the Global System: A Structural and Behavioral Analysis." *International Organization* 32:13–43.

Caporaso, James A., Charles F. Hermann, Charles W. Kegley, Jr., James N. Rosenau, and Dina A. Zinnes. 1987. "The Comparative Study of Foreign Policy: Perspectives on the Future." *International Studies Notes* 13:32–46.

Caraley, Demetrios. 1966. *The Politics of Military Unifications.* New York: Columbia Universtity Press.

Cardoso, Fernando H. 1973. "Associated-Dependent Development: Theoretical and Practical Implications." In *Authoritarian Brazil: Origins, Policies and Future*, ed. Alfred Stepan. New Haven, Conn.: Yale University Press.

Cardoso, Fernando H., and Enzo Faletto. 1979. *Dependency and Development in Latin America*. Berkeley: University of California Press.

Carr, E. H. 1939. *The Twenty Years Crisis, 1919–1939*. New York: St. Martin's Press.

Carroll, John S., and Richard L. Weiner. 1982. "Cognitive Social Psychology in Court and Beyond." In *Cognitive Social Psychology*, ed. Albert H. Hastorf and Alice M. Isen. New York: Elsevier North Holland.

Carter, Ralph G. 1989. "Senate Defense Budgeting, 1981–1988: The Impacts of Ideology, Party and Constituency Benefit on the Decision to Support the President." *American Politics Quarterly* 17:332–47.

Castañeda, Jorge. 1985. "Don't Corner Mexico!" *Foreign Policy* 61 (Fall): 75–90.

Chan, Steve. 1984. "Mirror, Mirror on the Wall…: Are Freer Countries More Pacific?" *Journal of Conflict Resolution* 28:617–48.

———. 1979. "Rationality, Bureaucratic Politics, and Police Systems: Explaining the Chinese Policy Debate, 1964–1966." *Journal of Peace Research* 16:333–47.

Cheney, Richard. 1990. "Using the Military Will Win the War on Drugs." In *War on Drugs: Opposing Viewpoints*, ed. Neal Bernards. San Diego: Greenhaven Press.

Chilcote, Ronald H. 1985. "Alternative Approaches to Comparative Politics." In *New Directions in Comparative Politics*, ed. Howard J. Wiarda. Boulder, Colo.: Westview.

Chittick, William O., and Keith R. Billingsley. 1989. "The Structure of Elite Foreign Policy Beliefs." *Western Political Quarterly* 42:201–24.

Christian, Cindy M., and Khalil Dokhanchi. 1991. The Structure of Foreign Policy Orientations of Middle Eastern and Latin American States: A Study of United Nations Roll-call Votes. Presented at the annual meeting of the Midwest Political Science Association, Chicago.

Chubb, John E., and Terry M. Moe. 1990. *Politics, Markets, and America's Schools*. Washington, D.C.: The Brookings Institution.

Churchill, Winston S. 1948. *The Second World War*, vol. 1, *The Gathering Storm*. Boston: Houghton Mifflin.

Cimbala, Stephen. 1987. *Artificial Intelligence and National Security*. Lexington, Mass.: Lexington Books.

Clapham, Christopher. 1977. "Comparative Foreign Policy and Developing States." In *Foreign Policy Making in Developing States*, ed. Christopher Clapham. Westmead, England: Saxon House.

Clark, Lorenne M., and Lynda Lange, eds. 1979. *The Sexism of Social and Political Theory: Women and Reproduction from Plato to Nietzsche*. Toronto: University of Toronto Press.

Clifford, Clark, with Richard Holbrooke. 1991. *Counsel to the President: A Memoir*. New York: Random House.

Cohen, Benjamin J. 1973. *The Question of Imperialism*. New York: Basic Books.

Cohen, Bernard C., and Scott A. Harris. 1975. "Foreign Policy." In *The Handbook of Political Science*, vol. 6, ed. Fred I. Greenstein and Nelson Polsby. Reading, Mass.: Addison-Wesley.

Cohn, Carol. 1987. "Sex and Death in the Rational World of Defense Intellectuals." *Signs* 12:687–718.

Coles, Robert. 1986. *The Political Life of Children.* Boston: Atlantic Monthly Press.

Connell, R. W. 1990. "The State, Gender and Sexual Politics: Theory and Appraisal." *Theory and Society* 19:507–44.

Connolly, William E. 1991. *Identity\Difference: Democratic Negotiations of Political Paradox.* Ithaca, N.Y., and London: Cornell University Press.

———. 1974. *The Terms of Political Discourse.* Lexington, Mass.: D. C. Heath.

Connor, Walker. 1972. "Nation-Building or Nation-Destroying." *World Politics* 24:319–55.

Conover, Pamela J., and Stanley Feldman. 1991. "Where Are the Schema? Critiques." *American Political Science Review* 85:1364–69.

Cooper, Andrew, F., Richard A. Higgott, and Kim Richard Nossal. 1993. *Relocating Middle Powers: Australia and Canada in a Changing World Order.* Vancouver: University of British Columbia Press.

Cooper, Richard N. 1977. "A New International Economic Order for Mutual Gain." *Foreign Policy* 26:65–139.

Coplin, William, Michael O'Leary, and Howard Shapiro. n.d. *PRINCE Project: International Transactions, Issue Specific Interactions and Power Data Sets, 1966–1972* (ICPSR 5006). Ann Arbor, Mich.: Inter-University Consortium for Political and Social Research.

Corkill David, and David Cubitt. 1988. *Ecuador: Fragile Democracy.* London: Latin American Bureau.

Corrigan, Philip, and Derek Sayer. 1985. *The Great Arch: English State Formation as Cultural Revolution.* Oxford and New York: Basil Blackwell.

Cottam, Martha. 1986. *Foreign Policy Decision Making: The Influence of Cognition.* Boulder, Colo.: Westview.

Cottam, Richard W. 1977. *Foreign Policy Motivation: A General Theory and a Case Study.* Pittsburgh: University of Pittsburgh Press.

Cox, Robert W., and Harold Jacobson. 1974. *The Anatomy of Influence: Decision Making in International Organizations.* New Haven, Conn.: Yale University Press.

Crabb, Cecil V., Jr., and Pat M. Holt. 1989. *Invitation to Struggle: Congress, the President and Foreign Policy.* 3d ed. Washington, D.C.: CQ Press.

Crabb, Cecil V., Jr., and Kevin Mulcahy. 1986. *Presidents and Foreign Policy Making.* Baton Rouge: Louisiana State University Press.

Crahan, Margaret E., and Peter H. Smith. 1992. "The State of Revolution." In *Americas: New Interpretive Essays*, ed. Alfred Stepan. New York: Oxford University Press.

Crane, Barbara B. 1984. "Policy Coordination by Major Western Powers in Bargaining with the Third World: Debt Relief and the Common Fund." *International Organization* 38:399–428.

Crapol, Edward P. 1992. *Women and American Foreign Policy: Lobbyists, Critics, and Insiders.* 2d ed. Wilmington, Del.: Scholarly Resources.

Cronin, Thomas E., and Sanford D. Greenberg, eds. 1969. *The Presidential Advisory System.* New York: Harper and Row.

Dahl, Robert A. 1971. *Polyarchy*. New Haven, Conn.: Yale University Press.

Dallek, Robert. 1983. *The American Style of Foreign Policy: Cultural Politics and Foreign Affairs*. New York: Knopf.

———. 1977. *Franklin Roosevelt and American Foreign Policy, 1932–1945*. New York: Oxford University Press.

Dallin, Alexander. 1981. "The Domestic Sources of Soviet Foreign Policy." In *The Domestic Context of Soviet Foreign Policy*, ed. Seweryn Bialer. Boulder, Colo.: Westview.

Daly, Judith Ayres, and Stephen J. Andriole. 1980. "The Use of Events/Interaction Research by the Intelligence Community." *Policy Sciences* 12:215–36.

D'Amico, Francine, and Peter Beckman, eds. 1995. *Women and World Politics*. New York: Bergin and Garvey.

David, Steven R. 1991. "Explaining Third World Realignment." *World Politics* 43:223–56.

Davies, John L., and Chad K. McDaniel. 1993. "The Global Event-Data System." In *International Event Data Developments*, ed. Richard L. Merritt, Robert G. Muncaster, and Dina A. Zinnes. Ann Arbor: University of Michigan Press.

Davis, Vincent. 1967. *The Admirals Lobby*. Chapel Hill: University of North Carolina Press.

Dawisha, Adeed. 1990. "Arab Regimes: Legitimacy and Foreign Policy." In *The Arab State*, ed. Giacomo Luciani. Berkeley: University of California Press.

Dawisha, Karen. 1980. "The Limits of the Bureaucratic Politics Model: Observations on the Soviet Case." *Studies in Comparative Communism* 13:300–46.

DeHaven, Mark J. 1991. "Internal and External Determinants of Foreign Policy: West Germany and Great Britain during the Two-Track Missile Controversy." *International Studies Quarterly* 35:87–108.

de Rivera, Joseph. 1968. *The Psychological Dimension of Foreign Policy*. Columbus, Ohio: Charles E. Merrill.

DeRouen, Karl, and Alex Mintz. 1991. Economic Dependence and Foreign Policy Compliance: A Survey of Problems and Evidence. Paper presented at the annual meeting of the Midwest Political Science Association, Chicago.

Destler, I. M. 1986. *American Trade Politics: System under Stress*. New York: Twentieth Century Fund.

———. 1983. "The Rise of the National Security Assistant, 1961–1981." In *Perspectives on American Foreign Policy*, ed. Charles W. Kegley, Jr. and Eugene R. Wittkopf. New York: St. Martin's Press.

———. 1972. *Presidents, Bureaucrats, and Foreign Policy*. Princeton, N.J.: Princeton University Press.

Destler, I. M., Priscilla Clapp, Hideo Sato, and Haruhiro Fukui. 1976. *Managing an Alliance: The Politics of U.S.–Japanese Relations*. Washington, D.C: Brookings.

Destler, I. M., Haruhiro Fukui, and Hideo Sato. 1979. *The Textile Wrangle: Conflict in Japanese–American Relations, 1969–1971*. Ithaca, N.Y.: Cornell University Press.

Destler, I. M., Leslie H. Gelb, and Anthony Lake. 1984. *Our Own Worst Enemy: The Unmaking of American Foreign Policy*. New York: Simon and Schuster.

Destler, I. M., and John S. Odell. 1987. *Anti-Protectionism: Changing Forces in United States Trade Politics.* Washington, D.C.: Institute of International Economics.

Deutsch, Karl W. 1968. *The Analysis of International Relations.* Englewood Cliffs, N.J.: Prentice-Hall.

————. 1966. *The Nerves of Government.* 2d ed. New York: Free Press.

Deutscher, Irwin. 1973. *What We Say/What We Do: Sentiments and Acts.* Glenview, Ill.: Scott, Foresman.

Dilulio, John J. 1989. "Recovering the Public Management Variable: Lessons from Schools, Prisons, and Armies." *Public Administration Review* 49:127–33.

DiMaggio, Paul J., and Walter W. Powell. 1991. "Introduction." In *The New Institutionalism in Organizational Analysis,* ed. Walter W. Powell and Paul J. DiMaggio. Chicago: University of Chicago Press.

Di Stefano, Christine. 1991. *Configurations of Masculinity: A Feminist Perspective on Modern Political Theory.* Ithaca, N. Y., and London: Cornell University Press.

Dixon, William J. 1993. "Democracy and the Management of International Conflict." *Journal of Conflict Resolution* 37:42–68.

————. 1986. "Reciprocity in United States–Soviet Relations: Multiple Symmetry or Issue Linkage." *American Journal of Political Science* 30:421–45.

Domhoff, G. William. 1978. *Who Really Rules? New Haven and Community Power Reexamined.* New Brunswick, N.J.: Transaction Books.

————. 1969. "Who Made American Foreign Policy 1945–1963?" In *Corporations and the Cold War,* ed. David Horowitz. New York: Monthly Review Press.

————. 1967. *Who Rules America?* Englewood Cliffs, N.J.: Prentice-Hall.

Domke, William K. 1988. *War and the Changing Global System.* New Haven, Conn.: Yale University Press.

Donahue, John D. 1989. *The Privatization Decision.* New York: Basic Books.

Doran, Charles F., Robert E. Pendley, and George E. Antunes. 1973. "A Test of Cross-National Event Reliability." *International Studies Quarterly* 17:175–203.

dos Santos, Teodoro. 1970. "The Structure of Dependence." *American Economic Review* 60: 231–36.

Downs, Anthony. 1967. *Inside Bureaucracy.* Glenview, Ill.: Scott, Foresman.

Dowty, Alan. 1984. *Middle East Crisis.* Berkeley: University of California Press.

Doxey, Margaret. 1989. "Constructive Internationalism: A Continuing Theme in Canadian Foreign Policy." *The Round Table* 311:288–304.

Doyle, Michael W. 1986. "Liberalism and World Politics." *American Political Science Review* 80:1151–69.

Duvall, Raymond. 1978. "Dependence and Dependencia Theory: Notes toward Precision of Concept and Argument." *International Organization* 32:51–78.

Duvall, Raymond, and John Freeman. 1983. "The Techno-Bureaucratic Elite and the Entrepreneurial State in Dependent Industrialization." *American Political Science Review* 77:569–87.

East, Maurice A. 1978. "National Attributes and Foreign Policy." In *Why Nations Act: Theoretical Perspectives for Comparative Foreign Policy*, ed. Maurice A. East, Stephen A. Salmore, and Charles F. Hermann. Beverly Hills, Calif.: Sage.

————. 1975. "Size and Foreign Policy Behavior: A Test of Two Models." In *International Events and the Comparative Analysis of Foreign Policy*, ed. Charles W. Kegley, Jr., Gregory A. Raymond, Robert M. Rood, and Richard A. Skinner. Columbia: University of South Carolina Press.

————. 1973. "Size and Foreign Policy Behavior: A Test of Two Models." *World Politics* 25:556–76.

East, Maurice A., and Charles F. Hermann. 1974. "Do Nation-Types Account for Foreign Policy Behavior?" In *Comparing Foreign Policies: Theories, Findings, and Methods*, ed. James N. Rosenau. New York: John Wiley and Sons for Sage.

East, Maurice A., Stephen A. Salmore, and Charles F. Hermann, eds. 1978. *Why Nations Act: Theoretical Perspectives for Comparative Foreign Policy Studies*. Beverly Hills, Calif.: Sage.

Eisenhardt, Kathleen M. 1989a. "Agency Theory: An Assessment and Review." *Academy of Management Review* 14:57–74.

————. 1989b. "Building Theories from Case Study Research." *Academy of Management Review* 14:532–50.

Eisenstein, Zillah R. 1981. *The Radical Future of Liberal Feminism*. Boston: Northeastern University Press.

Elshtain, Jean Bethke. 1992. "Sovereignty, Identity, Sacrifice." In *Gendered States*, ed. V. Spike Peterson. Boulder, Colo.: Lynne Rienner.

————. 1981. *Public Man, Private Woman: Women in Social and Political Thought*. Princeton, N.J.: Princeton University Press.

Enloe, Cynthia. 1990. *Bananas, Beaches and Bases: Making Feminist Sense of International Politics*. Berkeley: University of California Press.

————. 1987. "Feminists Thinking about War, Militarism, and Peace." In *Analyzing Gender*, ed. Beth B. Hess and Myra Marx Ferree. Newbury Park, Calif.: Sage.

Etheredge, Lloyd S. 1985. *Can Governments Learn? American Foreign Policy and Central American Revolutions*. New York: Pergamon Press.

————. 1978a. "Personality Effects on American Foreign Policy, 1898–1968: A Test of Interpersonal Generalization Theory." *American Political Science Review* 72:434–51.

————. 1978b. *A World of Men: The Private Sources of American Foreign Policy*. Cambridge, Mass.: MIT Press.

Evans, Peter B. 1993. "Building an Integrative Approach to International and Domestic Politics." In *Double-Edged Diplomacy*, ed. Peter B. Evans, Harold K. Jacobson, and Robert D. Putnam. Berkeley: University of California Press.

————. 1979. *Dependent Development: The Alliance of Multinational, State, and Local Capital in Brazil*. Princeton, N.J.: Princeton University Press.

Evans, Peter B., Harold K. Jacobson, and Robert D. Putnam, eds. 1993. *Double-Edged Diplomacy: International Bargaining and Domestic Politics*. Berkeley: University of California Press.

Evans, Peter B., Dietrich Rueschemeyer, and Theda Skocpol, eds. 1985. *Bringing the State Back In.* Cambridge: Cambridge University Press.

Everts, Philip P., ed. 1985. *Controversies at Home: Domestic Factors in the Foreign Policy of the Netherlands.* Boston: Martinus Nijhoff.

Falkowski, Lawrence S., ed. 1979. *Psychological Models in International Politics.* Boulder, Colo.: Westview.

Farrands, Christopher. 1988. "State, Society, Culture and British Foreign Policy." In *British Foreign Policy: Tradition, Change, and Transformation,* ed. Michael Smith, Steve Smith, and Brian White. Boston: Allen & Unwin.

Farrell, John C., and Asa P. Smith. 1967. *Image and Reality in World Politics.* New York: Columbia University Press.

Farrell, R. Barry, ed. 1966. *Approaches to Comparative and International Politics.* Evanston, Ill.: Northwestern University Press.

Feldman, Martha. 1993. "Organization Theory and the Presidency." In *Researching the Presidency: Vital Questions, New Approaches,* ed. George C. Edwards, John H. Kessel, and Bert A. Rockman. Pittsburgh: University of Pittsburgh Press.

Ferejohn, John A. 1987. "The Structure of Agency Decision Processes." In *Congress: Structure and Process,* ed. Mathew D. McCubbins and Terry Sullivan. Cambridge: Cambridge University Press.

Ferris, Elizabeth. 1984. "Mexico's Foreign Policies: A Study in Contradictions." In *The Dynamics of Latin American Foreign Policies: Challenges for the 1980s,* ed. Jennie K. Lincoln and Elizabeth G. Ferris. Boulder, Colo.: Westview.

Ferris, Elizabeth G., and Jennie K. Lincoln, ed. 1981. *Latin American Foreign Policies: Global and Regional Dimensions.* Boulder, Colo.: Westview.

Festinger, Leon. 1957. *A Theory of Cognitive Dissonance.* Stanford, Calif.: Stanford University Press.

Finkle, Jason L., and Richard W. Gable, ed. 1971. *Political Development and Social Change.* 2d ed. New York: Praeger.

Finlay, David J., Ole R. Holsti, and Richard R. Fagen. 1967. *Enemies in Politics.* Chicago: Rand McNally.

Fishbein, M., and I. Ajzen. 1975. *Belief, Attitude, Intention and Behavior: An Introduction to Theory and Research.* London: Addison-Wesley.

Fiske, Susan T. 1993. "Cognitive Theory and the Presidency." In *Researching the Presidency: Vital Questions, New Approaches,* ed. George C. Edwards, John H. Kessel, and Bert A. Rockman. Pittsburgh: University of Pittsburgh Press.

Fiske, Susan T., and Shelley E. Taylor. 1991. *Social Cognition.* 2d ed. New York: McGraw-Hill.

———. 1984. *Social Cognition.* New York: McGraw-Hill.

Fletcher Forum of World Affairs. 1993. "Special Issue: Gender in International Relations." 17.

Forsythe, David P. 1992. "Democracy, War, and Covert Action." *Journal of Peace Research* 29:385–95.

Frank, Andre Gunder. 1981. *Crisis in the Third World.* New York: Holmes and Meier.

————. 1969. *Latin America: Underdevelopment or Revolution.* New York: Monthly Review Press.

Frank, Thomas M., and Edward Weisband. 1979. *Foreign Policy by Congress.* New York: Oxford University Press.

Frankel, Glenn. 1990. "Is the Nation-State Headed for the Dustbin of History?" *Washington Post National Weekly,* Nov. 19–25, 16.

Frankel, Joseph. 1963. *The Making of Foreign Policy.* London: Oxford University Press.

Freedman, Jonathan L., J. Merrill Carlsmith, and David O. Sears. 1970. *Social Psychology.* Englewood Cliffs, N.J.: Prentice-Hall.

Freedman, Lawrence. 1976. "Logic, Politics and Foreign Policy Processes: A Critique of the Bureaucratic Politics Model." *International Affairs* 52:434–49.

Freidrich, Carl J., and Zbigniew K. Brzezinski. 1956. *Totalitarian Dictatorship and Autocracy.* New York: Praeger.

Frieden, Jeffry A. 1991. "Invested Interests: The Politics of National Economic Policies in a World of Global Finance." *International Organization* 45:425–52.

————. 1977. "The Trilateral Commission: Economics and Politics in the 1970's." *Monthly Review* 29 (7):1–18.

Friman, H. Richard. 1993. "Side-Payments Versus Security Cards: Domestic Bargaining Tactics in International Economic Negotiations." *International Organization* 47:387–410.

————. 1992. "Neither Compromise Nor Compliance: International Influence, Societal Influence and the Politics of International Drug Trade." In *The Limits of State Autonomy: Societal Groups and Foreign Policy Formulation,* ed. David Skidmore and Valerie M. Hudson. Boulder, Colo.: Westview.

Frost, Peter J., Larry F. Moore, Meryl Reis Louis, Craig C. Lundberg, and Joanne Martin, eds. 1991. *Reframing Organizational Culture.* Newbury Park, Calif.: Sage.

Fukui, Haruhiro. n.d. "Japanese Decision Making in the 1971 Exchange Rate Crisis." In *Leaders, Groups, and Coalitions: How Decision Units Shape Foreign Policy,* ed. Joe D. Hagan, Charles F. Hermann, and Margaret G. Hermann. Forthcoming.

————. 1978. "The GATT Tokyo Round: The Bureaucratic Politics of Multilateral Diplomacy." In *The Politics of Trade: U.S. and Japanese Policymaking for the GATT Negotiations,* ed. Michael Baker. New York: Occasional Papers of the East Asian Institute.

————. 1977a. "Foreign Policy Making by Improvisation: The Japanese Experience." *International Journal* 32:791–812.

————. 1977b. "Tanaka Goes to Peking: A Case Study in Foreign Policy Making." In *Policymaking in Contemporary Japan,* ed. T. J. Pempel. Ithaca, N.Y.: Cornell University Press.

————. 1970. *Party in Power: The Japanese Liberal-Democrats and Policy Making.* Berkeley: University of California Press.

Gaddis, John L. 1992/93. "International Relations Theory and the End of the Cold War." *International Security* 17(3):5–58.

————. 1987. "Expanding the Data Base: Historians, Political Scientists and the Enrichment of Security Studies." *International Security* 12:3–21.

————. 1982. *Strategies of Containment*. New York: Oxford University Press.

————. 1972. *The United States and the Origins of the Cold War*. New York: Columbia University Press.

Gaenslen, Fritz. 1992. "Decision-Making Groups." In *Political Psychology and Foreign Policy*, ed. Eric Singer and Valerie Hudson. Boulder, Colo.: Westview.

Galtung, Johan. 1971. "A Structural Theory of Imperialism." *Journal of Peace Research* 8:81–117.

Gamson, William A., and Andrei Modigliani. 1971. *Untangling the Cold War*. Boston: Little, Brown.

Garson, G. David. 1990. "Expert Systems: An Overview for Social Scientists." *Social Science Computer Review* 8:387–410.

Gelb, Leslie H., with Richard K. Betts. 1979. *The Irony of Vietnam: The System Worked*. Washington, D.C.: The Brookings Institution.

Geller, Daniel S. 1985. *Domestic Factors in Foreign Policy: A Cross-National Statistical Analysis*. Cambridge, Mass.: Schenkman Publishing.

Gellner, Ernest. 1983. *Nations and Nationalism*. Ithaca, N.Y.: Cornell University Press.

Gelman, Harry. 1984. *The Brezhnev Politburo and the Decline of Detente*. Ithaca, N.Y.: Cornell University Press.

George, Alexander L. 1993. *Bridging the Gap*. Washington, D.C.: United States Institute of Peace Press.

————. 1991. *Forceful Persuasion*. Washington, D.C.: United States Institute of Peace Press.

————. 1980a. "Domestic Constraints on Regime Change in U.S. Foreign Policy: The Need for Legitimacy." In *Change in the International Systems*, ed. Ole R. Holsti, Randolph M. Siverson, and Alexander L. George. Boulder, Colo.: Westview.

————. 1980b. *Presidential Decisionmaking in Foreign Policy: The Effective Use of Information and Advice*. Boulder, Colo.: Westview.

————. 1979a. "Case Studies and Theory Development: The Method of Structured, Focused Comparison." In *Diplomacy*, ed. Paul Lauren. New York: Free Press.

————. 1979b. "The Causal Nexus between Cognitive Beliefs and Decision-Making Behavior: The 'Operational Code' Belief System." In *Psychological Models in International Politics*, ed. Lawrence S. Falkowski. Boulder, Colo.: Westview.

————. 1972. "The Case for Multiple Advocacy in Making Foreign Policy." *American Political Science Review* 66:751–95.

————. 1969. "The 'Operational Code': A Neglected Approach to the Study of Political Leaders and Decision–Making." *International Studies Quarterly* 13:190–222.

George, Alexander L., David K. Hall, and William E. Simons. 1971. *The Limits of Coercive Diplomacy: Laos, Cuba, Vietnam*. Boston: Little, Brown.

George, Alexander L., and Timothy J. McKeown. 1985. "Case Studies and Theories of Organizational Decision Making." In *Advances in Information Processing in Organizations*, vol.2, ed. Richard F. Coulam and Robert A. Smith. Greenwich, Conn.: JAI Press.

George, Alexander L., and Richard Smoke. 1974. *Deterrence in American Foreign Policy*. New York: Columbia University Press.

Gerner, Deborah J. 1992a. "Foreign Policy Analysis: Exhilarating Eclecticism, Intriguing Enigmas." *International Studies Notes* 17:4–19.

———. 1992b. "Foreign Policy Analysis: Renaissance, Routine, or Rubbish." In *Political Science: Looking to the Future,* vol. 2, *Comparative Politics, Policy, and International Relations,* ed. William Crotty. Evanston, Ill.: Northwestern University Press.

Gerner, Deborah J., Philip A. Schrodt, Ronald A. Francisco, and Judith L. Weddle. 1994. "Machine Coding of Events from Regional and International Sources." *International Studies Quarterly* 38: 91–119.

Gilpin, Robert. 1987. *The Political Economy of International Relations.* Princeton, N.J.: Princeton University Press.

———. 1981. *War and Change in World Politics.* Cambridge: Cambridge University Press.

———. 1975. *U.S. Power and the Multinational Corporation.* New York: Basic Books.

Gilsenan, Michael. 1992. "The Grand Illusion." In *Taking Sides: Clashing Views on Controversial Issues in World Politics.* 4th ed. Guilford, Conn.: Dushkin.

Glad, Betty, and Charles Taber. 1990. "Images, Learning, and the Decision to Use Force: The Domino Theory of the United States." In *Psychological Dimensions of War,* ed. Betty Glad. Newbury Park, Calif.: Sage.

Gleason, Gregory. 1991. "Nationalism in Our Time." *Current World Leaders* 34:213–34.

Gleditsch, Nils Petter. 1992. "Democracy and Peace." *Journal of Peace Research* 29:369–76.

Goldmann, Kjell. 1988. *Change and Stability in Foreign Policy: The Problems and Possibilities of Detente.* Princeton, N.J.: Princeton University Press.

Goldmann, Kjell, Sten Berglund, and Gunnar Sjostedt. 1986. *Democracy and Foreign Policy: The Case of Sweden.* Brookfield, Vt.: Gower.

Goldstein, Joshua S. 1992. "A Conflict-Cooperation Scale for WEIS Events Data." *Journal of Conflict Resolution* 36:369–85.

———. 1991. "Reciprocity in Superpower Relations: An Empirical Analysis." *International Studies Quarterly* 35:195–209.

Goldstein, Joshua S., and John R. Freeman. 1990. *Three-Way Street: Strategic Reciprocity in World Politics.* Chicago: University of Chicago Press.

Golich, Vicki L. 1992. "From Competition to Collaboration: The Challenge of Commercial-Class Aircraft Manufacturing." *International Organization* 46:899–934.

Good, Robert C. 1962. "State-building as a Determinant of Foreign Policy in the New States." In *Neutralism and Non-Alignment,* ed. Laurence W. Martin. New York: Praeger.

Gould, Stephen J. 1989. *Wonderful Life.* New York: Norton.

Goulding, Marrack. 1993. "The Evolution of United Nations Peacekeeping." *International Affairs* 69:451–64.

Gourevitch, Peter. 1986. *Politics in Hard Times.* Ithaca, N.Y.: Cornell University Press.

———. 1978. "The Second Image Reversed: The International Sources of Domestic Politics." *International Organization* 32:881–911.

Graubard, Stephen R. 1993. "Preface. Special Issue: Reconstructing Nations and States." *Daedalus* 122:v–viii.

Grabendorff, W. 1984. "The Role of Regional Powers in Central America: Mexico, Venezuela, Cuba and Colombia." In *Latin American Nations in World Politics*, ed. H. Muñoz and J. Tulchin. Boulder, Colo.: Westview.

———. 1978. "Mexico's Foreign Policy: Indeed a Foreign Policy?" *Journal of Interamerican Studies and World Affairs* 2:85–91.

Grant, Rebecca. 1991. "The Sources of Gender Bias in International Relations Theory." In *Gender and International Relations*, ed. Rebecca Grant and Kathleen Newland. Bloomington and Indianapolis: Indiana University Press.

Gray, Colin S. 1977. *The Geopolitics of the Nuclear Era*. New York: Crane Russak.

Greenstein, Fred I. 1975. *Personality and Politics: Problems of Evidence, Inference, and Conceptualization*. New York: Norton.

Greenwood, Ted. 1975. *Making the MIRV: A Study of Defense Decision Making*. Cambridge, Mass.: Ballinger.

Gurr, Ted Robert. 1974. *Civil Strife Events, 1955–1970* (ICPSR 7531). Ann Arbor, Mich.: Inter-University Consortium for Political and Social Research.

Haas, Ernst. 1983. "Regime Decay: Conflict Management and International Organizations, 1945–81." *International Organization* 37:189–256.

———. 1958. *The Uniting of Europe*. Stanford, Calif.: Stanford University Press.

Haas, Ernst, and Philippe C. Schmitter. 1964. "Economics and Differential Patterns of Political Integration: Projections about Unity in Latin America." *International Organization* 18:705–37.

Haas, Peter M. 1992. "Introduction: Epistemic Communities and International Policy Coordination." *International Organization* 46:1–36.

———. 1990. *Saving the Mediterranean. The Politics of International Environmental Cooperation*. New York: Columbia University Press.

Hagan, Joe D. 1994. "Domestic Political Systems and War Proneness." *Mershon International Studies Review*. Forthcoming.

———. 1993. *Political Opposition and Foreign Policy in Comparative Perspective*. Boulder, Colo.: Lynne Rienner.

———. 1989. "Domestic Political Regime Changes and Third World Voting Realignments in the United Nations, 1946–1984." *International Organization* 43:505–41.

———. 1987. "Regimes, Political Oppositions and the Comparative Analysis of Foreign Policy." In *New Directions in the Study of Foreign Policy*, ed. Charles F. Hermann, Charles W. Kegley, Jr., and James N. Rosenau. Winchester, Mass.: Unwin Hyman.

Hagan, Joe D., Charles F. Hermann, and Margaret G. Hermann, eds. n.d. *Leaders, Groups, and Coalitions: How Decision Units Shape Foreign Policy*. Forthcoming.

Haggard, Stephen. 1991. "Structuralism and Its Critics: Recent Progress in International Relations Theory." In *Progress in Postwar International Relations*, ed. Emanuel Adler and Beverly Crawford. New York: Columbia University Press.

Halliday, Fred. 1988a. "Hidden from International Relations: Women and the International Arena." *Millennium* 17:419–28.

———. 1988b. "State and Society in International Relations: A Second Age." *Millennium* 16:215-29.

Halloran, Richard. 1989. "Colombians to Protect U.S. Personnel." *New York Times*, Sept. 2.

Halperin, Morton H. 1974. *Bureaucratic Politics and Foreign Policy*. Washington, D.C.: The Brookings Institution.

Hammond, Paul Y. 1963. "Super Carriers and B-36 Bombers: Appropriations, Strategy and Politics." In *American Civil-Military Decisions: A Book of Case Studies*, ed. Harold Stein. Tuscaloosa: University of Alabama Press.

Hampson, Fen Osler. 1988. "The Divided Decision-Maker: American Domestic Politics and the Cuban Crisis." In *The Domestic Sources of American Foreign Policy: Insights and Evidence*, ed. Charles W. Kegley, Jr., and Eugene R. Wittkopf. New York: St. Martin's Press.

Handel, Michael I. 1990. *Weak States in the International System*. London: Frank Cass.

Haney, Patrick J. 1994. "Decision-Making during International Crises: A Reexamination." *International Interactions* 19:177–91.

———. 1992. Organizing for Foreign Policy: Presidents, Advisers, and Crisis Decision-Making. Ph.D. diss., Indiana University.

Haney, Patrick J., Roberta Q. Herzberg, and Rick K. Wilson. 1992. "Advice and Consent: Unitary Actors, Advisory Models, and Experimental Tests." *Journal of Conflict Resolution* 36:603–33.

Hanrieder, Wolfram F. 1978. "Dissolving International Politics: Reflections on the Nation-State." *American Political Science Review* 72:1276–87.

———. 1967. *West German Foreign Policy, 1949–1963: International Pressure and Domestic Response*. Stanford, Calif.: Stanford University Press.

———. 1970. *The Stable Crisis: Two Decades of German Foreign Policy*. New York: Harper and Row.

Hanrieder, Wolfram F., and Graeme P. Auton. 1980. *The Foreign Policies of West Germany, France, Britain*. Englewood Cliffs, N.J.: Prentice-Hall.

Hardin, Garrett. 1977. "Living on a Lifeboat." In *Managing the Commons*, ed. Garrett Hardin and John Baden. New York: W. H. Freeman.

Harris, Milton, and Artur Raviv. 1978. "Some Results on Incentive Contracts with Applications to Education and Employment, Health Insurance, and Law Enforcement." *American Economic Review* 68:20–30.

Hart, Jeffrey A. 1977. "Cognitive Maps of Three Latin American Policy Makers." *World Politics* 30:115–40.

———. 1976. "Comparative Cognition: The Politics of International Control of the Oceans." In *The Structure of Decision*, ed. Robert Axelrod. Princeton, N.J.: Princeton University Press.

Hartley, Thomas, and Bruce Russett. 1992. "Public Opinion and the Common Defense: Who Governs Military Spending in the United States." *American Political Science Review* 86:905–15.

Hartsock, Nancy. 1983. *Money, Sex, and Power*. New York: Longman.

Hastie, Reid, and Nancy Pennington. 1991. "Cognitive and Social Processes in Decision Making." In *Perspectives on Socially Shared Cognition*, ed. Lauren B. Resnick, John M. Levine, and Stephanie D. Teasley. Washington, D.C.: American Psychological Association.

Hawes, Michael K. 1984. *Principal Power, Middle Power, or Satellite? Competing Perspectives in the Study of Canadian Foreign Policy*. Toronto: York Research Programme in Strategic Studies, York University.

Hayes, Robert H., Steven C. Wheelwright, and Kim B. Clark. 1988. *Dynamic Manufacturing*. New York: Free Press.

Hazelwood, Leo. 1975. "Diversion Mechanisms and Encapsulation Processes: The Domestic Conflict-Foreign Conflict Hypothesis Reconsidered." In *Sage International Yearbook of Foreign Policy Studies*, vol. 3, ed. Patrick McGowan. Beverly Hills, Calif.: Sage.

Heise, David. 1988. "Modeling Event Structures." *Journal of Mathematical Sociology* 13:138–68.

Hekman, Susan J. 1990. *Gender and Knowledge: Elements of a Postmodern Feminism*. Boston: Northeastern University Press.

Hellmann, Donald. 1969. *Japanese Foreign Policy and Domestic Politics: The Peace Agreement with the Soviet Union*. Berkeley: University of California Press.

Henderson, Phillip G. 1988. *Managing the Presidency: The Eisenhower Legacy*. Boulder, Colo.: Westview.

Heradstveit, Daniel. 1979. *The Arab-Israeli Conflict: Psychological Obstacles to Peace*. Oslo: Universititesforlaget.

Heradstveit, Daniel, and G. Matthew Bonham. 1986. "Decision-Making in the Face of Uncertainty: Attributions of Norwegian and American Officials." *Journal of Peace Research* 23:339–56.

Herek, Gregory M., Irving L. Janis, and Paul Huth. 1989. "Quality of U.S. Decision-Making during the Cuban Missile Crisis: Major Errors in Welch's Reassessment." *Journal of Conflict Resolution* 33:446–59.

———. 1987. "Decision Making during International Crisis." *Journal of Conflict Resolution* 31:203–26.

Herken, Gregg. 1992. *Cardinal Choices: Presidential Science Advising from the Atomic Bomb to SDI*. New York: Oxford University Press.

Hermann, Charles F. 1993. "Avoiding Pathologies in Foreign Policy Decision Groups." In *Diplomacy, Force, and Leadership: Essays in Honor of Alexander George*, ed. Dan Caldwell and Timothy McKeown. Boulder, Colo.: Westview.

———. 1990. "Changing Course: When Governments Choose to Redirect Foreign Policy." *International Studies Quarterly* 34:3–21.

———. 1987a. Observations from the First Generation of International Event Data Research. Paper presented at the DDIR Conference on Events Data, Columbus, Ohio.

———. 1987b. Political Opposition as Potential Agents of Foreign Policy Change: Developing a Theory. Paper presented at the annual meeting of the International Studies Association, Washington, D.C.

————. 1978a. "Decision Structure and Process Influences on Foreign Policy." In *Why Nations Act*, ed. Maurice A. East, Stephen A. Salmore, and Charles F. Hermann. Beverly Hills, Calif.: Sage.

————. 1978b. "Foreign Policy Behavior: That Which Is to Be Explained." In *Why Nations Act*, ed. Maurice A. East, Stephen A. Salmore, and Charles F. Hermann. Beverly Hills, Calif.: Sage.

————. 1972. *International Crises: Insights from Behavioral Research*. New York: Free Press.

————. 1969a. *Crises in Foreign Policy*. Indianapolis: Bobbs-Merrill.

————. 1969b. "International Crisis as a Situational Variable." In *International Politics and Foreign Policy*, ed. James N. Rosenau. New York: Free Press.

Hermann, Charles, Maurice A. East, Margaret G. Hermann, Barbara G. Salmore, and Stephen A. Salmore. 1973. *CREON: A Foreign Events Data Set*. Beverly Hills, Calif.: Sage.

Hermann, Charles F., and Margaret G. Hermann. 1967. "An Attempt to Simulate the Outbreak of World War I." *American Political Science Review* 61:400–16.

Hermann, Charles F., Margaret G. Hermann, and Richard K. Herrmann, eds. n.d. *Changing Course in Foreign Policy*. Forthcoming.

Hermann, Charles F., and Gregory Peacock. 1987. "The Evolution and Future of Theoretical Research in the Comparative Study of Foreign Policy." In *New Directions in the Study of Foreign Policy*, ed. Charles F. Hermann, Charles W. Kegley, Jr., and James N. Rosenau. Winchester, Mass.: Unwin Hyman.

Hermann, Margaret G. 1984a. "Independence, Interdependence." In *Describing Foreign Policy Behavior*, ed. Patrick Callahan, Linda P. Brady, and Margaret G. Hermann. Beverly Hills, Calif.: Sage.

————. 1984b. "Personality and Foreign Policy Decision Making: A Study of 54 Heads of Government." In *Foreign Policy Decision Making: Perception, Cognition, and Artificial Intelligence*, ed. Steve Chan and Donald A. Sylvan. New York: Praeger.

————. 1982. "Syria's Hafez al-Assad." In *Leadership and Negotiation: A New Look at the Middle East*, ed. Barbara Kellerman and Jeffrey Rubin. New York: Praeger.

————. 1980. "Explaining Foreign Policy Behavior Using the Personal Characteristics of Political Leaders." *International Studies Quarterly* 24:7–46.

————. 1978. "Effects of Personal Characterisitics of Political Leaders on Foreign Policy." In *Why Nations Act: Theoretical Perspectives for Comparative Foreign Policy*, ed. Maurice A. East, Stephen A. Salmore, and Charles F. Hermann. Beverly Hills, Calif.: Sage.

————, ed. 1986. *Political Psychology*. San Francisco: Jossey-Bass.

————, ed. 1977. *A Psychological Examination of Political Leaders*. New York: Free Press.

Hermann, Margaret G., and Charles F. Hermann. 1989. "Who Makes Foreign Policy Decisions and How: An Empirical Inquiry." *International Studies Quarterly* 33:361–87.

Hermann, Margaret G., Charles F. Hermann, and Joe D. Hagan. 1987. "How Decision Units Shape Foreign Policy Behavior." In *New Directions in the Study of Foreign*

Policy, ed. Charles F. Hermann, Charles W. Kegley, Jr., and James N. Rosenau. Winchester, Mass.: Unwin Hyman.

Hermann, Margaret G., and Thomas Preston. 1994. "Presidents, Advisers, and Foreign Policy: The Effect of Leadership Style on Executive Arrangements." *Political Psychology* 15:75–96.

Hermann, Tamar. 1992. "Public Opinion and Foreign Policy Formation: Peace Activism as a Test of Modification—The Israeli Case." In *The Limits of State Autonomy: Societal Groups and Foreign Policy Formulation,* ed. David Skidmore and Valerie M. Hudson. Boulder, Colo.: Westview.

Herrmann, Richard K. 1988. "The Empirical Challenge of the Cognitive Revolution: A Strategy for Drawing Inferences about Perceptions." *International Studies Quarterly* 32:175–203.

———. 1986. "The Power of Perceptions in Foreign-Policy Decision Making: Do Views of the Soviet Union Determine the Policy Choices of American Leaders?" *American Journal of Political Science* 30:841–75.

———. 1985. *Perceptions and Behavior in Soviet Foreign Policy.* Pittsburgh: University of Pittsburgh Press.

———. 1984. "Perceptions and Foreign Policy Analysis." In *Foreign Policy Decision Making: Perception, Cognition, and Artificial Intelligence,* ed. Donald A. Sylvan and Steve Chan. New York: Praeger.

Hess, Stephen. 1988. *Organizing the Presidency.* 2d ed. Washington, D.C.: The Brookings Institution.

Heur, Richards J., Jr. 1980. "Analyzing the Soviet Invasion of Afghanistan: Hypotheses from Causal Attribution Theory." *Studies in Comparative Communism* 13:347–55.

Hey, Jeanne A. K. 1993. "Foreign Policy Options under Dependence: A Theoretical Evaluation with Evidence from Ecuador." *Journal of Latin American Studies* 25:543–74.

———. 1992. Theories of Dependent Foreign Policy and the Case of Ecuador during the Hurtado and Febres Cordero Administrations. Ph.D. diss., Ohio State University.

Hey, Jeanne A. K., and Lynn M. Kuzma. 1993. "Anti-US Foreign Policy of Dependent States: Mexican and Costa Rican Participation in Central American Peace Plans." *Comparative Political Studies* 26:30–62.

Higgins, Rosalyn. 1993. "The New United Nations and Former Yugoslavia." *International Affairs* 69:465–84.

Higgott, Richard A., and Andrew F. Cooper. 1990. "Middle Power Leadership and Coalition Building: Australia, the Cairns Group, and the Uruguay Round of Trade Negotiations." *International Organization* 44:589–632.

Hilsman, Roger. 1990. *The Politics of Policy Making in Defense and Foreign Affairs: Conceptual Models and Bureaucratic Politics.* 2d ed. Englewood Cliffs, N.J.: Prentice-Hall.

———. 1971. *The Politics of Policy Making in Defense and Foreign Affairs.* New York: Harper and Row.

———. 1967. *To Move a Nation.* Garden City, N.Y.: Doubleday.

———. 1959. "The Foreign-Policy Consensus: An Interim Report." *Journal of Conflict Resolution* 3:361–82.

———. 1952. "Intelligence and Policy Making in Foreign Affairs." *World Politics* 5:1–45.

Hinckley, Ronald H. 1992. *People, Polls, and Policymakers: American Public Opinion and National Security.* New York: Lexington Books.

———. 1988. "Public Attitudes toward Key Foreign Policy Events." *Journal of Conflict Resolution* 32:295–318.

Hinton, Harold C. 1972. *China's Turbulent Quest: An Analysis of China's Foreign Policy since 1949.* New York: Macmillan.

Hobson, J. A. 1965. *Imperialism: A Study.* Ann Arbor: University of Michigan Press.

Hogarth, Robin M., and Melvin W. Reder. 1987. *Rational Choice: The Contrast between Economics and Psychology.* Chicago: University of Chicago Press.

Hoggard, Gary. 1974. "Differential Source Coverage in Foreign Policy Analysis." In *Comparing Foreign Policies,* ed. James N. Rosenau. New York: Wiley.

Holbraad, Carsten. 1984. *Middle Powers in International Politics.* New York: St. Martin's Press.

Holmes, John W. 1982. *The Shaping of Peace: Canada and the Search for World Order, 1943–1957.* Toronto: University of Toronto Press.

Holsti, K. J. 1986. "The Horsemen of the Apocalypse: At the Gate, Detoured, or Retreating?" *International Studies Quarterly* 30:355–72.

———. 1975. "Underdevelopment and the 'Gap' Theory of International Conflict." *American Political Science Review* 69:827–39.

———, ed. 1982. *Why Nations Realign: Foreign Policy Restructuring in a Postwar World.* London: Allen and Unwin.

Holsti, Ole R., 1992. "Public Opinion and Foreign Policy: Challenges to the Almond-Lipmann Consensus." *International Studies Quarterly* 36:439–66.

———. 1990. "Crisis Decision Making." In *Psychological Dimensions of War,* ed. Betty Glad. Beverly Hills, Calif.: Sage.

———. 1989. "Crisis Decision Making." In *Behavior, Society, and Nuclear War,* vol. 1, ed. Philip E. Tetlock, Charles Tilly, Robert Jervis, Jo L. Husbands, and Paul C. Stern. New York: Oxford University Press.

———. 1982. "Operational Code Approach: Problems and Some Solutions." In *Cognitive Dynamics and International Politics,* ed. Christer Jansson. New York: St. Martin's Press.

———. 1979. "Theories of Crisis Decision Making." In *Diplomacy,* ed. Paul Lauren. New York: Free Press.

———. 1976. "Foreign Policy Formation Viewed Cognitively." In *Structure of Decision: The Cognitive Maps of Political Elites,* ed. Robert Axelrod. Princeton, N.J.: Princeton University Press.

———. 1970. "The 'Operational Code' Approach to the Study of Political Leaders: John Foster Dulles' Philosophical and Instrumental Beliefs." *Canadian Journal of Political Science* 3:123–57.

———. 1967. "Cognitive Dynamics and Images of the Enemy: Dulles and Russia." In *Image and Reality in World Politics,* ed. John C. Farrell and Asa P. Smith. New York: Columbia University Press.

———. 1962. "The Belief System and National Images: A Case Study." *Journal of Conflict Resolution* 6:244–52.

Holsti, Ole R., Richard A. Brody, and Robert C. North. 1965. "Measuring Affect and Action in International Reaction Models: Empirical Materials from the 1962 Cuban Crisis." *Peace Research Society Papers* 2:170–90.

Holsti, Ole R., Robert C. North, and Richard A. Brody. 1968. "Perception and Action in the 1914 Crisis." In *Quantitative International Politics*, ed. J. David Singer. New York: Free Press.

Holsti, Ole R., and James N. Rosenau. 1990a. "The Emerging U.S. Consensus on Foreign Policy." *Orbis* 34:579–95.

———. 1990b. "The Structure of Foreign Policy Attitudes: American Leaders, 1976–1984." *Journal of Politics* 52:94–125.

———. 1986a. "Consensus Lost. Consensus Regained? Foreign Policy Beliefs of American Leaders, 1976–1980." *International Studies Quarterly* 30:375–409.

———. 1986b. "The Foreign Policy Beliefs of American Leaders: Some Further Thoughts on Theory and Method." *International Studies Quarterly* 30:473–84.

———. 1984. *American Leadership in World Affairs*. Boston: Allen and Unwin.

———. 1979. "Vietnam, Consensus, and the Belief Systems of American Leaders." *World Politics* 23:1–56.

Hopple, Gerald W. 1984. "Computer-Based Early Warning: A Staircase Display Option for International Affairs Crisis Projection and Monitoring." In *National Security Crisis Forecasting and Management*, ed. Gerald W. Hopple, Stephen J. Andriole, and Amos Freedy. Boulder, Colo.: Westview.

———, ed. 1982. *Biopolitics, Political Psychology, and International Politics*. New York: St. Martin's Press.

Hopple, Gerald W., Stephen J. Andriole, and Amos Freedy, eds. 1984. *National Security Crisis Forecasting and Management*. Boulder, Colo.: Westview.

Horowitz, Irving Louis. 1966. *The Three Worlds of Development*. New York: Oxford University Press.

Hosoya, Chihiro. 1976. "Japan's Decision-Making System as a Determining Factor in Japan United States Relations." In *Japan, America, and the Future World Order*, ed. Morton A. Kaplan and Kinhide Mushakoji. New York: Free Press.

Huber, George P. 1991. "Organizational Learning: The Contributing Processes and Literatures." *Organization Science* 2:88–115.

Hudson, Valerie M. 1992. "Birth Order and the Personal Characteristics of World Leaders." In *Political Psychology and Foreign Policy*, ed. Eric Singer and Valerie M. Hudson. Boulder, Colo.: Westview.

———. 1987. "Using a Rule-Based Production System to Estimate Foreign Policy Behavior." In *Artificial Intelligence and National Security*, ed. Stephen Cimbala. Lexington, Mass.: Lexington Books.

———, ed. 1991. *Artificial Intelligence and International Politics*. Boulder, Colo.: Westview.

Hudson, Valerie M., and Susan M. Sims. 1992. "Calculating Regime Response to Domestic Opposition: Anti-Americanism among U.S. Allies." In *The Limits of*

State Autonomy: Societal Groups and Foreign Policy Formulation, ed. David Skidmore and Valerie M. Hudson. Boulder, Colo.: Westview.

Hudson, Valerie M., Susan M. Sims, and John C. Thomas. 1993. "The Domestic Political Context of Foreign Policy-Making: Explicating a Theoretical Construct." In *The Limits of State Autonomy: Societal Groups and Foreign Policy Formulation*, ed. David Skidmore and Valerie M. Hudson. Boulder, Colo.: Westview.

Hufbauer, Gary Clyde, Jeffrey J. Schott, and Kimberly Ann Elliott. 1990. *Economic Sanctions Reconsidered: History and Current Policy*. Washington, D.C.: Institute for International Economics.

Hufbauer, Gary Clyde, and Jeffrey J. Schott, with Kimberly Ann Elliott. 1983. *Economic Sanctions in Support of Foreign Policy Goals*. Washington, D.C.: Institute for International Economics.

Hull, Cordell. 1948. *The Memoirs of Cordell Hull*, vol. 2. New York: Macmillan.

Hult, Karen M. 1993. "Advising the President." In *Researching the Presidency*, ed. George C. Edwards, John H. Kessel, and Bert A. Rockman. Pittsburgh: University of Pittsburgh Press.

Hunter, Robert E. 1988. *Organizing for National Security*. Washington, D.C.: Center for Strategic and International Studies.

Hunter, Shireen T. 1992. *Iran after Khomeini*. New York: Praeger.

Huntington, Samuel P. 1993. "The Clash of Civilizations?" *Foreign Affairs* 72:22–49.

———. 1991. *The Third Wave*. Norman: University of Oklahoma Press.

———. 1968. *Political Order in Changing Societies*. New Haven, Conn.: Yale University Press.

———. 1961. *The Common Defense: Strategic Programs in National Defense*. New York: Columbia University Press.

Hybel, Alex R. 1990. *How Leaders Reason: US Intervention in the Caribbean Basin and Latin America*. New York: Basil Blackwell.

Ikenberry, G. John. 1988. "An Institutionalist Approach to American Foreign Economic Policy." *International Organization* 42:219–43.

Ikenberry, G. John, David A. Lake, and Michael Mastanduno, eds. 1988. *The State and American Foreign Economic Policy*. Ithaca, N.Y.: Cornell University Press.

Inderfurth, Karl F., and Lock K. Johnson, eds. 1988. *Decisions of the Highest Order: Perspectives on the National Security Council*. Pacific Grove, Calif.: Brooks/Cole.

International Monetary Fund. 1987. *Direction of Trade Statistics Yearbook*. Washington, D.C.: International Monetary Fund.

International Studies Quarterly. 1983. "Symposium: Event Data Collections." *International Studies Quarterly* 27:147–77.

Ismael, Tareq Y., and Jacqueline S. Ismael. 1986. "Domestic Sources of Middle East Foreign Policy." In *International Relations of the Contemporary Middle East: A Study in World Politics*, ed. Tareq Y. Ismael. Syracuse, N.Y.: Syracuse University Press.

Jabber, Paul. 1978. "Conflict and Cooperation in OPEC: Prospects for the Next Decade." *International Organization* 32:377–99.

Jackson, Henry, ed. 1965. *The National Security Council*. New York: Praeger.

Jackson, Robert H., and Carl G. Rosberg. 1982. "Why Africa's Weak States Persist: The Empirical and the Juridical in Statehood." *World Politics* 35:1–24.

James, Patrick. 1988. *Crisis and War*. Kingston and Montreal: McGill-Queen's University Press.

James, Patrick, and John R. Oneal. 1991. "The Influence of Domestic and International Politics on the President's Use of Force." *Journal of Conflict Resolution* 35:301–32.

Janis, Irving L. 1989. *Crucial Decisions*. New York: Free Press.

———. 1982. *Groupthink: Psychological Studies of Policy Decisions and Fiascoes*. Boston: Houghton Mifflin.

Janis, Irving L., and Leon Mann. 1977. *Decisionmaking*. New York: Free Press.

Jayawardena, Kumari. 1986. *Feminism and Nationalism in the Third World*. London: ZED Books.

Jensen, Lloyd. 1981. *Explaining Foreign Policy*. Englewood Cliffs, N.J.: Prentice-Hall.

Jervis, Robert. 1991. "Domino Beliefs and Strategic Behavior." In *Dominoes and Bandwagons*, ed. Robert Jervis and Jack Snyder. New York: Oxford University Press.

———. 1976. *Perception and Misperception in International Politics*. Princeton, N.J.: Princeton University Press.

———. 1978. "Cooperation under the Security Dilemma." *World Politics* 30:167–214.

———. 1968. "Hypotheses on Misperception." *World Politics* 20:454–79.

Jervis, Robert, Richard Ned Lebow, and Janice Gross Stein, eds. 1985. *Psychology and Deterrence*. Baltimore: Johns Hopkins University Press.

Jervis, Robert, and Jack Snyder, eds. 1991. *Dominoes and Bandwagons: Strategic Beliefs and Great Power Competition in the Eurasian Rimland*. New York: Oxford University Press.

Job, Brian L. 1992. *The Insecurity Dilemma: National Security in Third World States*. Boulder, Colo.: Lynne Rienner.

Job, Brian L., and Douglas Johnson. 1991. "UNCLE-SAM: The Application of a Rule-Based Model to U.S. Foreign Policy." In *Artificial Intelligence and International Politics*, ed. Valerie Hudson. Boulder, Colo.: Westview.

Johansen, Robert C. 1980. *The National Interest and the Human Interest*. Princeton, N.J.: Princeton University Press.

Johnson, Chalmers. 1982. *MITI and the Japanese Miracle: The Growth of Industrial Policy, 1925–1975*. Stanford, Calif.: Stanford University Press.

Johnson, Christina J. 1992. *Power, Ideology, and the War on Drugs*. New York: Praeger.

Johnson, Loch K. 1989. *America's Secret Power: The CIA in a Democratic Society*. New York: Oxford University Press.

———. 1977. "Operational Codes and the Prediction of Leadership Behavior." In *A Psychological Examination of Political Leaders*, ed. Margaret G. Hermann. New York: Free Press.

Johnson, Richard T. 1974. *Managing the White House*. New York: Harper and Row.

Jones, Edward Ellsworth. 1972. *Attribution: Perceiving the Causes of Behavior.* Morristown, N.J.: General Learning Press.

Jones, Kathleen. 1990. "Citizenship in a Woman-Friendly Polity." *Signs* 15:781–812.

Kaarbo, Juliet, Ryan Beasley, and Margaret G. Hermann. 1990. Comparative Case Analysis and Theory-Building. Paper presented at the annual meeting of the International Studies Association, Washington, D.C.

Kahneman, Daniel, and Amos Tversky. 1984. "Choices, Values and Frames." *American Psychologist* 29:341–50.

Kahneman, Daniel, Paul Slovic, and Amos Tversky. 1982. *Judgement under Uncertainty: Heuristics and Biases.* Cambridge: Cambridge University Press.

Kaldor, Mary. 1991. "After the Cold War." *Feminist Review* 39:109–114.

Kandiyoti, Deniz. 1991a. "Identity and Its Discontents: Women and the Nation." *Millennium* 20:429–43.

———, ed. 1991b. *Women, Islam and the State.* Philadelphia: Temple University Press.

Karnow, Stanley. 1983. *Vietnam: A History.* New York: Viking Press.

Karns, Margaret P., and Karen A. Mingst. 1987. "International Organizations and Foreign Policy: Influence and Instrumentality." In *New Directions in Foreign Policy*, ed. Charles F. Hermann, Charles W. Kegley, Jr., and James N. Rosenau. Winchester, Mass.: Unwin Hyman.

———, eds. 1992. *The United States and Multilateral Institutions: Patterns of Changing Instrumentality and Influence.* London: Routledge.

Kasza, Gregory J. 1987. "Bureaucratic Politics in Radical Military Regimes." *American Political Science Review* 81:851–72.

Katzenstein, Peter J. 1976. "International Relations and Domestic Structures: Foreign Economic Policies of Advanced Industrial States." *International Organization* 30:1–45.

———, ed. 1978. *Between Power and Plenty: Foreign Economic Policies of Advanced Industrialized States.* Madison: University of Wisconsin Press.

Kaw, Marita. 1989. "Predicting Soviet Military Intervention." *Journal of Conflict Resolution* 33:402–29.

Kaysen, Carl. 1990. "Is War Obsolete? A Review Essay." *International Security* 14:42–64.

Kegley, Charles W., Jr. 1980. "The Comparative Study of Foreign Policy: Paradigm Lost?" Institute of International Studies Essay Series, no. 10. Columbia: University of South Carolina Press.

Kegley, Charles W., Jr., and Steven W. Hook. 1991. "U.S. Foreign Aid and U.N. Voting: Did Reagan's Linkage Strategy Buy Deference or Defiance?" *International Studies Quarterly* 35:295–312.

Kegley, Charles W., Jr., Gregory A. Raymond, Robert M. Rood, and Richard A. Skinner, eds. 1975. *International Events and the Comparative Analysis of Foreign Policy.* Columbia: University of South Carolina Press.

Kegley, Charles W., Jr., and Richard Skinner. 1976. "The Case for Analysis Problem." In *In Search of Global Patterns*, ed. James N. Rosenau. New York: Free Press.

Kegley, Charles W., Jr., and Eugene R. Wittkopf. 1991. *American Foreign Policy: Pattern and Process.* 4th ed. New York: St. Martin's Press.

Kellerman, Barbara, and Jeffery Z. Rubin, eds. 1988. *Leadership and Negotiation in the Middle East.* New York: Praeger.

Kelman, Herbert C. 1965b. "Social-Psychological Approaches to the Study of International Relations: Definition of Scope." In *International Behavior: A Social-Psychological Analysis*, ed. Herbert C. Kelman. New York: Holt, Rinehart and Winston.

———, ed. 1965a. *International Behavior: A Social-Psychological Analysis.* New York: Holt, Rinehart and Winston.

Kelman, Herbert C., and A. H. Bloom. 1973. "Assumptive Frameworks in International Politics." In *Handbook of Political Psychology*, ed. Jeanne N. Knutson. New York: Holt, Rinehart and Winston.

Kennan, George F. 1951. *American Diplomacy, 1900–1950.* Chicago: University of Chicago Press.

Kennedy, Paul. 1987. *The Rise and Fall of the Great Powers.* New York: Random House.

———. 1980. *The Rise of Anglo-German Antagonism, 1860–1914.* London: Unwin Hyman.

Keohane, Robert O. 1988. "International Institutions: Two Approaches." *International Studies Quarterly* 32:379–96.

———. 1987. "Theory of World Politics: Structural Realism and Beyond." In *Neorealism and Its Critics*, ed. Robert O. Keohane. New York: Columbia University Press.

———. 1984. *After Hegemony: Cooperation and Discord in the World Political Economy.* Princeton, N.J.: Princeton University Press.

———. 1966. "Political Influence in the General Assembly." *International Conciliation* 557.

Keohane, Robert O., and Joseph S. Nye. 1989. *Power and Interdependence.* 2d ed. Glenview, Ill.: Scott, Foresman.

———. 1977. *Power and Interdependence: World Politics in Transition.* Boston: Little, Brown.

———. 1974. "Transgovernmental Relations and International Organizations." *World Politics* 27:39–62.

Kernell, Samuel, and Samuel L. Popkin, eds. 1986. *Chief of Staff.* Berkeley: University of California Press.

Kessel, John H. 1984. "The Structures of the Reagan White House." *American Journal of Political Science* 28:231–58.

———. 1983. "The Structures of the Carter White House." *American Journal of Political Science* 27:431–63.

Khong, Yuen Foong. 1992. *Analogies at War: Korea, Munich, Dien Bien Phu, and the Vietnam Decisions of 1965.* Princeton, N.J.: Princeton University Press.

Kim, Kwan Bong. 1971. *The Korea-Japan Treaty Crisis and the Instability of the Korean Political System.* New York: Praeger.

Kim, Samuel K., ed. 1989. *China and the World: New Directions in Chinese Foreign Relations.* Boulder, Colo.: Westview.

Kindleberger, Charles P. 1981. "Dominance and Leadership in the International Economy: Exploitation, Public Goods, and Free Rides." *International Studies Quarterly* 25:242–52.

———. 1973. *The World in Depression, 1929–1939.* Berkeley: University of California Press.

King, Gary. 1989. "Event Count Models for International Relations: Generalizations and Applications." *International Studies Quarterly* 33:123–48.

King, Gary, Sidney Verba, and Robert O. Keohane. 1991. *Qualitative Inference in Qualitative Research.* Harvard University, Department of Government. Typescript.

Kiser, Larry L., and Elinor Ostrom. 1982. "The Three Worlds of Action." In *Strategies of Political Inquiry,* ed. Elinor Ostrom. Beverly Hills, Calif.: Sage.

Kittay, Eva F. 1987. *Metaphor: Its Cognitive Force and Linguistic Structure.* Oxford: Claredon Press.

Klineberg, Otto. 1950. *Tensions Affecting International Understanding.* New York: Social Science Research Council.

Klug, Francesca. 1989. " 'Oh to be in England': The British Case Study." In *Woman-Nation State,* ed. Nira Yuval-Davis and Floya Anthias. London: Macmillan.

Knorr, Klaus. 1975. *The Power of Nations.* New York: Basic Books.

Knutson, Jeane N., ed. 1973. *Handbook of Political Psychology.* San Francisco: Jossey-Bass.

Korany, Bahgat. 1986a. "Foreign Policy Decision Making Theory and the Third World: Payoffs and Pitfalls." In *How Foreign Policy Decisions Are Made in the Third World,* ed. Bahgat Korany. Boulder, Colo.: Westview.

———. 1983. "The Take-off of Third World Studies? The Case of Foreign Policy." *World Politics* 35:464–87.

———, ed. 1986b. *How Foreign Policy Decisions Are Made in the Third World.* Boulder, Colo.: Westview.

Korany, Bahgat, and Ali E. Hillal Dessouki, eds. 1984. *The Foreign Policies of Arab States.* Boulder, Colo.: Westview.

Krasner, Stephen D. 1988. "Sovereignty: An Institutional Perspective." *Comparative Political Studies* 21:66–94.

———. 1985. *Structural Conflict: The Third World against Global Liberalism.* Berkeley: University of California Press.

———. 1984. "Approaches to the State: Alternative Conceptions and Historical Dynamics." *Comparative Politics* 16:223-46.

———. 1978. *Defending the National Interest: Raw Materials Investments and U.S. Foreign Policy.* Princeton, N.J.: Princeton University Press.

———. 1976. "State Power and the Structure of International Trade." *World Politics* 28:317–47.

———. 1971. "Are Bureaucracies Important? (Or Allison Wonderland)." *Foreign Policy* 7:159–79.

Krause, Keith, David DeWitt, and W. Andy Knight. 1990. Canada, the United Nations and the Evolution of International Governance. Paper presented at the International Research Conference on the Future of the United Nations, Ottawa.

Krippendorff, Klaus. 1980. *Content Analysis: An Introduction to Its Methodology.* Beverly Hills, Calif.: Sage.

Kuhn, Thomas S. 1962. *The Structure of Scientific Revolutions.* Chicago: University of Chicago Press.

Kuklinski, James, Robert Luskin, and John Bolland. 1991. "Where Is the Schema? Going beyond the 'S' Word in Political Psychology." *American Political Science Review* 85:1341–56.

Kurian, George T. 1992. *Encyclopedia of the Third World.* 4th ed. New York: Facts on File.

LaFeber, Walter. 1989. "The Rise and Fall of American Power: 1963–1975." In *America in Vietnam*, ed. William A. Williams, Thomas McCormick, Lloyd Gardner, and Walter LaFeber. New York: Norton.

Lake, David A. 1992. "Powerful Pacifists: Democratic States and War." *American Political Science Review* 86:24–37.

Lakoff, George. 1991. "Metaphor and War: The Metaphor System Used to Justify War in the Gulf." *Peace Research* 23:25–32.

Lakoff, George, and Mark Johnson. 1980. *Metaphors We Live By.* Chicago: University of Chicago Press.

Lamborn, Alan C. 1991. *The Price of Power: Risk and Foreign Policy in Britain, France, and Germany.* Boston: Allen and Unwin.

Lampton, D. M. 1973. "The U.S. Image of Peking in Three International Crises." *Western Political Quarterly* 26:28–50.

Lane, Robert E. 1962. *Political Ideology: Why the American Common Man Believes What He Does.* New York: Free Press.

Lanphier, Vernard A. 1975. "Foreign Relations Indicator Project." In *Theory and Practice of Events Research*, ed. Edward E. Azar and Joseph Ben-Dak. New York: Gordon and Breach.

Lapid, Yosef. 1991. Theorizing the "National" in International Relations Theory: Reflections on Nationalism and Neorealism. Paper presented at the annual meeting of the International Studies Association, Vancouver.

———. 1989. "The Third Debate: On the Prospects of International Theory in a Post-Positivist Era." *International Studies Quarterly* 33:235–54.

Larson, Deborah Welch. 1994. "The Role of Belief Systems and Schemas in Foreign Policy Decision-Making." *Political Psychology* 15:17–34.

———. 1988. "Problems of Content Analysis in Foreign-Policy Research: Notes from the Study of the Origins of the Cold War." *International Studies Quarterly* 32:241–55.

———. 1985. *Origins of Containment: A Psychological Explanation.* Princeton, N.J.: Princeton University Press.

Laszlo, Ervin, Robert Baker, Jr., Elliott Eisenberg, and Vankata Raman. 1978. *The Objectives of the New International Order.* New York: Pergamon Press.

Latham, Robert. 1993. "Democracy and War-Making: Locating the International Liberal Context." *Millennium* 22 (2):139–64.

Lau, Richard R., and R. Erber. 1985. "An Information Processing Approach to Political Sophistication." In *Mass Media and Political Thought*, ed. S. Kraus and R. Perloff. Beverly Hills, Calif.: Sage.

Lau, Richard R., and David O. Sears. 1986a. "An Introduction to Political Cognition." In *Political Cognition*, ed. Richard R. Lau and David O. Sears. Hillsdale, N.J.: Lawrence Erlbaum.

————. 1986c. "Social Cognition and Political Cognition: The Past, the Present, and the Future." In *Political Cognition*, ed. Richard R. Lau and David O. Sears. Hillsdale, N.J.: Lawrence Erlbaum.

————, eds. 1986b. *Political Cognition*. Hillsdale, N.J.: Lawrence Erlbaum.

Laurance, Edward J. 1990. "Events Data and Policy Analysis." *Policy Sciences* 23:111–32.

Lave, Charles A., and James G. March. 1975. *An Introduction to Models in the Social Sciences*. New York: Harper and Row.

Lawson, Fred H. 1984. "Syria's Intervention in the Lebanese Civil War, 1976: A Domestic Conflict Explanation." *International Organization* 38:451–80.

Lebovic, James H. 1993. Before the Storm: Momentum and the Onset of the Gulf War. Paper presented at the annual meeting of the International Studies Association, Acapulco.

Lebow, Richard Ned. 1981. *Between Peace and War: The Nature of International Crisis.* Baltimore: Johns Hopkins University Press.

Lehnert, Wendy, and Beth Sundheim. 1991. "A Performance Evaluation of Text Analysis." *AI Magazine* 12:81–94.

Leites, Nathan. 1953. *A Study of Bolshevism*. Glencoe, Ill.: Free Press.

————. 1951. *The Operational Code of the Politburo*. New York: McGraw-Hill.

Lenczowski, George. 1990. *American Presidents and the Middle East*. Durham, N.C.: Duke University Press.

Leng, Russell J. 1993a. *Interstate Crisis Behavior, 1816–1980*. New York: Cambridge University Press.

————. 1993b. "Reciprocating Influence Strategies in Interstate Crisis Bargaining." *Journal of Conflict Resolution* 37:3–41.

————. 1987. *Behavioral Correlates of War, 1816–1975* (ICPSR 8606). Ann Arbor, Mich.: Inter-University Consortium for Political and Social Research.

Lentner, Howard H. 1984. "The Concept of the State: A Response to Stephen Krasner." *Comparative Politics* 16:367–77.

Levine, John M., and Richard L. Moreland. 1990. "Progress in Small Group Research." *Annual Review of Psychology* 41:585–634.

Levitsky, Melvyn. 1991. "U.S. Efforts in the International Drug War." In *Searching for Alternatives: Drug-Control Policy in the United States*, ed. Melvyn Krauss and Edward Lazear. Stanford, Calif.: Hoover Institution Press.

Levy, Jack S. 1989. "The Diversionary Theory of War: A Critique." In *Handbook of War Studies*, ed. Manus I. Midlarsky. Boston: Unwin Hyman.

———. 1988. "Domestic Politics and War." In *The Origin and Prevention of Major Wars*, ed. Robert I. Rotberg and Theodore K. Rabb. New York: Cambridge University Press.

———. 1986. "Organizational Routines and the Causes of War." *International Studies Quarterly* 30:193–222.

Levy, Jack S., and Lily Vakili. 1990. External Scapegoating by Authoritarian Regimes: Argentina in the Falklands/Malvinas Case. Unpublished manuscript, Rutgers University.

Light, Paul C. 1982. *The President's Agenda*. Baltimore: Johns Hopkins University Press.

Lijphart, Arend. 1975. "The Comparable-Cases Strategy in Comparative Research." *Comparative Political Studies* 8:158–77.

———. 1963. "The Analysis of Bloc Voting in the General Assembly." *American Political Science Review* 62:902–17.

Lincoln, Jennie K., and Elizabeth G. Ferris, eds. 1984. *The Dynamics of Latin American Foreign Policies: Challenges for the 1980s*. Boulder, Colo.: Westview.

Linden, Carl A. 1966. *Khrushchev and the Soviet Leadership, 1957–1964*. Baltimore: Johns Hopkins University Press.

Lips, Hilary. 1991. *Women, Men, and Power*. Mountain View, Calif.: Mayfield.

Lister, Ruth. 1993. "Tracing the Contours of Women's Citizenship." *Policy and Politics* 21:3–16.

Lloyd, Genevieve. 1984. *The Man of Reason: "Male" and "Female" in Western Philosophy*. Minneapolis: University of Minnesota Press.

Lodge, Milton, and Kathleen McGraw. 1991. "Where Is the Schema? Critiques." *American Political Science Review* 85:1357–64.

Longley, Jeanne, and Dean G. Pruitt. 1980. "Groupthink: A Critique of Janis's Theory." *Review of Personality and Social Psychology* 1:74–93.

Lowi, Theodore J. 1967. "Making Democracy Safe for the World: National Politics and Foreign Policy." In *Domestic Sources of Foreign Policy*, ed. James N. Rosenau. New York: Free Press.

MacDonald, Douglas. 1991. "The Truman Administration and Global Responsibilities: The Birth of the Falling Domino Principle." In *Dominoes and Bandwagons*, ed. Robert Jervis and Jack Snyder. New York: Oxford University Press.

MacKay, R. A. 1969. "The Canadian Doctrine of the Middle Powers." In *Empire and Nations*, ed. H. L. Dyck and P. Krosby. Toronto: University of Toronto Press.

Maghroori, Ray. 1982. "Introduction: Major Debates in International Relations." In *Globalism Versus Realism*, ed. Ray Maghroori and Bennett Ramberg. Boulder, Colo.: Westview.

Magnuson, Ed. 1990. "More and More, a Real War." *Time,* Jan. 11, 22.

Majeski, Stephen J. 1987. "A Recommendation Model of War Initiation: The Plausibility and Generalizability of General Cultural Rules." In *Artificial Intelligence and National Security*, ed. Stephen Cimbala. Lexington, Mass.: Lexington Books.

Mallery, John C. n.d. "Beyond Correlation: Bringing Artificial Intelligence to Events Data." *International Interactions.* Forthcoming.

Mander, John. 1969. *The Unrevolutionary Society: The Power of Latin American Conservatism in a Changing World.* New York: Knopf.

Maoz, Zeev. 1990. "Framing the National Interest: The Manipulation of Foreign Policy Decisions in Group Settings." *World Politics* 43:77–110.

————. 1989. "Joining the Club of Nations: Political Development and International Conflict, 1816–1976." *International Studies Quarterly* 33:199–231.

————. 1981. "The Decision to Raid Entebbe: Decision Analysis Applied to Crisis Behavior." *Journal of Conflict Resolution* 25:677–707.

Maoz, Zeev, and Nasrin Abdolali. 1989. "Regime Types and International Conflict, 1916–1976." *Journal of Conflict Resolution* 33:3–35.

Maoz, Zeev, and Bruce Russett. 1993. "Normative and Structural Causes of Democratic Peace, 1946–1986." *American Political Science Review* 87:624–38.

————. 1992. "Alliance, Contiguity, Wealth, and Political Stability: Is the Lack of Conflict among Democracies a Statistical Artifact?" *International Interactions* 17:245–67.

March, James G., and Johan P. Olsen. 1989. *Rediscovering Institutions.* New York: Free Press.

March, James G., and Herbert A. Simon. 1958. *Organizations.* New York: Wiley.

Mares, David. 1988. "Middle Powers under Regional Hegemony: To Challenge or Acquiesce in Hegemonic Enforcement." *International Studies Quarterly* 32:453–71.

Marra, Robin F. 1985. "A Cybernetic Model of the U.S. Defense Expenditure Policymaking Process." *International Studies Quarterly* 29:357–84.

Martin, Joanne. 1992. *Cultures in Organizations: Three Perspectives.* Oxford: Oxford University Press.

————. 1982. "Stories and Scripts in Organizational Settings." In *Cognitive Social Psychology,* ed. A. Hastorf and A. Isen. London: Routledge.

Martin, Lawrence W. 1962. *Neutralism and Nonalignment.* New York: Praeger.

Mastanduno, Michael, David A. Lake, and G. John Ikenberry. 1989. "Toward a Realist Theory of State Action." *International Studies Quarterly* 33:457–74.

May, Ernest. 1973. *"Lessons" of the Past.* New York: Oxford University Press.

Mayall, James. 1990. *Nationalism and International Society.* Cambridge: Cambridge University Press.

Mayer, Frederick W. 1992. "Managing Domestic Differences in International Negotiations: The Strategic Use of Internal Side-Payments." *International Organization* 46:793–818.

Mayhall, Stacey. 1993. "Gendered Nationalism and 'New' Nation-States: 'Democratic Progress' in Eastern Europe." *Fletcher Forum of World Affairs* 17:91–99.

Mayr, Ernst. 1982. *The Growth of Biological Thought.* Cambridge, Mass.: Harvard University Press.

McCalla, Robert B. 1992. *Uncertain Perceptions: U.S. Cold War Crisis Decision Making.* Ann Arbor: University of Michigan Press.

McCamy, James L. 1964. *Conduct of the New Diplomacy.* New York: Harper and Row.

McClelland, Charles A. 1970. Some Effects on Theory from the International Event Analysis Movement. Mimeo, University of Southern California.

———. 1968a. "Access to Berlin: The Quantity and Variety of Events, 1948–1963." In *Quantitative International Politics*, ed. J. David Singer. New York: Free Press.

———. 1968b. International Interaction Analysis: Basic Research and Some Practical Uses. Mimeo, University of Southern California.

———. 1976. *World Event/Interaction Survey Codebook* (ICPSR 5211). Ann Arbor, Mich.: Inter-University Consortium for Political and Social Research.

———. 1969. International Interaction Analysis in the Predictive Mode. Mimeo, University of Southern California.

———. 1967a. Event-Interaction Analysis in the Setting of Quantitative International Relations Research. Mimeo, University of Southern California.

———. 1967b. World-Event-Interaction-Survey: A Research Project on the Theory and Measurement of International Interaction and Transaction. Mimeo, University of Southern California.

McClintock, Anne. 1991. "'No Longer in a Future Heaven': Women and Nationalism in South Africa." *Transition* 51:104–23.

McCormick, James M. 1985. "Congressional Voting on the Nuclear Freeze Revolutions." *American Politics Quarterly* 13:122–36.

McGinnis, Michael D. 1993. "Policy Uncertainty in Two-Level Games: Examples of Correlated Equilibria." *International Studies Quarterly* 37:29–54.

McGinnis, Michael D., and John T. Williams 1993. "Policy Uncertainty in Two-level Games: Examples of Correlated Equilibria." *International Studies Quarterly* 37:29–54.

McGlen, Nancy E., and Meredith Reid Sarkees, eds. 1993. *Women in Foreign Policy: The Insiders.* New York: Routledge.

McGowan, Patrick J. 1975. "Meaningful Comparisons in the Study of Foreign Policy: A Methodological Discussion of Objectives, Techniques, and Research Designs." In *International Events and the Comparative Analysis of Foreign Policy*, ed. Charles W. Kegley, Jr., Gregory A. Raymond, Robert M. Rood, and Richard A. Skinner. Columbia: University of South Carolina Press.

———. 1974. "Problems in the Construction of Positivist Foreign Policy Theory." In *Comparing Foreign Policies: Theories, Findings, and Methods*, ed. James N. Rosenau. New York: Wiley.

McGowan, Patrick J., and Howard B. Shapiro. 1973. *The Comparative Study of Foreign Policy: A Survey of Scientific Findings.* Beverly Hills, Calif.: Sage.

McGowan, Patrick, Harvey Starr, Gretchen Hower, Richard L. Merritt, and Dina A. Zinnes. 1988. "International Data as a National Resource." *International Interactions* 14:101–13.

McGowan, Patrick, and Stephen G. Walker. 1981. "Radical and Conventional Models of U.S. Foreign Economic Policy Making." *World Politics* 33:347–82.

McGuire, William J. 1969. "The Nature of Attitudes and Attitude Change." In *Handbook of Social Psychology*, vol. 3, 2d ed., ed. G. Lindzey and E. Aronson. Chicago: Rand McNally.

McLellan, David. 1977. "The 'Operational Code' Approach to the Study of Political Leaders: Dean Acheson's Philosophical and Instrumental Beliefs." *Canadian Journal of Political Science* 4:52–75.

Mefford, Dwain. 1987. "Analogical Reasoning and the Definition of the Situation: Back to Snyder for Concepts and Forward to Artificial Intelligence for Method." In *New Directions in the Study of Foreign Policy*, ed. Charles F. Hermann, Charles W. Kegley, Jr., and James N. Rosenau. Winchester, Mass.: Unwin Hyman.

Mehta, J. S., ed. 1985. *Third World Militarization: A Challenge to Third World Diplomacy.* Austin: University of Texas Press.

Melan, Eugene H. 1989. "Process Management: A Unifying Framework for Improvement." *National Productivity Review* 8:395–406.

Melanson, Richard A. 1991. *Reconstructing Consensus: American Foreign Policy since the Vietnam War.* New York: St. Martin's Press.

Meltsner, Arnold J. 1990. *Rules for Rulers.* Philadelphia: Temple University Press.

Menkhaus, Kenneth J., and Charles W. Kegley, Jr. 1988. "The Compliant Foreign Policy of the Dependent State Revisited: Empirical Linkages and Lessons from the Case of Somalia." *Comparative Political Studies* 21:315–46.

Merchant, Carolyn. 1980. *The Death of Nature: Women, Ecology and the Scientific Revolution.* New York: Harper and Row.

Merritt, Richard L., Robert G. Muncaster, and Dina A. Zinnes, eds. 1993. *International Event Data Developments.* Ann Arbor: University of Michigan Press.

Merton, Robert K. 1957. *Social Theory and Social Structure.* Rev. ed. Glencoe, Ill.: Free Press.

Metz, S. 1986. "The Anti-Apartheid Movement and the Populist Instinct in American Politics." *Political Science Quarterly* 101:379–95.

Michalski, Ryszard S. 1989. "Two-Tiered Concept Meaning, Inferential Matching, and Conceptual Cohesiveness." In *Similarity and Analogical Reasoning*, ed. Stella Vosniadou and Anthony Ortony. New York: Cambridge University Press.

Milburn, Michael A. 1991. *Persuasion and Politics: The Social Psychology of Public Opinion.* Pacific Cove, Calif.: Brooks/Cole.

Miller, A. 1991. "Where Are the Schema? Critiques." *American Political Science Review* 85:1369–76.

Milliband, Ralph. 1969. *The State in Capitalist Society.* New York: Basic Books.

Mills, C. Wright. 1959. *The Power Elite.* New York: Oxford University Press.

Mills, William deB. 1990. "Rule-Based Analysis of Sino-Soviet Negotiations." *Social Science Computer Review* 8:181–95.

Mingst, Karen A. 1993. Implementing International Environmental Treaties: The Role of NGOs. Paper presented at the annual meeting of the International Studies Association, Acapulco.

———. 1976. "Cooperation or Illusion: An Examination of the Intergovernmental Council of Copper Exporting Countries." *International Organization* 30:263–87.

Mintzberg, Henry, Duru Raisinghani, and Andre Theoret. 1976. "The Structure of 'Unstructured' Decision Processes." *Adminstrative Science Quarterly* 21:246–75.

Mitrany, David. 1966. *A Working Peace System.* Chicago: Quadrangle.

Moe, Terry M. 1989. "The Politics of Bureaucratic Structure." In *Can the Government Govern?* ed. John E. Chubb and Paul E. Peterson. Washington, D.C.: The Brookings Institution.

Moens, Alexander. 1991. "President Carter's Advisers and the Fall of the Shah." *Political Science Quarterly* 106:211–37.

Moghadam, Valentine M., ed. 1994. *Gender and National Identity: Woman in Muslim Society.* Forthcoming. London: ZED Books.

Mohanty, Chandra Talpade, Anne Russo, and Lourdes Torres, eds. 1991. *Third World Women and the Politics of Feminism.* Bloomington: Indiana University Press.

Montville, Joseph V. 1991. "Transnationalism and the Role of Track-Two Diplomacy." In *Approaches to Peace: An Intellectual Map*, ed. W. Scott Thompson and Kenneth M. Jensen. Washington, D.C.: U.S. Institute of Peace.

———. 1987. "The Arrow and the Olive Branch: A Case for Track Two Diplomacy." In *Conflict Resolution: Track Two Diplomacy*, ed. John W. McDonald, Jr. and Diane B. Bendahmane. Washington, D.C.: Center for the Study of Foreign Affairs.

Moon, Bruce E. 1987. "Political Economy Approaches to the Comparative Study of Foreign Policy." In *New Directions in the Study of Foreign Policy*, ed. Charles F. Hermann, Charles W. Kegley, Jr., and James N. Rosenau. Winchester, Mass.: Unwin Hyman.

———. 1985. "Consensus or Compliance? Foreign Policy Change and External Dependence." *International Organization* 39:297–329.

———. 1983. "The Foreign Policy of the Dependent State." *International Studies Quarterly* 27:315–40.

Moon, Chung-In. 1988. "Complex Interdependence and Transnational Lobbying: South Korea in the United States." *International Studies Quarterly* 32:67–89.

Moore, David W. 1974a. "Governmental and Societal Influences on Foreign Policy in Open and Closed Nations." In *Comparing Foreign Policies: Theories, Findings, and Methods*, ed. James N. Rosenau. Beverly Hills, Calif.: Sage.

———. 1974b. "National Attributes and Nation Typologies: A Look at the Rosenau Genotypes." In *Comparing Foreign Policies: Theories, Findings, and Methods*, ed. James N. Rosenau. Beverly Hills, Calif.: Sage.

Moran, Theodore H., ed. 1985. *Multinational Corporations: The Political Economy of Foreign Direct Investment.* Lexington, Mass.: Lexington Books.

Moreland, Richard L., and John M. Levine. 1982. "Role Transitions in Small Groups." In *Role Transitions: Explorations and Explanations,* ed. Vernon L. Allen and Evert van de Vliert. New York: Plenum.

Morgan, Patrick M. 1987. *Theories and Approaches to International Politics: What Are We to Think?* 4th ed. New Brunswick, N. J., and Oxford: Transaction Books.

———. 1977. *Deterrence: A Conceptual Analysis.* Beverly Hills, Calif.: Sage.

Morgan, T. Clifton. 1992. "Democracy and War: Reflections on the Literature." *International Interactions* 18:197–203.

Morgan, T. Clifton, and Kenneth Bickers. 1982. "Domestic Discontent and the External Use of Force." *Journal of Conflict Resolution* 36:25–52.

Morgan, T. Clifton, and Sally Howard Campbell. 1991. "Domestic Structure, Decisional Constraints, and War: So Why Kant Democracies Fight." *Journal of Conflict Resolution* 35:187–211.

Morgan, T. Clifton, and Valerie L. Schwebach. 1992. "Take Two Democracies and Call Me in the Morning: A Prescription for Peace." *International Interactions* 17:305–20.

Morgenthau, Hans J. 1985. *Politics among Nations: The Struggle for Power and Peace.* 6th ed. Revised by Kenneth W. Thompson. New York: Knopf.

———. 1967. *Politics among Nations: The Struggle for Power and Peace.* 4th ed. New York: Knopf.

———. 1951. *In Defense of the National Interest.* New York: Knopf.

———. 1948. *Politics among Nations.* New York: Knopf.

Morse, Edward L. 1973. *Foreign Policy and Interdependence in Gaullist France.* Princeton, N.J.: Princeton University Press.

Morrow, James. 1989. "Capabilities, Uncertainty, and Resolve." *American Journal of Political Science* 33:941–72.

Mosse, George L. 1985. *Nationalism and Sexuality: Respectability and Abnormal Sexuality in Modern Europe.* New York: Howard Fertiz.

Most, Benjamin A., and Harvey Starr. 1989. *Inquiry, Logic and International Politics.* Columbia: University of South Carolina Press.

———. 1984. "International Relations Theory, Foreign Policy Substitutability and 'Nice' Laws." *World Politics* 36:383–406.

Motyl, Alexander J. 1992. "The Modernity of Nationalism: Nations, States and Nation-States in the Contemporary World." *Journal of International Affairs* 45:307–23.

Mouffe, Chantal. 1992. "Feminism, Citizenship, and Radical Democratic Politics." In *Feminists Theorize the Political,* ed. Judith Butler and Joan W. Scott. New York and London: Routledge.

Mueller, John. 1989. *Retreat from Doomsday: The Obsolescence of Major War.* New York: Basic Books.

———. 1971. *War, Presidents, and Public Opinion.* New York: Wiley.

Muller, Harald, and Thomas Risse-Kappen. 1993. "From the Outside In and from the Inside Out: International Relations, Domestic Politics, and Foreign Policy." In *The Limits of State Autonomy: Societal Groups and Foreign Policy Formulation,* ed. David Skidmore and Valerie M. Hudson, Boulder, Colo.: Westview.

Muñoz, Heraldo, and Joseph S. Tulchin, eds. 1984. *Latin American Nations in World Politics.* Boulder, Colo.: Westview.

Munton, D. 1978. *Measuring International Behavior: Public Sources, Events and Validity.* Dalhousie University: Centre for Foreign Policy Studies.

Nathan, James A., and James K. Oliver. 1987. *Foreign Policy Making and the American Political System.* Boston: Little, Brown.

———. 1978. "Bureaucratic Politics: Academic Windfalls and Intellectual Pitfalls." *Journal of Political and Military Sociology* 6:81–91.

Neack, Laura. 1994. "UN Peacekeeping: In the Interest of Community or Self?" *Journal of Peace Research* 31.

———. 1993. "Delineating State Groups through Cluster Analysis." *Social Science Journal* 30:347–71.

———. 1992. "Empirical Observations on 'Middle State' Behavior at the Start of a New International System." *Pacific Focus* 7:5–22.

———. 1991. Beyond the Rhetoric of Peacekeeping and Peacemaking: Middle States in International Politics. Ph.D. diss., University of Kentucky.

Nelson, Barbara J. 1989. "Women and Knowledge in Political Science." *Women and Politics* 9:1–25.

Nettl, J. P. 1971. "The State as a Conceptual Variable." In *Comparative Foreign Policy: Theoretical Essays*, ed. Wolfram F. Hanrieder. New York: David McKay.

———. 1968. *International Systems and the Modernizing of Societies*. New York: Basic Books.

Neustadt, Richard E. 1970. *Alliance Politics*. New York: Columbia University Press.

Neustadt, Richard, and Ernest May. 1986. *Thinking in Time: The Uses of History for Decision Makers*. New York: Free Press.

Nicholson, Linda. 1986. *Gender and History*. New York: Columbia University Press.

———, ed. 1990. *Feminism/Postmodernism*. New York: Routledge.

Nincic, Miroslav. 1992. *Democracy and Foreign Policy: The Fallacy of Political Realism*. New York: Columbia University Press.

Nisbett, Richard E., and Lee Ross. 1980. *Human Inference: Strategies and Shortcomings in Social Judgement*. Englewood Cliffs, N.J.: Prentice-Hall.

Nitze, Paul H. 1989. *From Hiroshima to Glasnost*. New York: Weidenfeld and Nicholson.

North, Robert. 1967. "Perception and Action in the 1914 Crisis." *Journal of International Affairs* 21:103–22.

Northedge, F. S. 1976. *The International Political System*. London: Faber and Faber.

Nye, Joseph S., Jr. 1990. *Bound to Lead: The Changing Nature of American Power*. New York: Basic Books.

Oakerson, Ronald. 1987. *The Organization of Local Public Economies*. Washington, D.C.: Advisory Commission on Intergovernmental Relations.

O'Donnell, Guillermo. 1980. "Comparative Historical Formations of the State Apparatus and Socio-Economic Change in the Third World." *International Social Science Journal* 32:717–29.

O'Donnell, Guillermo, Philippe C. Schmitter, and Laurence Whitehead, eds. 1986. *Transitions from Authoritarianism*. 4 vols. Baltimore: Johns Hopkins University Press.

Okin, Susan Moller. 1979. *Women in Western Political Thought*. Princeton, N.J.: Princeton University Press.

Okolo, Julius E., and Stephen Wright. 1990. *West African Regional Cooperation and Development*. Boulder, Colo.: Westview.

Orbovich, Cynthia B., and Richard K. Molnar. 1992. "Modeling Foreign Policy Advisory Processes." In *Political Psychology and Foreign Policy*, ed. Eric Singer and Valerie Hudson. Boulder, Colo.: Westview.

Organski, A. F. K. 1968. *World Politics*. New York: Knopf.

Ori, Kan. 1976. "Political Factors in Postwar Japan's Foreign Policy Decisions." In *Japan, America, and the Future World Order*, ed. Morton A. Kaplan and Kinhide Mushakoji. New York: Free Press.

Osgood, Charles E. 1966. *Perspective in Foreign Policy*. Palo Alto, Calif.: Pacific Books.

Oskamp, Stuart. 1977. *Attitudes and Opinions*. Englewood Cliffs, N.J.: Prentice-Hall.

Ostrom, Charles W., and Brian Job. 1986. "The President and the Political Use of Force." *American Political Science Review* 80:541–66.

Ostrom, Elinor. 1986. "An Agenda for the Study of Institutions." *Public Choice* 48:3–25.

Ott, J. Steven. 1989. *The Organizational Culture Perspective*. Pacific Grove, Calif.: Brooks/Cole.

Oudsten, E. 1989. "European Attitude on Nuclear Defense." In *Public Opinion and Nuclear Weapons*, ed. Catherine Marsh and Colin Fraser. London: Macmillan.

Paige, Glenn D. 1968. *The Korean Decision, June 24–30, 1950*. New York: Free Press.

Palumbo, Dennis J. 1975. "Organization Theory and Political Science." In *The Handbook of Political Science*, vol. 2, ed. Fred I. Greenstein and Nelson W. Polsby. Reading, Mass.: Addison-Wesley.

Papadakis, Maria, and Harvey Starr. 1987. "Opportunity, Willingness, and Small States: The Relationship between Environment and Foreign Policy." In *New Directions in the Study of Foreign Policy*, ed. Charles F. Hermann, Charles W. Kegley, Jr., and James N. Rosenau. Winchester, Mass.: Unwin Hyman.

Pateman, Carole. 1989. *The Disorder of Women*. Stanford, Calif.: Stanford University Press.

———. 1988. *The Sexual Contract*. Stanford, Calif.: Stanford University Press.

Paterson, Thomas G. 1988. *Meeting the Communist Threat: Truman to Reagan*. New York: Oxford University Press.

Payer, Cheryl. 1974. *The Debt Trap*. New York: Monthly Review Press.

Pazzani, Michael. 1989. "Learning from Historical Precedent." In *AI Systems in Government Conference Proceedings*, ed. H. James Antonisse, John W. Benoit, and Barry Silverman. Washington, D.C.: IEEE Computer Society Press.

Pear, T. H. 1950. *Psychological Factors of War and Peace*. London: Hutchinson.

Peffley, Mark, and Jon Hurwitz. 1992. "International Events and Foreign Policy Beliefs: Public Response to Changing Soviet-U.S. Relations." *American Journal of Political Science* 36:431–61.

Pellicer, Olga. 1985. "A Note on Mexico: Expectations and Reality." In *Towards an Alternative for Central America and the Caribbean*, ed. George Irvín and Xabier Gorostiaga. London: Allen and Unwin.

———. 1981. "Mexico's Position." *Foreign Policy* 44 (summer): 88–92.

Pempel, T. J. 1977. "Japanese Foreign Policy: The Domestic Bases for International Behavior." In *Between Power and Plenty: Foreign Economic Policies of Advanced Industrial States*, ed. Peter J. Katzenstein. Madison: University of Wisconsin Press.

Penelope, Julia. 1990. *Speaking Freely: Unlearning the Lies of the Fathers' Tongues*. New York: Teachers College, Columbia University Press.

Perl, Raphael. 1989. "International Narcopolicy and the Role of the U. S. Congress." In *The Latin American Narcotics Trade and U. S. National Security*, ed. Donald Mabry. New York: Greenwood Press.

Perlmutter, Amos. 1974. "The Presidential Center and Foreign Policy: A Critique of the Revisionist and Bureaucratic-Political Orientations." *World Politics* 27:87–106.

Peters, B. Guy. 1990. "Administrative Culture and Analysis of Public Organizations." *Indian Journal of Public Administration* 36:420–28.

Peterson, Sophia. 1975. "Research on Research: Events Data Studies, 1961–1972." In *Sage International Yearbook on Foreign Policy Studies*, ed. Patrick J. McGowan. Beverly Hills, Calif.: Sage.

Peterson, V. Spike. 1993. "The Politics of Identity in International Relations." *Fletcher Forum of World Affairs* 17:1–12.

———. 1992b. "Introduction." In *Gendered States: Feminist (Re)Visions of International Relations Theory*, ed. V. Spike Peterson. Boulder, Colo.: Lynne Rienner.

———. 1992c. "Security and Sovereign States: What Is at Stake in Taking Feminism Seriously?" In *Gendered States: Feminist (Re)Visions of International Relations Theory*. Boulder, Colo.: Lynne Rienner.

———. 1992d. "Transgressing Boundaries: Theories of Knowledge, Gender, and International Relations." *Millennium* 21:183–206.

———, ed. 1992a. *Gendered States: Feminist (Re)Visions of International Relations Theory*. Boulder, Colo.: Lynne Rienner.

Peterson, V. Spike, and Anne Sisson Runyan. 1993. *Global Gender Issues*. Boulder, Colo.: Westview.

Pettman, Jan Jindy. 1992. "Women, Nationalism and the State: Towards an International Feminist Perspective." Occasional Paper 4 in Gender and Development Studies. Bangkok: Asian Institute of Technology.

Pettman, Ralph. 1991. *International Politics: Balance of Power, Balance of Productivity, Balance of Ideologies*. Boulder, Colo.: Lynne Rienner.

Phillips, Warren R. 1987. "Alternative Futures in the Middle East: The Results from Three Simulations." In *Artificial Intelligence and National Security*, ed. Stephen Cimbala. Lexington, Mass.: Lexington Books.

Pierre, Andrew J. 1982. *The Global Politics of Arms Sales*. Princeton, N.J.: Princeton University Press.

Pika, Joseph A. 1988. "Management Style and the Organizational Matrix: Studying White House Operations." *Administration and Society* 20:3–29.

Plowden, William, ed. 1987. *Advising the Rulers*. Oxford: Basil Blackwell.

Political Psychology. 1992. "Special Issue on Prospect Theory and Political Psychology." June.

Porter, Roger B. 1980. *Presidential Decision-Making: The Economic Policy Board.* New York: Cambridge University Press.

Poulantzas, Nicos. 1969. "The Problem of the Capitalist State." *New Left Review* 58:67–78.

Powell, Robert. 1990. *Nuclear Deterrence Theory.* New York: Cambridge University Press.

Prados, John. 1991. *Keepers of the Keys: A History of the National Security Council from Truman to Bush.* New York: Morrow.

Pratt, Cranford. 1989. "Middle Power Internationalism and North-South Issues: Comparisons and Prognosis." In *Internationalism under Strain: The North-South Policies of Canada, the Netherlands, Norway, and Sweden,* ed. Cranford Pratt. Toronto: University of Toronto Press.

Pratt, John W., and Richard J. Zeckhauser. 1985. "Principals and Agents: An Overview." In *Principals and Agents: The Structure of Business,* ed. John W. Pratt and Richard J. Zeckhauser. Boston: Harvard Business School Press.

Price-Williams, D. R. 1985. "Cultural Psychology." In *Handbook of Social Psychology,* vol. 3, 2d ed., ed. G. Lindzey and E. Aronson. Chicago: Rand McNally.

Puchala, Donald, and Roger Coate. 1989. The Challenge of Relevance: The United Nations in a Changing World Environment. Paper presented at the annual meeting of the Academic Council on the United Nations System, Ottawa.

Purkitt, Helen. 1992. "Artificial Intelligence and Intuitive Foreign Policy Decision-Makers Viewed as Limited Information Processors." In *Artificial Intelligence and International Politics,* ed. Valerie M. Hudson. Boulder, Colo.: Westview.

Putnam, Robert D. 1988. "Diplomacy and Domestic Politics: The Logic of Two-Level Games." *International Organization* 42:427–69.

———. 1973. *The Beliefs of Politicians: Ideology, Conflict, and Democracy in Britain and Italy.* New Haven, Conn.: Yale University Press.

Pye, Lucian W. 1986. "Political Psychology in Asia." In *Political Psychology,* ed. Margaret G. Hermann. San Francisco: Jossey-Bass.

Quandt, William B. 1993. *Peace Process.* Washington, D.C.: The Brookings Institution; Berkeley: University of California Press.

———. 1981. *Saudi Arabia in the 1980s: Foreign Policy, Security, and Oil.* Washington, D.C.: The Brookings Institution.

———. 1977. *Decade of Decisions.* Berkeley: University of California Press.

Ragin, Charles C. 1987. *The Comparative Method: Moving beyond Qualitative and Quantitative Strategies.* Berkeley: University of California Press.

Rai, Kul B. 1980. "Foreign Aid and Voting in the UN General Assembly, 1967–1976." *Journal of Peace Research* 17:269–77.

Rainey, Hal G. 1984. "Organization Theory and Political Science." *Policy Studies Journal* 13:5–22.

Randall, Vicky. 1987. *Women and Politics: An International Perspective.* 2d ed. Chicago: University of Chicago Press.

Ray, James Lee. 1989. "The Abolition of Slavery and the End of International War." *International Organization* 43:405–39.

———. 1981. "Dependence, Political Compliance, and Economic Performance: Latin America and Eastern Europe." In *The Political Economy of Foreign Policy Behavior*, ed. Charles W. Kegley, Jr. and Patrick J. McGowan. Beverly Hills, Calif.: Sage.

Raymond, Gregory A. 1975. "Introduction: Comparative Analysis and Nomological Explanation." In *International Events and the Comparative Analysis of Foreign Policy*, ed. Charles W. Kegley, Jr., Gregory A. Raymond, Robert M. Rood, and Richard A. Skinner. Columbia: University of South Carolina Press.

Report of the Commission on the Organization of the Government for the Conduct of Foreign Policy. 1975. Washington, D.C.: U.S. Government Printing Office.

Resnick, Phillip. 1986. "The Functions of the Modern State: In Search of a Theory." In *The State in Global Perspective*, ed. Ali Kazancigil. Brookfield, Vt.: Gower.

Rhoodie, Eschel M. 1989. *Discrimination against Women: A Global Survey.* Jefferson, N.C.: McFarland.

Richardson, Neil R. 1981. "Economic Dependence and Foreign Policy Compliance: Bringing Measurement Closer to Conception." In *The Political Economy of Foreign Policy Behavior*, ed. Charles W. Kegley, Jr. and Patrick J. McGowan. Beverly Hills, Calif.: Sage.

———. 1978. *Foreign Policy and Economic Dependence.* Austin: University of Texas Press.

———. 1976. "Political Compliance and U.S. Trade Dominance." *American Political Science Review* 70:1098–109.

Richardson, Neil R., and Charles W. Kegley, Jr. 1980. "Trade Dependence and Foreign Policy Compliance: A Longitudinal Analysis." *International Studies Quarterly* 24:191–222.

Richardson, Neil R., Charles W. Kegley, Jr., and Ann C. Agnew. 1981. "Symmetry and Reciprocity as Characteristics of Dyadic Foreign Policy Behavior." *Social Science Quarterly* 62:128–38.

Ripley, Brian. 1988. Rethinking Groupthink: Methods and Evidence. Paper presented at the annual meeting of the International Studies Association/Midwest, Columbus, Ohio.

Ripley, Brian, and Kyle Gardner. 1992. Profiles in Chaos: Kennedy and the Diem Coup. Paper presented at the annual meeting of the Northeast Political Science Association, Providence.

Risse-Kappen, Thomas. 1994. "Ideas Do Not Float Freely." *International Organization* 48:185–214.

———. 1991. "Public Opinion, Domestic Structure, and Foreign Policy in Liberal Democracies." *World Politics* 43:479–512.

Robinson, James A., and Richard S. Snyder. 1965. "Decision-Making in International Politics." In *International Behavior: A Social-Psychological Analysis*, ed. Herbert C. Kelman. New York: Holt, Rinehart and Winston.

Roeder, Philip G. 1988. *Soviet Political Dynamics: Development of the First Leninist Polity.* New York: Harper and Row.

———. 1985. "The Ties that Bind: Aid, Trade, and Political Compliance in Soviet Third World Relations." *International Studies Quarterly* 29:191–216.

———. 1984. "Soviet Policies and Kremlin Politics." *International Studies Quarterly* 28:171–93.

Rogers, Elizabeth S. 1992. "The Conflicting Roles of American Ethnic and Business Interests in U.S. Economic Sanctions Policy: The Case of South Africa." In *The Limits of State Autonomy: Societal Groups and Foreign Policy Formulation,* ed. David Skidmore and Valerie M. Hudson. Boulder, Colo.: Westview.

Rogowski, Ronald. 1989. *Commerce and Coalitions: How Trade Affects Domestic Alignments.* Princeton, N.J.: Princeton University Press.

Rokeach, Milton. 1968. *Beliefs, Attitudes, and Values.* San Francisco: Jossey-Bass.

Rosati, Jerel. 1993. *The Politics of United States Foreign Policy.* Fort Worth, Tex.: Harcourt Brace Jovanovich.

———. 1990. "Continuity and Change in the Foreign Policy Beliefs of Political Leaders: Addressing the Controversy over the Carter Administration." *Political Psychology* 9:471–505.

———. 1987. *The Carter Administration's Quest for Global Community: Beliefs and Their Impact on Behavior.* Columbia: University of South Carolina Press.

———. 1984. "The Impact of Beliefs on Behavior: The Foreign Policy of the Carter Administration." In *Foreign Policy Decision Making: Perception, Cognition, and Artificial Intelligence,* ed. Donald A. Sylvan and Steve Chan. New York: Praeger.

———. 1981. "Developing a Systematic Decision-Making Framework: Bureaucratic Politics in Perspective." *World Politics* 33:234–52.

Rosati, Jerel, Joe D. Hagan, and Martin Sampson, eds. n.d. *Foreign Policy Restructuring.* Columbia: University of South Carolina Press. Forthcoming.

Rosecrance, Richard. 1986. *The Rise of the Trading State.* New York: Basic Books.

Rosecrance, Richard, and Arthur Stein, eds. 1993. *The Domestic Bases of Grand Strategy.* Ithaca, N.Y.: Cornell University Press.

Rosenau, James N. 1989. "Global Changes and Theoretical Challenges: Toward a Post-international Politics for the 1990s." In *Global Challenges and Theoretical Challenges,* ed. Ernst-Otto Czempiel and James N. Rosenau. Lexington, Mass.: D. C. Heath.

———. 1988. "The State in an Era of Cascading Politics: Wavering Concept, Widening Competence, Withering Colossus, or Weathering Change?" *Comparative Political Studies* 21:13–44.

———. 1987a. "Introduction: New Directions and Recurrent Questions in the Comparative Study of Foreign Policy." In *New Directions in the Study of Foreign Policy,* ed. Charles F. Hermann, Charles W. Kegley, Jr., and James N. Rosenau. Winchester, Mass.: Unwin Hyman.

———. 1987b. "Toward Single-Country Theories of Foreign Policy: The Case of the USSR." In *New Directions in the Study of Foreign Policy,* ed. Charles F. Hermann, Charles W. Kegley, Jr., and James N. Rosenau. Boston: Allen and Unwin.

———. 1984. "A Pre-Theory Revisited: World Politics in an Era of Cascading Interdependence." *International Studies Quarterly* 28:245–305.

———. 1976. "Restlessness, Change, and Foreign Policy Analysis." In *In Search of Global Patterns*, ed. James N. Rosenau. New York: Free Press.

———. 1969a. *Linkage Politics: Essays on the Convergence of National and International Systems*. New York: Free Press.

———. 1969b. "Toward the Study of National-International Linkages." In *Linkage Politics: Essays on the Convergence of National and International Systems*, ed. James N. Rosenau. New York: Free Press.

———. 1968a. "Comparative Foreign Policy: Fad, Fantasy or Field?" *International Studies Quarterly* 12:296–329.

———. 1968b. "Moral Fervor, Systemic Analysis, and Scientific Consciousness in Foreign Policy Research." In *Political Science and Public Policy*, ed. Austin Ranney. Chicago: Markham.

———. 1967b. "Foreign Policy as an Issue Area." In *Domestic Sources of Foreign Policy*, ed. James N. Rosenau. New York: Free Press.

———. 1967c. "The Premises and Promises of Decision-Making Analysis." In *Contemporary Political Analysis*, ed. J. C. Charlesworth. New York: Free Press.

———. 1966. "Pre-theories and Theories and Foreign Policy." In *Approaches to Comparative and International Politics*, ed. R. Barry Farrell. Evanston, Ill.: Northwestern University Press.

———, ed. 1974. *Comparing Foreign Policies: Theories, Findings, and Methods*. New York: Sage, John Wiley and Sons.

———, ed. 1967a. *Domestic Sources of Foreign Policy*. New York: Free Press.

Ross, Dennis. 1980. "Coalition Maintenance in the Soviet Union." *World Politics* 32:258–80.

Ross, Stephen A. 1973. "The Economic Theory of Agency: The Principal's Problem." *American Economic Review* 63:134–39.

Rothgeb, John M., Jr. 1993. *Defining Power: Influence and Force in the Contemporary International System*. New York: St. Martin's Press.

———. 1989. *Myths and Realities of Foreign Investment in Poor Countries: The Modern Leviathan in the Third World*. New York: Praeger.

———. 1987. "Trojan Horse, Scapegoat, or Non-foreign Entity: Foreign Policy and Investment Penetration in Poor Countries." *Journal of Conflict Resolution* 31:227–65.

Rothstein, Robert. 1977. *The Weak in the World of the Strong*. New York: Columbia University Press.

———. 1968. *Alliances and Small Powers*. New York: Columbia University Press.

Rummel, R. J. 1979. *National Attributes and Behavior*. Beverly Hills, Calif.: Sage.

———. 1972a. *The Dimensions of Nations*. Beverly Hills, Calif.: Sage.

———. 1972b. "U.S. Foreign Relations: Conflict, Cooperation, and Attribute Distance." In *Peace, War, and Numbers*, ed. Bruce M. Russett. Beverly Hills, Calif.: Sage.

———. 1969. "Some Empirical Findings on Nations and Their Behavior." *World Politics* 21:226–41.

Runyan, Anne S., and V. Spike Peterson. 1991. "The Radical Future of Realism: Feminist Subversions of IR Theory." *Alternatives* 16:67–106.

Russett, Bruce M. 1993a. "Can a Democratic Peace Be Built?" *International Interactions* 18:277–82.

———. 1993b. *Grasping the Democratic Peace: Principles for a Post–Cold War World.* Princeton, N.J.: Princeton University Press.

———. 1990. *Controlling the Sword: The Democratic Governance of National Security.* Cambridge, Mass.: Harvard University Press.

———. 1982. International Interactions and Processes: The Internal vs. External Debate Revisited. Paper presented at the annual meeting of the American Political Science Association, Denver.

———. 1970. "International Behavior Research: Case Studies and Cumulation." In *Approaches to the Study of Political Science,* ed. Michael Haas and Henry S. Kariel. Scranton, Pa.: Chandler Publishing Company.

Russett, Bruce M., and Thomas W. Graham. 1989. "Public Opinion and National Security Policy: Relationships and Impacts." In *The Handbook of War Studies,* ed. Manus Midlarsky. London: Unwin Hyman.

Russett, Bruce M., and R. J. Monsen. 1975. "Bureaucracy and Polyarchy as Predictors of Performance: A Cross-National Examination." *Comparative Political Studies* 8:5–31.

Russett, Bruce, and Harvey Starr. 1992. W*orld Politics: The Menu for Choice.* 4th ed. New York: W. H. Freeman.

Salmore, Barbara, and Stephen Salmore. 1978. "Political Regimes and Foreign Policy." In *Why Nations Act: Theoretical Perspectives for Comparative Foreign Policy,* ed. Maurice East, Stephen Salmore, and Charles Hermann. Beverly Hills, Calif.: Sage.

———. 1972. Structure and Change in Regimes: Their Effects on Foreign Policy. Paper presented at the annual meeting of the American Political Science Association, San Francisco.

———. 1970. Political Accountability and Foreign Policy. Paper presented at the annual meeting of the American Political Science Association, Los Angeles.

Sampson, Martin W., III, and Stephen G. Walker. 1987. "Cultural Norms and National Roles: A Comparison of Japan and France." In *Role Theory and Foreign Policy Analysis,* ed. Stephen G. Walker. Durham, N.C.: Duke University Press.

Sankoff, David, and Joseph B. Kruskal, eds. 1983. *Time Warps, String Edits and Macromolecules: The Theory and Practice of Sequence Comparison.* New York: Addison-Wesley.

Savas, E. E. 1987. *Privatization.* Chatham, N.J.: Chatham House.

Sawyer, Jack. 1967. "Dimensions of Nations: Size, Wealth, and Politics." *American Journal of Sociology* 73:145–72.

Saxonhouse, Arlene. 1985. *Women in the History of Political Thought: Ancient Greece to Machiavelli.* New York: Praeger.

Scalapino, Robert A., ed. 1977. *The Foreign Policy of Modern Japan.* Berkeley: University of California Press.

Schandler, Herbert Y. 1977. *The Unmaking of a President: Lyndon Johnson and Vietnam*. Princeton, N.J.: Princeton University Press.

Schein, Edgar H. 1992. *Organizational Culture and Leadership: A Dynamic View*. 2d ed. San Francisco: Jossey-Bass.

Schelling, Thomas C. 1966. *Arms and Influence*. New Haven, Conn.: Yale University Press.

Schiebinger, Londa. 1989. *The Mind Has No Sex: Women in the Origins of Modern Science*. Cambridge, Mass.: Harvard University Press.

Schilling, Warner R. 1962a. "The Politics of National Defense: Fiscal 1950." In *Strategy, Politics and Defense Budgets*, ed. Warner R. Schilling, Paul T. Hammond, and Glenn H. Snyder. New York: Columbia University Press.

———. 1962b. "Scientists, Foreign Policy, and Politics." *American Political Science Review* 56:287–300.

Schilling, Warner R., Paul Y. Hammond, and Glenn H. Snyder. 1962. *Strategy, Politics, and Defense Budgets*. New York: Columbia University Press.

Schmiltroch, Linda, ed. 1991. *Statistical Record of Women Worldwide*. Detroit: Gale Research.

Schmitter, Philippe C. 1970. "A Revised Theory of Regional Integration." *International Organization* 24:836–68.

Schneider, William. 1983. "Conservatism, Not Interventionism: Trends in Foreign Policy Opinion, 1974–1982." In *Eagle Defiant: United States Foreign Policy in the 1980s*, ed. Kenneth A. Oye, Robert J. Lieber, and Donald Rothchild. Boston: Little, Brown.

Schoppa, Leonard J. 1993. "Two-Level Games and Bargaining Outcomes: Why Gaiatsu Succeeds in Japan in Some Cases but Not Others." *International Organization* 47:353–86.

Schrodt, Philip A. 1994a. *Patterns, Rules and Learning: Computational Models of International Politics*. Ann Arbor: University of Michigan Press.

———. 1994b. "Statistical Characteristics of Events Data." *International Interactions* 20:35–53.

———. 1991. "Pattern Recognition in International Event Sequences: A Machine Learning Approach." In *Artificial Intelligence and International Politics*, ed. Valerie M. Hudson. Boulder, Colo.: Westview.

———. 1990. "Parallel Event Sequences in International Crises." *Political Behavior* 12:97–123.

———. 1989. "Short-Term Prediction of International Events Using a Holland Classifier." *Mathematical and Computer Modelling* 12:589–600.

———. 1985. "Precedent-Based Logic and Rational Case: A Comparison." In *Dynamic Models of International Conflict*, ed. Michael Don Ward and Urs Luterbacher. Boulder, Colo.: Lynne Rienner.

———. 1983. The Effects of Arms Transfers on Supplier-Recipient Behavior. Paper presented at the annual meeting of the International Studies Association, Mexico City.

Schrodt, Philip A., and Deborah J. Gerner. 1994. "Validity Assessment of a Machine-Coded Event Data Set for the Middle East, 1982–1992." *American Journal of Political Science* 38: 825–54.

Schrodt, Philip A., and Alex Mintz. 1988. "A Conditional Probability Analysis of Regional Interactions in the Middle East." *American Journal of Political Science* 32:217–30.

Schuman, Frederick L. 1941. *International Politics*. New York: McGraw-Hill.

Schuman, Howard, and Cheryl Rieger. 1992. "Historical Analogies, Generational Effects, and Attitudes toward War." *American Sociological Review* 57:315–26.

Schwartz, Morton. 1975. *The Foreign Policy of the U.S.S.R.: Domestic Factors*. Encino, Calif.: Dickenson California Press.

Schweller, Randall L. 1992. "Domestic Structure and Preventive War: Are Democracies More Pacific?" *World Politics* 44:235–69.

Schwenk, Charles. 1988. *The Essence of Strategic Decision Making*. Lexington, Mass.: Lexington Books.

Sears, David O., and R. E. Whitney. 1973. *Political Persuasion*. Morristown, N.J.: General Learning Press.

Shapiro, Michael J., and G. Matthew Bonham. 1973. "Cognitive Process and Foreign Policy Decision-Making." *International Studies Quarterly* 17:147–74.

Shaw, Timothy M., and Olajide Aluko, eds. 1984. *The Political Economy of African Foreign Policy*. New York: St. Martin's Press.

Shepard, Graham H. 1988. "Personality Effects on American Foreign Policy, 1969–84: A Second Test of Interpersonal Generalization Theory." *International Studies Quarterly* 32:91–123.

Sherman, Frank L., and Laura Neack. 1993. "Imagining the Possibilities: The Possibilities of Isolating the Genome of International Conflict From the SHERFACS Dataset." In *International Event Data Developments*, ed. Richard L. Merritt, Robert G. Muncaster, and Dina A. Zinnes. Ann Arbor: University of Michigan Press.

Shimko, Keith L. 1994. "Metaphors and Foreign Policy Decision Making." *Political Pyschology*. 15: 657–73

———. 1992. "Reagan on the Soviet Union and the Nature of International Conflict." *Political Psychology* 13:353–77.

———. 1991. *Images and Arms Control: Perceptions of the Soviet Union in the Reagan Administration*. Ann Arbor: University of Michigan Press.

Shoup, Laurence H., and Minter, William. 1977. *Imperial Brain Trust: The Council on Foreign Policy*. New York: Monthly Review Press.

Showers, Caroline and Nancy Cantor. 1985. "Social Cognition: A Look at Motivated Strategies." *Annual Review of Psychology* 36:275–305.

Shull, Steven A. 1989. "Presidential Influence Versus Bureaucratic Discretion: President-Agency Relations. *American Review of Public Administration* 19:197–215.

Shweder, Richard A., and Marin A. Sullivan. 1993. "Cultural Psychology: Who Needs It?" *Annual Review of Psychology* 44:497–593.

Sickels, Robert J. 1974. *Presidential Transactions.* Englewood Cliffs, N.J.: Prentice-Hall.

Sigal, Leon V. 1970. "The Rational Policy Model and the Formosa Straits Crisis." *International Studies Quarterly* 14:121–56.

Sigler, John H., John O. Field, and Murray L. Adelman. 1972. *Applications of Events Data Analysis: Cases, Issues and Programs in International Interaction.* Beverly Hills, Calif.: Sage.

Simes, Dimitri K. 1986. "The Domestic Environment of Soviet Policy Making." In *U.S.-Soviet Relations: The Next Phase,* ed. Arnold L. Horelick. Ithaca, N.Y.: Cornell University Press.

Simon, Herbert. 1985. "Human Nature in Politics: The Dialogue of Psychology with Political Science." *American Political Science Review* 79:293–304.

———. 1957a. "A Behavioral Model of Rational Choice." In *Models of Man: Social and Rational.* New York: Wiley.

———. 1957b. *Models of Man: Social and Rational.* New York: Wiley.

Singer, Eric, and Valerie M. Hudson, eds. 1992. *Political Psychology and Foreign Policy.* Boulder, Colo.: Westview.

Singer, J. David. 1991. "Peace in the Global System: Displacement, Interregnum, or Transformation?" In *The Long Postwar Peace,* ed. Charles W. Kegley, Jr. New York: HarperCollins.

———. 1961. "The Level-of-Analysis Problem in International Relations." In *The International System: Theoretical Essays,* ed. Klaus Knorr and Sidney Verba. Princeton, N.J.: Princeton University Press.

Singer, Marshall R. 1972. *Weak States in a World of Powers: The Dynamics of International Relationships.* New York: Free Press.

Siverson, Randolph M., and Harvey Starr. 1994. "Regime Change and the Restructuring of Alliances." *American Journal of Political Science* 38:145–61.

Skidmore, David. 1994. "The Politics of National Security Policy: Interest Groups, Coalitions and the SALT II Debate." In *The Limits of State Autonomy: Societal Groups and Foreign Policy Formulation,* ed. David Skidmore and Valerie M. Hudson. Boulder, Colo.: Westview.

Skocpol, Theda. 1985. "Bringing the State Back In: Strategies of Analysis in Current Research." In *Bringing the State Back In,* ed. Peter Evans, Dietrich Rueschemeyer, and Theda Skocpol. New York: Cambridge University Press.

———. 1979. *States and Social Revolutions: A Comparative Analysis of France, Russia, and China.* Cambridge: Cambridge University Press.

Small, Melvin, and J. David Singer. 1976. "The War-Proneness of Democratic Regimes, 1816–1965." *Jerusalem Journal of International Relations* 1:50–69.

Smith, Anthony D. 1991. "The Nation: Invented, Imagined, Reconstructed?" *Millennium* 20:353–68.

Smith, Michael, Steve Smith, and Brian White, eds. 1988. *British Foreign Policy: Tradition, Change, and Transformation.* London: Unwin and Hyman.

Smith, Steve. 1984/85. "Policy Preferences and Bureaucratic Position: The Case of the American Hostage Rescue Mission." *International Affairs* 61:9–25.

Snare, Charles. 1992. "Personality and Foreign Policy Behavior: Comparing and Contrasting Three Methods of Assessment At-a-Distance." In *Political Psychology and Foreign Policy*, ed. Eric Singer and Valerie M. Hudson. Boulder, Colo.: Westview.

Snyder, Glenn H. 1961. *Deterrence and Defense: Toward a Theory of National Security.* Princeton, N.J.: Princeton University Press.

Snyder, Glenn H., and Paul Diesing. 1977. *Conflict among Nations: Bargaining, Decision Making, and System Structure in International Crises.* Princeton, N.J.: Princeton University Press.

Snyder, Jack. 1991. *Myths of Empire: Domestic Politics and International Ambition.* Ithaca, N.Y.: Cornell University Press.

———. 1978. "Rationality at the Brink: The Role of Cognitive Processes in Failures of Deterrence." *World Politics* 30:344–65.

Snyder, Richard C., H. W. Bruck, and Burton Sapin. 1962a. "Decision-Making as an Approach to the Study of International Politics." In *Foreign Policy Decision-Making: An Approach to the Study of International Politics*, ed. Richard C. Snyder, H. W. Bruck, and Burton Sapin. New York: Macmillan.

———. 1954. *Decision-Making as an Approach to the Study of International Politics.* Foreign Policy Analysis Series no. 3. Princeton, N.J.: Princeton University Press.

———, eds. 1962b. *Foreign Policy Decision Making.* New York: Free Press.

Snyder, Richard C., and Glenn D. Paige. 1958. "The United States Decision to Resist Aggression in Korea: The Application of an Analytical Scheme." *Administrative Science Quarterly* 3:341–78.

Sobel, Richard. 1989. "The Polls—A Report: Public Opinion about United States Intervention in El Salvador and Nicaragua." *Public Opinion Quarterly* 54:114–28.

Solo, Pam. 1988. *From Protest to Policy: Beyond the Freeze to Common Security.* Cambridge, Mass.: Ballinger.

Sontag, Susan. 1989. *Illness as a Metaphor and AIDS and Its Metaphors.* New York: Doubleday.

Spanier, John. 1987. *Games Nations Play.* Washington, D.C.: Congressional Quarterly Press.

Spanier, John, and Joseph Nogee, eds. 1981. *Congress, the Presidency, and American Foreign Policy.* New York: Pergamon.

Spechler, Dina Rome. 1987. "The Politics of Intervention: The Soviet Union and the Crisis in Lebanon." *Studies in Comparative Communism* 20:115–43.

Sprout, Harold, and Margaret Sprout. 1971. *Toward a Politics of the Planet Earth.* New York: Van Nostrand.

———. 1969. "Environmental Factors in the Study of International Relations." In *International Politics and Foreign Policy*, ed. James N. Rosenau. New York: Free Press.

———. 1965. *The Ecological Perspective on Human Affairs.* Princeton, N.J.: Princeton University Press.

———. 1957. "Environmental Factors in the Study of International Politics." *Journal of Conflict Resolution* 1:309–28.

———. 1956. *Man-Milieu Relationship Hypotheses in the Context of International Politics.* Princeton, N.J.: Princeton University Press.

Starbuck, William H., and Paul C. Nystrom. 1981. *Handbook of Organizational Design.* 2 volumes. New York: Oxford University Press.

Starr, Harvey. 1991. Modeling Domestic and Foreign Policy Linkages: Choice, Substitutability, and Nested Games. Paper presented at the annual meeting of the American Political Science Association, Washington, D.C.

———. 1990. Modeling the Internal-External Linkage: Rethinking the Relationship between Revolution, War and Change. Paper presented at the annual meeting of the American Political Science Association, San Francisco.

———. 1984. *Henry Kissinger: Perceptions of International Politics.* Lexington: University Press of Kentucky.

Staudt, Kathleen. 1989. "Women in High-Level Political Decision Making: A Global Analysis." Vienna: United Nations Report EGM/EPPDM/1989/WP.2.

Stein, Arthur A. 1993. "Domestic Constraints, Extended Deterrence, and the Incoherence of Grand Strategy: The United States, 1938–1950." In *The Domestic Bases of Grand Strategy,* ed. Richard Rosecrance, and Arthur A. Stein. Ithaca, N.Y.: Cornell University Press.

Steinbruner, John D. 1974. *The Cybernetic Theory of Decision.* Princeton, N.J.: Princeton University Press.

Steiner, Miriam. 1977. "The Elusive Essence of Decision." *International Studies Quarterly* 21:389–422.

Stempel, John D. 1981. *Inside the Iranian Revolution.* Bloomington: Indiana University Press.

Sternberg, Robert. 1977. *Intelligence, Information Processing, and Analogical Reasoning.* Hillsdale, N.J.: Lawrence Erlbaum.

St. John, Ronald Bruce. 1992. *The Foreign Policy of Peru.* Boulder, Colo.: Lynne Rienner.

Stockholm International Peace Research Institute. 1992. *SIPRI Yearbook 1992: World Armaments and Disarmament.* Oxford, England: Oxford University Press.

Stoessinger, John G. 1971. *Nations in Darkness: China, Russia, and America.* New York: Random House.

———. 1967. "China and America: The Burden of Past Misperceptions." *Journal of International Affairs* 21:72–91.

Stuart, Douglas, and Harvey Starr. 1981–82. "The 'Inherent Bad Faith Model' Reconsidered: Dulles, Kennedy, and Kissinger." *Political Psychology* 3:1–33.

Sullivan, Michael P. 1990. *Power in Contemporary International Politics.* Columbia: University of South Carolina Press.

———. 1976. *International Relations: Theories and Evidence.* Englewood Cliffs, N.J.: Prentice-Hall.

Sundelius, Bengt. n.d. "Whiskey on the Rocks: Sweden's Response to a Trapped Soviet Submarine." In *Leaders, Groups, and Coalitions: How Decision Units Shape Foreign Policy,* ed. Joe D. Hagan, Charles F. Hermann, and Margaret G. Hermann. Forthcoming.

———, ed. 1982. *Foreign Policies of Northern Europe.* Boulder, Colo.: Westview.

Sylvan, Donald A., and Steve Chan, eds. 1984. *Foreign Policy Decision Making: Perception, Cognition and Artificial Intelligence.* New York: Praeger.

Sylvan, Donald A., Ashok Goel, and B. Chandrasekaran. 1990. "Analyzing Political Decision Making from an Information-Processing Perspective: JESSE." *American Journal of Political Science* 34:79–123.

Sylvan, Donald A., and Stuart J. Thorson. 1992. "Ontologies, Problem Representation, and the Cuban Missile Crisis." *Journal of Conflict Resolution* 36:709–32.

Sylvester, Christine. 1994. *Feminist Theory and International Relations in a Postmodern Era.* Cambridge: Cambridge University Press.

———. 1991/92. "Feminist Theory and Gender Studies in International Relations." *International Studies Notes* 16/17:32–38.

Szulc, Tad. 1965. *The Winds of Revolution: Latin America Today—and Tomorrow.* New York: Praeger.

Taber, Charles S. 1992. "POLI: An Expert System Model of U.S. Foreign Policy Belief Systems." *American Political Science Review* 86:888–904.

Talbott, Strobe. 1984. *Deadly Gambits: The Reagan Administration and the Stalemate in Nuclear Arms Control.* New York: Knopf.

Tanaka, Akihiko. 1984. "China, China Watching and CHINA-WATCHER." In *Foreign Policy Decision Making: Perception, Cognition and Artificial Intelligence*, ed. Donald A. Sylvan and Steve Chan. New York: Praeger.

Taylor, Charles L., and Michael C. Hudson. 1972. *World Handbook of Political and Social Indicators.* 2d ed. New Haven, Conn.: Yale University Press.

Tetlock, Philip E. 1986. "Psychological Advice on Foreign Policy: What Do We Have to Contribute?" *American Psychologist* 41:557–67.

———. 1985. "Integrative Complexity of American and Soviet Foreign Policy Rhetoric: A Time-Series Analysis." *Journal of Personality and Social Psychology* 49:1565–85.

———. 1983a. "Cognitive Style and Political Ideology." *Journal of Personality and Social Psychology* 45:118–26.

———. 1983b. "Psychological Research on Foreign Policy: A Methodological Overview." In *Review of Personality and Social Psychology*, vol. 4. Beverly Hills, Calif.: Sage.

Tetlock, Philip E., and Charles B. McGuire, Jr. 1985. "Cognitive Perspectives on Foreign Policy." In *Political Behavior Annual*, ed. S. Long. Boulder, Colo.: Westview.

Tetlock, Philip E., and Ariel Levi. 1982. "Attribution Bias: On the Inclusiveness of the Cognition-Motivation Debate." *Journal of Experimental Social Psychology* 18:68–88.

Tetreault, Mary Ann, ed. 1994. *Women and Revolution in Africa, Asia, and the New World.* Columbia: University of South Carolina Press.

Therborn, Goran. 1986. "Neo-Marxist, Pluralist, Corporatist, Statist Theories and the Welfare State." In *The State in Global Perspective*, ed. Ali Kazancigil. Brookfield, Vt.: Gower.

Thomas, Caroline. 1987. *In Search of Security: The Third World in International Relations.* Boulder, Colo.: Lynne Rienner.

Thorne, Christopher. 1988. *Border Crossings: Studies in International History.* New York: Oxford University Press.

Thorson, Stuart, and Donald A. Sylvan. 1982. "Counterfactuals and the Cuban Missile Crisis." *International Studies Quarterly* 26:537–71.

Tickner, J. Ann. 1992. *Gender in International Relations: Feminist Perspectives on Achieving Global Security.* New York: Columbia University Press.

Tilly, Charles. 1992. "Futures of European States." *Social Research* 59:705–17.

———, ed. 1975. *The Formation of National States in Western Europe.* Princeton, N.J.: Princeton University Press.

Tomlin, Brian W. 1985. "Measurement Validation: Lessons from the Use and Misuse of UN General Assembly Roll-Call Votes." *International Organization* 39:189–206.

Trout, B. Thomas. 1975. "Rhetoric Revisited: Political Legitimation and the Cold War." *International Studies Quarterly* 19:251–84.

True, Jacqui. 1993. "National Selves and Feminine Others." *Fletcher Forum of World Affairs* 17:75–89.

Tsebelis, George. 1990. *Nested Games: Rational Choice in Comparative Politics.* Berkeley: University of California Press.

Tuchman, Barbara Wertheim. 1984. *The March of Folly: From Troy to Vietnam.* New York: Knopf.

Tullock, Gordon. 1987. *The Politics of Bureaucracy.* Lanham, Md.: University Press of America.

Tweraser, Kurt. 1974. "Changing Patterns of Political Beliefs: The Foreign Policy Operational Codes of J. William Fulbright, 1943–1967." *Sage Professional Papers in American Politics* (Series no. 04-016). Beverly Hills, Calif.: Sage.

United Nations. 1991. *The World's Women: 1970–1990 Trends and Statistics.* New York.

United Nations, Various years. *Yearbook of National Accounts Statistics.* New York: United Nations Publications.

United Nations, Various years. *U.N. Statistical Yearbook.* New York: United Nations Publications.

U.S. Congress. 1990. Senate, Committee on the Judiciary. *Hearings on the One-year Drug Strategy Review.* 101st Cong., 2d Sess. Sept. 5, 6.

Unseld, Sigrid D., and John C. Mallery. 1992. "Interaction Detection in Complex Datamodels" (AI Memo no. 1298). Cambridge, Mass.: MIT Artificial Intelligence Laboratory.

Valenta, Jiri. 1984. "Soviet Decision Making and the Hungarian Revolution." In *The First War between Socialist States: The Hungarian Revolution of 1956 and Its Impact*, ed. Bela K. Kiraly, Barbara Lotze, Nandor F. Dreisziger. New York: Brooklyn College Press.

———. 1980a. "From Prague to Kabul: The Soviet Style of Invasion." *International Security* 5:114–41.

————. 1980b. "Soviet Decision Making on the Intervention in Angola." In *Communism in Africa*, ed. David E. Albright. Bloomington: Indiana University Press.

————. 1979. *Soviet Intervention in Czechoslovakia, 1968: Anatomy of a Decision.* Baltimore: Johns Hopkins University Press.

Valenzuela, J. Samuel, and Arturo Valenzuela. 1978. "Modernization and Dependency: Alternative Perspectives in the Study of Latin American Underdevelopment." *Comparative Politics* 10:535–57.

Van Belle, Douglas. 1993. "Domestic Imperatives and Rational Models of Foreign Policy Decision Making." In *The Limits of State Autonomy: Societal Groups and Foreign Policy Formulation*, eds. David Skidmore and Valerie M. Hudson. Boulder, Colo.: Westview.

Vandenbroucke, Lucien S. 1984. "Anatomy of a Failure: The Decision to Land at the Bay of Pigs." *Political Science Quarterly* 99:471–91.

Van Dyke, Vernon. 1966. *International Politics.* New York: Appleton-Century-Crofts.

Van Wyk, Koos, and Sarah Radloff. 1993. "Symmetry and Reciprocity in South Africa's Foreign Policy." *Journal of Conflict Resolution* 37:382–96.

Vasquez, John A. 1992. *The War Puzzle.* Cambridge: Cambridge University Press.

Vaughan, Diane. 1990. "Autonomy, Interdependence, and Social Control: NASA and the Space Shuttle 'Challenger.'" *Administrative Science Quarterly* 35:225–57.

Vellut, Jean-Luc. 1967. "Smaller States and the Problem of War and Peace: Some Consequences of the Emergence of Smaller States in Africa." *Journal of Peace Research* 2:253–69.

Verba, Sidney. 1985. "Comparative Politics: Where Have We Been, Where Are We Going?" In *New Directions in Comparative Politics*, ed. Howard J. Wiarda. Boulder, Colo.: Westview.

Vernon, Raymond, Debora L. Spar, and Gregory Tobin. 1991. *Iron Triangles and Revolving Doors: Cases in U.S. Foreign Economic Policymaking.* New York: Praeger.

Vertzberger, Yaacov Y. I. 1990. *The World in Their Minds: Information Processing, Cognition, and Perception in Foreign Policy Decisionmaking.* Stanford, Calif.: Stanford University Press.

————. 1984a. "Bureaucratic-Organizational Politics and Information Processing in a Developing State." *International Studies Quarterly* 28:69–95.

————. 1984b. *Misperceptions in Foreign Policymaking: The Sino-Indian Conflict, 1959–1962.* Boulder, Colo.: Westview.

Vickers, Jean. 1991. *Women and the World Economic Crisis.* London: ZED Books.

Vickers, Jill McCalla. 1990. "At His Mother's Knee: Sex/Gender and the Construction of National Identities." In *Women and Men: Interdisciplinary Readings on Gender*, ed. Greta Hoffmann Nemiroff. Toronto: Fitzhenry and Whiteside.

Vincent, Jack E. 1979. *Project Theory: Interpretations and Policy Relevance.* Washington, D.C.: University Press of America.

Vosniadou, Stella, and Anthony Ortony. 1989. "Similarity and Analogical Reasoning: A Synthesis." In *Similarity and Analogical Reasoning*, ed. Stella Vosniadou and Anthony Ortony. New York: Cambridge University Press.

Voss, James F., and Ellen Dorsey. 1992. "Perception and International Relations: An Overview." In *Political Psychology and Foreign Policy*, eds. Eric Singer and Valerie Hudson. Boulder, Colo.: Westview.

Wagner, A. R. 1974. *Crisis Decision-Making*. New York: Praeger.

Walby, Sylvia. 1992. "Women and Nation." *International Journal of Comparative Sociology* 33:81–100.

Walker, Stephen G. 1990. "The Evolution of Operational Code Analysis." *Political Psychology* 11:403–17.

———. 1987. "Role Theory and the Origins of Foreign Policy." In *New Directions in the Study of Foreign Policy*, ed. Charles F. Hermann, Charles W. Kegley, Jr., and James N. Rosenau. Winchester, Mass.: Unwin Hyman.

———. 1983. "The Motivational Foundations of Political Belief Systems: A Re-Analysis of the Operational Code Construct." *International Studies Quarterly* 27:179–201.

———. 1977. "The Interface between Beliefs and Behavior: Henry Kissinger's Operational Code and the Vietnam War." *Journal of Conflict Resolution* 21:129–68.

———. 1975. Cognitive Maps and International Realities: Henry A. Kissinger's Operational Code. Paper presented at the annual meeting of the American Political Science Association, San Francisco.

Wallace, William. 1976. *The Foreign Policy Process in Britain*. London: Allen and Unwin.

Wallerstein, Immanuel. 1979. *Capitalist World-Economy*. Cambridge: Cambridge University Press.

———. 1976. *The Modern World-System: Capitalist Agriculture and the Origins of the European World-Economy in the 16th Century*. New York: Academic Press.

———. 1974. *The Modern World System*. New York: Academic Press.

Walt, Stephen. 1992. "Revolution and War." *World Politics* 44:321–68.

———. 1987. *The Origins of Alliances*. Ithaca, N.Y.: Cornell University Press.

Waltz, Kenneth N. 1993. "The Emerging Structure of International Politics." *International Security* 18:44–79.

———. 1988. "The Origins of War in Neorealist Theory." *Journal of Interdisciplinary History* 18:615–28.

———. 1986. "A Response to My Critics." In *Neorealism and Its Critics*, ed. Robert O. Keohane. New York: Columbia University Press.

———. 1979. *Theory of International Politics*. New York: Random House.

———. 1967. *Foreign Policy and Democratic Politics: The American and British Experience*. Boston: Little, Brown.

———. 1959. *Man, the State, and War: A Theoretical Analysis*. New York: Columbia University Press.

Ward, Michael Don. 1982. "Cooperation and Conflict in Foreign Policy Behavior." *International Studies Quarterly* 26:87–126.

Ward, Richard Edmund. 1992. *India's Pro-Arab Policy*. New York: Praeger.

Weber, Robert Philip. 1990. *Basic Content Analysis*. Newbury Park, Calif.: Sage.

Weede, Erich. 1992. "Some Calculations on Democracy and War Involvement." *Journal of Peace Research* 29:377–83.

———. 1984. "Democracy and War Involvement." *Journal of Conflict Resolution* 28:649–64.

Weekly Compilation of Presidential Documents (WCPD). 1982. Washington D.C.: U. S. Government Printing Office.

Weil, Herman M. 1975. "Can Bureaucracies Be Rational Actors?" *International Studies Quarterly* 19:432–68.

Weinstein, Franklin B. 1976. *Indonesian Foreign Policy and the Dilemma of Dependence: From Sukarno to Soeharto.* Ithaca, N.Y.: Cornell University Press.

———. 1972. "The Uses of Foreign Policy in Indonesia: An Approach to the Analysis of Foreign Policy in the Less Developed Countries." *World Politics* 24:356–81.

Welch, David A. 1992. "The Organizational Process and Bureaucratic Politics Paradigms: Retrospect and Prospect." *International Security* 17 (fall): 112–46.

———. 1989. "Crisis Decision Making Reconsidered." *Journal of Conflict Resolution* 33:430–45.

Welch, William. 1970. *American Images of Soviet Foreign Policy.* New Haven, Conn.: Yale University Press.

White, Ralph K. 1968. *Nobody Wanted War: Misperception in Vietnam and Other Wars.* Garden City, N.Y.: Doubleday.

———. 1966. "Misperception and the Vietnam War." *Journal of Social Issues* 22 (3):1–67.

———, ed. 1986. *Psychology and the Prevention of War: A Book of Readings.* New York: New York University Press.

Whyte, Glen. 1989. "Groupthink Reconsidered." *Academy of Management Review* 14:40–56.

Wiarda, Howard J. 1985. "Comparative Politics Past and Present." In *New Directions in Comparative Politics,* ed. Howard J. Wiarda. Boulder, Colo.: Westview.

Wicker, Alan L. 1969. "Attitudes versus Actions: The Relationship between Verbal and Overt Behavioral Responses to Attitude Objects." *Journal of Social Issues* 254:41–78.

Wilkenfeld, Jonathan. 1973. "Domestic and Foreign Conflict." In *Conflict Behavior and Linkage Politics,* ed. Jonathan Wilkenfeld. New York: McKay.

———. 1968. "Domestic and Foreign Conflict Behavior of Nations." *Journal of Peace Research* 1:56–59.

Wilkenfeld, Jonathan, Gerald W. Hopple, Paul J. Rossa, and Stephen J. Andriole. 1980. *Foreign Policy Behavior: The Interstate Behavior Analysis Model.* Beverly Hills, Calif.: Sage.

Williamson, Samuel R. 1979. "Theories of Organizational Process and Foreign Policy Outcomes." In *Diplomacy,* ed. Paul Lauren. New York: Free Press.

Willis, F. Roy. 1971. *Italy Chooses Europe.* New York: Oxford University Press.

Wilson, James Q. 1989. *Bureaucracy.* New York: Basic Books.

Winter, David G. 1992. "Personality and Foreign Policy: Historical Overview of Research." In *Political Psychology and Foreign Policy*, ed. Eric Singer and Valerie M. Hudson. Boulder, Colo.: Westview.

Wirth, David. 1992. "The GATT Tuna Dolphin Decision." Typescript.

Wirtz, James J. 1991. *The Tet Offensive: Intelligence Failure in War.* Ithaca, N.Y.: Cornell University Press.

Wise, Charles R. 1990. "Public Service Configurations and Public Organizations." *Public Administration Review* 50:141–55.

Wisotsky, Steven. 1986. *Breaking the Impasse in the War on Drugs.* New York: Greenwood Press.

Wittkopf, Eugene R. 1990. *Faces of Internationalism: Public Opinion and American Foreign Policy.* Durham, N.C.: Duke University Press.

———. 1987. "Elites and Masses: Another Look at Attitudes toward America's World Role." *International Studies Quarterly* 31:131–59.

———. 1986. "On the Foreign Policy Beliefs of the American People: A Critique and Some Evidence." *International Studies Quarterly* 30:425–45.

———. 1973. "Foreign Aid and United Nations Votes: A Comparative Study." *American Political Science Review* 67:868–88.

Wohlstetter, Roberta. 1962. *Pearl Harbor: Warning and Decision.* Stanford, Calif.: Stanford University Press.

Wolf-Phillips, Leslie. 1987. "Why 'Third World'?: Origin, Definition and Usage." *Third World Quarterly* 9:1311–27.

World Bank. 1992. *World Development Report 1992.* New York: Oxford University Press.

World Bank. 1988. *World Development Report 1988.* New York: Oxford University Press.

Wright, Quincy. 1955. *The Study of International Relations.* New York: Appleton.

Wright, Stephen. 1992. "The Foreign Policy of Africa." In *Foreign Policy in World Politics*, ed. Roy C. Macridis. 8th ed. Englewood Cliffs, N.J.: Prentice-Hall.

Yaniv, Avner, and Yael Yishai. 1981. "Israeli Settlements in the West Bank: The Politics of Intransigence," *Journal of Politics* 43:1104–28.

Yergin, Daniel. 1977. *Shattered Peace: The Origins of the Cold War and the National Security State.* Boston: Houghton Mifflin.

Young, Oran. 1986. "International Regimes." *World Politics* 39:104–22.

———. 1978. "Anarchy and Social Choice: Reflections on the International Polity." *World Politics* 30:241–63.

Yuval-Davis, Nira. 1991. "The Citizenship Debate: Women, Ethnic Processes and the State." *Feminist Review* 39:58–68.

Yuval-Davis, Nira, and Floya Anthias, eds. 1989. *Woman-Nation-State.* London: Macmillan.

Zacher, Mark. 1979. *International Conflicts and Collective Security, 1946–77.* New York: Praeger.

Zakaria, Fareed. 1992. "Realism and Domestic Politics." *International Security* 17:177–98.

Zimmerman, William. 1987. "Issue Area and Foreign Policy Process: A Research Note in Search of a General Theory." *American Political Science Review* 67:1204–12.

Zinnes, Dina A. 1976. *Contemporary Research in International Relations*. New York: Free Press.

▶ INDEX